Nine Centuries of Man

Nine Centuries of Man

Manhood and Masculinities in Scottish History

Edited by Lynn Abrams and Elizabeth Ewan

EDINBURGH
University Press

Edinburgh University Press is one of the leading university presses in the UK. We publish academic books and journals in our selected subject areas across the humanities and social sciences, combining cutting-edge scholarship with high editorial and production values to produce academic works of lasting importance. For more information visit our website: edinburghuniversitypress.com

Edinburgh University Press Ltd
The Tun – Holyrood Road
12 (2f) Jackson's Entry
Edinburgh EH8 8PJ

First published in hardback by Edinburgh University Press 2017

Typeset in 10.5/13pt Sabon by
Servis Filmsetting Ltd, Stockport, Cheshire
and printed and bound in Great Britain by
CPI Group (UK) Ltd, Croydon CR0 4YY

A CIP record for this book is available from the British Library

ISBN 978 1 4744 0389 4 (hardback)
ISBN 978 1 4744 3783 7 (paperback)
ISBN 978 1 4744 0390 0 (webready PDF)
ISBN 978 1 4744 0391 7 (epub)

Contents

List of Figures   vii
Acknowledgements   viii
Notes on the Contributors   x

Introduction: Interrogating Men and Masculinities in
Scottish History   1
Lynn Abrams and Elizabeth Ewan

Part I Models

1 'Be Wise in Thy Governing': Managing Emotion and
Controlling Masculinity in Early Modern Scottish Poetry   21
Sarah Dunnigan

2 Reformed Masculinity: Ministers, Fathers and Male Heads
of Households, 1560–1660   39
Janay Nugent

3 The Importance and Impossibility of Manhood: Polite and
Libertine Masculinities in the Urban Eighteenth Century   58
Rosalind Carr

4 The Taming of Highland Masculinity: Interpersonal
Violence and Shifting Codes of Manhood, c. 1760–1840   80
Lynn Abrams

Part II Representations

  5 Making a Manly Impression: The Image of Kingship on
     Scottish Royal Seals of the High Middle Ages   101
     Cynthia J. Neville

  6 Contrasting Kingly and Knightly Masculinities in
     Barbour's *Bruce*   122
     Sergi Mainer

  7 Negotiating Independence: Manliness and Begging Letters in
     Late Eighteenth- and Early Nineteenth-Century Scotland   142
     Katie Barclay

  8 A Wartime Family Romance: Narratives of Masculinity and
     Intimacy during World War Two   160
     Lynn Abrams

Part III Lived Experiences

  9 Social Control and Masculinity in Early Modern Scotland:
     Expectations and Behaviour in a Lowland Parish   183
     Harriet Cornell

 10 A 'Polite and Commercial People'? Masculinity and
     Economic Violence in Scotland, 1700–60   203
     Tawny Paul

 11 Music Hall, 'Mashers' and the 'Unco Guid': Competing
     Masculinities in Victorian Glasgow   223
     Tanya Cheadle

 12 'That Class of Men': Effeminacy, Sodomy and Failed
     Masculinities in Inter- and Post-War Scotland   242
     Jeffrey Meek

 13 Speaking to the 'Hard Men': Masculinities, Violence and
     Youth Gangs in Glasgow, c. 1965–75   258
     Angela Bartie and Alistair Fraser

Index   278

Figures

5.1	Seal of Duncan II, king of Scots	103
5.2	Seal of Edgar, king of Scots	107
5.3	Seal of Alexander II, king of Scots	109
5.4	Seal of Alexander III, king of Scots	112
8.1	George Johnstone Brown and Seaforth Sinclair Brown on their wedding day, 1939	163
8.2	British Army Garrison, Trinidad, 1944	168

Acknowledgements

Gender has been central to our research for many years though it is only recently that men have achieved prominence. This collection grew out of two separate initiatives by the editors. Lynn Abrams (with Alexandra Shepard) of the Centre for Gender History at the University of Glasgow organised a series of workshops in 2012–13 on Scottish masculinity in historical perspective supported by the Royal Society of Edinburgh, which brought together historians, sociologists, youth workers, health researchers, policy makers and others on the frontline including the head of the Strathclyde Youth Violence Reduction Unit. We were struck by certain continuities (as well as differences) across the centuries, and the value of comparisons across time. Elizabeth Ewan, thanks to the Institute for Scottish Historical Research at the University of St Andrews where she had a visiting Fellowship in Winter 2014, and with funds from St Andrews, a Standard Research Grant on Scottish Masculinities 1400–1600 from the Social Sciences and Humanities Research Council of Canada, and the College of Arts University Research Chairs fund, University of Guelph, organised a day conference on masculinities in Scottish history in March 2014, where ideas for this collection were first debated. We are very grateful to John Watson of Edinburgh University Press who attended the conference and has supported us in this project ever since, even when some unavoidable obstacles delayed our progress. The present collection includes revised papers from contributors to both projects as well as others which were submitted later.

We are grateful to Edinburgh University Press and the Trustees of the Scottish Historical Trust for permission to publish a shortened version of Lynn Abrams' article 'The Taming of Highland Masculinity', which originally appeared in the *Scottish Historical Review*, 92 (2013). We would also like to thank the University of Guelph Special Collections and the University of Glasgow Photographic Unit for providing high-quality digital images for our six illustrations.

We especially want to thank all of our contributors for their enthusiasm, timeliness, willingness to address the revisions suggested by external referees and the collection editors, and calm responses to last-minute queries. We are indebted to the anonymous readers for their insightful comments, some contributors who stepped in late in the day, Tanya Cheadle who was responsible for copy-editing the manuscript before submission, Belinda Cunnison, copy-editor for EUP and Gavin Jack, Assistant Commissioning Editor at EUP, for his valuable help and patience in getting the book to press.

This book is of course dedicated to the men in our lives, Callum and Kris, who sometimes stepped out of traditional male gender roles to enable us to finish it.

Notes on the Contributors

Lynn Abrams is Professor of Modern History at the University of Glasgow. She has published widely in the field of gender history and oral history including *Myth and Materiality in a Woman's World: Shetland 1800–2000* (2005); *Gender in Scottish History since 1700* (Edinburgh University Press, 2006); and *Oral History Theory* (2nd edition, 2016).

Katie Barclay is an ARC DECRA Fellow in the ARC Centre of Excellence for the History of Emotions, University of Adelaide. She is the author of *Love, Intimacy and Power* (Manchester, 2011) and numerous articles on gender, emotion and family life. Her current research explores intimacy amongst lower order Scots.

Angela Bartie is Lecturer in Scottish History at the University of Edinburgh. She is author of *The Edinburgh Festivals: Culture and Society in Post-war Britain* (Edinburgh University Press, 2013) and co-editor (with Eleanor Bell) of *The International Writers' Conference Revisited: Edinburgh, 1962* (2012). She has published on Glasgow youth gangs, policing of youth in post-war Britain, and oral history in Scotland.

Rosalind Carr is Senior Lecturer in History at the University of East London, and the author of *Gender and Enlightenment Culture in Eighteenth-Century Scotland* (Edinburgh University Press, 2014). As well as Scottish masculinities, her previous work has included studies of women's role in Scottish politics across the eighteenth century.

Tanya Cheadle had a first career in broadcasting, making history documentaries for the BBC and Channel 4. She now teaches history at the University of Glasgow, having recently completed her doctorate on sexual progressives in late Victorian Scotland. Her current research focuses on sex, gender and alternative religion and spiritualities in the nineteenth century.

Harriet Cornell is a Carnegie Postdoctoral Fellow in History at the University of Edinburgh where she is working on the collaborative project 'Agriculture and teind reform in early modern Scotland'. Her doctoral thesis, 'Gender, sex and social control: East Lothian, 1610–1640' was awarded the Jeremiah Dalziel Prize in British History in 2012.

Sarah Dunnigan is Senior Lecturer in English Literature at Edinburgh University. She has published on diverse aspects of medieval and early modern Scottish literature, with particular interests in women's writing and traditional culture. Her books include *Eros and Poetry at the Courts of Mary Queen of Scots and James VI* (2003).

Elizabeth Ewan is University Research Chair in Scottish Studies and History at the University of Guelph in Canada. Her research focuses on gender and crime and urban history in medieval and early modern Scotland. Publications include the co-edited *Women in Scotland c. 1100–1750* (1999) and *The Biographical Dictionary of Scottish Women* (Edinburgh University Press, 2006).

Alistair Fraser is currently Lecturer in Criminology and Sociology at the University of Glasgow and Honorary Assistant Professor in Criminology at the University of Hong Kong. His research focuses on issues of youth, crime and globalisation, with a particular focus on 'youth gangs'. Publications include *Urban Legends: Gang Identities in the Post-Industrial City* (2015).

Sergi Mainer currently teaches Hispanic Literature, Spanish language and translation at Edinburgh University. His research concentrates on the social and political dimension of literature and the construction of class, gender, national and cultural identities. Publications include *Nation, Chivalry and Knighthood: The Scottish Romance Tradition c. 1375–c. 1550* (2010).

Jeffrey Meek is a Research Assistant in Economic and Social History at the University of Glasgow. He has published on the history of homo-sexuality in nineteenth- and twentieth-century Scotland, including his monograph *Queer Voices in Post-War Scotland: Male Homosexuality,*

Religion and Society (2015) and on the effects of World War One on Scottish families

Cynthia J. Neville holds the George Munro Chair in History and Political Economy at Dalhousie University in Canada. She has published extensively on the legal and social history of later medieval Scotland. Recent books include *Native Lordship in Medieval Scotland* (2005), *Land, Law and People in Medieval Scotland* (Edinburgh University Press, 2010) and, with Grant G. Simpson, *Regesta Regum Scottorum*, Vol. IV, Pt 1, *The Acts of Alexander III, King of Scots 1249–1286* (Edinburgh University Press, 2011).

Janay Nugent is Associate Professor of History and the Institute for Child and Youth Studies at the University of Lethbridge in Canada. She is co-editor with Elizabeth Ewan of *Finding the Family in Medieval and Early Modern Scotland* (2008) and *Children and Youth in Premodern Scotland* (2015).

Tawny Paul is Senior Lecturer in Economic and Social History at the University of Exeter. She holds a PhD in economic and social history from the University of Edinburgh. Her research broadly considers the social and economic history of eighteenth-century Britain, with a focus on themes of gender, debt and the social order.

Introduction: Interrogating Men and Masculinities in Scottish History

Lynn Abrams and Elizabeth Ewan

IN JUNE 1844 GEORGE MacLennan appeared before Dingwall sheriff court accused of assaulting John Williamson, a farm servant, causing him serious injury. MacLennan proffered this statement in his defence. 'I had been at the Muir of Ord market that day and had had a dram. Williamson seeing this said to me I was drunk and further provoked me by saying I was a tailor and not a man.' MacLennan answered him 'that if he would not be quiet I would show to him what I was'. When Williamson refused to react to MacLennan's provocations, MacLennan took hold of the spade with which Williamson was working and in the ensuing struggle Williamson was struck in the mouth.[1] A commonplace confrontation between two men on a roadside in rural Scotland provides us with an entry point into everyday understandings of masculinity. George MacLennan felt insulted by Williamson's insinuation that he was not a real man because he was a tailor – presumably an effeminate trade to be contrasted with Williamson's physical labour – and furthermore, that he could not hold his drink. The verbal altercation descended into a physical one as the pair allegedly tussled over the spade, but in this case it is the slight perceived by MacLennan that should interest us rather than the fight alone. George MacLennan felt insulted by a man who cast aspersions on his manliness and that manliness, in this case, was defined as being able to take a drink, undertaking physical labour and being up for a fight. It is rare for the historian to come across such an unequivocal statement regarding what men in the past understood as constituting masculinity. More often we use descriptions of male behaviour or representations of ideal and alternative masculinities as indicators of masculine gender norms. George MacLennan regarded himself as just as much of a man as John Williamson, notwithstanding his occupation and his drunken demeanour. And he sought to prove it by provoking Williamson to a fight.

Men are everywhere in the narratives of Scotland's past, but at the same time they are nowhere, or at least their gendered selves, roles and practices are less frequently interrogated than women's.[2] In other words men are of course ever present in the story of Scotland but as characters in a landscape that they populate in the guise of normative actors, their actions unremarked upon as manifestations of gendered norms or expectations. And yet, as theorists and historians of gender have explained, masculinity needs to be in our sights as a set of practices and roles, expectations and attributes, which shape the ways in which men act towards one another and women and children, and the ways in which their actions are represented and understood. The male subject and the male experience need to be particularised rather than subsumed into a generalised gender-neutral account, and historians must be attentive to men in all their identities and roles as carriers of gender. Not all men have the same gender; gender identities for men as much as for women are plural, multifaceted and complex, rarely static and always contingent upon particular social, economic, political and cultural conditions. Gender intersects with age, marital status, race, religion, sexuality and a host of other variables so that relations amongst men are as interesting as those between men and women. Indeed masculinity is not dependent on its assumed opposite – femininity – for, as R. W. Connell alerted us, there are many variants of masculinity, which exist in dynamic relations with each other. However, for Connell, 'at any given time, one form of masculinity rather than others is culturally exalted'.[3] Connell's concept of hegemonic and subordinate (as well as marginalised and complicit) masculinities has been influential in framing our interpretations of relations amongst men in a range of contexts, though we should remind ourselves that hegemonic masculinity is never fixed but 'always contestable', allowing for a picture of fluid or dynamic relations whereby the dominance of a particular model is always liable to be challenged.

Notwithstanding this however, the commonest application of the concept of hegemonic masculinity is in relation to the holding of power and maintenance of authority at all levels, from the state to marriage, and thus the upholding and maintenance of patriarchy. But investigations of power relations at a micro level in a range of temporal and geographical contexts have questioned this notion of a patriarchal dividend whereby benefits accrue to those men who ascribe to dominant codes.[4]

In the context of research into men and masculinities in Scotland over the *longue durée*, it is noticeable that Connell's model, or at least the language of dominant and subordinate, hegemonic and transgressive, has been easily incorporated (though often without explicit acknowledgement) into studies of certain kinds of male behaviours. Violence, deviance and a range of transgressive practices are perhaps easily understood as manifestations of subordinate masculinities or as articulations of the dynamism of gender as it is acted out amongst men in contest.[5] And of course deviant masculine behaviours are often the most visible to researchers, evident in the religious and secular legal sources, newspaper accounts and in literary and visual representations. Men who engaged in physical violence when dominant cultural codes were emphasising restraint, who engaged in homosexual encounters within a heteronormative culture or who abjured their family responsibilities in the context of the respectability of breadwinning and providing, are always present in our sources, easy to spot but easy too to translate into a stereotype of the violent or irresponsible hard man of legend. Likewise, our sources are quick to reveal new models at the moment when their advocates are challenging for ascendancy, such as the model of civility so effectively propagated by some Enlightenment writers when older models continue to be ascribed to.[6]

Beacons of civility or its perceived converse represent ideals and anti-ideals, often exaggerated on account of where they are articulated: in the courts, for instance, or in didactic literature. Everyday behaviour, practised by men in commonplace contexts – in the workplace, at home – excites little comment and thus is more likely to be ignored by historians. But it is arguably the rituals of the everyday, the routines of work and relationships, which offer a less contested view of manhood and identify the attributes and behaviours that attracted consent in certain communities or groups. Anthropologists have succeeded in uncovering these patterns where historians have largely focused on the extremes and the exceptions (albeit to highlight the norms). For instance, Anthony Cohen's study of the island community of Whalsay in Shetland in the 1970s revealed embedded patterns of male behaviour that were rooted in the work and community life of that island. Fishing and crofting, which employed the majority of men at that time, created temporal and spatial practices (such as *dellin* or digging the peats), through which men performed a masculinity that was understood by the group, and despite the negligible economic value of some of the activities they were continued to maintain a group cohesion that was so important in a marginal place.[7] Sustaining the distinctive dialect of Whalsay, continuing to hold sprees – peripatetic parties – and the rituals associated with funerals all serve to maintain a community identity that implicitly rests upon men's activities. Daniel Wight's community study of a Lanarkshire mining village lays bare the strains on widely accepted gender roles in a traditional industrial setting. When the mine closed, many of the tenets of a working-class masculinity forged in the hard conditions of work and its compensatory leisure were called into question. Men, whose masculinity was expressed physically (working underground, drinking and smoking) as well as spatially (at work at the pit and in the working men's club) struggled to adapt to unemployment, a lack of independent spending power and pressures to be more involved in the domestic sphere. Wight describes unemployed men as having a demeaned masculinity; unable to express their role as workers through drinking and reluctant to take on 'female roles', such as the grocery shopping.[8] Both Cohen's and Wight's analyses benefit from close observation of their subjects (in both cases, extended time living amongst the communities) and the result reveals a more nuanced understanding of how masculinities are sustained and reworked over time in the face of challenges to long-held understandings of gendered behaviour.

Masculinity – or elements of a masculine identity – is relatively easy to read into a behaviour or a practice – a punch thrown, a job done – but it is more challenging to respond to Shepard and Harvey's 2005 injunction to pay less attention to 'masculinity as a set of cultural attributes' and more to subjective identities.[9] Feminist historians have privileged expressions of the self as a means of accessing female subjectivity, free or at least liberated from dominant male framings of experience. Until recently less attention was paid to male subjectivity, but Michael Roper's challenge to historians to pay attention to the psychic or unconscious dimensions of the subject has been taken up, especially by historians of the modern period who are able to work with various forms of personal testimony – letters, diaries, oral histories and autobiography – as a means of revealing subjective identity.[10] Katie Barclay's interrogation of early modern Scottish marriages mined the correspondence of middling and elite couples and reached beneath the surface of the patriarchal marriage model to reveal the subjectivities of husbands anxious to maintain their social role and patriarchal authority, sometimes revealing aspects of their subjectivities that offer us a range of spousal models, from the patronising to the conciliatory, the authoritarian to the egalitarian.[11] And Hilary Young's exploration of young men's subjectivity via their reading habits in the middle decades of the twentieth century offers alternatives to some of the stereotypes of the masculine persona – men who identified with sporting and adventure heroes and who negotiated their boyhood identities though their consumption of popular literature. Incorporating Dan Dare or Alf Tupper into their everyday life expanded possibilities; here, in the penny papers and comics were alternative and sometimes fantastical masculine role models that could offer boys pathways to social mobility.[12] This shift in research trajectories to the domestic and intimate spaces of men's lives arguably facilitates this focus on subjectivity as it is in this sphere that men are more likely to drop the façade of a masculinity appropriate for public consumption and reflect on themselves.

The chapters contained in this volume are influenced by all of these trends, perhaps a beneficial consequence of Scottish historiography arriving a little late to the party. The history of masculinity largely developed from work in women's and gender history in the 1980s and 1990s and the concurrent development of 'men's studies'.[13] In the last two decades the field has burgeoned, so that key works on men and masculinity – while still clustering in the modern period – suggest comparisons across time, from the medieval period to the present day, and space.[14] Research that explicitly problematises men as gendered subjects in the Scottish context is now quite extensive, albeit largely focused on the urban environment, from the Enlightenment to the present.[15] Influenced by the burgeoning field of women's and feminist history in Scotland, scholars turned their attention to gendered relations in a range of contexts, from religion to politics, the family to the Empire, and argued that taking gender seriously as a category of analysis requires understanding men as well as women as a gendered sex.[16] This set in train a rich vein of scholarship seeking to recover men's experiences *as men* (a kind of recovery history in reverse), which in turn had the potential to recast some of the conventional narratives of the Scottish story: most notably the Protestant Reformation, the Scottish Enlightenment, the rise (and fall) of industrial labour, the Scots and Empire, amongst others.[17] New paths have also been opened up, particularly by those who have shifted their attention towards private and domestic matters, to sexualities and the intimacies of personal relationships where masculinities must be interrogated in order to access and interpret experience.[18] Before 1700, historians have been slower to capitalise on the theoretical insights and methodological advances that facilitate the study of men as gendered actors, with the exceptions of historians of the family and of children and youth.[19] Given the constraints of historical sources for the earlier periods we should not be surprised that literary scholars have been more open than historians to reading for masculinity and the latter are beginning to mine narrative sources such as religious autobiographies for uncovering personal emotions and relationships.[20]

This collection draws from a number of different approaches. Much research, especially by literary scholars and historians influenced by their work, has focused on cultural representations of masculinity, both the models that were presented as ideal forms of masculinity and the images presented by men of themselves. Other work has looked more closely at the actual practice of masculinity by individuals and how it could be influenced by other determinants such as age, social status, and economic and social factors.[21] In the chapters that follow the authors examine both prescription and practice, representation and experience, recognising that gender is a relational category and that behaviours, beliefs and experiences need to be considered in relation to the social world, which incorporates discourses on manhood in the form of images, literary representations, didactic instruction and a host of other framing devices that act to shape the ways in which men act as men at any given time. The book as a whole examines the relationship between masculinity and power, arguing that while patriarchy has benefited men, especially in respect to women, it has also disadvantaged men in various ways.[22] It argues that masculinity has been defined not only in opposition to women, but also in relation to and in competition with other men.[23] It suggests that different forms of masculinity could coexist both between different men and in individual men, and that these masculinities could compete, contradict and undermine each other.[24]

There is a legitimate question about the Scottish flavour of this discussion. The pervasiveness of modern stereotypes of the Scottish man cannot be ignored, and have arguably skewed popular and scholarly interpretations of men in the past. *Braveheart* has a lot to answer for. The 1995 film brought medieval Scotland to the attention of a new generation, both inside and outside Scotland, but the hyper-masculine image of the military hero fed into the already existing stereotype of the 'martial Scot', characterised by the fierce kilted warrior.[25] In more modern times the fictional characters of Begbie and Renton, psychopath and drug addict respectively, stars of Irvine Welsh's novel *Trainspotting*, were freighted with a different kind of meaning as representatives of a post-industrial dystopia. Beyond these extremes, though, Scotland has a host of more positive male exemplars to draw on, all containing a kernel at least of a trait lauded in Scottish culture: the self-educated man; the 'lad o' pairts', the respectable trade unionist, the Enlightenment intellectual. All appear in the contributions to this collection, often as spectres or foils for a more considered and complex interrogation of some aspect of masculine character, but sometimes as real characters in a landscape of memory and imagination that privileges some representations over others and ignores the commonplace and unremarkable.[26]

One might say that such stereotypes should not concern the historian but literary and visual representations contribute to popular discourse and, via the cultural circuit, inform understandings and interpretations of behaviour. The former gang member, for instance, reflecting back on his life is well aware of the particular stereotype associated with that tribe but also present-day Scottish government policies reference more positive understandings of Scottish men, such as the image of the 'civic Scot'. And notwithstanding the particularities of the Scottish legal, religious and education systems (in comparison with those of England), there are certain peculiarities of the Scottish economic, social and cultural environment that have, we suggest, shaped masculinities in this country. Amongst these are the strong bonds of kinship, the clan, the blood feud, the centuries of warfare with England, the large-scale emigration of men to continental armies or merchant towns, and later to the far-flung lands of the Empire. The Scottish Enlightenment, centred on Edinburgh but with tentacles in all the urban centres, created a climate of debate that positioned men's behaviour towards one another and to women as central to civilised discourse. Scotland's industrial character, with a reliance on the extractive and heavy industries, shaped a labouring masculinity that regarded hardness of bodies and minds as the necessary prerequisites to survive in the dangerous trades. The place of the Presbyterian kirk since the Reformation, with its influence within communities and households until the nineteenth century, gave some men moral and coercive power.[27] Moreover, we should not underestimate the importance of place and landscape in the shaping of the Scottish man. The Highlands, islands and the *Gàedhaeltacht*, with their distinctive clan and farming system (and language and culture); the industrial heartland, which forged a class identity amongst labouring men but also alienation following de-industrialisation; the cities with their soulless post-war estates, which offered men little respite and sustained territorialism and sectarianism.[28] The contingency and relationality of masculinities must always be borne in mind, and so we accept that most men's sense of self is shaped, at least in part, by their cultural influences and their relationships with others while being permeable to influences from outwith Scotland.

The present collection expands this field of historical enquiry by exploring perceptions of and practices associated with masculinity in Scotland, uniquely across the *longue durée*, c. 1100–c. 2000. It examines the potential of a range of sources and methodologies for the study of masculinity (including personal testimony, literary and visual sources, legal depositions, didactic material and printed media), and introduces new topics of enquiry including youth, family and household, honour, friendship and sexuality, government and authority. Individual contributions demonstrate that ideas about and practices of appropriate (and inappropriate or deviant) masculine behaviour have varied by social status and class, age, region and other factors, and it therefore examines 'masculinities' rather than attempting to identify one homogeneous masculinity. All the contributors accept the notion that masculinity is a fluid, permeable and contingent construct and their chapters reveal the existence of multiple models across time and place, often conflicting or in tension with one another, resulting in contests between men and sometimes even within an individual's subject identity. James Boswell, featured in Rosalind Carr's chapter, cannot have been the only man to have experienced an ongoing and self-conscious struggle between two versions of his self: the polite, respectable husband and professional man about Edinburgh and the self-loathing libertine who drank and consorted with prostitutes.

The book is structured to illustrate some of the models of masculinity to which men might aspire (or which they might reject), the ways in which men themselves have represented their masculinity, and the lived experiences both of those who have upheld and those who have resisted the socially accepted gender norms of their time. Where the sources allow, the voices of men themselves have been brought to bear on these topics. Many of the chapters, of course, address more than one of these issues simultaneously. Part I includes amongst its masculine models sixteenth-century courtiers, Protestant ministers and 'godly households' of the post-Reformation period, polite and libertine male elites of eighteenth-century Edinburgh and Glasgow, late eighteenth-century Highlanders, and the commercial and labouring classes of nineteenth-century Inverness.

Drawing on recent work on the history of emotions, Sarah Dunnigan's discussion of sixteenth-century lyric poetry examines advice given by the poets to elite young men, encouraging them to aspire to an ideal of moderate and self-governed masculinity. Dangers came both from women, as tempters to illicit sexuality, and from other men who could tempt them to evil actions. Janay Nugent shows how barriers between the clergy and parishioners were broken down after the Protestant Reformation of 1560, with the new ministers, mostly married men with families, providing a model of 'reformed masculinity' to their congregations, especially the male heads of household. Men were now responsible for the spiritual care and moral guidance of their household, as well as its physical and economic maintenance.

The following two chapters both discuss conflicting models of masculinity that coexisted, in some cases within the one individual. Rosalind Carr examines the Scottish Enlightenment ideal of polite masculinity as discussed in contemporary writings, a masculinity that eschewed violence and excess and encouraged refined, well-mannered comportment. At the same time, many elite men were taking advantage of opportunities for sexual licence provided by gentlemen's clubs such as the Beggar's Benison or the female and male prostitutes in the growing cities of Edinburgh and Glasgow. James Boswell's diary provides a very personal glimpse into this world, casting light on the contradictions and tensions between models of masculinity and the repercussions for men who had aspirations to manly respectability. Taking the Highland areas around Inverness as an example, Lynn Abrams looks at how an older model of masculine behaviour common throughout Scotland, which legitimised some forms of violence in defence of family honour, was gradually being replaced by a new model of disciplined masculinity, with increased sensibilities around male interpersonal violence, indicating growing intolerance of violent behaviour by local elites. At the same time, new social dynamics in Inverness itself created points of conflict between labourers, artisans and town officers.

Men may internalise models of masculinity, but they also have to be seen to do so. The performance of gender is crucial to one's place in society. Masculinity is written about, depicted in images, and constructed through personal letters and other such sources. Part II examines representations of masculinity (which, in contrast with women and femininity, is usually undertaken by men themselves: a kind of self-referencing and in some cases self-fashioning). Cynthia Neville examines how medieval kings of Scots drew on European trends in self-fashioning in order to project power, designing personal seals to express their kingly authority, a power bound up with medieval ideals of masculinity. Equestrian imagery depicted the king as a mounted knight, the epitome of medieval military masculinity. The king, seated in majesty, held the symbols of authority, including the sword, which became increasingly prominent, referencing the virility of the male ruler, a particularly pressing issue for preserving the royal bloodline. Sergi Mainer's chapter also examines kingship, taking as its subject the earliest vernacular historical poem, *The Bruce*, written c. 1375 by John Barbour, which tells the story of King Robert the Bruce and his trusted companion James Douglas during the First War of Independence (1296–1328). Barbour uses Bruce and Douglas to show how young princes and noble warriors develop into trusted authority figures, capable of governing others, and finally transcending gender itself as their religious piety and goodness took them into heaven at death.

As Katie Barclay points out in her examination of the begging letters sent by poor men to elite patrons in the nineteenth century, it can be difficult to see, in a modern society that prizes individual independence, how dependence and vulnerability can be an acceptable form of masculinity. But in an ordered hierarchical society where everyone knows their place, dependence is not antithetical to concepts of manliness, but rather one of a series of strategies practised by those in need to provide for themselves and others. Moreover, the charitable relationship is a mutually beneficial one; while emphasising their own gratitude and humility, the petitioners give the elite the opportunity to demonstrate their patriarchal responsibilities in providing for the less fortunate. Letters also form the basis of Lynn Abrams' chapter, which focuses on the wartime correspondence between a serviceman stationed in Trinidad during World War Two and his wife. Separated from his family, George Brown constructed his own image as a romantic lover, caring husband, and responsible father, a type of private emotional masculinity that was becoming more acceptable by the mid-twentieth century. In all of these contributions we can observe men actively engaging with a variety of masculine models, trying them out for size and self-consciously assuming identities, be that powerful ruler, humble supplicant or sensitive lover. Representations then, are actively created by men with an interest in how they are portrayed and some degree of control over the process, which must influence how we interpret such sources.

Moving from models and representations, Part III examines how the lived experiences of men were shaped by gendered expectations. Harriet Cornell's chapter offers a case study of an early seventeenth-century countryman, John Airth, as he moves from the excesses of youth, which result in frequent appearances in the church court for sexual sins and violent behaviour, to responsible male householder upholding the expectations of the community for its adult men. Airth's story highlights how expectations and practices of masculinity change across the life course with the mature man able to cast off his youthful indiscretions and take on a new identity as a respected elder in the community. Tawny Paul takes as her context eighteenth-century Edinburgh, showing how the ideals of polite behaviour and respectable livelihood based on trade obscured the reality of violence between men, not only verbal and physical, but also of a commercial form. Just as Rosalind Carr demonstrates, Edinburgh was a multi-layered urban environment in this period, a city where commercial competition rubbed up against refined politeness. In this context new forms of legally sanctioned violence in the form of litigation and punishment offered men new ways of defending their honour or asserting their authority. A century later in Glasgow, class and respectability clashed in another context. Tanya Cheadle examines the conflict that broke out over risqué music hall performances in Victorian Glasgow between an elite and bourgeois group of men who wished to enforce their moral standards, the working-class men who rejected these standards, and the bourgeois men who crossed social boundaries to join them. Here (as with the cases of Edinburgh and Inverness) we can observe how, in a rapidly changing environment, alternative masculinities are constantly jostling for ascendancy but also how men's identities as men were shaped through experience – in this case by enjoying lewd performances surrounded by hundreds of other men in a heightened atmosphere.

The final two chapters examine those who stood apart from mainstream society. Jeffrey Meek examines men prosecuted for sodomy in mid-twentieth-century Scotland. As he demonstrates, many of the male prostitutes challenged the strict gender binary by dressing in ways associated with women; it was often this gender transgression, rather than the homosexual act itself, which was regarded with horror by heterosexual men. Moreover the definition of deviance was influenced by social class. Clients from 'respectable' society often emerged from court cases with their reputations and masculinity intact. Angela Bartie and Alistair Fraser's chapter looks at the young men who were the epitome of one of the Scottish stereotypes, the youth gangs of 1960s Glasgow. Here violence once more plays a crucial role in establishing one's masculinity, although again individuals could demonstrate both an aggressive masculinity in competition with other young men in their social groups, and a separate gentler domestic masculinity at home. Indeed it is noticeable how many former gang members, interviewed by the authors, had abandoned their gang past to establish new identities as respectable husbands and fathers. The ideals of masculinity that men adopted for themselves changed over the life cycle, as well as over the centuries.

Taken together, the contributions to this volume demonstrate the many different masculinities that shaped the experiences and actions of men (and women) in the Scottish past. But these masculinities did not exist in a vacuum; rather they intersected with and were influenced by many other factors. As many of the chapters demonstrate, individuals are always in a stage of becoming, and their values and ideals and thus their practices change and evolve over time. King Robert Bruce,

John Airth of East Lothian and the boys of the Glasgow gangs assume new styles or modes of masculinity as they age (and in the latter case are able to consciously reflect on the changes they have experienced), while the sixteenth-century advice poems and the eighteenth-century Enlightenment writers attempt to persuade their readers to embrace a particular type of moderate masculinity. Marriage and fatherhood brings new responsibilities as men must not only govern themselves, but also govern their households and their communities. Patriarchal values support such roles for adult men, but not all are able to uphold these particular roles successfully, and some men find themselves dependent on other men, as the eighteenth-century begging letters show, although this did not necessarily threaten their masculine identity. Men also construct their own ideals of domestic masculinity, influenced by wider changes in society, such as the romantic intimate husband and father who appears in George Brown's letters to his beloved wife.

Ideals and practices of masculinity also vary by class and social status. This collection considers a wide range of men, including medieval kings, Enlightenment literati, early modern villagers, gang members, criminalised men, merchants, clansmen and labourers. The disturbances caused by the Glasgow music hall performances cast a particularly illuminating light on how different masculinities can come into conflict, but also show how men could both accept and reject the masculine ideals of their social class. Moreover, social status could sometimes protect those who wished to move outside these ideals, such as the 'respectable' men caught up in sodomy trials, or the libertine elite of eighteenth-century towns. But rejecting these ideals could also come at a price, if society considered individuals to have gone too far, as many from the early twentieth-century homosexual community found, especially those who crossed the gender binary divide.

One result of this gender binary is the tendency to define masculinity as the opposite to femininity. So male tears occupy an awkward place in Barbour's *Bruce*, with the poet emphasising that shedding them is a sign of manly emotion, not female weakness. By the twentieth century, though, George Brown was unapologetic and unselfconscious about expressing his most intimate thoughts to his wife, albeit in writing. But masculinity is also crucially defined in company with and in competition with other men. This collection provides many examples of homosocial society, including the elite chivalric brotherhood of medieval Europe, the sex clubs of Enlightenment Scotland, craft associations, the tavern, the largely male audiences of music halls, and youth gangs. Competition can lead to violence; one of the interesting findings that emerges from the research of our contributors is how pervasive violence seems to have been in the lives of men in the past (in reality or as a threat), but also how many different forms violence could take, from the verbal violence of defamation and threats, to the interpersonal violence of brawls, individual assaults and duels, to the commercial violence visited on economic competitors and creditors. It is this propensity to violence that works of advice throughout the centuries counselled young men in particular to learn to control and govern within themselves. Violence between men in Scotland is still a concern in the twenty-first century, though the methods to counter it have become less didactic and more embedded in community initiatives that engage those most at risk.[29] It remains the case that for young men in Scotland, violence towards other men but also perpetrated against themselves (evidenced by the high suicide rate and the documented reluctance of men to seek medical interventions) is too frequently a response to social isolation and economic marginalisation.[30]

Violence often resulted when a man's honour and reputation were called into question by others. Honour could be bound up with both the individual and the larger family or network in which one was involved. Slights to one's clan or kin began many fights, both in the Highland hinterland and in the streets of Inverness. Reputation also had more immediate economic consequences, as the experience of those involved in the commercial world of eighteenth-century Edinburgh shows. Loss of reputation could lead to loss of the ability to make a living. In contrast with slights to a woman's reputation, which were often of a sexual nature, men across the centuries have been vulnerable to reputational loss across a range of factors, which included the willingness to physically stand up to another man, the ability to support one's household (including controlling one's spouse and servants), and having economic integrity.

Reputation and honour are both outward and inward manifestations of masculinity, experienced by the individual but perceived by the members of society at large. One question addressed by the long temporal scope of this collection is the issue of interiority. Some historians have suggested that masculine ideals and values were increasingly internalised during a 'civilising process', which Norbert Elias and others have argued occurred in Western society during the late seventeenth and eighteenth centuries (coinciding with the Scottish Enlightenment) with masculinity being primarily an outward performance in earlier times. Certainly the sources that shed light on an individual's private thoughts and feelings are much less extensive before the eighteenth century, but the Reformed church as well as medieval and early modern literature placed much emphasis on the cultivation of the well-being of one's own soul and personal piety, which suggests greater continuity than has hitherto been suggested. If historians had access to more of the personal writings of medieval and early modern men, the extent to which they internalised the masculine values and expectations of their own day and social status might be clearer. In the end, as can be seen throughout this collection, each man must construct his version of masculinity for himself.

NOTES

1. NRS, SC 25/56/1 Dingwall Sheriff Court: Criminal Court Indictments 1829–51: Criminal Letters, Procurator Fiscal against George MacLennan, 6 July 1844 – Assault.
2. For a recent review of the literature on gender (but with a strikingly small section devoted to masculinity) see Katie Barclay, Tanya Cheadle, Eleanor Gordon, 'The state of Scottish history: gender', *Scottish Historical Review*, 92 (Supplement): (2013), pp. 83–107.
3. R. W. Connell, *Masculinities* (Cambridge: Polity Press, 1995), pp. 77–81.
4. See especially Alexandra Shepard, *Meanings of Manhood in Early Modern England* (Cambridge: Cambridge University Press, 2003).
5. See for instance, Annmarie Hughes, 'The "non-criminal" class: wife-beating in Scotland c. 1800–1949', *Crime, History and Societies* 14:2 (2010), pp. 31–54; Andrew Davies, 'Street gangs, crime and policing in Glasgow during the 1930s: the case of the Beehive Boys', *Social History*, 23 (1998), pp. 251–67.
6. See John Dwyer, *Virtuous Discourse: Sensibility and Community in Late Eighteenth Century Scotland* (Edinburgh: Edinburgh University Press, 1987); Rosalind Carr, *Gender and Enlightenment Culture in Eighteenth-Century Scotland* (Edinburgh: Edinburgh University Press, 2014).
7. Anthony P. Cohen, *Whalsay: Symbol, Segment and Boundary in a Shetland Island Community* (Manchester: Manchester University Press, 1987).
8. Daniel Wight, *Workers Not Wasters: Masculine Respectability, Consumption and Employment in Central Scotland* (Edinburgh: Edinburgh University Press, 1993), pp. 204–5.
9. Karen Harvey and Alexandra Shepard, 'What have historians done with masculinity? Reflections on five centuries of British history, circa 1500–1950', *Journal of British Studies*, 44:2 (2005), pp. 274–80, at 280.
10. Michael Roper, 'Slipping out of view: subjectivity and emotion in gender history', *History Workshop Journal*, 59:1 (2005), pp. 57–72.
11. Katie Barclay, *Love, Intimacy and Power: Marriage and Patriarchy in Scotland, 1650–1850* (Manchester: Manchester University Press, 2011).

12. Hilary Young, 'Representation and reception. An oral history of gender in British children's story papers, comics and magazines in the 1940s and 1950s' (unpublished doctoral thesis, University of Strathclyde, 2006) and 'Being a man: everyday masculinities', in Lynn Abrams and Callum G. Brown (eds), *A History of Everyday Life in Twentieth Century Scotland* (Edinburgh: Edinburgh University Press, 2010), pp. 131–52.

13. Harry Brod, *The Making of Masculinities: The New Men's Studies* (Boston: Allen & Unwin, 1987); Mairtin Mac an Ghaill, *Understanding Masculinities: Social Relations and Cultural Arenas* (Philadelphia: Open University Press, 1996). The most influential historian has probably been John Tosh. See his *Manliness and Masculinities in Nineteenth Century Britain* (Harlow: Pearson, 2005) for a selection of his work.

14. The literature here is extensive, but examples include: R. M. Karras, *From Boys to Men: Formations of Masculinity in Late Medieval Europe* (Philadelphia: University of Pennsylvania Press, 2003); S. H. Hendrix and C. Karant-Nunn (eds), *Masculinity in the Reformation Era* (Kirksville: Truman State University Press, 2005); Philip Carter, *Men and the Emergence of Polite Society Britain 1660–1800* (Harlow: Pearson Education, 2001); Michael Roper and John Tosh (eds), *Manful Assertions: Masculinities in Britain since 1800* (London: Routledge, 1991).

15. For example: Lynn Abrams, '"There was nobody like my Daddy": fathers, the family and the marginalisation of men in modern Scotland', *Scottish Historical Review*, 78 (1999), pp. 219–42; Barclay, *Love, Intimacy and Power*; Carr, *Gender and Enlightenment Culture*; Andrew Davies, 'Youth gangs, masculinity and violence in late Victorian Manchester and Salford', *Journal of Social History*, 32:2 (1998) pp. 349–69; Ronald Johnstone and Arthur McIvor, 'Dangerous work, hard men and broken bodies: masculinity in the Clydeside heavy industries, c. 1930–1970s', *Labour History Review*, 69:2 (2004), pp. 135–51; Maureen M. Martin, *The Mighty Scot: Nation, Gender, and the Nineteenth-Century Mystique of Scottish Masculinity* (New York: SUNY Press, 2005); Andrew Perchard, '"Broken men" and "Thatcher's children": memory and legacy in Scotland's coalfields', *International Labor and Working Class History*, 84 (2013), pp. 78–98; Hilary Young, 'Hard man, new man: re/composing masculinities in Glasgow, c. 1950–2000', *Oral History*, 35:1 (2007), pp. 71–81.

16. Lynn Abrams, Eleanor Gordon, Deborah Simonton, Eileen Yeo (eds), *Gender in Scottish History since 1700* (Edinburgh: Edinburgh University Press, 2006).

17. Carr, *Gender and Enlightenment Culture*; Ronald Johnston and Arthur McIvor, *Lethal Work: A History of the Asbestos Tragedy in Scotland* (East Linton: Tuckwell Press, 2000); John M. Mackenzie, 'The imperial pioneer and hunter and the British masculine stereotype in late Victorian and Edwardian times', in J. A. Mangan and J. Walvin (eds), *Manliness and*

Morality: Middle Class Masculinity in Britain and America, 1800–1940 (Manchester: Manchester University Press, 1987) pp. 176–98.

18. Jeffrey Meek, *Queer Voices in Postwar Scotland: Male Homosexuality, Religion and Society* (Basingstoke: Palgrave, 2015); Eleanor Gordon and Gwyneth Nair, *Murder and Morality in Victorian Britain: the Story of Madeleine Smith* (Manchester: Manchester University Press, 2011); Tanya Cheadle, 'Realizing a "more than earthly paradise of love": Scotland's sexual progressives, 1880–1914' (unpublished doctoral thesis, University of Glasgow, 2014).

19. Elizabeth Ewan and Janay Nugent (eds), *Finding the Family in Medieval and Early Modern Scotland* (Aldershot: Ashgate, 2008); Janay Nugent and Elizabeth Ewan (eds), *Children and Youth in Premodern Scotland* (Martlesham: Boydell Press, 2015).

20. R. J. Goldstein, 'Normative heterosexuality in history and theory: the case of Sir David Linsday of the Mount' in J. J. Cohen and B. Wheeler (eds), *Becoming Male in the Middle Ages* (New York: Routledge, 1997), pp. 349–65; Sarah Dunnigan, 'Sons and daughters, "young wyfis" and "barnis": lyric, gender and the imagining of youth in the Maitland manuscripts', in Nugent and Ewan, *Children and Youth*, pp. 187–203; David Mullan, *Narratives of the Religious Self in Early Modern Scotland* (Farnham: Ashgate, 2010).

21. For instance, Alexandra Shepard, 'From anxious patriarch to refined gentleman? Manhood in Britain c. 1500–c. 1700', *Journal of British Studies*, 44 (2005), pp. 281–95.

22. Elizabeth Foyster, *Manhood in Early Modern England: Honour, Sex and Marriage* (London: Longman, 1999).

23. Derek G. Neal, *The Masculine Self in Late Medieval England* (Chicago: University of Chicago Press, 2008).

24. Todd Reeser, *Moderating Masculinity in Early Modern Culture* (Chapel Hill: University of North Carolina Press, 2006); J. Murray (ed.), *Conflicted Identities and Multiple Masculinities in the Medieval West* (New York: Garland Publishing, 1999).

25. T. Edensor, 'Reading Braveheart: representing and contesting Scottish identity', *Scottish Affairs*, 21 (1997), pp. 135–58; Esther Breitenbach and Lynn Abrams, 'Gender and Scottish identity', in Abrams et al. (eds), *Gender in Scottish History*, pp. 17–42.

26. See Andrew Blaikie, *The Scots Imagination and Modern Memory* (Edinburgh: Edinburgh University Press, 2013).

27. Callum G. Brown, 'Religion', in Abrams et al. (eds), *Gender in Scottish History*, pp. 84–110. Leah Leneman and Rosalind Mitchison, *Sexuality and Social Control: Scotland 1660–1780* (Oxford: Blackwell, 1989).

28. For example, Angela Bartie, 'Moral panics and Glasgow gangs: exploring "the new wave of Glasgow hooliganism", 1965–1970', *Contemporary British History*, 24:3 (2010), pp. 385–408; Alistair Fraser, 'Street habitus:

gangs, territorialism and social change in Glasgow', *Journal of Youth Studies*, 16:8 (2013), pp. 970–85.

29. For the Glasgow Violence Reduction Unit see http://www.actiononviolence.org.uk (last accessed 21 April 2016).

30. 'Male suicide rate hits 10 year high', *The Scotsman*, 20 February 2015.

PART I

Models

1

'Be Wise in Thy Governing': Managing Emotion and Controlling Masculinity in Early Modern Scottish Poetry

Sarah Dunnigan

IN ONE OF THE most important artistic survivals from sixteenth-century Scotland, David Lyndsay's drama, *Ane Satyre of the Thrie Estaitis*, there is a protracted seduction scene in which a young man is tempted by a female protagonist who is sensuality incarnate.[1] This occurs within the allegorical template of the play's first part: it portrays a monarch's fall within a larger drama about rightful sovereignty, and the nature of social and political justice. In staging the king's undoing through desire, this scene exemplifies one of the most pervasive ways in which masculinity is imagined in early modern Scottish literature. Yet specifically as a portrayal of vulnerable masculinity, it has been overlooked, perhaps because it depicts a highly conventional late medieval moral and gendered conflict between reason and sensuality. It may also reflect the broader lack of critical attention given to masculine bodies, selves, and identities in early modern Scottish writing compared to recent scholarship in English and French Renaissance cultures.[2] While work on women writers and representations of femininity has begun to reveal some interrelationships between gender and cultural agency, the subject of masculinity, either 'as an analytical category' or as a sphere of literary representation, is relatively unexplored.[3] Literature, however, can interestingly refract and reflect sociocultural norms and ideals. As a beginning step in exploring the relationship between masculinity and the early modern literary imagination, this chapter discusses lyric poetry drawn from two important poetic miscellanies: the Bannatyne and Maitland manuscripts.[4] In the present context this chapter cannot comprehensively survey their diverse material, or provide a detailed account of provenance and context (further sources are suggested in endnotes). Its focus is on selected poems that are thematically preoccupied with questions of sexual desire and social conduct. This subject matter most vividly illuminates the fault lines and fragilities of the masculine identities that are projected as both normative and ideal – men in the roles of lovers, fathers and sons.

The lyric genre, however, presents only one variety of literary and cultural representation amid diverse other kinds in early modern Scotland; as Sallie Westwood puts it, '[m]asculinity ... exists in a plurality of forms'.[5] In focusing on a small range of lyrics drawn from two miscellanies assembled in civic and courtly environments in the 1560s and 1580s, the early modern masculinity that they articulate is obviously confined to socially and culturally dominant groups. On the surface, then, these lyrics seem to portray a version of hegemonic masculinity, to use R. W. Connell's term. However, because these imaginative lyric voices only aspire towards, rather than attain, their patriarchal ideals of conduct, 'subordinate' masculinity, with its associated emotional and social anxieties, becomes the real subject of these poems. Alexandra Shepard's helpful twofold definition of masculinity – as 'ranging from a set of cultural attributes associated with normative notions of maleness to the subjective experience of male identity' – explains why this chapter focuses on the lyric genre.[6] In relation to the first of Shepard's categories, these poems strikingly provide a particular kind of 'emotional script' for normative masculine conduct: in other words, they prescribe ways in which their male speakers and addressees should 'present' themselves in the social and emotional public worlds to which these poems imaginatively gesture. In that respect, they are preoccupied with the rhetorical and affective 'display' of masculine identity.

Secondly, the first-person lyric poem is a genre in which questions of identity and interiority are almost always paramount. In this particular context, however, some qualification is required. With the exception of the father–son tutelary poem by Sir Richard Maitland, the selection of lyrics discussed here is anonymous and therefore cannot be said to represent the views of historically identifiable subjects. In any case, we can rarely assume the emotional transparency or 'authenticity' of voice in lyric poetry. In the early modern context in particular, the first-person poetic subject is usually viewed as a rhetorical construction, a deliberately 'fashioned' persona. The notion of poetic 'subjectivity' is therefore complex, as indeed is the idea of reading emotion 'historically'; in the early modern period the term 'emotion' did not exist, and 'passion' and 'affection' were instead the more common verbal currency of affect.[7] Nevertheless, this chapter is interested in the associations drawn between masculinity and emotion – in the particular 'affects' that these lyrics both approve and condemn in terms of what should be 'experienced' by their ideal masculine subject. It alludes to William M. Reddy's concept of 'emotional regimes', and Barbara H. Rosenwein's influential work on 'emotional community'.[8] This is understood as a socially cohesive network forged by shared 'systems of feeling . . . bound by the emotions that they [those members of the emotional community] value, devalue, or ignore; the nature of the affective bonds between people that they recognise; and the modes of emotional expression that they expect, encourage, tolerate, and deplore'.[9]

MASCULINITY, DESIRE AND EMOTIONAL COMMUNITY: THE BANNATYNE LYRICS

The Bannatyne manuscript is arguably the richest surviving collection of fifteenth- and sixteenth-century Scottish poetry.[10] Its compiler George Bannatyne (1545–1607/8) can be located within Edinburgh's 'urban and legal circles', which had 'connections to church, court, and literature'.[11] Accordingly, Theo van Heijnsbergen argues, Bannatyne's collecting and editorial procedures reflect 'socially conservative yet culturally open-minded tastes', and constitute a view of literature 'as both moral counsel and entertainment'.[12] In the manuscript's fourth section, the so-called 'ballattis of lufe', there are poems devoted respectively to the excoriation and praise of women. When Bannatyne chose and arranged material for inclusion, he may have had the phenomenon of the *querelle des femmes* in mind. Without an understanding of the *querelle*'s precedent, these fifty or so poems (of variable length) appear an odd, shocking, and discomfiting mixture of antifeminist diatribe and satire in the first part, and religious and moral exaltation in the second. The *querelle* tradition emerged out of, and remained entangled within, the discourses of misogyny – formed out of classical, philosophical, theological and medical sources – which, from the twelfth century onwards, comprise what Alcuin Blamires terms 'the phenomenon of medieval antifeminism'.[13] Although in ideological terms, this is a relatively 'unified' discourse (that is, in its intent to articulate hatred of women), its outlets of expression in the later Middle Ages were varied and diverse. These courtly, scholarly, and clerical disputes varied (at least rhetorically) in 'seriousness' for, as Blamires points out, '[t]here can be little doubt that the intelligentsia did regard the rhetorical formulae of misogyny as a game, or at least that they considered misogyny a suitable arena in which to show off their literary paces'.[14] They were carried over into contemporary vernacular literary discourses. They flourished especially in satirical, comic and moral genres that explored the subject of desire (*Le Roman de la Rose* is famously a point of illustration). Why, then, is the Bannatyne manuscript so obsessively concerned with the 'facultie of famenene' [the character of womanhood] (vol. 4, p. 10, line 17)?[15] The presence of Mary, Queen of Scots as the reigning monarch during the period of its apparent compilation has been suggested as one possible reason that would give these poems topicality.[16] Although at one level they simply reconstitute what Jill Mann has aptly described as 'this vast echo-chamber of anti-feminist commonplace',[17] this poetry – so thematically concerned with female duplicity and treachery; with adultery and infidelity; and with disordered and intolerable marriages (or, specifically, wives) – would find its parallel in the queen accused of adulterous murder.

This is one supposition for the manuscript's striking inclusion of antifeminist materials in its pursuit of 'counsel' and 'entertainment', to use van Heijnsbergen's terms; another might be that their particular arrangement purposefully foregrounds and anatomises male desire – what shores up its 'normative' expression, and what disorders it (in other words, desire for women). These poems are always in pursuit of a longed-for but unattainable emotional or psychological equilibrium. This returns us to the notion of 'the echo-chamber' – not, this time, of medieval antifeminism but of the traditions of medieval love lyric, which the Bannatyne corpus inherits and transforms. Its male speakers, ungoverned by desire, inhabit the voices of earlier amatory tradition; in particular, the genre of the late medieval courtly love lyric in terms of thematic content and style.[18] In these lyrics (as well as the proverbs, apothegms, and riddles of this section), desire is often portrayed in 'passionate' terms, using Michael Schoenfeldt's summation of early modern passion as 'any feeling by which the mind is powerfully affected or moved; ... a vehement, commanding, or overpowering force whose power is to be feared'.[19] It is also depicted as a game whose rules of conduct need to be observed with care and caution. In many ways, they adhere to a formulaic discourse of obedience and subjugation which focuses on the uneven distribution of sexual and emotional power between male lover and female beloved; hence the Bannatyne love corpus is full of unidentified lovers who contemplate their own imminent extinction at the mercy of a vindictive female figure. In the 'restricted and repetitive vocabulary'[20] that characterises this erotic discourse, sexual desire and femininity are often figuratively associated through metaphors of sickness, contagion, and pollution. The early modern notion of the materiality of the passions[21] often finds violent expression ('Thruch his entrellis [scho] taklid the hart rute' [she tore up the roots of his heart by means of the entrails], vol. 4, p. 25, line 56). Male desire for women is tantamount to a death-wish:

> thair is no differance
> Betuix the gallowis and the spowsing claith . . .
> [There is no difference between the gallows and the marriage cloth . . .]
>   (vol. 4, p. 37, line 40)

Desire is portrayed as a destructive fire, and an experience of piercing and wounding; in these lyrics, the male body is the site of emotional expressiveness.

Because these poems are best understood within the rhetorical and thematic conventions of the late medieval and early modern love lyric, they might be judged to represent only a restricted and generic type of literary masculinity. But the Bannatyne corpus arguably seeks to present a kind of resolution or 'escape' from this self-destructive male desire and, accordingly, gestures towards some ways in which literary and broader 'sociocultural' notions of masculinity might intersect. Although, as already suggested, these lyrics can rarely be read as 'historically lived' experiences of emotions (in these instances, desire, love, fear), they can nonetheless serve as *representations* of those emotions. As imaginative embodiments of affect, they project the illusion of feeling that is still vividly depicted:

> Teiris over my visage ranis
> And makis the blud within my vanis / To dry . . .
> [Tears over my visage rain and make the blood within my veins to dry . . .]
>   (vol. 4, p. 10, lines 6–7)

Moreover, their central affective experience is vulnerability. These poems repeatedly present a male subject being confronted with a mirror of his own emotional or psychological inadequacies – his various states of 'unpreparedness' to 'manage' the passions that the figure of woman evokes. Moreover, this 'failure' is not just portrayed in terms of women's fearful powers (the paradigm of woman-as-temptress in late medieval and early modern love discourse) but conceived as a failure of emotional self-governance[22] – of the disciplining or 'regulation' of the passions. As Mark Breitenberg puts it in his study of early modern 'anxious' masculinities, 'masculine identity is portrayed as a potential site of disorder and misrule, a "state" in and of itself whose competing elements must display proper obedience and "subjection" to the internal authorities of reason and self-control'.[23] These lyrics might also be situated within the context of the prevailing early modern theory of the passions, largely conceived according to a model of opposition between Neostoicism and Neo-augustinianism. The former adheres to a Stoic conception of the passions as 'perturbations', needing to be controlled and expelled by a cultivated indifference or *apatheia*; the latter conceives of affective experience as spiritually beneficial, shaped by the 'proportion of emotion that determines the ethical status of the subject'.[24] It is obvious, therefore, that these lyrics adhere to the former emotional 'regime', strongly suggesting that masculinity can only re-assume its normative and 'regulated' state by the expulsion of this passion or affect.

This is also corroborated by the persistent ways in which these poems urge masculine self-preservation. A strong sense of rhetorical community is created by which the 'individuality' of the lyric voice is subsumed into a plural one. A kind of collective masculine voice becomes its own self-legitimising authority. For even though the masculine voices or selves that populate this section mourn and lament (and hence represent a vocality that is usually considered feminine in cultural terms), this vulnerability is shared; one poem alludes to 'wemen quhilk [which] ar our oppressioun'.[25] This has the effect of making the regulation of disordering passions a kind of edict. Their obsession with expunging desire is achieved by means of a kind of homosocial rhetorical and 'emotional community' of exchange. Even in the manuscript's pro-feminine section (in which women are the subject of praise rather than excoriation, the source of nurture, goodness, and inspiring 'knychtheid'), the creation of an 'emotional community' is similarly achieved:

> For we aucht first to think on quhat maner
> Thay bring ws furth and quhat pane thay indure
> First in our birth and syne fro yeir to yeir
> [We should first think how they brought us into the world and what pain
>   they suffered first in giving birth to us and then in subsequent years][26]

These masculine voices also apportion themselves a particular kind of rhetorical authority. These are presented as written emblems of repudiation against women – 'I wret it as a man steidfast' (vol. 4, p. 22, line 74):

> Ane proclamatioun / Vnto all natioun / I mak heir by this bill. (vol. 4, p. 19,
>   line 19)

Alexander Scott devises a persona who excuses himself:

> I wat gud wemen will not wyt me
> Nor of this sedull be eschamit

[I hope good women won't blame me nor be ashamed of this bill] (vol. 4, p. 13, lines 73–4)

What is interesting here is the way in which language itself bolsters the articulation of masculine disquiet; the act of the poem's creation, of giving poetic shape to desires and anxieties, is paradoxically an exercise in power. These poems become an elaborate series of rhetorical ploys that strive to 'authorise' a certain kind of masculine identity (one that is hegemonic and normative), all the while imagining affective states and experiences which betray a subordinate identity.

These poems also articulate their anxieties within a social framework. Just as Bannatyne (and therefore by implication his manuscript) is associated with Edinburgh's urban, legal, and civic environments, so too do these apparently 'private' poems gesture towards a public world of scrutiny and judgement. Several are concerned with female conduct, and how it might endanger masculine propriety. The traditional association between women and garrulity is expressed in interesting terms such that men are themselves drawn into the 'secreit' discourses that women then violate:

To bid men keip their secreit counsaillis
Syne schaw the same agane till uthiris . . .
[To bid men keep their secret counsels then show the same again to others
. . .] (vol. 4, p. 11, lines 21–2)[27]

The 'proper', ordered, and well-governed masculine self, these lyrics suggest, should be capable of being publicly enacted or performed. This is why the language of governance and governing is so striking in these poems, and why desire is portrayed as a form of 'misgovirnance' (vol. 4, p. 9, line 7). This returns us to the poems' manifest fear of unregulated passion:

So day be day scho plaid with me buk hud
With Mony skornis and mokkis behind my bak
Hir subtell wylis gart me spend all my gud
Quhill that my clayis grew threidbair on my back . . .
[Daily she played 'blindman's buff' with me, scorning and mocking me
behind my back; her covert guile forced me to spend all my goods until
my clothes on my back were threadbare . . .] (vol. 4, p. 30, lines 57–60).[28]

If masculine identity is conceived as a form of social governance, and therefore about the preservation of a coherent and well-regulated public identity, then its failure to be enacted in this way ultimately becomes a source of shame.

FATHERS, SONS AND 'EMOTIONAL REGIMES'

This story about the 'control' of masculine passions can be located elsewhere in medieval and early modern Scottish literary writing. Joanna Martin has identified a late medieval tradition of erotic renunciation in favour of philosophical and rational self-governance so that *The Kingis Quair*, for example (the fifteenth-century allegorical love vision poem ascribed to James I) can also be interpreted as a fable of ideal political rule.[29] This is echoed in the amatory poetic culture of the later Jacobean court in the 1580s and 1590s in which the writing of love poetry is seen as morally and ethically charged by the king himself, James VI, who in his own early lyric poems constructs an imperious poetic masculinity. But there is also another particular lyric genre in which the 'regulation' of masculinity is paramount and which, in turn, presents a further variant on the idea of masculinity's 'emotional regimes'. This is found in a small body of poems, written for or to young men who are specifically addressed as sons; in other words, poems written from the perspective of a father to a male child. The father–son advice poem constitutes a genre in itself, inherited from earlier medieval literature in which an older, wiser preceptor instructs a younger, naive man – age is set in opposition to youth, and all that this implies morally and philosophically. In the Bannatyne manuscript, for example, there are poems that exhort, cajole and scold men in 'the flour . . . of yowthed' [in the flower . . . of youth] and 'In thy flowris of lust'.[30] One such young man, or rather a 'ventriloquised' lyric voice, regrets that:

> Evir fader me gat
> Or moder me wend in clais . . .
> [Ever father me begot or mother wrapped me in swaddling clothes . . .] (vol.
>   4, p. 7, lines 41–2)[31]

that is, he regrets that he was born, since he suffers so much 'for ane womans saik'. The voice of the paternal preceptor is therefore a powerful example of an 'early modern governing masculinity'.[32]

Although this is a conventional late medieval genre, its manifestation within the context of the family manuscript miscellany offers a further perspective on these interrelated ideas of emotional community and emotional regime. The Maitland Folio manuscript contains a lyric that begins 'My sone gif yow to the court will ga', anonymously attributed and inscribed 'how the father teichit the sone' (MF XLVII).[33] And it presents its counsel in more formal terms:

Myn awin deir sone I the requeir
Thir documentis that thow wald leyr
And keip thame weill bayth less and mair . . .
[My own dear son, I require you to learn these documents and keep them
    well both less and more . . .] (MFXLVII p. 173, lines 121–3)

The son must keep his father's counsel, the word of paternal 'law', close:

Everie day tak tent thairto
Suppois that thow haue meikle ado.
[Every day take heed thereto, even if you have much to do.] (MF II lines
    3–4)

In this case, the lyric genre of paternally prescriptive masculinity, however, has the more historically identifiable resonance of the Maitland Folio and Quarto manuscripts. Both are associated with Sir Richard Maitland of Lethington (c. 1496–1586), a prominent lawyer and courtier who held a range of political positions throughout a variety of administrations and reigns (including that of Mary Queen of Scots). He was an extraordinary lord of session, a keeper of the privy seal until Mary's abdication, factor and chamberlain of the royal abbey of Haddington, and significantly he was also a writer, both of historical chronicle and poetry. Maitland's work often explores contemporary politics and religion, and survives in these two collections: the Folio, which seems to have been begun in the 1570s but contains poetry which relates to events datable to 1555, and the Quarto, which has the date 1586 inscribed in it, appropriately ending at his death.[34] At some point he wrote a poem for his son, undated, but copied out in each of the manuscripts, Folio and Quarto (MF XIV; MQ II), where it is entitled 'The Laird of Lethingtounis Counsale to his Sone, Beand in the Court'. Which son is addressed, of the three whom he had with his wife, Mariota, or Mary, is unclear, despite the evidence that an eighteenth-century editor produced to the contrary: 'To his son William beand in court'.[35] This was William Maitland (1525–73), 'secretary Lethington' to Queen Mary, whose Marian support eventually cost him his freedom, and then his life (he died in Leith prison). There was also Thomas, who died in Italy in 1572, and John who lived until 1586. It would, of course, help a great deal if it were known for sure which son was the recipient of this poem, thereby giving it socio-historical flesh and bone; and Joanna Martin also suggests that 'sone' here may merely indicate a younger man, addressed by a more experienced figure, and is characteristic of the mode of address of such poems.[36] But the poem still remains suggestive for the 'emotional regime', which it projects as the only way to survive, and prosper. It is a highly crafted, 'public' text but one that at its core concerns the careful navigation of feeling: the way in which words, actions and gestures are invested with social symbolism, and in which conduct and emotions might be 'managed'. It exemplifies a particular sociocultural template of masculinity, which demonstrates, as Vaught argues, that the emotional articulation of masculinity is determined by professional and social class.[37]

The poem begins from the moment at which the Maitland son has departed for court. It exhorts him to take careful notice of the paternal advice that follows, as if articulating the father's fears that his son's courtly career might be in trouble. In general terms, the entrance into court life is a rite of passage, a threshold-crossing into a particular stage of maturity and so, accordingly, the poem is concerned with a formative masculinity.[38] The subsequent 'rules' for courtly living, including the precept that he 'Be wyse and tentie in thy gouerning' [Be wise and careful in your governing] (line 29), and that he should keep his counsel closely guarded for a high-status position at court, are subject to the flux and instability of court life. The lyric begins with a series of maxims, and paints a world of figurative instability. The son, compared to an easily blown tree, reflects the fragility that characterises the environment to which he now belongs. In this, the particular specificity of this father–son poem transmutes a more general late medieval lyric tradition of moral complaint about the impermanence and instability of life. Accordingly, the poem's subject is a Maitland son who is 'already' an emblem of a wider philosophical literary tradition – the son is portrayed as a kind of Boethius figure, a vulnerable youth in need of philosophical instruction, except it is not Lady Philosophy but his father who will be the source of revelation.

Maitland's lyric demonstrates how masculinity should be constituted within a particular sociopolitical and cultural order, and how inevitably it must function as an emblem of that order. The poem suggests the court is a particular testing ground of the son's strength. This echoes a deep-rooted tradition of anti-courtly, or anti-curial writing: in a satirical, political vein of medieval and Renaissance literature, courts are the loci of treachery and deceit, rife with factions and general corruption. Another Folio poem (MF LXXVI), framed as a folktale, tells how the youngest of three brothers has the bad luck to end up in court (as opposed to the elder two – one becomes a rich cleric, the other a rich merchant):

Thre brether war we
All borne of ane cuntre [the same country]

The hardest fortoun fell me
The grit god be my gyde. (lines 5–8)

Elsewhere in the manuscripts [Quarto and Folio], Maitland is happy to assume the role of general moral commentator. But more is symbolically at stake in his son's conduct. For it embodies not just broader ethical or philosophical concerns but a particular family honour. All these Maitland and Bannatyne poems speak of the anxiety, not that the son will inherit the sins of the father but that it might happen vice versa – the good name of the father might be 'contaminated' by association; a reverse lineage, as it were. The poem demonstrates the ways in which the family shapes an 'individual's subjection within a set of hierarchical social relations',[39] exemplifying Shepard's assertion that men's 'self-governance' was seen as 'a precondition of successful household management and of access to the full patriarchal dividend'.[40] Collectively these poems speak of the power and prestige of 'the Maitland lyne and lineage'. This concerns the creation and perpetuation of a 'family community', defined by shared social and emotional values. There are, however, no poems about daughters, or from a mother to a daughter, even though we know that they were in fact in the possession and ownership of Helen and Marie Maitland, and therefore entrusted to the care of Maitland's daughters, and not his sons. Masculinity carries the particular honour of family but also, according to Maitland's poem, the broader social, moral, ethical, and political well-being of the realm. The loyal and well-disciplined son is also a model courtier, subject and politician. The need for an ordered, and orderly, masculinity is therefore paramount, and so the language of both constraint and restraint, discipline and caution, is woven through this lyric.

This enables the expression of a particular kind of masculine emotional regime. Maitland's poem is all about the 'disciplining' of the son; how he might mould himself in order to find acceptability within, and to find mastery over, this courtly world. In that sense, the poem is a miniature emblem of the Renaissance 'conduct book', and so has echoes of the way in which the Bannatyne poetry, as argued earlier, might be seen as a 'moral mirror' for men. In medieval and early modern Europe there was a pervasive tradition of treatises and manuals that sought to 'mould' the 'conduct' of young men and young women; Erasmus' *De civilitate morum puerilium*, first published in 1530 and extremely popular right through to the eighteenth century, was concerned with the cultivation of 'civility' and 'propriety' in male youth.[41] But much of it is about the prescription of normative behaviour for young men: how to comport actions and gestures within a social world which surveys and scrutinises conduct, one in which 'appearances' signify 'essences'.[42] In that sense, what this chapter is calling a miniature masculine conduct book poem prescribes a normative 'emotional script'. And it is on this point that the Maitland poem differs from the Bannatyne corpus in terms of its emotional regime. For it is a 'conduct lyric', which is actually far more concerned with the moral and spiritual self than the bodily or public or social self. 'External' actions, words and deeds may be the things that determine the son's career at the court but they ought to be the consequence of carefully managed judgement, reflection and feeling. For the masculinity presented here is not vulnerable in the way that we commonly find (as in the Bannatyne poems, which exhort young men to discipline their bodily desires). Maitland's poem does not address the dangers of lust, for example; indeed, neither erotic desire nor women are mentioned. For once, according to the logic of these poems, a young man's world is not jeopardised by women. Rather the danger comes from 'vther mannis fais . . . wicket men who draw the far on syde' [other men's faces . . . wicked men who draw you far aside] (line 14). Fragility lies *within*, and masculine self-governance requires 'management' of other things. Its anxiety about how the young man should exercise restraint in language seems to go beyond the usual courtly conduct book prescriptions for eloquent speech:

> In thy speiking luik that thow be nocht vane
> Behald and heir and to thy tung tak tent . . .
> [. . .]
> Be nocht ane scorner nor feinyeit flatterer
> Nor yit ane rounder of Inuentit talis . . .
> [In your speaking, look that you be not vain. Observe and hear and be
>   careful of your tongue . . . Be not a scorner nor a deceitful sycophant, nor
>   yet a creator of made-up stories . . .] (lines 3–4, 9–10)

Such warnings about duplicitous, or 'ill-managed', speech rather ironically invert Renaissance anxieties about the subversive or transgressive nature of female speech (hence the traditional conduct book prescription of silence as a female ideal). But in this public, courtly sphere, masculine rhetoric is invested with a moral power. Ideal male speech, or 'fair wourdis' (line 31), is judicious and temperate, and its exemplary masculinity is moderate, and moderated.[43] The poem points to all the potentially precarious pitfalls but provides answers on avoidance of all. Here we see most vividly how it becomes less of a conduct book, intent on rules for regulating bodily and social selves, and more of a devotional or religious exercise, as it were. The poem presents a fusion of two 'regulatory' discourses: social and religious. Because being 'gud of lyf' appears more important than any other moral imperative, this becomes a poem concerned with spiritual rather than erotic 'affect'. It is about care of the soul, or attention to the inward spirit. Ultimately the burden of responsibility for such self-governance lies within the self; fathers might preach but this is about personal responsibility. 'Think at the last thy doing will be spyit', Maitland's poem warns, expressive of both the prying court and the eyes of God come Judgement Day; the implication is that there is never anywhere to hide. Arguably, by the poem's end, masculinity is subsumed into a non-gendered individuality before God, purity of heart and soul portrayed as the ultimate goal of the son's 'gudly living'.

CONCLUSION

This chapter has suggested that some of the affective and cultural 'meanings' of masculinity in early modern Scotland can be glimpsed in two examples of the literary miscellany. Lyric poetry appears to offer a distinctive imaginative projection of emotional states, which in turn are invested with social and cultural import. Both the Bannatyne and Maitland texts discussed here suggest in different ways how and why certain emotions need to be 'managed' in order for their masculine selves to attain stability and wholeness. In pointing to 'the early modern investment in emotional expression as either a generic marker of social status or the sentient matter of communal bonds',[44] they suggest some other fruitful areas of investigation in terms of early modern Scottish masculinities: for example, expressions of male friendship. The Bannatyne male voices – preceptors, interlocutors, complainants – constitute an 'emotional community' of masculinity, intent on the creation and maintenance of an affective 'regime' from which heterosexual erotic desire must be expelled; in that sense, women become the symbolic scapegoat for its collective 'failure' of masculinity. Maitland's paternal advice poem, on the other hand, perhaps only tells us that he had high expectations for his son, or that he took the demands of fatherhood very seriously. But because this manuscript poetry as a whole sits on a fascinating threshold between private and public, the poem also suggests the double-edged nature of the courtly, performative masculine self: how it is outwardly perceived, and how inwardly it might be 'governed'. In that respect, the poem portrays both the external and internal locations of masculinity's social and emotional identities within this particular courtly context. Proper 'self-governance' is also about shoring up a particular assumed position of privilege: the poem is the external symbol or sign, as it were, of the son's determined and legitimate place in a highly stratified social order. And it gestures towards that recurring implicit association between masculinity and vulnerability, but in a more nuanced way than the Bannatyne lyrics, with their terminal point of misogyny. To use Barbara Correll's description of Renaissance conduct books, such poetry is concerned with 'specifying what one does – and especially, what one does not do' and 'expos[ing] what one is not yet and would like to become'.[45] Maitland's poem is really a series of imperatives, addressed to the future and therefore ideal self that his son might become but which acknowledges his fragility in the face of actual experience. Most likely the career of William, Thomas, or John, whichever son this poem may have been intended for, fell between the gaps of such lived and imagined experience. Early modern lyric poetry can help us see the projected ideal forms that hegemonic masculinity, or authoritative manhood, could assume: how emotions should be managed and what feelings are 'legitimate'. And in its imaginative depiction of lovers, fathers and sons, it gives voice to the anxieties that surround its inevitable failure to be sustained.

NOTES

1. For a recent edition of Lyndsay's play, see Greg Walker (ed.), *Anthology of Medieval Drama* (Oxford: Blackwell, 2000).
2. See, for example, Catherine Bates, *Masculinity and the Hunt. Wyatt to Spenser* (Oxford: Oxford University Press, 2013), and *Masculinity, Gender, and Identity in English Renaissance Lyric* (Cambridge: Cambridge University Press, 2007); Gerry Milligan and Jane Tylus (eds), *The Poetics of Masculinity in Early Modern Italy and Spain* (Toronto: Centre for Reformation and Renaissance Studies, 2010); Ian McAdam, *Magic and Masculinity in Early Modern Drama* (Pittsburgh: Duquesne University Press, 2009); Frederick Kiefer (ed.), *Masculinities and Femininities in the Middle Ages and Renaissance* (Turnhout: Brepols, 2009); Jennifer C. Vaught, *Masculinity and Emotion in Early Modern English Literature* (Aldershot: Ashgate, 2008); Bruce R. Smith, *Shakespeare and Masculinity* (Oxford: Oxford University Press, 2000). Important earlier studies include Susan Dwyer Amussen, 'The cultural politics of manhood in early modern England', in Amussen and Mark A. Kishlansky (eds), *Political Culture and Cultural Politics in Early Modern England* (Manchester: Manchester University Press, 1995), pp. 213–33; Lynn Enterline, *The Tears of Narcissus: Melancholia and Masculinity in Early Modern Writing* (Stanford, CA:

Stanford University Press, 1995); Mark Breitenberg, *Anxious Masculinity in Early Modern England* (Cambridge: Cambridge University Press, 1996). More work has been done on Scottish masculinity and literature in the post-1800 period, for example: Carole Jones, *Disappearing Men: Gender Disorientation in Scottish Fiction 1979–1999* (New York: Rodopi, 2009); Maureen M. Martin, *The Mighty Scot: Nation, Gender, and the Nineteenth-Century Mystique of Scottish Masculinity* (Albany: State University of New York Press, 2009).

3. Karen Harvey and Alexandra Shepard, 'What have historians done with masculinity? Reflections on five centuries of British history, circa 1500–1950', *Journal of British Studies*, 44:2 (2005), pp. 274–80, at 274–5.

4. On Scottish early modern manuscript culture, see Priscilla Bawcutt, 'Manuscript miscellanies in Scotland from the fifteenth to the seventeenth century', in Sally Mapstone (ed.), *Older Scots Literature* (Edinburgh: John Donald, 2005), pp 189–210; Sebastiaan J. Verweij, '"The inlegebill scribbling of my impromptu pen": the production and circulation of literary miscellany manuscripts in Jacobean Scotland, c. 1580–c. 1630' (unpublished doctoral thesis, University of Glasgow, 2008).

5. Sallie Westwood, '"Feckless fathers": masculinities and the British state', in Máirtín Mac an Ghaill (ed.), *Understanding Masculinities: Social Relations and Cultural Arenas* (Buckingham: Open University Press, 1996), pp. 21–34, at 24.

6. Alexandra Shepard, 'From anxious patriarchs to refined gentlemen? Manhood in Britain, circa 1500–1700', *Journal of British Studies*, 44:2 (2005), pp. 281–95, at 288.

7. There is growing interdisciplinary work on the history of emotions: see, for example, 'Introduction: reading the early modern passions', in Gail Kern Paster, Katherine Rowe and Mary Floyd-Wilson (eds), *Reading the Early Modern Passions: Essays in the Cultural History of Emotion* (Philadelphia: University of Pennsylvania Press, 2004), pp. 1–20, at 2.

8. William M. Reddy, *The Navigation of Feeling: A Framework for the History of Emotions* (Cambridge: Cambridge University Press, 2001); Barbara H. Rosenwein, *Emotional Communities in the Early Middle Ages* (Ithaca, NY: Cornell University Press, 2006), and 'Worrying about emotions in history', *American Historical Review*, 107 (2002), pp. 821–45.

9. B. Rosenwein, 'Problems and methods in the history of emotions', *Passions in Context*, 1 (2010), pp. 1–32, at 11.

10. For the manuscript and its sociocultural contexts, see Theo van Heijnsbergen, 'The interaction between literature and history in Queen Mary's Edinburgh: the Bannatyne Manuscript and its prosopographical context', in A. A. MacDonald, M. Lynch and I. B. Cowan (eds), *The Renaissance in Scotland: Studies in Literature, Religion, History and Culture offered to John Durkan* (Leiden: Brill, 1994), pp 183–225. All quotations are taken from the Scottish Text Society edition, *The Bannatyne Manuscript, writtin*

in tyme of pest 1568 by George Bannatyne, W. Tod Ritchie (ed.), 4 vols (Edinburgh: Blackwood, 1928–34); the relevant volume, page, and line reference are given.

11. Theo van Heijnsbergen, 'Bannatyne, George (1545–1607/8)', in *Oxford Dictionary of National Biography* (Oxford University Press, 2004; online edition, October 2006), http://www.oxforddnb.com/view/article/1309 (last accessed 7 July 2015)

12. Ibid.

13. Alcuin Blamires (ed.), with Karen Pratt and C. W. Marx, *Woman Defamed and Woman Defended: An Anthology of Medieval Texts* (Oxford: Clarendon Press, 1992), p. 1.

14. Ibid. p. 12.

15. The Dictionary of the Scots Language glosses 'facultie' as 'personal character; ability, skill; branch of learning; social position', www.dsl.ac.uk (last accessed 23 January 2016).

16. See David Parkinson, 'A lamentable storie: Mary Queen of Scots and the inescapable *Querelle des Femmes*', in L. A. J. R. Houwen, A. A. MacDonald and Sally Mapstone (eds), *A Palace in the Wild: Essays on Vernacular Culture and Humanism in Late-medieval and Renaissance Scotland* (Leuven: Peeters, 2000), pp 141–60; Sarah M. Dunnigan, *Eros and Poetry at the Courts of Mary, Queen of Scots, and James VI* (Basingstoke: Palgrave Macmillan, 2002).

17. Jill Mann, *Geoffrey Chaucer* (New York; London: Harvester Wheatsheaf, 1991), note 17.

18. See further Theo van Heijnsbergen, 'The Bannatyne manuscript lyrics: from literary convention to personal expression' in G. D. Caie (ed.), *The European Sun* (East Linton: Tuckwell Press), pp. 423–44.

19. Michael Schoenfeldt, '"Commotion Strange": Passion in *Paradise Lost*', in Paster et al. (eds), *Reading the Early Modern Passions*, pp. 43–67, at 50.

20. Sarah Kay, 'Desire and subjectivity', in Simon Gaunt and Sarah Kay (eds), *The Troubadours: An Introduction* (Cambridge: Cambridge University Press, 1999), pp. 212–27, at 213.

21. Cf. Gail Kern Pastor, 'The body and its passions', *Shakespeare Studies*, 29 (2001), pp. 44–50; see also her *Humoring the Body: Emotions and the Shakespearean Stage* (Chicago: University of Chicago Press, 2004).

22. On ideas of masculine governance and 'self-mastery' in general in the early modern period, see Susan Broomhall and Jacqueline Van Gent (eds), *Governing Masculinities in the Early Modern Period: Regulating Selves and Others* (Farnham: Ashgate, 2011), pp. 16ff.

23. Ibid. p. 18.

24. Schoenfeldt, '"Commotion Strange"', p. 53. See further William J. Bouwsma, 'Two faces of humanism', in *A Usable Past: Essays in European Cultural History* (Berkeley: University of California Press, 1990), pp. 19–73; Michael Schoenfeldt, *Bodies and Selves in Early Modern England:*

Physiology and Inwardness in Spenser, Shakespeare, Herbert, and Milton (Cambridge: Cambridge University Press, 1999), pp. 15–19; Paster et al. (eds), *Reading the Early Modern Passions*, pp. 12ff; Vaught, *Masculinity and Emotion*, pp. 13–14; Margaret R. Graver, *Stoicism and Emotion* (Chicago: University of Chicago Press, 2007). See Richard Strier, 'Against the rule of reason: praise of passion from Petrarch to Luther to Shakespeare to Herbert', in Paster et al. (eds), *Reading the Early Modern Passions*, pp. 23–42, for an account of Renaissance 'anti-Stoicism' in which emotional and affective expression was seen as valuable.

25. Vol. 4, p. 33, line 18.
26. Vol. 4, p. 65, lines 8–10. This particular poem (again attributed to Chaucer) directly addresses a male interlocutor but seems to mock male mourning and self-pity as if to portray misogyny as a kind of sham ritual of 'manhood'.
27. The poem suggests this is a 'vice' that women inherit from their mothers.
28. Also 'Quhy sowld I schamefully thus me avance' (vol. 4, p. 9, line 5).
29. Cf. Joanna Martin, *Kingship and Love in Scottish Poetry, 1424–1540* (Aldershot: Ashgate, 2008). See also Elizabeth Elliott, 'Eros and self-government: Petrarchism and Protestant self-abnegation in William Fowler's *Tarantula of Love*', *Scottish Literary Review*, 4.1 (2012), pp. 1–14.
30. Vol. 3, p. 246, ascribed to 'Mersar'; vol. 4, p. 24, line 17, wrongly ascribed to 'chawseir'.
31. Ascribed to 'stewart'.
32. Cf. Broomhall and Van Gent (eds), *Governing Masculinities*.
33. The Maitland Quarto manuscript is held in Cambridge, Magdalene College, Pepys Library, MS 1408, and the Folio in Cambridge, Magdalene College, Pepys Library, MS 2553. The manuscripts were edited by W. A. Craigie, with introductory material, notes, and glossary, in 1919: *The Maitland Folio Manuscript*, 2 vols (Edinburgh and London), and *The Maitland Quarto Manuscript* (Edinburgh). A new edition of the Quarto for the Scottish Text Society has been edited by Joanna M. Martin (Woodbridge: Boydell Press, 2015). Quotations from the Folio are based on Craigie's edition; from the Quarto on Martin's edition. For citation purposes, the abbreviations MF and MQ are given parenthetically in the essay, followed by the Roman number each poem has been assigned, then the relevant line references.
34. See further Martin (ed.), *The Maitland Quarto*, pp. 3–19; Joanna M. Martin, and Katherine A. McClune, 'The Maitland Folio and Quarto manuscripts in context' in A. S. G. Edwards (ed.), *Tudor Manuscripts 1485–1603* (London: British Library, 2009), pp. 237–63; Joanna Martin, 'The Maitland Quarto manuscript and the literary culture of the Reign of James VI', in David Parkinson (ed.), *James VI and I. Literature and Scotland: Tides of Change, 1567–2013* (Leuven: Peeters, 2013), pp. 65–81, and 'The presentation of the family in Maitland writings', in Janet Hadley Williams

and Derrick McClure (eds), *Fresche Fontanis: Studies in the Culture of Medieval and Early Modern Scotland* (Newcastle upon Tyne: Cambridge Scholars Publishing, 2013), pp. 319–30.

35. As Martin notes, John Pinkerton, who edited the manuscript in 1786, retitles it 'Counsale to his sone [William] Beand in the Court. Written about the yeir 1555', repeated in Joseph Bain's 1830 edition, *The Poems of Sir Richard Maitland of Lethington*. See Martin (ed.), *The Maitland Quarto*, p. 307.

36. Martin (ed.), *The Maitland Quarto*, p. 307.

37. Cf. Vaught, *Masculinity and Emotion*, pp. 3ff.; cf. also Joshua Scodel, *Excess and the Mean in Early Modern English Literature* (Princeton: Princeton University Press, 2002).

38. On this aspect, see further Sarah M. Dunnigan, 'Sons and daughters, "young wyfis" and "barnis": lyric, gender, and the imagining of youth in the Maitland manuscripts', in Janay Nugent and Elizabeth Ewan (eds), *Children and Youth in Medieval and Early Modern Scotland* (Woodbridge: Boydell Press, 2015), pp. 187–204.

39. Breitenberg, *Anxious Masculinity*, p. 18.

40. Alexandra Shepard, *Meanings of Manhood in Early Modern England* (Oxford: Oxford University Press, 2003), p. 85.

41. See Daniel Juan Gil, 'Before intimacy', *English Literary History*, 69:4 (2002), pp. 861–87. On English conduct books which dispensed advice on male 'gentility and civility', see Shephard, *Meanings of Manhood*, pp. 88ff.

42. Norbert Elias's *The Civilizing Process*, first published in 1939, is the classic scholarly account; cf. Edmund Jephcott's translation (Oxford: Blackwell, 1994).

43. Cf. Todd W. Reeser, *Moderating Masculinity in Early Modern Culture* (Chapel Hill: University of North Carolina, 2006).

44. Paster et al. (eds), *Reading the Early Modern Passions*, pp. 12–13.

45. Barbara Correll, *The End of Conduct: Grobianus and the Renaissance Text of the Subject* (Ithaca, NY: Cornell University Press, 1996), p. 46.

2

Reformed Masculinity: Ministers, Fathers and Male Heads of Households, 1560–1660

Janay Nugent

I cannot use my Paternal Authority to better purpose, then in adjuring you and straightly charging and requiring you, to be constant and zealous in the Religion now left established in this Kingdome.[1]

ARCHIBALD CAMPBELL, 1ST MARQUESS of Argyll, wrote these words to his children as he awaited execution for treason in 1661. The position of the powerful Clan Campbell was threatened due to Argyll's political failings during Cromwell's occupation of Scotland, beginning in 1651 and lasting until the 1660 Restoration. His thirty-two-year-old son, Archibald, was the family's hope for sociopolitical salvation.[2] In his advice on how to resurrect the family's legacy, the marquess began with religion, '[t]his being your greatest concernment the director of all your actions'.[3] He went on to argue that devoutness, zeal, and piety in the practice of religion were critical in being respected as a man, 'remember this, that he that is not truly religious, will hardly be esteemed', and indeed if one is hypocritical in their faith, this will be poorly reflected in 'your greatness and honour'.[4] For his son to earn his way back into the ranks of noble society and salvage the future of Clan Campbell, the marquess believed that piety would lead the way, offering him the metaphor, 'like the Diamond out-shines the lustre of all other Jewels. A religious heart and a clear conscience will make you truly conspicuous'.[5] The Marquess of Argyll penned these words just over one hundred years after the Reformation Parliament met and adopted the *Scots Confession of Faith*. During the intervening years, being a strong, powerful, and successful man became inextricably linked to being a devout reformed Christian.

As this collection attests, Scottish masculinity has meant many different things in different contexts, and it has been a powerful force in shaping the culture and institutions of the country. Within the early modern context there were a plurality of gender experiences and expectations for men.[6] Scholars of early modern British masculinity have largely focused on how manhood both shaped, and was shaped by, the social, economic, and political order.[7] Manliness and its connection to early modern religion in Europe have been explored in Scott Hendrix and Susan Karant-Nunn's edited collection, *Masculinity in the Reformation Era*.[8] This chapter brings that conversation to bear on Scotland. After 1560, masculinity became an important influence in constructing the reformed 'godly community'. With multiple masculinities existing simultaneously, the 'reformed man' was an ideal exalted by the kirk above all other variants of masculine identity.

In 1559–60 the official adoption of Protestantism by the Reformation Parliament meant that the kirk was faced with the enormous task of converting the religion, and the religious culture, of the people. The *Scots Confession*, adopted by parliament in 1560, explained that to create a 'godly community' kirk leaders needed to 'repress vice and nourish virtue'.[9] Ministers were critical role models for lay families in reforming the population, but it was not only their godly behaviour that shaped the reformed kirk, it was also their struggle with sin and their resulting relationship with God that provided a model for all Scots. The programme of conversion was a complex and multifaceted undertaking,[10] yet it is clear that families were widely recognised as a critical resource in the reformation of the nation.[11] As historians of the continental Reformation have demonstrated, families were where religion was taught, practised, discussed and reinforced on a daily level; this is where the godly behaviour of individuals could be monitored at all times.[12] Men were to take an active role in reforming their households, with the minister as model for the ideal male head of household.

Kirk leaders depended on lay masters of households to enforce the reformed agenda within their homes. To 'repress vice and nourish virtue', people must internalise the new faith and behave in a way that reflected positively upon God's chosen community. Fathers were likened to ministers and families were their seminaries. Heads of households were not just reformed men – they were men who actively brought about the Reformation. In 1641, the kirk produced the instructional manual, *Familie Exercise*, which argued that without these 'little seminaries ... the word of God in the Kirk [was not] duly regarded'.[13] The reformed religion depended on family government and duty.

Prior to the Reformation men were already the legal, economic, political, and moral heads of their households. Reformers added spiritual leadership to this repertoire. For centuries men had been expected to be good Christians, but now this took on a decidedly reformed shape. Within the broader continental context, Lyndal Roper argues that the early sixteenth-century Reformation is often viewed as both 'a religious credo and a social movement, [but it] must be understood as a theology of gender'.[14] This chapter tests the slightly later Scottish context to explore the local minister as the ideal reformed man, and how this ideal was both contested and embraced by male heads of households. Reformed ideals of piety and discipline were gendered in expectation, with masculinity embracing submission and obedience as well as strength through leadership.

MINISTERS AS REFORMED HEADS OF HOUSEHOLDS

Ministers were essential to establishing the three marks of the true church, which included 'the preaching of the Word, the sacraments rightly administered and discipline'.[15] They were powerful leaders in the community and the local nexus of reforming work. Essential to the creation of the 'godly community', ministers expounded lessons from the pulpit, while clerical marriage made them models for married men on how to run a godly household. In his 1589 *A Spiritvall Propine of a Pastour to his People*, James Melville explained how this model would bring reformation to the entire realm:

> Reverend Fathers, and loving brethren of the Eldership, mindful of the weight of your charge, and of the solemn oath and obligation, made before God, his Angels and Kirk relating to that matter. Take faithful and diligent care that this word of life dwell plentifully, first in your own hearts, and next in your families: from which as fountains of living waters, it may flow unto the hearts, houses and families committed in particular to every one of your charge.[16]

The baptism of John Knox's first child, reconstructed in Jane Dawson's recent biography of the reformer, demonstrates clearly how his son's entrance into the reformed community flowed from the father's faith and provided a model for all of those in attendance.[17] Standing under the pulpit, before the congregation, Knox officially brought his son into the Christian community where all were reminded of their part in God's covenant. Ministers, elders, and other men such as readers were often presented as models for male heads of households to emulate, but unlike in French reformed communities, where elders were the most powerful and ubiquitous models of masculinity, in Scotland it was the ministers who emerged as the primary model of reformed masculinity.[18]

The ministerial traits of piety and discipline were particularly significant to the creation of reformed masculinity. Piety nourished virtue while discipline repressed vice, thus establishing and enforcing the godly community. Piety and discipline built upon a variety of already existing ideals of masculinity, such as authority over one's household, religious observance, self-control, and community leadership.[19] These broadly recognised masculine traits mapped effectively onto ideals espoused by the kirk and embodied by the pastors, thus creating a masculine ideal that was distinctively reformed.

Personal piety, the internalisation and private celebration of faith, was critical to reformed masculinity and leading a godly household. Despite contemporary and modern assumptions that women were 'more prone to piety' in the early modern era,[20] piety was also a key aspect of what it was to be a reformed man. Elizabeth Foyster recognised the advantage that piety had in constructing early modern English masculinity, but in Scotland piety was more than an advantage, it was integral to men's reformed identity.[21] Fathers and masters of households were to emulate ministers in practising, embracing and internalising the new faith. The internalisation and private celebration of faith were critical to being a man and led to the creation of godly households throughout the realm as men actively nurtured personal piety within their households. As with gender ideals more generally, masculine piety was seen as active and authoritative, while feminine piety was submissive and obedient.[22]

Ministers modelled reformed masculinity, in part, through various manifestations of personal piety. To be 'fruitful in the work of the Lord', the minister was to 'bring home the word of God to his own heart and conscience by prayers and meditation'.[23] Ministers also demonstrated piety through the practice of family worship. As Steven Ozment argued, Lutheran fathers were to 'methodically inculcate virtues and values'.[24] This was true for most Protestant groups, but it was incumbent upon Scottish men to lead family exercise as the General Assembly, the head body of the kirk, expected that ministers were 'using godly exercises in their families, and teaching of their wives, children, and servants, in using ordinary prayers, and the reading of the scriptures'.[25] To ensure that ministers met these obligations, the General Assembly ordered examinations of the households of ministers to test whether they had sufficient religious instruction.[26]

Piety was also embedded in the way men conducted themselves, thus developing further markers of idealised masculine behaviour. Clothing was an outer representation of the seriousness with which one embraced the reforming cause. Ministers and those 'serving in the function of the Kirk' were to make appropriate choices in apparel. In 1575, the General Assembly provided an extensive list of what it deemed acceptable clothing, accessories, and colours for ministers, readers, and their wives to wear, 'that the good word of God be not slandered by them and their immoderateness; and their wives to be subject to the same order'. In addition to avoiding rich fabrics such as silk, velvet, and taffeta, those in positions of power within the kirk were to avoid costly ornamentation such as extravagant embroidery or passments [lace or braid adornments]. The wearing of rings, or gold, silver, or metal buttons was discouraged, as was the expensive gilding of knives and whingers [short swords], and the excessive use of fabric such as in doublets. Red, blue, or yellow clothing was to be avoided as it suggested a lightness of mind; instead it was recommended to ministers and their wives that 'their whole habit be of a grave colour, such as black, russet, sad grey, sad brown'.[27] Clothing embodied the inner life of a reformed person, a piety that resulted in seriousness of mind, frugality, and humility. It was critical that ministers modelled this trait. The stakes were high, as those who wore 'gorgeous and vain apparel' attracted the wrath of God, and in 1596 were even blamed for contributing to the famine.[28]

Closely linked to the trait of piety was discipline. Male heads of households had been the source of discipline in their families long before the Reformation, but after 1560 this was reshaped to advance the reformed agenda and became the means by which one both 'repress[ed] vice and nourish[ed] virtue'.[29] Masters were to use discipline to order and rule their household, ensuring that religious instruction was followed and that everyone in the household acted in a way that reflected positively upon the godly community. In 1649 the Canongate kirk session ordered that visitation be taken of each family in the parish where discipline would be examined. Observation of the Sabbath, family instruction, private worship, and how sinners and scandal in the family were disciplined would all be examined.[30] In 1641, *Familie Exercise* noted that:

> [if] godliness may be practised, there must be exercise of discipline in wisdom and patience, by admonition, reproof, and correction for such faults as are proper to be censured in the Family and if servants will not amend, by removing them. And for this end, diligent observing and watching over their ways is necessary.[31]

To be effective in one's discipline, male household heads needed to be capable of 'ordering and ruling of the house in wisdom'.[32]

As both heads of their households and of the kirk sessions, ministers were particularly well placed to model the disciplinarian aspect of reformed masculinity. In 1598 the kirk session of St Cuthbert's interviewed elders, deacons, and other 'honest men' about the ministers and whether there was 'scandal in their lives and doctrine or in their families'.[33] If sin happened within their own household, ministers were expected to fully enforce kirk discipline. In 1591 the Synod of Lothian and Tweeddale investigated what order had been taken with the minister of Linlithgow and what behaviour he had exhibited to his daughter when she was found guilty of fornication. Patrick Kinlochie testified that he discharged his daughter from the house as soon as he found out about the fault, and that the presbytery could attest to 'what grief that was to him'. The synod then ordered him to pursue the man before the judges for a promise of marriage made to his daughter.[34] As a minister, it was incumbent upon Kinlochie to enforce discipline and to ensure that all kirk expectations for such a situation be fulfilled. The General Assembly ordered ministers to govern their families with diligence in all matters, especially in using godly exercises in their families, in teaching their wives, children, and servants ordinary prayers and to read scriptures, in removing offensive persons out of their families, and in providing good example. They were to be visited by the presbyteries and if they did not enforce kirk discipline within their families they were to be removed from the ministry, having been 'judged not meet to govern the house of God, according to the rule of the apostle'.[35]

Control and discipline over one's household began with the behaviour of the master himself, as sin became entwined with unmasculine traits. The General Assembly noted the problem of 'deboshed [immoral] men, as make not conscience of their life and ruling of their families, and especially of education of their children, lying, slandering, and backbiting and breaking of promises'.[36] Yet those who had strayed could reclaim the ideal of reformed masculinity through submission to discipline. 'Masculinity [wa]s ultimately governable',[37] and personal submission to kirk authority demonstrated conformity. Particularly scandalous were ministers who sinned and avoided repentance. As models for all other men, by failing to control themselves and to submit to discipline, they put the success of the Reformation at stake.

In 1645 the Presbytery of Ayr launched a series of investigations into ministerial misbehaviour. The context of a particularly strong Covenanting region during the height of the Montrose campaigns provides exceptionally detailed records of investigations into the behaviour of ministers who did not support the Covenanting cause. Although these investigations were entwined with politics, their detailed nature provides an excellent opportunity to tease out ideals of reformed masculinity.[38] On 24 September, an eight-month investigation into the scandalous behaviour of Robert Hamilton, minister of Monkton, preoccupied the court. Hamilton had engaged in suspicious behaviour with his servant girl, Grissell Black. Black was not deemed to be 'of rank and quality beseeming his [Hamilton's] place and age', which the presbytery noted greatly increased the scandal, as did her betrothal to another man with whom banns had been publicly proclaimed.[39] Robert Hamilton had clearly stained the godly community by scandalous carriage that was amplified by the unsuitability of their match. Men throughout Europe were expected to be in control of their sexual actions, even when seen as tempted by women who were perceived to be impure.[40] Losing control had economic, social and religious consequences for most early modern communities. Yet there was a distinctively reformed element to sexual infidelity in Scotland. Sexual infidelity reflected poorly upon God's chosen community and threatened the viability of the 'godly household'.

Reformed masculinity demanded chastity outside of marriage, running an orderly household free of sin, obedience to socially prescribed roles and control over one's personal desires. Hamilton failed in all these behaviours. As head of his household, he was expected to model and enforce good behaviour; instead he brought sin within its walls. As a minister, his inability to model the godly household had ramifications for the entire community, which was further complicated by his anti-Covenanting behaviour. Hamilton's apparent royalist sympathies in the War of the Three Kingdoms became entwined with his failure as a reformed man. When the Session of Monkton refused to proclaim his banns with Black, he beseeched two colleagues from neighbouring parishes to marry them. When this request was denied, on the evening of the Battle of Kilsyth, 15 August 1645,

> when the enemy was lying at Bothwell, and the people of God in this parts lying in the fields, ready to venture themselves and estates, for the defence of the gospel, [Mr Hamilton] did then write a scurrilous letter to Mr William Scot, to come and marry him on the foresaid party, that they might be merry and jovial two or three days together in these sad and melancholy times.[41]

In addition to dishonesty and disobedience, Hamilton also failed in his duties as a reformed minister. The Marquess of Montrose had just led the royalist forces to their high point of the civil war and Hamilton's actions were an egregious offence to the kirk leaders. Kilsyth was many miles from Monkton, yet the royalist army had been laying waste to the countryside and the Covenanters as they marched across the country. As they neared Ayrshire, the Presbytery of Ayr chastised the minister: '[Mr Hamilton] did never come towards them of his charge that were in the fields neither to exhort nor encourage them to stand to the defence of the Lord's cause against the public enemy as the rest of the ministers did.'[42] The presbytery noted that his ministry 'could no ways be profitable to the Lord's people, till he were purged of the said scandal', and he was 'suspended, from all exercise of the function of the Ministry'.[43] This decree was prompted when the parishioners of Monkton rioted on a Sunday, preventing Hamilton from preaching and requiring the presbytery to order that no further violence be taken against the minister.[44]

At the same time the Presbytery of Ayr also heard complaints against Mr John McCone, minister at Straiton:

> now aged and paralytic, notwithstanding he had been seven times previously admonished by the Presbytery for his scandalous carriage in drinking and tipling [habitual drinking] too frequently in alehouses about the kirk of Straiton, yet continued still in that vice resorting ordinarily both Sabbath day and weekday in the ale house, and remaining there the weekday from morning to evening, except a little in the noon time he used to go home and take a sleep, and thereafter returned.[45]

Excessive drinking was sinful behaviour and a poor model for the community. The consumption of alcohol is an excellent example of the sometimes conflicting markers of masculinity. In early modern Europe, drinking alcohol was an integral aspect of masculine sociability. As a social lubricant that helped build community ties, it accompanied business transactions and celebrations of changes in the life course such as births, marriages, and deaths. It was how social time was passed during festivals or days off work. Drinks were also shared amongst household members on a daily basis.[46] Bonds of family, friendship, economic partnerships, and community were often forged over a jug of ale, yet alcohol was only to be consumed in moderation, as excess could lead to sin and uncontrolled behaviour. Temperate drinking indicated self-control, a moderate personality, frugality, and trustworthiness. Drunkenness was unmasculine as it threatened social stability through uncontrolled, raucous, wasteful, violent, and licentious behaviour.[47] Early modern Europeans were fixated on bringing order to society and this included controlling excessive drink.[48] In reformed Scotland, the sins of excessive drink were also believed to stain the 'godly community'. As A. Lynn Martin argues, drinking behaviour is socially mediated.[49] Reformed Scots applied important markers of masculinity to drinking culture by

identifying how moderation of consumption contributed to the creation of the godly community through the nourishment of virtue and the
repression of vice.

In addition to his unmasculine behaviour through sinful drunkenness,
alcohol also led to John McCone's failures as a reformed minister. Not
only did McCone frequent the ale house on the Sabbath, but he was also
charged with refusing to leave the pub to examine parishioners.[50] The
lure of drunkenness could keep men from doing their jobs, but within
the Reformation context it also kept ministers from completing their
duties. With the minister acting in this manner, the disciplinary system
in Straiton was failing and reformed teachings were being neglected.
McCone was seen as a 'mocker of piety'; he neglected his family duties,
and he spoke openly against the presbytery – even arguing that the
Covenanters were not fighting for God.[51]

In both cases the ministers' sinful behaviour was entwined with anti-
Covenanting sentiments. The Presbytery of Ayr pursued a lengthy investigation of 'the enormities and corruptions in the ministers and the
remedies thereof'.[52] Wanting to ensure that ministers 'behave ourselves
as becomes the men of God', the presbytery focused on the worldliness
of these two ministers. Particular points of concern about their behaviour included a 'slighting of God's worship in their families', a 'want
of gravity in carriage and apparel, dissoluteness in hair, and shakings
about the knees, lightness in the apparel of their wives and children'.[53]
The ministers had been 'made vile and contemptible' through 'tipling
and bearing company in inappropriate timing, drinking in taverns and
alehouses'.[54] Although the dissoluteness of hair and shakings about
the knees suggest Cavalier styles, these cases reveal the importance of
ministers in modelling the ideal of reformed masculinity. Their lack of
piety, sobriety, chastity outside of marriage, seriousness of purpose as
indicated by their clothing and hair styles, control over their families
and congregations, and personal discipline were as significant a threat
to the godly community as were their royalist sympathies. Such concerns
about the '[n]egligence in the lives of the ministry' existed long before
the Covenanting period.[55]

Although ministerial sin was a threat to the reformed agenda, those
who submitted to discipline continued to provide an important model
of reformed masculinity to other men in the godly community. Sin was
natural; it was how one dealt with the sin that mattered. The extensive
system of discipline constructed throughout the nation depended on
the idea articulated by the General Assembly that a person could 'by
God's grace repent of his impiety, and return to that company of the

faithful; from which, by his heinous offence, he has so horribly fallen'.[56] All humans are sinners, which meant that the misbehaviour of kirk leaders was to be expected to a certain degree. The Presbytery of Ayr's investigation into 'the enormities and corruptions in the ministers and the remedies thereof' provided the framework for understanding how ministers fit into the reality of sin:

> The first and main sin are reaching both to our personal carriage and call-ings we judge to be not studying how to keep command and fellowship with God in Christ, but walking in a natural way without employing Christ and drawing virtue from him for sanctification and preaching in spirit and power. And in our lives first fruitless conversing in company and complying with the sins of all sorts, nor behaving ourselves as becomes the men of God.[57]

Being a man of God did not come from the minister's duties in knowing and interpreting the Bible, leading sermons, or enforcing kirk discipline; rather it came first from one's personal struggle with sin and the result-ing relationship this created with God. Ministers were men first, and then pastors.

Unrepentant ministers posed a significant threat to the reformed agenda as their lack of humility, obedience, and repentance would 'destroy their authority and bring disgrace on the ministry'.[58] Yet sinful ministers were also a beacon of hope for those who had temporarily lost their way. Karen Spierling demonstrates that piety and obedience were a critical aspect of reformed masculinity in Geneva and this observation also holds for Scotland.[59] By obeying kirk leaders and submitting to dis-cipline, ministers served as a powerful example. On 20 October 1572, the General Assembly ordered that adultery and all other sin rampant in the country be tried, 'And especially, that it may be known that ministers who ought to be good examples, as well by doctrine as life, to provoke others to godly conversation, be not exempted, but rather first tried'.[60] Ministers would misbehave; they just needed to be dealt with as were all others who strayed from the path of righteousness. Therefore, as min-isters were to make visitations to their flock, presbyteries also required elders to make visitations and report on one another and their ministers so that order could be taken with the guilty.[61] The realisation that none of God's elect were free from sin, and that even the most fiercely pious ministers struggled with giving in to sin and temptation could be com-forting to those who had doubts about their own sinful ways.

A clear example of this is seen with Alexander Jardine, minister of Kilspindie, Inchture, and Rait in the Presbytery of Perth. Jardine had admitted his guilt in fornicating with a virgin.[62] A model of repentance,

Jardine observed the typical expectations of the kirk in such a situation: he married the woman and submitted himself to public discipline. Once he had repented, the General Assembly asked the Superintendent to reinstate him to his ministry. Despite his status as a religious leader in the community, the General Assembly recorded no special chastisement or punishment for his behaviour. Once he had submitted to discipline, he could resume overseeing the discipline of others. Indeed, one can imagine that a sinner fearful of the results of his or her own lapses might find it comforting to know that even the person doling out discipline had been welcomed back into the Christian community.

The experience of sin was even expected to improve the abilities of ministers to preach effectively. Margo Todd notes that the Reformation in Scotland went a long way to eliminating the distinction between clergy and laity, and the sinfulness of clerics helped to break down these barriers even further.[63] The Ayr presbytery noted the powerful influence of a repentant minister, 'that every minister be humbled for his former failings and make his peace with God that the more effectually he may preach repentance, and may stand in the gap to turn away the wrath running betwixt the porch and the altar'.[64] As Spierling found for Geneva, there was a clear link between masculinity and obedience, which makes the discussion of masculinity in reformed communities 'interesting and more complicated than one might expect'.[65] Reformed men were to be obedient and submissive to kirk discipline while simultaneously holding positions of authority over their families.

FATHERS AND MALE HEADS OF HOUSEHOLDS AS REFORMED MEN

Within early modern Europe, married men were expected to 'take on the social burden of upholding the structure and values of the community'.[66] Within the Scottish religious context, this meant that male heads of households were expected to embrace the idealised model that ministers had provided of the reformed man. As with ministers, piety and discipline were foremost in this model of masculinity. Masters should nurture a culture of piety in the family, performing 'all the parts of family exercise, as to read, to catechise, to pray with and for the family, to exercise discipline, to show and set forth the works of God, and to direct and order the times and manner of humiliation'.[67] To demonstrate their piety, frugality, and seriousness of mind, men were to emulate the comportment of ministers and their families by giving 'good example in all godliness and gravity'.[68]

The godly discipline of ministers and their families was also to be emulated. Local kirk session records are full of examples of masters bringing discipline to their households, which at times required men to submit to discipline themselves. Obedience to other men, even in the running of their household, was a critical aspect of reformed masculinity.[69] Helen Stewart's master was ordered to put her out of service in St Cuthbert's until she had satisfied for her fornication;[70] Helen Bryson's father was to remove her from his house in North Leith as she was an unrepentant fornicator in Canongate;[71] masters in Aberdeen promised to report ungodly behaviour by their apprentices to the kirk session;[72] William White was to pay a fine for his wife's fighting upon the Sabbath,[73] while John Williamson and John Stewart promised that their wives, servants, and families would not quarrel in the future.[74] The General Assembly was clear that discipline was to be applied beyond the obvious sins of 'whoredom and bloodshed', for there were many sins offensive to God including the 'blasphemy of God, banning, profaning of the Sabbath, disobedience to parents, idle, unruly ones without calling, [and] drunkards'.[75] Male heads of households were to enforce discipline when these transgressions occurred, thus advancing the reformed agenda. Control over one's wife and household was an integral aspect of discipline and reformed masculinity.[76]

Although male household heads were expected to embrace the ideal of the reformed man, pastors across the Calvinist regions of Europe were often frustrated when 'members of the congregation habitually baulked when asked . . . to change their everyday habits and devotional patterns'.[77] This was particularly evident in Scotland during periods of crisis, such as during the War of the Three Kingdoms in the 1640s when the kirk session of St Nicholas noted, 'family exercises [were] being neglected and many mocked, the Lord's Sabbaths profaned and fornicators, adulterers, incest, drunkenness and other heinous sins still abounding'.[78] Sin was seen as rampant throughout the country, but the general willingness of adult men to submit to kirk discipline meant that they were aware of the expectations placed upon them and to some extent they were willing to emulate the ideal of the reformed man.

This ideal was often tested when it came into conflict with more traditional, secular forms of masculinity. For example, Sabbath observance was critical to reformed masculinity as this was how one demonstrated personal piety and facilitated family exercise. Yet in a subsistence society leisure time was rare. As Todd has demonstrated, the new reformed culture often came into conflict with traditional ways of engaging in leisure time.[79] Most people worked long hours to support themselves and their families, and the Sabbath was their only day of rest. Participating in sports and games allowed early modern men to engage in the male culture of competition. Punctuated by displays of strength, skill, and physical prowess, this was a critical opportunity for men to earn the respect of their peers and to cultivate masculine friendships which had important economic and social functions. Sports and competition did not innately conflict with the ideals of the reformed man; it was participating in these events on the Sabbath that was the problem. In St Cuthbert's, despite his own attendance at church, John Robson was called before the kirk session as his yard was used on the Sabbath for French kyles as well as row bowls.[80] Both games were widely played by men in St Cuthbert's on the Sabbath.[81] In South Leith golf on the Sabbath appeared before the session court,[82] in Newbattle playing cards was tried by the session,[83] and in North Leith two men were disciplined for playing a Sabbath game of football.[84]

Drinking on Sundays was another common male activity. Business deals and social connections were often fostered over a pint of ale and were an integral aspect of secular masculinity. Moderate drinking was an important masculine practice and was not in conflict with reformed masculinity. The problem emerged when drink led to uncontrolled behaviour, especially when this occurred as Sabbath breaking. In 1599 five men in St Cuthbert's confessed their offence of drinking and fighting, thereby 'violating and breaking of the Sabbath day in time of preaching'.[85]

Despite such offences to the godly community, godly discipline created a system whereby men could participate in both traditional secular masculinity and reformed masculinity. Men could engage in drinking, gaming, and other forms of social and cultural masculinity as long as they practised moderation, order and obedience. As in Geneva, 'neither the consistory nor Calvin himself expected Genevans to be sinless; their realistic hope was that faithful, Reformed Genevans would participate willingly in the disciplining of the church and community'.[86] As in other European reformed communities, this system of discipline allowed citizens who had sinned to be accepted back into the community. For men, the action of submission reinforced the ideals of reformed masculinity.

CONCLUSION

The ideals of the reformed man built upon traditional ideals of masculinity and what it was to be a good Christian. Yet after the Reformation, manliness took on a particular set of reformed traits. As reformed men, male heads of households were integral to the success of the reformed agenda. As Callum Brown notes, 'religion matters to gender history, and gender matters to religious history'.[87] Within Scotland the ideal of the reformed man consisted of a number of traits and attributes, all of which were intended to further the reformed cause. By internalising the faith and encouraging those in their families to do the same, male heads of households contributed to the domestication of the Reformation.[88] Ministers offered the model of personal piety, order and control over one's household, seriousness of mind, frugality, humility, temperate drinking, chastity outside of marriage, trustworthiness, self-discipline and submissiveness to kirk discipline. This list of characteristics entwined existing masculine traits with distinctly reformed goals. Through these personal traits individuals would create a pious community and one where individual behaviour reflected the goals of the godly community. In 1558, prior to the official adoption of the *Scots Confession*, the reformed 4th Earl of Argyll wrote to his son that 'he should study to set forward the public and true preaching of the Evangel of Jesus Christ, and to suppress all superstition and idolatry, to the uttermost of his power'.[89] Roughly one hundred years later, this same family had moved from simply seeking to support the reformed cause to fully embracing a form of reformed masculinity that was embedded in the religious culture of Scotland.

NOTES

1. National Library of Scotland [NLS], RY.III.H.21. Archibald Late Marquis of Argyle, *Instructions to a Son* (Edinburgh: reprinted in London for D. Trench, 1661), p. 29.
2. Allan I. Macinnes, *The British Confederate: Archibald Campbell, Marquess of Argyll, c. 1607–1661* (Edinburgh: John Donald, 2011), p. 303.
3. Argyle, *Instructions to a Son*, p. 29. To make the text more accessible, spelling in direct quotations has been modernised.
4. Argyle, *Instructions to a Son*, p. 31.
5. Argyle, *Instructions to a Son*, p. 32. For more on the connection between masculinity and religious advice literature see Jeremy Gregory, '*Homo religiosus*: masculinity and religion in the long eighteenth century', in Tim Hitchcock and Michèle Cohen (eds), *English Masculinities, 1660–1800* (London: Longman, 1999), pp. 85–110.
6. Alexandra Shepard, *Meanings of Manhood in Early Modern England* (Oxford: Oxford University Press, 2003), p. 2.
7. Shepard, *Meanings of Manhood*, especially pp. 87–9; Elizabeth A. Foyster, *Manhood in Early Modern England: Honour, Sex and Marriage* (London: Longman, 1999); Bernard Capp, 'The double standard revisited: plebeian

women and male sexual reputation in early modern England', *Past and Present*, 162 (1999), pp. 70–100; Alexandra Shepard, 'Manhood, credit and patriarchy in early modern England c. 1580–1640', *Past and Present*, 167 (2000), pp. 75–106; Tim Reinke-Williams, 'Misogyny, jest-books and male youth culture in seventeenth-century England', *Gender & History*, 21:2 (2009), pp. 324–39; Katie Barclay, *Love, Intimacy and Power: Marriage and Patriarchy in Scotland, 1650–1850* (Manchester: Manchester University Press, 2011); Rosalind Carr, *Gender and Enlightenment Culture in Eighteenth-Century Scotland* (Edinburgh: Edinburgh University Press, 2014).

8. Scott H. Hendrix and Susan C. Karant-Nunn (eds), *Masculinity in the Reformation Era* (Kirksville: Truman State University Press, 2008).

9. *The Scots Confession of 1560*, trans. James Bulloch (Edinburgh: Church of Scotland, 1984).

10. Margo Todd, *The Culture of Protestantism in Early Modern Scotland* (New Haven: Yale University Press, 2002) and John McCallum, *Reforming the Scottish Parish: The Reformation in Fife, 1560–1640* (Farnham: Ashgate, 2010).

11. See Janay Nugent, '"The mistresse of the family hath a speciall hand": family, women, mothers, and the establishment of a "godly community of Scots"', in Stuart Macdonald and Daniel MacLeod (eds), *Keeping the Kirk: Scottish Religion at Home and in the Diaspora* (Guelph: Guelph Centre for Scottish Studies, 2014), pp. 39–62; Janay Nugent and Megan Clark, 'A loaded plate: food symbolism and the early modern Scottish household', *Journal of Scottish Historical Studies*, 30:1 (2010), pp. 43–63.

12. Steven Ozment, *When Fathers Ruled: Family Life in Reformation Europe* (Cambridge, MA: Harvard University Press, 1983); Lyndal Roper, *The Holy Household: Women and Morals in Reformation Augsburg* (Oxford: Clarendon Press, 1989).

13. *Familie Exercise, or, The Service of God in Families* (Edinburgh: Robert Bryson, 1641), p. 10.

14. Roper, *The Holy Household*, pp. 1, 5.

15. McCallum, *Reforming the Scottish Parish*, p. 11.

16. James Melville, *A Spiritvall Propine of a Pastour to his People* (Edinburgh: Robert Walde-graue, Printer to the Kings Majestie, 1589).

17. Jane Dawson, *John Knox* (New Haven: Yale University Press, 2015), pp. 1–4.

18. Raymond A. Mentzer, 'Masculinity and the reformed tradition in France', in Hendrix and Karant-Nunn (eds), *Masculinity in the Reformation Era*, pp. 120–39. Elders were male leaders of the community who aided in asserting kirk discipline. Readers read prayers and passages from scripture when a minister was unavailable to preach.

19. Foyster, *Manhood in Early Modern England*, pp. 207–18.

20. Christine Peters, *Patterns of Piety: Women, Gender and Religion in Late*

Medieval and Reformation England (Cambridge: Cambridge University Press, 2003), pp. 5–6.

21. Foyster, *Manhood in Early Modern England*, p. 7.

22. The importance of submission in masculine piety is discussed below, pp. 47–9.

23. Ayrshire Archives Centre [AAC], CH2/532/1, Ayrshire Presbytery, 24 September 1645, p. 221.

24. Ozment, *When Fathers Ruled*, pp. 132–3.

25. Duncan Shaw (ed.), *The Acts and Proceedings of the General Assemblies of the Church of Scotland, 1560–1618* [APGACS] (Edinburgh: Scottish Record Society, 2004), 26 March 1596, ii: p. 1023.

26. *APGACS*, 13 November 1602, ii: p. 1336.

27. *APGACS*, 6 August 1575, i: pp. 398–9.

28. *APGACS*, 31 March 1596, ii: p. 1031.

29. *The Scots Confession*.

30. National Records of Scotland [NRS], CH2/122/4, Canongate Kirk Session, 4 December 1649, p. 24.

31. *Familie Exercise*, p. 14.

32. *Familie Exercise*, p. 17. For paternal discipline in early modern Germany see Ozment, *When Fathers Ruled*, pp. 135–54.

33. NRS, CH2/718/2, St Cuthbert's Kirk Session, 13 July 1598, p. 75.

34. James Kirk (ed.), *The Records of the Synod of Lothian and Tweeddale, 1589–1596, 1640–1649* (Edinburgh: Stair Society, 1977), 11 April 1591, pp. 24–5.

35. *APGACS*, 26 March 1596, ii: p. 1023; repeated again, almost verbatim forty-two years later in NRS, CH2/84/31, Dalkeith Kirk Session, *The Principal Acts of the Solemne Generall Assembly of the Kirk of Scotland: indicted by the Kings Majestie, and convened at Glasgow the xxi of November 1638. Visited, collected and extracted forth of the Register of the Acts of the Assembly, by the clerk thereof* (Edinburgh: Heirs of Andrew Hart, 1639), p. 34.

36. NRS, CH2/84/31, *The Principal Acts of the Solemne Generall Assembly*, p. 33.

37. Sarah M. Dunnigan, 'Sons and daughters, "young wyfs" and "barnis": lyric, gender, and the imagining of youth in the Maitland manuscripts', in Janay Nugent and Elizabeth Ewan (eds), *Children and Youth in Premodern Scotland* (Woodbridge: Boydell & Brewer, 2015), pp. 197–204, at 193.

38. Covenanters signed the 'National Covenant' in 1638, which objected to Stuart interference in the Scottish Presbyterian church. In 1644–5 the royalist James Graham, 1st Marquess of Montrose, fought Covenanting armies across Scotland in the name of King Charles I.

39. AAC, CH2/532/1, 24 September 1645, p. 216.

40. Scott Hendrix, 'Masculinity and patriarchy in reformation Germany', in

Hendrix and Karant-Nunn (eds), *Masculinity in the Reformation Era*, pp. 71–91; Capp, 'The double standard revisited', pp. 70–100.

41. AAC, CH2/532/1, 24 September 1645, p. 216.

42. Ibid. p. 216.

43. Ibid. p. 217.

44. Ibid. p. 217.

45. Ibid. p. 214.

46. Benjamin Roberts, 'Drinking like a man: the paradox of excessive drinking for seventeenth-century Dutch youths', *Journal of Family History*, 29:3 (2004), pp. 237–52, at 238–40; B. Ann Tlusty, 'Drinking, family relations, and authority in early modern Germany', *Journal of Family History*, 29:3 (2004), pp. 253–73, at 254–6; A. Lynn Martin, *Alcohol, Violence, and Disorder in Traditional Europe* (Kirksville: Truman State University Press, 2009).

47. Roberts, 'Drinking like a man', pp. 240–52; Tlusty, 'Drinking, family relations, and authority', pp. 256–73; Martin, *Alcohol, Violence, and Disorder*; A. Lynn Martin, *Alcohol, Sex, and Gender in Late Medieval and Early Modern Europe* (Basingstoke: Palgrave, 2001).

48. Martin, *Alcohol, Violence, and Disorder*, pp. 3–14.

49. Martin, *Alcohol, Violence, and Disorder*, p. 14.

50. Parishioners were usually examined on their good behaviour as well as on their knowledge, of the Lord's Prayer or the Ten Commandments, for example.

51. AAC, CH2/532/1, 24 September 1645, p. 214.

52. Ibid. p. 219.

53. Cavalier clothing styles were considered extravagant with long flowing hair and a variety of ornamentations around the knees (which are likely to be the shakings referenced) such as petticoat breeches fringed with ribbons pointing to the knees. See Patrick Little, 'Cromwell's "Gay Attire"', *History Today*, 58:9 (2008), pp. 45–51.

54. AAC, CH2/532/1, 24 September 1645, p. 219. My thanks to Michael Graham for sharing his insights into these cases.

55. *APGACS*, 14 May 1601, ii: p. 1267. See also 20 June 1587, ii: p. 817; 24 March 1596, ii: pp. 1021–3.

56. *APGACS*, i: p. 127.

57. AAC, CH2/532/1, 24 September 1645, p. 219.

58. John Calvin, *Institutes of the Christian Religion*, 4.3.12; *First Book of Discipline* (1561), in *The Books of Discipline, and of Common Order; the Directory for Family Worship; the Form of Process; and the Order of Election of Superintendents, Ministers, Elders, and Deacons* (Edinburgh: Edinburgh Printing and Publishing Company, 1836), pp. 28–9; see also Raymond Mentzer, 'Reorganizing the pastorate: innovations and challenges in the French reformed churches', in Konrad Eisenbichler (ed.), *Collaboration, Conflict, and Continuity in the Reformation* (Toronto:

Centre for Reformation and Renaissance Studies, 2014), pp. 195–216, at 207.

59. Karen Spierling, 'Father, son, and pious Christian: concepts of masculinity in reformation Geneva', in Hendrix and Karant-Nunn (eds), *Masculinity in the Reformation Era*, pp. 97–107.

60. *APGACS*, 20 October 1572, i: p. 302.

61. AAC, CH2/532/1, 24 September 1645, p. 221; see also *First Book of Discipline*, pp. 63–7; *APGACS*, ii: p. 1334.

62. *APGACS*, 31 December 1563, i: pp. 59–60; *APGACS*, 29 June 1564, i: pp. 69–70.

63. Todd, *The Culture of Protestantism*, pp. 362–74.

64. AAC, CH2/532/1, 24 September 1645, p. 221.

65. Spierling, 'Father, son, and pious Christian', p. 98.

66. Scott Hendrix, 'Masculinity and patriarchy in reformation Germany', *Journal of the History of Ideas*, 56:2 (1995), pp. 177–93, at 186.

67. *Familie Exercise*, p. 18. See also NRS, CH2/718/3, St Cuthbert's Kirk Session, 4 December 1649, p. 24.

68. *Familie Exercise*, p. 17.

69. Melville, *A Spiritvall Propine*, pp. 45–6; *The Scots Confession*.

70. NRS, CH2/718/2, 6 September 1590, ff. 44v–45r.

71. NRS, CH2/621/1, North Leith Kirk Session, 14 November 1605 to 3 January 1606, pp. 385–92 (author's pagination).

72. John Stuart (ed.), *Selections from the Records of the Kirk Session of Aberdeen 1562–1659* (Aberdeen: Spalding Club, 1846), pp. 36–7.

73. NRS, CH2/718/4, St Cuthbert's Kirk Session, 6 March 1620, f. 42r.

74. NRS, CH2/621/1, 7 November 1605, p. 384 (author's pagination).

75. NRS, CH2/84/31, *The Principal Acts of the Solemne Generall Assembly*, p. 33.

76. Callum G. Brown, 'Religion', in Lynn Abrams, Eleanor Gordon, Deborah Simonton and Eileen Janes Yeo (eds), *Gender in Scottish History since 1700* (Edinburgh: Edinburgh University Press, 2006), pp. 84–110, at 99; Shepard, *Meanings of Manhood*, p. 83.

77. Mentzer, 'Reorganizing the pastorate', p. 201.

78. NRS, CH2/84/1, St Nicholas Kirk Session, 20 October 1644, f. 18r.

79. Todd, *The Culture of Protestantism*, pp. 183–226.

80. NRS, CH2/718/2, 10 July 1606, p. 238. French kyles and row bowls were variations of skittles or bowling. See John Burnett, *Riot, Revelry and Rout: Sport in Lowland Scotland before 1800* (East Linton: Tuckwell Press, 2000), pp. 38–45.

81. NRS, CH2/718/2, 6 June 1605, p. 194; NRS, CH2/718/2, 27 June 1605, p. 197; NRS, CH2/718/2, 17 July 1606, p. 239; NRS, CH2/718/2, 24 July 1606, p. 240.

82. NRS, CH2/716/2, South Leith Kirk Session, 8 October 1609, f. 29v.

83. NRS, CH2/276/1, Newbattle Kirk Session, 1 March 1618, p. 25.

84. NRS, CH2/621/1, 27 June 1611, pp. 599–600.
85. NRS, CH2/718/2, 1 July 1599, p. 99.
86. Karen Spierling, 'Friend and foe: reformed Genevans and Catholic neighbours in the time of Calvin', in Randall C. Zachman (ed.), *John Calvin and Roman Catholicism: Critique and Engagement, Then and Now* (Grand Rapids, MI: Baker Academic, 2008), pp. 79–98, at 91.
87. Brown, 'Religion', p. 85.
88. Roper, *The Holy Household*, p. 3.
89. William Croft Dickinson (ed.), John Knox, *History of the Reformation in Scotland*, 2 vols. (London: Thomas Nelson, 1949), i: 138. My thanks to the anonymous reader who provided this very useful reference.

3

The Importance and Impossibility of Manhood: Polite and Libertine Masculinities in the Urban Eighteenth Century

Rosalind Carr

SHIFTING IDEALS OF BEHAVIOUR and sentiment served to assert manhood amongst different groups of men in eighteenth-century Scotland, and men could adopt different manly personas depending on locale and time of day. Take, for instance, James Boswell, who embodied polite and libertine manhood. His days in Edinburgh often progressed from heterosocial suppers and visits to the theatre with his wife and other women, to homosocial meetings of the Freemasons, Faculty of Advocates or intellectual societies, followed by drinking in a tavern or coffeehouse and sometimes sexual intercourse with women, including prostitutes.[1]

Rather than a binary opposition, Georgian archetypes of the polite gentleman and the libertine stood at two ends of a continuum of possible masculinities, and landed and professional men could perform characteristics of these identities depending on the specific context. Boswell wished to achieve an ideal of refined, virtuous manhood but from his time as a young man visiting London through to married, professional life as a lawyer in Edinburgh, his behaviour displayed adherence to a libertinism of convivial tavern-based sociability and extramarital sex.[2] Boswell was not necessarily atypical, and this chapter will explore the fluidity of manhood in his and other elite men's lives in eighteenth-century urban Scotland.

Recent studies of English masculinities during this period have explored libertine, impolite, polite and domestic manhood. These histories highlight significant differences in the performance of ideal manhood manifested by the masculinities of the libertines and bohemians of London, and landed gentlemen and merchants displaying self-control through economic management of household and estate, and fatherly leadership.[3] These and other studies demonstrate that multiple masculinities were available to landed, professional and middling men.[4] This was as true for Scotland as for England, and this chapter will explore the continuum of polite and libertine expressions of manhood in eighteenth-century Scotland through an examination of violence, independence, sexuality and friendship. To do so it will draw on a variety of sources with a focus on men's life writing, a source that offers an entrée into their articulation and negotiation of gender identity.

Elite men are the focus of this chapter but an important subtext is the significant continuities across classes and locales in ideals and expressions of manhood. In regard to violence, there appears to have been a general decline in interpersonal violent conflict during the century, as Lynn Abrams and Tawny Paul have shown in this volume and elsewhere.[5] A lack of clear statistical data makes it difficult to conclusively assert a decline in male violence, but there was an emerging discourse of opposition. In the urbane world of the Enlightenment literati this was intimately connected to changing ideas of male honour, and these changes were reflected in debates on whether duelling was justifiable.

The novelist Henry Mackenzie considered duelling honourable in certain contexts, but noted in his *Anecdotes* that 'Duels rarely happened in Edinburgh'.[6] Some men, mostly army officers, continued to duel during the eighteenth century, and the importance of defending male honour in a public context, if not contest, was understood even by those who opposed the practice.[7] Even Enlightenment philosophers, who typically condemned duelling, understood the reasons for it; moral philosopher and Glasgow professor, Adam Smith concluded in his lectures on jurisprudence, delivered in the early 1760s, that men's propensity to duel was exacerbated by the law's failure to adequately address infringements of honour, especially concerning men's physical autonomy, stating that the law gave 'but a very small satisfaction' for assaults on reputation, and citing the relatively small £10 fines levied for spitting, punching someone in the face, or nose pulling.[8] Yet while understood, men's violent response to infringements of personal autonomy was increasingly condemned, especially in periodical literature.[9] As in London, elite men were increasingly willing to use the courts and other means to publicly assert their honour and settle disputes.[10]

Changing conceptions of male honour can be seen early in the century in response to the death of James, Duke of Hamilton. Representing the parliamentary opposition to the Anglo-Scottish Union, in November 1706 Hamilton asked fellow members of the Scottish Parliament, 'Shall we in Half an Hour yield what our Forefathers maintain'd with their Lives and Fortunes for many ages; are none of the Descendants here of those worthy Patriots who defended the Liberty of their Country against all Invaders?'[11] In November 1712 he and his opponent, Lord Mohun, lay dead following a duel in Hyde Park, triggered by political conflict and a property dispute.[12] In his speeches to parliament, Hamilton drew on imagery of a manly Scotland defending the independence of Mother Caledonia against a rapacious England. This Scotland of anti-Union rhetoric was defined by the courage of mythic 'Heroick ancestors' who had maintained Scotland's independence for two thousand years.[13] As leader of the Country Party opposition, Hamilton embodied this heroism.

During the parliament's Union debates, Hamilton was sometimes carried by the Edinburgh crowd from parliament to Holyrood Palace, and a poem of 1707 declared him 'a man of great Renown; and has been born for *Scotland's* Good'.[14] Yet Hamilton also displayed libertine characteristics: he ran up large debts in London and initially refused his parents' demands to leave the royal court, marry and return to Scotland. He is now remembered mainly as the man who blocked a last-minute walk-out intended to stop the Articles of Union being passed. He did so because, although ideologically opposed to Union, he did not want to lose his estates in Lancashire, and he desired the favour of Queen Anne's court.[15]

The nature of his death is illustrative of Hamilton's conflicted masculine personas. The duel symbolised martial courage, yet it was also represented as a tragedy, as emblematic of Hamilton's misguided honour. These two discourses are present in the pamphlet *A Full and Exact Relation of the Duel* published in 1713. Here the author celebrates Hamilton, writing that his death 'is universally lamented because he was a Prince of unquestionable Bravery, and on all occasions appear'd for the Honour of his Countrey [sic]'. Yet it is his 'affable and Courteous Temper, and other Noble Qualities, [that] make his Loss so much the more bewailed'.[16] Narrating the circumstances of the duel, the author records the attendant surgeon's concern that he did not intervene before the event to prevent 'the Effusion of so much Noble and Illustrious Blood'.[17]

Although the pamphlet portrays Hamilton as a man of courage and honour, the circumstance of his death is not depicted as a manifestation of these virtues. Rather than a display of courage, duels are presented as the product of the 'Rashness of Mistaken Honour'.[18] This critique is indicative of the growing influence of politeness and the pamphlet reproduces a text from a 1711 edition of the *Spectator* journal, 'Pharamond's Edict Against Duels'. Speaking in the voice of Pharamond, the author argues that in the act of duelling, the Rules of Good Society and Virtuous Conversation are hereby inverted; the Loose, the Vain and the Impudent, insult the Careful, the Discreet and the Modest; that all Virtue is suppress'd, and all Vice supported in the one Act of being capable to dare to the Death.[19]

This pamphlet illustrates a process whereby the emergent discourse of politeness sought to remodel the noble warrior into a man of inner virtue.[20] This warrior never entirely disappeared from conceptions of male honour; instead, there was a desire to combine male refinement with courage.

The impact of refinement on courage was a primary concern in the moral philosophy of Adam Ferguson, Church of Scotland minister, professor at the University of Edinburgh and leader of the Edinburgh Poker Club, which campaigned for a Scottish militia. He located the true expression of honour in martial, savage society rather than the commercial civility celebrated by Adam Smith and David Hume, who themselves were concerned to show that courage would be enhanced in commercial society, rather than replaced.[21] Location was important here, with martial manhood particularly relevant in the Highlands, initially as a threat to the British Crown during the 1745 Jacobite rebellion and then as a source of British imperial power in the form of Highland regiments during the Seven Years and American wars.[22]

For urban gentry and professional men especially, the combined impact of an expanding commercial economy, politeness and Enlightenment notions of sympathy, amended definitions of honour, and, like the English landed gentry the governance of behaviour 'according to internalised codes of male honour', remained crucial.[23] The connection between behaviour, particularly self-control, and manhood was not only relevant for the elite; Paul has demonstrated that for Edinburgh's lower-middling sorts, economic and social credit were intertwined, and the ideal man was 'honest, fair dealing, and sociable. He provided for his family and adhered to codes of appropriate sexual behaviour'.[24] Economics connected the public and domestic man, and manly authority within the household depended upon sound economic management. This made credit crucial across the classes.[25]

Economic credit was connected to independence. Though typically associated with the landed gentleman, some men's independence was limited to their position as head of a household, with this more democratic definition increasing in power in the early nineteenth century.[26] A member of the professional classes, for the Reverend Alexander Carlyle economic independence was inseparable from the maintenance of a manliness free of obsequiousness. Commenting on his initial aversion to the prospect of being a private tutor in a landed household, Carlyle recorded: 'A little experience corrected this prejudice, for I knew many afterwards who had passed through that station yet retained a manly independency in both mind and manner.'[27] This association of manliness with independence is also apparent in the assessment of language by high court judge and founding member of the Select Society, Lord Kames, in his study of the causes of different manners between nations and across time. Reflecting on the influence of government, he compares the French and English languages, commenting that monarchical government makes the French submissive while the 'freedom of the English government' makes their language 'more manly'.[28]

The importance of independence (economic and of manner) is also apparent in David Hume's short autobiography 'My Own Life'. Recorded shortly before his death in 1776, Hume emphasised the various steps taken to enable him to pursue 'philosophy and general learning' despite his relatively small fortune, with particular attention paid to the success or not of his publications. Combined with economic independence, refinement of character was central to his identity. Hume asserts that he was 'a man of mild dispositions, of command of temper, of an open, social, and cheerful humour, capable of attachment, but little susceptible of enmity, and of great moderation in all my passions'.[29] Here he defines his life according to the maxims of male refinement informed by Scottish Enlightenment moral philosophy, whereby older notions of independence and courage were blended with a new emphasis on politeness in social interaction and an importance placed on inner sensibility rather than affectation.

This was an ideal of urban, elite identity, and the conflict between different expressions of manhood apparent in the courageous patriot–libertine identity of James, Duke of Hamilton at the start of the century did not disappear. But rather than the courageous patriot, the polite gentleman became a dominant archetype and an expression of a North British post-Union identity.[30] The pull of polite, virtuous manhood and the freedoms of the libertine were explored by the Reverend Thomas Somerville in his autobiographical musings on his student days at Edinburgh in the 1750s:

> I often reflect on this period as the pleasantest, no less than the most profitable of my early life. I had leisure to pursue my studies without interruption; and being of a social disposition, I enjoyed much of the company of friends of my own age and station. If the time of my liberty had been prolonged, it

is more than probable that the love of pleasure might have relaxed my application to study; for I was, perhaps to a culpable degree, fond of convivial
meetings, and my company began to be courted by many young men of a
similar disposition, who were not under the restraints which my principles,
pecuniary circumstances, and professional views imposed upon me.[31]

Convivial meetings could threaten the rectitude of a young man and
damage his financial credit, not because of the conduct at meetings
themselves, which was normally polite, but because meetings typically
adjourned to taverns. This was not a simple chronology of youthful
excess followed by adult sobriety. Instead the transitional phase of university was a period when the conflicting pressures of libertinism and
virtuous manhood were accentuated. For Somerville, '[t]he Theological
Society was not only a school of mental improvement, but a nursery of
brotherly love and kind affections'. Yet these advantages were 'diminished, perhaps counterbalanced' by the 'tavern adjournments, which
succeeded our weekly meetings in the College, [and] were the cause of
expense, and sometimes of excess and irregularity, unsuitable to our
circumstances and professional views'.[32]

A minister's son, Somerville's choices were restricted by his rank and
profession. In order to maintain his identity as an upstanding member
of the clergy he needed to distance himself from libertine conviviality.[33]
Since the Restoration, libertinism had been associated with the aristo-
cratic rake, and his behaviour an assertion of social, as well as sexual
power.[34] A full embodiment of this identity was not available to men
like Somerville, because of both his religious adherence and his social
rank. Politeness, on the other hand, was typically associated with elite
culture, but as a set of behavioural codes enacted in spaces such as spa
towns and assembly rooms, it could be performed by professionals
and middling sorts with financial means and leisure time.[35] A powerful
cultural ideal, politeness required courtesy and elegance in speaking, a
generosity towards friends, and an easy sociability in company.[36]

Examining the life writing of Boswell and Somerville, differences in the
men's responses to the limitations of professional and polite manhood
are starkly apparent. Both men studied at Edinburgh University during
the 1750s, attending literary societies, and later contributing to the published output of the Scottish Enlightenment.[37] They were both members
of the professional classes, though Boswell was also landed, inheriting
his family's Auchinleck estate in 1782. They both married, Somerville
in 1770 and Boswell in 1769, and both desired to embody the ideal of
virtuous, polite manhood. Where Somerville succeeded, Boswell often

failed; he wanted to be an upstanding lawyer and a good husband but found it difficult to resist the temptations of drink and extramarital sex. In January 1768, when he was still a bachelor, he regretted the impact of drink on his professional reputation, recording that he 'felt myself a very rake as I pleaded a cause before Lord Monboddo'.[38] This behaviour continued into married life. On one occasion Boswell arrived home intoxicated and threw chairs at his wife. Remembering nothing but hearing his wife, Margaret Montgomerie, recount his actions the following day, he considered it a 'monstrous account of a man'.[39] Yet he did not wholly disown his libertine tendencies. In 1776, recalling a contemporary assumption that Asia was a site of licentiousness, Boswell defended his 'Asiatic satisfactions' declaring them 'quite consistent with devotion and with a fervent attachment to my valuable spouse'.[40]

Boswell's journals record the enactment of appropriate models of masculinity for different contexts. Although there was significant overlap between the libertine and the polite gentleman, Boswell's embrace of both created tension in his conception of self, and his relationships with his father and wife became sites where this tension was played out.[41] This is illustrated by his experiences in December 1775. On 2 December, following a night when he had gambled until four in the morning, Boswell wrote that he 'was ill from such rakishness and knew that my dear wife would suffer. Yet I could not quit gaming.'[42] Gaming was not his only vice; as is well known, Boswell also displayed a sexual libertinism. The next day he acknowledged a sexual liaison. Two days later his wife found the journal, leading him to claim that it gave 'an opportunity to check in the beginning what might have produced much mischief', and that he 'loved my wife with renewed fervour'.[43] His wife's discovery of his infidelity disrupted Boswell's attempt to combine libertine and domestic manhood, but his sobriety and fidelity were short-lived. On 11 December he attended a play with his Freemasons' lodge and then visited a coffeehouse where he drank brandy punch. Recounting this, he wrote that he 'felt a kind of desponding impression that I was unfit for being a married man'.[44]

Boswell faced a tension in his masculine identity partly because he enjoyed the leisure opportunities of urbanity. Along with gambling and sex, this cultural scene also offered polite activities. During December 1775, Boswell drank port and tea with Hume, and attended a debate at the heterosocial Pantheon public debating society. Demonstrating an ability to combine libertine and polite worlds simultaneously, Boswell's entry for 27 December records that he 'was very drunk and wandered in the streets about three hours following girls but luckily retaining rationality enough to keep clear of them'.[45]

The nature of the sources means that we should expect differences between Boswell and Somerville's life narratives; Somerville wrote his memoir in old age, and was therefore retrospectively constructing an ideal self, while Boswell's self-formation emerges in short diary entries, written day-to-day. Also, Somerville was a church minister while Boswell was a lawyer and member of the gentry, making the latter relatively free to engage in deviant behaviour.[46] Yet Boswell's regular self-admonition demonstrates that he aspired to construct a self in alignment with the norms of a modernising but still deeply Presbyterian Scotland. Central to this was the conflict between the urbane life and a Calvinist work ethic that underpinned the Enlightenment commitment to self and social improvement. This was a central theme in Boswell's relationship with his father, Alexander, Lord Auchinleck. Like James Hamilton at the end of the seventeenth century being urged by his parents to assume the duties required of the heir apparent, in 1763 Boswell faced demands to return from London, study law and follow the trajectory of his father's professional life. It was intended that through the habit of study, James Boswell would form a rational, industrious, and therefore virtuous character; that he never fully achieved this, and also struggled with the self-command demanded in polite social intercourse, led to (and was probably the product of) chronic melancholy, or, in modern parlance, depression.[47] Boswell's life highlights the multiplicity of masculine personas available to elite men, but it also reminds us of the tension between the pursuit of pleasure and manly self-command.

These two forces, pulling men towards either end of the continuum of elite masculine identities are illustrated by the associational culture of clubs and societies that rapidly expanded over the course of the eighteenth century.[48] The most well known is the Select Society. Established in 1754, it was composed of leading philosophers including Smith and Hume, alongside the artist Allan Ramsay and leading nobility, such as James, sixth duke of Hamilton (grandson of the duke who died in a duel in 1712), and Boswell. This intellectual society was governed by rules designed to ensure polite debate and enable its members to develop refinement in a homosocial space, free from the effeminising influence of women.[49] That politeness had to be learned and enforced is illustrated by Rule XII of the Society, which exhorted members to 'observe a strict Silence during the debate and, no member shall leave the Room during the time that another is speaking'.[50] But this was not the only form of homosocial associational activity in Edinburgh, and intellectual societies were joined by convivial clubs, such as the Soaping Club founded by Boswell when he was a law student at Edinburgh, with the motto 'Every man soap his own beard' (or 'Let everyman indulge his own humour').[51]

One association that was expressly libertine was the Wig Club established in Edinburgh in 1775. The members of this club were mainly landed gentleman or officers, backgrounds typical of eighteenth-century libertines.[52] The name refers to a wig allegedly made from the pubic hair of the courtesans of Charles II, which was kept and venerated by the club in its rituals which included drinking from phallic 'prick glasses'. Although a libertine club that celebrated sexuality, the Wig was not clandestine. Its rituals were secret but its existence was not, and like the Select Society it used the newspaper press to advertise its meetings. It also kept regular minutes and charged members a subscription, like more respectable associations. This location within, rather than marginal to, the associational culture of Enlightenment Edinburgh is also indicated by the club's meeting location, Fortune's Tavern in the Old Town, the same tavern used by the Poker Club.[53]

Enlightenment culture was not separate from the world of prostitution either, as shown by Boswell's journals. That Boswell was not atypical in lending his custom to this practice is indicated by the fact that many women held in Edinburgh's Tolbooth prison were accused of prostitution.[54] Rather than being a clear example of libertinism as opposed to politeness, prostitution highlights the blurred boundary between these two masculine identities. In *Ranger's Impartial List of the Ladies of Pleasure in Edinburgh*, published in 1775, this blurring is emphasised for erotic effect, with women's sexual prowess and gentility both depicted. Miss Anderson of Miss Adam's brothel was praised 'not only on account of her beauty but for her agreeable company', and male readers were assured that 'no one is more fond of enjoyment, although she is extremely modest and decent'.[55]

Ranger's Impartial List defended female prostitution in the context of sexual libertinism. Arguing that sex enhanced men's happiness and virtue, the author asserted:

> With her the youth is taught the lesson of the mind practised in genuine taste, and learns the right use of things. Here the drunkard drops a while his swinish appetite, and gazes like a man upon beauty. The lawyer in the case of love, forgets his quirks and equivocations, and is for that short space honest and upright.[56]

This argument deploys Enlightenment notions of improvement and the formation of character, seen, for instance, in Hume's philosophy, whereby commerce, leisure time and exposure to the arts enhanced civility and humanity.[57]

Outlining the process of social progress, Hume wrote that as 'refined arts advance', men become increasingly knowledgeable and sociable, leading them to seek out the company of women, with the effect that 'the tempers of men, as well as their behaviour, refine apace'.[58] Following Joseph Addison in the *Spectator* periodical, this female influence was typically associated with women's participation in polite society, especially mixed-sex conversation.[59] Yet the language used in *Ranger's Impartial List* tells us that it could be associated with heterosexual as well as heterosocial engagement. Hume did not defend prostitution but was relaxed about male sexual liberty. Explaining that refinement reduced excess in men's pursuit of all pleasures, he accepted that male sexual infidelity increased in polite times but countered that 'drunkenness, on the other hand, is much less common: A vice more odious, and more pernicious both to mind and body.'[60] In an era when adultery remained a capital crime, this was a radical statement. More conservatively, female sexual infidelity was to be discouraged because men needed to be assured of their paternity of children in order to financially support their family and develop domestic affection.[61]

Yet there was no consensus on female sexuality. Church of Scotland minister and Enlightenment participant, Robert Wallace, argued in favour of sexual pleasure, asserting in 'Of Venery, or the commerce of the two sexes' (c. 1760) that 'the most bashful virgin or chastest matron has often more lust or inclination to Venery than the greatest prostitute'.[62] And while he was uneasy about sexual promiscuity, Wallace supported divorce and questioned the naturalness of monogamy.[63] This discussion was in keeping with the challenge to an imposed Christian morality set by the European Enlightenment, but there was not a simple chronology towards greater freedom; as G. S. Rousseau and Roy Porter emphasise, 'sexual attitudes and activities during the Enlightenment were no simple matter', and in Scotland arguments such as Wallace's were in the minority.[64] Kames, who was described in John Ramsay's character sketches of the Lords of Session as an ideal polite man of letters, took a more conservative position.[65] He believed that the indulgence of the female sexual appetite would lead women to become barren; ever keen to put ideas into practice (Kames was an active agricultural improver), he exiled his daughter, Jane Home (alias Heron) after she had an adulterous affair and divorced in 1772 (she had previously had an affair with Boswell in 1761).[66] Amongst the lower-middling classes a conservative attitude seems to have prevailed also, with Paul's study showing a clear gender divide in defamation cases concerning sexual insults, with only five per cent of cases brought by men begun by a sexual insult compared to half of those brought by women.[67] In practice, sexual liberty was a largely elite male phenomenon, but it was not approved of by all men and nor was it entirely limited to the landed and professional classes or the urban realm.

The city of Edinburgh was the most obvious location for male libertinism in Scotland. Not only was it the main site of printing in Scotland, it was home to professional organisations like the College of Surgeons, and contained a university, and, by mid-century, regular theatre and dancing assemblies, along with a plethora of clubs and societies. Glasgow was also a growing city with a university but offered fewer opportunities for urbane libertinism, dominated as it was by the kirk and merchant community.[68] If moral philosopher and professor at the University, Thomas Reid, is to be believed, there was very little drinking in Glasgow. In a letter to Andrew Skene from the College in November 1764, Reid commented that since he came to Glasgow that year, he had 'not heard any swearing in the streets, nor seen a man drunk (excepting *inter nos* one Prof—r [Moor])'.[69]

Just as cities were not necessarily sites of libertinism, the countryside was not entirely lacking in opportunities. The most infamous sex club of eighteenth-century Scotland is the Beggar's Benison, and though eventually establishing branches in Edinburgh and Glasgow, it initially began in the relatively small community of the East Neuk of Fife. Established in 1732, the Beggar's Benison was a space where local gentry, merchants, customs officers and Church of Scotland elders celebrated 'a cheerful sexual hedonism' by engaging in masturbation rituals founded upon a shared belief that the primary purpose of sex was pleasure.[70] As with Boswell, these men typically combined libertinism with respectable, married manhood.

The patchy records of the Beggar's Benison depict a homosocial sexual world, and we should not assume that for some men their social intimacy was not also, or exclusively, homosexual. Our understanding of homosexual practices in Britain during this period is dominated by England, particularly London, where we have evidence of persecuted men in the pillory, a cross-dressing subculture of molly houses, and a marginal discourse in favour of homosexual freedom.[71] In Edinburgh, homosexuals were not as present in public space as they were in parts of London from at least the 1720s.[72] Edinburgh had libertine clubs, convivial societies and all the trappings of the Habermasian public sphere, factors which, Tim Hitchcock argues, contributed to the rise of the molly culture in London, yet no homosexual subculture emerged (at least not a visible one).[73] Simultaneously, sodomy does not appear to have been prosecuted in Scotland during the eighteenth century. This is despite its remaining a capital crime against divine law, punished, legal professor John Erskine explained, by society rather than God because, like adultery, it consisted of 'a positive act, hurtful to the peace of society'.[74] However, unlike the adulterer, the sodomite had no place on the continuum of acceptable manhood.

In his 1797 *Commentaries on the Law of Scotland*, David Hume (nephew of the philosopher) placed sodomy in the category of 'Fornication, Drunkenness and Unnatural Lusts', alongside bestiality.[75] Declaring that bestiality and sodomy 'by our law, like that of most other countries in Europe, justly expose the offender to be punished with death, as one whose very presence is a pollution to his fellow-creatures', he recorded that there had been only two cases of prosecution for sodomy, one in 1560 and the other in 1630.[76] Hume was not entirely correct; there were at least two prosecutions for buggery in the seventeenth century. In November 1645, the Scottish Parliament granted a commission to try and judge apprentice Gavin Bell for 'the vile and filthy crime of buggery'.[77] Significantly the 1630 case that Hume includes prosecuted Michael Erskine for 'witchcraft and filthy sodomy'.[78] This suggests that Alan Bray's argument that the sodomite was imagined as a source of destructive disorder in the early modern mental universe can be applied to the Scottish case. In this world the sodomite's two companions were the Papist and the witch.[79]

Over the century the divine crimes of adultery and bestiality were prosecuted in the High Court of Justiciary, but seemingly no cases are recorded for sodomy or buggery.[80] Though there were few prosecutions in the seventeenth century, the apparent change to none in the eighteenth, when prosecutions began to increase in England, begs the question as to why sodomy was ignored.[81] This is particularly significant when we consider that from 1817, when John Trott was convicted of 'attempted sodomy', there are relatively regular prosecutions.[82] The Presbyterian kirk in eighteenth-century Scotland was not afraid to punish sexual offences; kirk sessions continued to enforce sexual morality throughout the century.[83] This suggests that sodomy was considered too abhorrent to prosecute, and this tendency to ignore homosexuality's existence became more powerful once the spectre of witchcraft declined in prominence in Scots' imaginative universe and was no longer a capital crime.[84]

Although the public sodomite was probably not visible in Enlightenment Edinburgh, effeminate men were. In Robert Fergusson's

poetic portrayal of Edinburgh in *Auld Reekie* (1773) drunk, effeminate
men are depicted as macaronis:

> At night the macaroni drunk,
> In pools or gutters aftimes sunk:
> Hegh, what a fright he now appears,
> Whan he his corpse dejected rears!
> Look at that head and think if there
> The pomet slaistered up his hair! (lines 119–24)[85]

Like the libertine, the macaroni's identity is located in the night, when
alternative codes of masculinity reigned in taverns and wynds. Yet he
does not display the power of the libertine; instead the macaroni is
lying in a gutter, his hair ruined. The macaroni was a caricature but
this caricature 'drew on recognizable social behaviour'.[86] Depicted by
Fergusson, the macaroni represents a failure of manhood due to his
excessive refinement, but this effeminacy does not necessarily cast him
as a sodomite. As Philip Carter maintains, the effeminate fop was typically a failed heterosexual, corrupted by luxury, and too enamoured of
feminine fashions to affectively bond with women in a complementary
manner.[87] In Scottish Enlightenment philosophy, this complementary
gender identity, particularly in the context of marriage, was considered
to be both an indicator and a driver of progress.[88]

As well as heterosexual bonds, intimacy between men was an important site for the determination of manhood. We find a possible reference to homosexual desire in Kames' essay on manners, *Sketches of
the History of Man* (1774), in which he contemplated the tendency of
luxury to encourage selfishness and confine man's perspective so that
he 'admits not of friendship, and scarce of any other social passion'.[89]
This idea was common to Scottish Enlightenment critiques of luxury,
where, using Rome as an example, moralists warned that increased
wealth could introduce licentious manners that, in turn, would eventually destroy commercial civilisation.[90]

Kames contrasted the selfishness of luxury with that of the so-called
savage state, asserting that savages direct their selfishness outward: 'the
whole force of his social affection being directed to a single object,
becomes extremely fervid. Hence the unexampled friendship between
Achilles and Patroclus in the *Iliad*; and hence many such friendships
amongst savages.'[91] However, the relationship between Achilles and
Patroclus has not always been read as sexual, so Kames' reference is
opaque; it is possible that he is alluding to passionate but platonic
friendship with this example.[92] Either way, the passionate and exclusive

nature of the relationship rendered it uncivilised. The rational, sympathetic attachment of ideal male friendship 'was used to distinguish civilised Europeans, in their own eyes, from the uncivilised nations of other parts of the world'.[93]

Influenced by Classical writers such as Cicero and Aristotle, Enlightenment-defined friendship was associated with virtue and equality, and character traits such as avarice or a commitment to debauchery disqualified men from true mutual attachment. While the rise of the novel explored and disseminated ideas of emotional and female friendship, the philosophical ideal was one of rational, mutual affection between men.[94] Kames' ideal of friendship was similar to that of Adam Smith, who celebrated a moderate expression of friendship founded upon interdependence and independence, removing deference and encouraging cooperation in an urban, commercial world.[95]

A belief in the improving quality of large circles of friendship was shared by Hume, and founded upon the notion that sociability was innate. As Kames reasoned, 'nature, which designed us for society, has linked us together in an intimate manner, by the sympathetic principle, which communicates the joy and sorrow of one to many'.[96] A significant impact of the Enlightenment on Scottish manhood was that these sociable relationships came to be considered crucial to the formation of a manly character; only in interactions with others could the self, the subject of the Scottish science of man, be judged.[97]

Untangling intimate platonic friendship and physical, sexual intimacy is difficult for a period when men may have lacked an appropriate language to express homosexual desires and experiences in representations of the self, thus possibly concealing or transferring these via the language of intimate friendship. It is also likely that, as in early modern England, homosexual practices were not always understood as sodomy or an expression of homosexuality by the men engaging in them, a process described by Bray as a 'cleavage between an individual's behaviour and his awareness of its significance'.[98]

This problem faced historian G. S. Rousseau when he examined a club of students from Scotland, England and France, including Alexander Carlyle, John Wilkes and the Baron D'Holbach, who all studied at Leiden and Utrecht universities in the 1740s, and their tutor, Scottish moralist, Andrew Baxter.[99] To properly comprehend queer sexualities and the male experience more research is needed on the wider context of male intimacy, particularly for men such as Hume and Smith who did not marry but instead earned their manly reputation within professional, polite and predominantly homosocial, worlds. Rousseau makes a strong case for understanding same-sex desire in the eighteenth century through a focus on male subjectivities, of which friendship was a crucial expression.[100] In Presbyterian Scotland, the sodomite may have been so abhorrent as to have encouraged a silence on homosexual desires, but this could have created space for a comprehension of queer acts within the context of intimate friendship.

Although typically confirmed through marriage and the heading of a household, manhood could, alternatively, be validated in a homo-social context by financial independence, professional standing and the achievement of reputation. What was crucial was the public display of a manly character such as Hume's self-definition as a man 'of mild dispositions', 'command of temper' and a 'cheerful humour'.[101] This moderation in the sentiments distinguished the polite man from the effeminate fop, and it was manifested in Hume's life through homo- and heterosocial social engagement, from membership of leading intellectual societies to friendship with gentry women such as Elizabeth Fletcher.[102] This combination of same- and mixed-sex sociability enabled men to obtain a balance between the influence of feminine sensibility and manly self-command, and avoid the stamp of effeminacy that physician and philosopher, William Alexander, warned would result if 'perpetually confined to their [women's] company'.[103]

While there was fluidity, men needed to be careful that they did not step outside the boundaries of acceptable masculinity: just as there could be slippage between polite and libertine, so too could the polite man become a fop, and the fop a sodomite. This slippage is apparent in Smollett's *Roderick Random* (1748), which contains a rare Scottish reference to the sodomite in the characters of Captain Whiffle and Earl Strutwell, who highlight the dangers of same-sex intimacy in a novel in which male–male relationships take centre stage.[104] Written in the aftermath of Culloden, this novel can be read as an argument for a British masculinity founded upon industry, self-control and autonomy, in opposition to the self-interested sodomite.[105]

Within the heteronormative boundaries of culturally approved manhood, some masculinities appear more powerful than others; whether expressed through domestic economy, an industrious work ethic and/ or polite social interaction, independence and self-command loom large in definitions of manhood. Yet exactly how these were understood dif-fered; independence, for instance, could be defined by the holding of land or the earning of an income, or the freedom to, in Boswell's words, 'be in some degree whatever character we choose'.[106] Men's lived experi-ence, too, did not always equate with aspirational ideals. Men may have

aspired to gentility but have been fond of homosocial tavern conviviality, they may have read the *Spectator* or *Scots Magazine*, and attended
dancing assemblies, but still felt the need to defend their honour in a
duel or drunken fight. To be manly was crucial but to define manhood
in the singular was, and is, impossible.

NOTES

1. James Boswell, *Boswell's Edinburgh Journals: 1767–1786*, Hugh Milne
   (ed.) (Edinburgh: Mercat Press, 2001).
2. Philip Carter, 'James Boswell's manliness', in Tim Hitchcock and Michèle
   Cohen (eds), *English Masculinities 1660–1800* (London: Longman, 1999),
   pp. 111–30.
3. Faramerz Dabhoiwala, *The Origins of Sex: A History of the First
   Sexual Revolution* (London: Allen Lane, 2012); Simon Dickie, *Cruelty
   and Laughter: Forgotten Literature and the Unsentimental Eighteenth
   Century* (Chicago: University of Chicago Press, 2011); Henry French
   and Mark Rothery, *Man's Estate: Landed Gentry Masculinities 1600–
   1900* (Oxford: Oxford University Press, 2012); Vic Gatrell, *The First
   Bohemians: Life and Art in London's Golden Age* (London: Allen Lane,
   2013); Karen Harvey, *The Little Republic: Masculinity and Domestic
   Authority in Eighteenth-Century Britain* (Oxford: Oxford University
   Press, 2012).
4. Helen Berry, 'Rethinking politeness in eighteenth-century England: Moll
   King's coffee house and the significance of "flash talk"', *Transactions
   of the Royal Historical Society*, 11 (2001), pp. 65–82; Kate Davison,
   'Occasional politeness and gentlemen's laughter in 18th century England',
   Historical Journal, 57:4 (2014), pp. 921–45; Karen Harvey, 'Ritual
   encounters: punch parties and masculinity in the eighteenth century', *Past
   and Present*, 214:1 (2012), pp. 165–203.
5. Lynn Abrams, 'The taming of Highland masculinity: interpersonal violence and shifting codes of manhood, c. 1760–1840', *Scottish Historical
   Review*, 92:1 (2013), pp. 100–22 and see Abrams' 'Highland Masculinity'
   and Tawny Paul's chapters in this collection.
6. Henry Mackenzie, *The Anecdotes and Egotisms of Henry Mackenzie,
   1745–1831*, John Dwyer (ed.) (Bristol: Thoemmes Press, 1996), p. 69.
7. Rosalind Carr, *Gender and Enlightenment Culture in Eighteenth-Century
   Scotland* (Edinburgh: Edinburgh University Press, 2014), pp. 142–74.
8. Adam Smith, *Lectures on Jurisprudence*, R. L. Meek, D. D. Raphael and
   P. G. Stein (eds) (Indianapolis: Liberty Classics, 1982), p. 122.
9. Donna T. Andrew, 'The code of honour and its critics: the opposition to
   duelling in England, 1700–1850', *Social History*, 5:3 (1980), pp. 409–34.
10. Robert B. Shoemaker, 'The taming of the duel: masculinity, honour and

ritual violence in London, 1660–1800', *Historical Journal*, 45:3 (2002), pp. 525–45.

11. James, Duke of Hamilton [1706] quoted in George Lockhart, *Scotland's Ruine: Lockhart of Carnwath's Memoirs of the Union*, Daniel Szechi (ed) (Aberdeen: Aberdeen University Press, [1714] 1995), p. 252.

12. Hamilton was a Tory and Mohun a Whig. Stephen Banks, *A Polite Exchange of Bullets: The Duel and the English Gentleman, 1750–1850* (Woodbridge: Boydell Press, 2010), pp. 18–19.

13. A good example is Lord Belhaven's Mother Caledonia speech; John Hamilton, Lord Belhaven, *The Late Lord Belhaven's Memorable Speeches in the Last Parliament of Scotland* (Edinburgh: G. Hamilton & J. Balfour, 1741).

14. Anon., *A Poem upon the most Potent Prince, James D[uk]e of Hamilton, Anent the Union of Great Britain* (Edinburgh, 1707). Original italics.

15. See Christopher Whatley, *The Scots and the Union* (Edinburgh: Edinburgh University Press, 2007), p. 47; Rosalind K. Marshall, *The Days of Duchess Anne: Life in the Household of the Duchess of Hamilton 1656–1716* (East Linton: Tuckwell Press, 2000), pp. 168–88; Rosalind Carr, 'Gender, national identity and political agency in eighteenth-century Scotland (unpublished doctoral thesis, University of Glasgow, 2008), pp. 90–6.

16. Anon., *A Full and Exact Relation of the Duel Fought in Hyde-Park on Saturday, Nov. 15, 1712 Between his Grace, James, Duke of Hamilton, and the Right Honourable, Charles, Lord Mohun, In a Letter to a Member of Parliament* (London: E. Curll, 1713), p. 12.

17. Anon., *Full and Exact Relation*, p. 10.

18. Ibid. p. 13.

19. Ibid. p. 18.

20. For the impact of the *Spectator* in Scotland and the emergence of politeness, see Nicholas Phillipson, 'Politics, politeness and the early eighteenth-century anglicisation of Scottish culture', in Roger A. Mason (ed.), *Scotland and England, 1286–1815* (Edinburgh: John Donald, 1987), pp. 226–46.

21. Adam Ferguson, *An Essay on the History of Civil Society*, Fania Oz-Salzberger (ed.) (Cambridge: Cambridge University Press, [1767] 1995); John Robertson, *The Scottish Enlightenment and the Militia Issue* (Edinburgh: John Donald, 1985), pp. 63–91.

22. Rosalind Carr, 'The gentleman and the soldier: patriotic masculinities in eighteenth-century Scotland', *Journal of Scottish Historical Studies*, 28:2 (2008), pp. 101–21.

23. French and Rothery, *Man's Estate*, p. 87.

24. K. Tawny Paul, 'Credit, reputation and masculinity in British urban commerce: Edinburgh, c. 1710–70, *The Economic History Review*, 66:1 (2013), pp. 226–248, at 234. This corresponds with Harvey's findings for England. Harvey, *The Little Republic*.

25. For the landed classes see Katie Barclay, *Love, Intimacy and Power: Marriage and Patriarchy in Scotland, 1650–1850* (Manchester: Manchester University Press, 2011).

26. Matthew McCormack, *The Independent Man: Citizenship and Gender Politics in Georgian England* (Manchester University Press, 2005).

27. Alexander Carlyle, *Autobiography of the Rev. Dr Alexander Carlyle Minister of Inveresk* (Edinburgh: William Blackwood, 1861), p. 63.

28. Henry Home, Lord Kames, *Sketches of the History of Man*, Book I, Sketch V, 'Manners', 3rd edition, James A. Harris (ed.) (Indianapolis: Liberty Fund, [1788] 2007), pp. 172–3.

29. David Hume, 'My Own Life' [1776] in *Essays Moral, Political and Literary*, Eugene F. Miller (ed.) (Liberty Fund: Indianapolis, 1987) www.econlib.org/library/LFBooks/Hume/hmMPL0.html#My Own Life, by David Hume (last accessed 16 January 2015).

30. Carr, 'Gender, national identity and political agency', pp. 130–73.

31. Reverend Thomas Somerville, *My Own Life and Times 1741–1814*, R. B. Sher (ed.) (Thoemmes Press, [1861] 1996), p. 53.

32. Somerville, *My Own Life*, pp. 42–4.

33. Ibid. pp. 44–5.

34. Susan Kingsley Kent, *Gender and Power in Britain 1640–1990* (London: Routledge, 1996), pp. 29–33; Faramerz Dabhoiwala, 'The construction of honour, reputation and status in late seventeenth- and early eighteenth-century England', *Transactions of the Royal Historical Society*, 6 (1996), pp. 201–13, at 205–7.

35. Paul Langford, 'The uses of eighteenth-century politeness', *Transactions of the Royal Historical Society*, 12 (2002), pp. 311–31.

36. Philip Carter, *Men and the Emergence of Polite Society, Britain 1660–1800* (Harlow: Pearson, 2001), pp. 21–2.

37. See for example, James Boswell, *A View of the Edinburgh Theatre During the Summer Season 1759* (London: A. Morely, 1760); *An Account of Corsica* (London: Foulis, 1768); *The Life of Dr Samuel Johnson, LL.D.* (London: Charles Dilly, 1792); Thomas Somerville, *The Effects of the French Revolution, with respect to the interests of humanity, liberty, religion, and morality* (Edinburgh: William Creech, 1793); *The History of Great Britain During the Reign of Queen Anne* (London: A. Strahan and T. Caddell, 1798).

38. Boswell, *Edinburgh Journals*, pp. 68–9.

39. Ibid. p. 205.

40. Quoted in ibid. p. 253.

41. Katie Barclay, 'Sex, identity and enlightenment in the long eighteenth century', in Jodi A. Campbell, Elizabeth Ewan and Heather Parker (eds), *The Shaping of Scottish Identities: Family, Nation and the Worlds Beyond* (Guelph: Centre for Scottish Studies, 2011), pp. 29–42, at 35–6; Anthony

LaVopa, 'The not-so-prodigal son: James Boswell and the Scottish Enlightenment', in Thomas Ahnert and Susan Manning (eds), *Character, Self and Sociability in the Scottish Enlightenment* (New York: Palgrave, 2011), pp. 85–103.

42. Boswell, *Edinburgh Journals*, p. 21; 'The not-so-prodigal son', 5.
43. Ibid. p. 215.
44. Ibid. pp. 217–18.
45. Ibid. p. 223.
46. The power of the church to punish deviancy was displayed when the Reverend John Home, author of *Douglas*, was forced to resign after the play's performance in Edinburgh in 1756.
47. LaVopa, 'The not-so-prodigal son', pp. 85–103.
48. Davis D. McElroy, *Scotland's Age of Improvement: A Survey of Eighteenth-Century Literary Clubs and Societies* (Pullman, WA: Washington State University Press, 1969).
49. Carr, *Gender and Enlightenment*, 36–72.
50. National Library of Scotland, Minutes of the Select Society, MS Adv.23.1.1.
51. Frederick A. Pottle, *James Boswell: The Earlier Years 1740–1769* (London: William Heinemann, 1966), p. 58.
52. Dabhoiwala, *Origins of Sex*, pp. 118–21; Paul, 'Credit, reputation and masculinity', pp. 233–6.
53. David Stevenson, *The Beggar's Benison: Sex Clubs of Enlightenment Scotland and their Rituals* (East Linton: Tuckwell Press, 2001), pp. 193–214. See also, Carr, *Gender and Enlightenment*, pp. 36–72, 118–28.
54. Edinburgh City Archives, 'Edinburgh Burgh Court Black Books', SL232, Vol. 3, 1736–55.
55. Anon., *Ranger's Impartial List of the Ladies of Pleasure in Edinburgh, with a Preface by a celebrated Wit* (Edinburgh, 1775), p. 17. See also, Carr, *Gender and Enlightenment*, pp. 128–40.
56. Anon., *Ranger's Impartial List*, v.
57. Christopher J. Berry, *The Idea of Commercial Society in the Scottish Enlightenment* (Edinburgh: Edinburgh University Press, 2013).
58. David Hume, 'Of refinement in the arts' [1752], in *Essays Moral, Political and Literary*, Miller (ed.), p. 271.
59. Lawrence Klein, 'Gender, conversation and the public sphere in early eighteenth-century England', in J. Still and M. Worton (eds), *Textuality and Sexuality: Reading Theories and Practices* (Manchester: Manchester University Press, 1993), pp. 100–15; Katharine Glover, *Elite Women and Polite Society in Eighteenth-Century Scotland* (Woodbridge: Boydell Press, 2011), especially pp. 79–109.
60. Hume, 'Of refinement in the arts', p. 272.
61. S. A. M. Burns, 'The human female', in L. M. G. Clark and L. Lange (eds) *The Sexism of Social and Political Theory: Women and Reproduction from Plato to Nietzsche* (Toronto: University of Toronto Press, 1979), pp.

55–7. For female sexuality, see Barclay, 'Sex, identity and enlightenment', pp. 29–42.

62. Quoted in Nora Smith, 'Sexual mores in the eighteenth century: Robert Wallace's "Of Venery"', *Journal of the History of Ideas*, 39:3 (1978), pp. 419–33, at 424.

63. Smith, 'Sexual mores'.

64. G. S. Rousseau and Roy Porter, 'Introduction', in Rousseau and Porter (eds), *Sexual Underworlds of the Enlightenment* (Manchester: Manchester University Press, 1987), p. 5.

65. LaVopa, 'The not-so-prodigal son', p. 88.

66. Smith, 'Sexual mores', p. 426; Pottle, *Boswell*, pp. 78–9.

67. Paul, 'Credit, reputation and masculinity', p. 234.

68. Richard Sher, 'Commerce, religion and enlightenment in eighteenth-century Glasgow', in Thomas M. Devine and Gordon Jackson (eds), *Glasgow Vol. 1: Beginnings to 1830* (Manchester: Manchester University Press, 1996), pp. 326–8.

69. Thomas Reid to Andrew Skene, 14 November 1764, in *Electronic Enlightenment*, Robert McNamee et al. (eds), version 2.4. (University of Oxford, 2013) www.e-enlightenment.com.catalogues.ulrls.lon.ac.uk/item/ reidthEU0010035b_1key001cor/ (last accessed 4 October 2015).

70. Stevenson, *Beggar's Benison*, p. 69.

71. Rictor Norton, *Mother Clap's Molly House: The Gay Subculture in England 1700–1830* (London: Gay Men's Press, 1992); Randolph Trumbach, 'Modern sodomy: the origins of homosexuality, 1700–1800', in Matt Cook (ed.), *A Gay History of Britain: Love and Sex Between Men Since the Middle Ages* (Greenworld: Oxford, 2007), pp. 77–106; Tim Hitchcock, *English Sexualities, 1700–1800* (Basingstoke: Macmillan, 1997), pp. 58–75.

72. Gatrell, *First Bohemians*, p. xx.

73. Hitchcock, *English Sexualities*, p. 75.

74. John Erskine, *An Institute of the Law of Scotland: In Four Books*, 7th edition (Edinburgh: Edinburgh Printing and Publishing Company, [1773] 1838), p. 1079, see also p. 1105.

75. David Hume, *Commentaries on the Law of Scotland, Respecting Crimes* (Edinburgh: Bell & Bradfute, [1797] 1819), vol. 1, p. xiv.

76. Ibid. p. 465.

77. *The Records of the Parliaments of Scotland to 1707*, Keith M. Brown et al (eds) (University of St Andrews, 2007–2015), 1645/11/28, http://www.rps.ac.uk/trans/1645/11/28 (last accessed 16 February 2015).

78. Hume, *Commentaries*, vol. 1, p. 466.

79. Ibid. p. 466; Alan Bray, *Homosexuality in Renaissance England* (London: Gay Men's Press, 1982), pp. 25–7. This corresponds to discussion of sexual activity at the black Sabbath in sixteenth-century texts, when claims emerged that male witches had homosexual relations with the

Devil, see Brian P. Levack, *The Witch-Hunt in Early Modern Europe*, 3rd edition, (Harlow: Pearson, 2006), pp. 52–3.

80. More research is needed before we can conclusively assert a lack of prosecutions but this initial assertion is supported by the (inconclusive) 'Scottish Criminal Cases Index', NRS, and informal discussion with experts in Scottish legal history, including Professor John Cairns.

81. Hitchcock, *English Sexualities*, p. 60.

82. NRS, AD14/17/163A.

83. Rosalind Mitchison and Leah Leneman, *Sexuality and Social Control: Scotland 1660–1780* (Oxford: Blackwell, 1989).

84. The Scottish Witchcraft Act of 1563 was repealed in 1736. For a discussion of the early modern English abhorrence of sodomy see Bray, *Homosexuality*, pp. 58–62.

85. Christopher Maclachlan (ed.), *Before Burns: Eighteenth-Century Scottish Poetry* (Edinburgh: Canongate, 2002), p. 214.

86. Dror Wahrman, *The Making of the Modern Self: Identity and Culture in Eighteenth-Century England* (New Haven: Yale University Press, 2004), p. 62.

87. Carter, *Men and the Emergence of Polite Society*, pp. 139–49.

88. Silvia Sebastiani, 'Race, women and progress in the Scottish Enlightenment', in Sarah Knott and Barbara Taylor (eds), *Women, Gender and Enlightenment* (Basingstoke: Palgrave, 2005), pp. 75–96, at 75–83.

89. Kames, 'Manners', p. 204.

90. See for example, John Millar, *The Origin of the Distinction of Ranks*, 4th edition (Edinburgh, [1779] 1806), p. 103; Kames, 'Manners', pp. 178–9.

91. Kames, 'Manners', p. 204.

92. David M. Halperin, *One Hundred Years of Homosexuality and Other Essays on Greek Love* (London: Routledge, 1990), pp. 75–87.

93. David Garrioch, 'From Christian friendship to secular sentimentality: Enlightenment re-evaluations', in Barbara Caine (ed.), *Friendship: A History* (Oakville, CT: Equinox, 2009), pp. 165–214, at 200.

94. Ibid. pp. 165–214.

95. John Dwyer, 'Ethics and economics: bridging Adam Smith's *Theory of Moral Sentiments* and *Wealth of Nations*', *Journal of British Studies*, 44:4 (2005), pp. 662–87; Lisa Hill and Peter McCarthy, 'Hume, Smith and Ferguson: friendship in a commercial society', *Critical Review of International Social and Political Philosophy*, 2:4 (1999), pp. 33–49.

96. Henry Home, Lord Kames, *Essays on the Principles of Morality and Natural Religion, Corrected and Improved, in a Third Edition. Several Essays Added Concerning the Proof of a Deity*, Mary Catherine Moran (ed.) (Indianapolis: Liberty Fund, 2005) http://oll.libertyfund.org/titles/1352#Home_0995_68 (last accessed 7 August 2015).

97. Susan Manning and Thomas Ahnert, 'Introduction: character, self and

sociability in the Scottish Enlightenment', in Ahnert and Manning (eds), *Character, Self and Sociability*, pp. 1–30, at 6.

98. Bray, *Homosexuality*, p. 68.
99. G. S. Rousseau, '"In the house of Madam Vander Tasse, on the Long Bridge": a homosocial university club in early modern Europe', in Kent Gerard and Gert Hekma (eds), *The Pursuit of Sodomy: Male Homosexuality in Renaissance and Enlightenment Europe* (New York: Harrington Park Press, 1989), pp. 311–47.
100. George Rousseau, '"Homoplatonic, homodepressed, homomorbid": some further genealogies of same-sex attraction in Western civilisation', in Katherine O'Donnell and Michael O'Rourke (eds), *Love, Sex, Intimacy and Friendship Between Men, 1550–1800* (Basingstoke: Palgrave, 2003), pp. 12–52.
101. Hume, 'My Own Life'.
102. Glover, *Elite Women and Polite Society*, pp. 118–19.
103. William Alexander, *The History of Women, From the Earliest Antiquity to the Present Time; giving some account of almost every interesting particular concerning that sex among all nations, ancient and modern*, 3rd edition, vol. 1 (London: C. Dilly and R. Christopher, 1781), p. 475.
104. George E. Haggerty, 'Smollett's world of masculine desire in *The Adventures of Roderick Random*', *Eighteenth Century: Theory and Interpretation*, 53:3 (2012), pp. 317–30.
105. Juliet Shields, 'Smollett's Scots and sodomites: British masculinity in *Roderick Random*', *The Eighteenth Century*, 46:2 (2005), pp. 175–88.
106. *Boswell's London Journals 1762–63*, quoted in Ahnert and Manning (eds), *Character, Self and Sociability*, p 14.

4

The Taming of Highland Masculinity: Interpersonal Violence and Shifting Codes of Manhood, c. 1760–1840

Lynn Abrams

HISTORIANS GENERALLY ACCEPT THAT interpersonal violence was a common feature of relationships between men in the past and that the contexts in which violence was perpetrated can reveal something about the mentalities and social roles of men in past societies.[1] Nevertheless, it is also agreed that the modes of and occasions for violence vary according to their context, and thus there is a need to understand precisely the conditions that facilitate and legitimate interpersonal violence between men in different locales and time periods.[2] While male violence appears to be ubiquitous – men form the overwhelming majority of perpetrators and victims of violent behaviour – its meaning is historically specific.

This chapter examines a type of modernising society – the Scottish Highlands in the period 1760–1840 – in which a code of violence governed by an indigenous culture of manhood was gradually superseded by a new culture with a new code concerning violence. This was in part the consequence of changing economic and social conditions in the Highlands as well as the imposition of a judiciary and law enforcers serving the aspirant bourgeois ideology of local elites and the demands of a distant state. It argues that violence against the (male) person was regarded as commonplace and to some degree legitimate in the rural Highland counties until at least the 1820s, that men of the rural labouring classes regarded violence as a means to protect or affirm their status, to restore honour or to avenge a wrong, and that this had previously been accepted or tolerated by Highland elites. But this association between a certain model of manhood and interpersonal violence was challenged increasingly from around 1800 by those who advocated civility and restraint amongst men, especially in the growing Highland town of Inverness, the centre of an emerging middle-class culture with changing social sensibilities. The borderline between acceptable and unacceptable, legitimate and illegitimate male violence shifted as a new conception of what constituted respectable manhood was disseminated. In the wake of the Jacobite risings and the repressive measures aimed at taming the Highlands, there was a more subtle and longer-term taming of every-day Highland manhood. Certainly, the Highlands exhibited some very particular characteristics in respect of the conduct of men and the social, economic and political context in which that conduct was performed. But this is not an exceptional case. Rather, this analysis of male inter-personal violence is suggestive of more general trends in the disciplining of manhood in late eighteenth- and early nineteenth-century Scotland.

APPROACHES TO MALE VIOLENCE

Historians of masculinity and violence in England have characterised the period from the late eighteenth century as encompassing the rise of civility, politeness and refinement, when interpersonal violence was increasingly frowned upon and expressions of anger and aggression were diverted into the courts. Being a respectable man meant eschewing vio-lence for restraint, walking away from a confrontation and, if necessary, pursuing a grievance in the courts rather than with fists.[3] This model fits a historical narrative characterised by a shift from a 'rough-and-ready seventeenth-century manhood' to 'a polite and civil eighteenth-century masculinity'.[4] It presumes increasing emphasis on manners and civility in interpersonal relations and a decline in resort to physical violence, but it also highlights a transition from the concept of manhood (a state externally validated and articulated through public behaviour and social action) to the concept of masculinity (an internalised subjective identity) and in turn a move from the external to the internal policing of the individual. Thus in the sixteenth and seventeenth centuries there is a concern with reputation and honour, publicly defended in words and actions; by the eighteenth, there is a 'modern' concern with interiority, or masculinity as an expression of the self that implies the internalisation of certain attributes.

This narrative of change rests in large part on evidence from the elites and middling sorts of the English metropole, though in Edinburgh too, as Tawny Paul's and Rosalind Carr's chapters in this collection demonstrate, the model of manhood that saw violence replaced by the advocacy of self-restraint and recourse to the law was in evidence. However, to date the relationship between Scottish labouring men and violence has been subject to surprisingly limited historical investigation.

Clearly, alternative or subversive modes of masculine behaviour could have existed alongside the model promoted by the urban elite. Indeed, the culture of refinement and civility necessarily established itself *in opposition to* customary violence; 'civilised' thinking engaged with and worried about violence, categorising it and identifying it as a remnant of a savage society, either backward or working-class. In eighteenth-century Scotland the Highlands were perceived and represented by others as untamed and undisciplined, a place where manhood had not yet found expression in disciplined labour, respectable domesticity or the restraint of physical aggression.[5]

This chapter considers the *social practices* of masculinity, the ways in which men acted out codes of manhood in order to establish social status, as opposed to the prescriptive roles and discursive constructions of masculinity that are discussed elsewhere in this collection.[6] It argues that the threat and use of physical violence between men in the Highland counties remained a feature of male public culture at least until the 1820s, albeit diminishing over time, and that the use of violence in an everyday context was part and parcel of a male culture of recreation and status reinforcement.[7] That said, however, codes of manhood are not homogeneous. In the tension between an increasing emphasis on restraint and civility adopted by the gentry and middling classes from the middle decades of the eighteenth century and the continuation of the resort to violence amongst the poor, divergent masculine codes are accentuated. In the courts, ongoing tensions in Highland society between customary codes of manliness and new models of manhood were played out. This tension reached its peak in the burgeoning Highland town of Inverness.

The discussion is based primarily on the scrutiny of legal records relating to cases of violent assault, most involving men of the middling and lower classes from across the Highland counties, which were heard in the burgh, sheriff or High Court of Justiciary.[8] These range from the most trivial (an argument about the price of a fish) to the most serious (a conflict resulting in a man's death). The inconsistent and incomplete character of the legal records prevents a quantitative analysis of the geographical or chronological distribution of legal cases or conclusions about the frequency of violent incidents *per capita*; the cases pursued in the legal system that have left written traces are a fraction of those that occurred, though it is impossible to be certain what that fraction is.[9] Analysis of Inverness burgh court records shows a very low but fairly consistent prosecution of assault between the 1770s and 1830s, but from 1800 onwards this court was almost solely concerned with cases of debt and removal.[10] The sheriff court, where most assault cases from the rural areas and the town would have been addressed, appears to record a higher incidence of cases prosecuted, especially in the 1820s and 1830s, but the incompleteness of the records means it is impossible to determine the actual incidence of violence or even if the legal system had greater efficacy in these decades.[11] The most serious cases, those concerning aggravated assault or resulting in death or serious injury, were referred to the High Court of Justiciary on circuit in Inverness, and these provide more fulsome material including witness statements. But here too the usual provisos apply. An analysis of all the assault cases heard by the High Court across Scotland indicates a significant increase in incidence of both investigations and prosecutions between 1810 and 1839 – as at the local level – but while this may indicate a real increase in violent assault, it is just as likely to be a consequence of a greater propensity to prosecute in these decades.[12] What one can say with certainty is that in its perpetrators, victims and witnesses, this is overwhelmingly a male realm of behaviour.[13]

Nevertheless, despite these shortcomings some important insights can be gained into the boundaries between acceptable and unacceptable violent behaviour, if only because those cases that reached the courts crossed a line, because something went wrong (someone was seriously or fatally injured) or because one party deemed himself humiliated and sought public retribution. More significantly, recourse to the law by one party may indicate that there was change afoot in Highland culture; if 'satisfaction' could not be gained one way (with violence), it could by another (in the courts). This is everyday manhood in transition. The evidence from defendants, victims and witnesses provides descriptions of everyday social conduct and face-to-face interactions amongst men that developed into violent confrontation. Few incidences are transparent to the historian in terms of providing a clear expression of men's sense of manhood. Instead, we are forced to decode descriptions of actions and statements given in court that have already been mediated, especially in Gaelic-speaking areas where the testimony has been translated at the point of transcription, before the historian reads the text of a witness precognition or a defence statement. Nevertheless, it is often the mundane or unremarkable incident that provides an acute insight into the meanings men assigned to their actions.

THE HIGHLAND CONTEXT

The political, social and economic convulsions experienced in the Highlands following the Jacobite period form the backdrop to this analysis. The policy of state-sponsored repression of all vestiges of Jacobite interest, and subsequent attempts to improve or civilise the Highlands, are mirrored by approaches to male interpersonal violence seen in the civil arena of everyday life.[14] The suppression was a violent and punitive affair, a dismantling of the Highland way of life with profound effects on social structures and social relationships, and arguably resulting in the disintegration of Highland society.[15] The policy – involving confiscation of estates, forcible removal of peoples from the land, destruction of crops and property, and arrest, sentencing and deportation of alleged Jacobite sympathisers – legitimised violence carried out in the name of the state, whereas the outlawing of the carrying of arms and the wearing of the plaid aimed to reduce Highland men to impotence. Although the latter was largely a symbolic measure it did undermine one of the signifiers of Highland manhood at a time when the state was exerting its power as never before. The military presence in Inverness, Fort George and the Highland counties from 1746 and the activities of recruiting parties across the region following the passing of the Scottish Militia Act in 1797, exemplified the imposition of state power through violence involving arms.[16]

The 'civilising' stage of the process had a different but no less profound impact. The promotion of commercial production in agriculture, fisheries and manufacture, and investment in road construction were intended to foster capitalism and ensure the transformation of a clan-based system into one based on commercial competition.[17] This had far-reaching consequences, not least the decline of a social system based on kin allegiances and changes in agricultural land use, leading to community relocation. Between the 1780s and 1820s incidents of riot and popular resistance to evictions, grain shortages, military recruitment and arrests of whisky smugglers are indicative of this social upheaval. Popular disquiet expressed itself in social disobedience, and this environment undoubtedly nurtured interpersonal conflict, despite the rise of evangelical religiosity encouraging a self-restraining masculinity.[18] In towns like Inverness, the growth of small-scale industry, economic competition amongst artisans, and the emergence of a merchant and professional class, fed this volatile environment where face-to-face conflict was common.

In the second half of the eighteenth century, social interactions amongst men were still shaped in part by a continuum of customary forms of dealing with grudges and the existence of long-standing kin groups. Despite the destruction of the social basis of the clan system, 'the mental attitudes and beliefs engendered by the Highlands' traditional social system could not be so easily erased'.[19] The traditional feud – a legitimised form of violence promoted by kinship bonds and a culture of revenge – still existed as a social memory.[20] Yet the combination of customary modes of dispute resolution and economic and social dislocation resulted in what Robert Dodgshon has termed 'social banditry' – a resort to collective retribution with few or no rules that was far less regulated than traditional feuding.[21] Bonds of kinship remained strong, but the economic and social structures upon which the clan system rested had been swept away. Hospitality – one of clanship's remaining vestiges – expressed itself increasingly in a society lubricated by strong drink. Whisky, most of it produced in illegal stills, was easily available and cheap.[22]

SOCIAL VIOLENCE

Aside from the collective riots and disturbances, much reported male interpersonal violence bears a superficial resemblance to the traditional feud. One kin group wreaks vengeance on another kin group in a planned violent confrontation, which serves to maintain the honour of the avenging party and operates according to an agreed set of rules.[23] The social importance of clan or kin loyalty was often cited by defendants to legitimise violence that might once have been described as customary. Incidents that appear to be spontaneous drunken brawls were revealed to be informed by a history of enmity and the acceptance of violent retaliation for a slight upon oneself or one's clansman. So it was in the case of a series of violent confrontations in 1828 at a wedding at Mallaig between the McPhails and McDonalds from Morar, and the McGillivrays from neighbouring Arisaig. The incidents have all the characteristics of a form of social violence not uncommon in the rural Highlands: clan loyalty and revenge, young men, ritualistic confrontation, concepts of fair play, all lubricated by alcohol and played out in a recreational context.[24]

The two sets of family members had gathered for the marriage of Angus McPhail. The night 'was passed with great conviviality and friendship', but at some point a confrontation occurred and members of the McGillivray clan set upon one of the Morar McDonalds – James McDonald – during which he was knocked down 'and lay as if lifeless on the ground'. Donald McDonald, on observing James being maltreated, exclaimed: '"Oh my God! What shall I do seeing my blood thus spilt"'. Donald was then set upon by Alexander McPhail, who allegedly 'trampled and kicked his body with iron heeled and toed shoes when his sons were keeping him tied to the ground'. According to the alleged perpetrator who admitted being 'somewhat intoxicated', Donald McDonald 'was very noisy and bragging that there was no a son of a bitch of them that came across the river Morar, meaning the Arisaig men, but he could thrash and take the breeches off'. Following this, a reconciliation amongst all parties was effected and all shook hands and mutually forgave one another before breakfasting together. On the journey home though, the recollection of the night's affray aroused the participants once again, and a second fight broke out, this time between James McDonald and Alexander McPhail's son. Donald McDonald leapt to his kinsman's defence, but the McPhails surrounded the two McDonalds, and in the ensuing fight Donald McDonald was killed.

Although this confrontation was undoubtedly fuelled initially by excessive alcohol consumption and high spirits, its progress was informed by family enmities, the acceptability of violent retaliation for a physical or verbal slight upon oneself or one's clansman, and certain ritualistic, confrontational behaviour. Brothers aided brothers, few actions were regarded as taboo (fists, stones and iron tacketed boots were used as weapons), men squared up to one another in ritualistic fashion, throwing off their coats and rolling up their sleeves. Indeed, such behaviour was regarded as unexceptional, the procurator fiscal's office noting that this case had arisen 'from too free use of spirits at a wedding' – though remarking that 'the McPhails and McGillivrays are very proper subjects of discipline as they are considered turbulent, quarrelsome people in the district where they live'.[25] What seems clear is that filial and sibling connections were strong, that identification with a locality still held meaning for these men and that, at a time when the economic basis of their manhood was insecure, the resort to more physical manifestations of being a man may have served to strengthen the bonds of the relationship they had with one another.[26]

Another instance of this kind of social violence came to light with the indictment of three McLeod brothers for a case of assault in Glenelg, near Kyle of Lochalsh, in 1821. It was alleged that Donald, Norman and Kenneth McLeod deliberately assaulted Duncan and Roderick Murchison and Alexander McLeod (unrelated to the assailants) with a planned attack involving stones and clubs, until Alexander 'was blinded with his own blood'.[27] During the trial a history of grudges between the two groups of men was revealed. Witnesses recalled hearing Donald McLeod state that 'he long ago bore Alexander [McLeod] a grudge and that he was determined that night to have his revenge'. Furthermore, Donald declared that one year previously he had been drinking with other tenants when he received a message that his brother Norman had been murdered. In fact Norman was not dead but it was alleged he had been assaulted by Roderick Murchison, hence the McLeods believed it was justifiable to conduct a revenge attack on the Murchisons when the opportunity arose.

Violence emanating from long-standing feuds was still in evidence in the 1830s. In 1836 in the parish of Urquhart, near Dingwall, brothers Alexander and John Chisholm attacked Alexander McDougal so seriously that two of his ribs were broken. The attack was said to be motivated by revenge for an earlier insult. The incident started when sixty-one-year-old McDougal and a young boy of twelve were on their way to cut wood and stopped at a smuggling hut 'to get a dram'. There they encountered John Chisholm and others drinking whisky and 'the worse for liquor'. 'Chisholm then accused [McDougal] of having formerly struck his [Chisholm's] father and that he would now be revenged of him', whereby he struck McDougal. When Alexander Chisholm arrived, John told his brother that 'he should not protect a man who had struck his father on which Alexander gave [McDougal] a severe kick with his foot'.[28]

Despite the incidence of violence resulting from long-standing feuds, examination of the range of assaults across the Highlands reveals a pattern of behaviour that might be better described as recreational or social violence. In the comparable context of nineteenth-century Ireland, this kind of violence was widely tolerated in a society that was pre-industrial and distanced from the state and its legal machinery. Perhaps more importantly, such violence provided one of the few opportunities for young unmarried men 'to assert their masculinity or achieve any individual status'.[29] Although the economic status of the men who appeared in Scottish courts is not always stated, tenants, servants and labourers are the most common occupational categories, and it is likely that the majority belonged to a subset of the rural poor – men who were economically insecure, without stable employment and often unmarried. Their sense of manhood stemmed from their place within the kin group, their physical prowess, their ability to take a drink and their willingness to defend either their own honour or that of a family member. This was not feuding in the traditional sense, although the manner in which some groups of men went about their business was reminiscent of customary patterns of behaviour and a traditional approach to justice and retribution as practised amongst the Highland clans in their heyday.[30]

Recreational violence was sometimes coloured by traditional enmities between families, but more often perpetrators acted with little forethought and often under the influence of alcohol. A petty altercation could easily turn into serious violence. On the streets of Campbeltown in 1807, Neil Maclean called out to Irishmen Peter Downie and James Marmont, thinking one of them was an acquaintance. It was, however, a case of mistaken identity, and the pair took offence and refused to accept an apology. For his error Maclean was beaten on the head with a candlestick and a sharp stone. It was reported that Downie had placed one foot on Maclean's neck while striking him on the head with the other foot and asking Marmont: 'is the bugger dead?' Both men denied intoxication, only admitting they had imbibed a few drams, but there seemed to be no other explanation for their unbridled assault on a man they did not know.[31] This was alcohol-fuelled aggression with no justi-fication or legitimacy which, if it had any purpose at all, seemed to be aimed at establishing themselves as men to be feared in the community and earning for themselves a reputation as what would become known in later generations as 'hard men'.

NEW CODES OF RESTRAINT

There is little evidence of a civilising impulse attempting to regulate this kind of recreational violence in the rural Highlands. The kirk session rarely commented upon or attempted to ameliorate violent behaviour amongst males unless it impinged upon concerns close to the church, such as Sabbath breaking or holy rituals.[32] Drinking at funerals, for example, was specifically remarked upon by the Glenelg kirk session in 1832 following 'improper and indecent conduct' consisting of quar-relling and fighting amongst intoxicated mourners at the funeral of the wife of a weaver.[33] The criminal courts rarely expressed any views on the acceptability or otherwise of this kind of behaviour, merely treating more harshly those cases regarded as going beyond acceptable limits. One such instance is offered in the case of John and William Fraser in 1787, who sought to frighten the weaver William Shaw, from whom the Frasers demanded a sheep.[34] The pair 'blackened their faces and disguised their persons with sheets, plaid or blankets and a hairy hide in the way of an apron . . . tied around their bodies with leather belts'. When Shaw refused to comply and threw the men out of his house John Fraser threatened 'that he would have the said William Shaw's wife' and furthermore reportedly told Shaw, 'You ugly weaver, I'll be upsides with you and will soon see you again'. They returned the following night, once more in disguise only this time brandishing an iron spit as a weapon. And this time the Frasers used violence, leaving William Shaw beaten and cut with a knife and lying in his own blood.[35] Cases such as this were deemed beyond the realms of fair play. Setting about a lone victim or donning a disguise to conceal one's identity violated the rules of the fair fight.

However, the fact that these cases reached the courts suggests an intolerance for certain kinds of male violent crime. It was no longer legitimate merely to avenge a slight and neither was intoxication necessarily an excuse. In this way the judicial system began to offer alternative models of manhood, in the first instance by actively clamping down on violence perpetrated by the elites, most notable in the turn against the culture of duelling, discussed in Carr's chapter in this volume.[36] The duel was a public and ritualised form of gentlemanly violence, a cultural practice resting upon notions of honour but increasingly frowned upon by advocates of Enlightenment politeness and inner virtue, who regarded the duel as representing all that was immoral, artificial and undisciplined in the new civilised public spaces of the towns. Although prosecutions for murder following duels were not uncommon, in Scots law it was also illegal to issue a challenge. By 1800 efforts were being made to repress duelling in the name of public order. This is reflected in the warrant issued to arrest Duncan Forbes of Culloden in 1805 merely on the suspicion that he intended to fight a duel with Duncan Munro of Culcairn.[37] There was a history to this case which gives greater significance to the sheriff's attempts to prevent a staged contest between these two men, both of local gentry families. A previous duel involving the Forbes family in 1798 had resulted in the death of one of the assailants. The victorious dueller was subsequently acquitted at his trial for murder.[38] The sheriff's actions in the 1805 case indicated that there was diminishing tolerance for such violent and very public dispute resolution. A new model of honourable manhood, one that eschewed violence, was the more acceptable in polite society.

New models of manly behaviour were also exhibited by soldiers. Large numbers of military personnel were stationed in the Highlands, primarily in recruiting parties for the Highland regiments and garrisons such as that at Fort George.[39] In May 1819, the officers organised a day of sports, dubbed the 'Fort George Olympics' by the *Inverness Courier*. While the 'more fashionable' attendees enjoyed a ball in the evening, the private soldiers performed an amateur play. This event was clearly a public relations success while at the same time showcasing a more disciplined model of manhood, where competitive sports replaced undisciplined high jinks.[40] But outside the garrison the presence of the military had the potential to cause problems of law and order in local communities. Amongst officers, there was a tradition of duelling and 'demanding satisfaction' over sometimes very minor slights. But just as duelling became heavily targeted in the 1810s and 1820s, so too a new standard of behaviour in encounters with local men was becoming evident from soldiers across the ranks. The actions of Sergeant William Miller and Corporal John Munro when they were abused and assaulted while recruiting at a rood fair at Watten near Thurso in 1822 suggests a new model of manhood was on display, one that refused to rise to the bait, that walked away from confrontation. In a case of assault brought against two local men, Miller explained that 'he heard some person at a little distance calling out "damn the soldiers"', whereby he was sur-rounded by a crowd, struck on the head, and brought to the ground. 'Immediately after getting up he [Sergeant Miller] walked off out of the crowd without attempting to resent the treatment he had met', and his colleague Munro likewise, when threatened by a man, said 'that he was not a man for fighting'.[41] Their restraint counted for little amongst their assailants who proceeded to hit them with sticks.

It would be taking this argument too far to argue that Highland recruits themselves necessarily absorbed this model of manhood during their military service. The case of Ewan MacLean – a recruit belonging to the 79th Regiment who violently assaulted a man in a public house in Drumnadrochit in 1797 with a muck hack (a two-pronged dung fork), fracturing his skull – suggests otherwise, and further cases of drunken assaults and riot by soldiers in Inverness show that the model of restraint demonstrated by Miller and Munro was far from universal.[42] But, as Rosalind Carr points out, one of the main motivations of recruits was the attainment of 'independent manhood' by means of the promise of land in return for service.[43] Independence in the form of marriage, a household and land was a key tenet of respectable manhood – a model that stood in opposition to the undisciplined behaviour represented by those who abused and attacked military representatives and officers of the law in their parishes.

These various cases highlight two tensions concerning male violence in the Highlands. The first is that between modern and premodern conceptions of the place of violence in the conduct of relations between men; we are seeing here the imposition of novel codes deriving from a new culture based on male restraint, decorum and social respectability – a culture that deprecated violence in all social situations, save only that of self-defence. The second tension concerns class, involving repre-sentatives of the judiciary and law enforcement who would no longer tolerate the settling of plebeian scores, family feuds, and the obtaining of 'satisfaction', through the customary use of recreational violence. Man-on-man violent behaviour had previously been so common as to be almost ritualistic in nature. By the early nineteenth century, the judiciary, the military and social elites were no longer willing to tolerate it.

THE TAMING OF URBAN MASCULINITY

Criticism of rowdy and undisciplined behaviour emerged as a much more common refrain in the town of Inverness than in other Highland areas. The tensions described above were at their height in the town where conflict between 'civilised' urban society and rowdy rural society spilled over into face-to-face altercations. After 1746 Inverness began to benefit from improvements to communications, infrastructure and employment opportunities, and by 1791 it was characterised by increasing prosperity consequent upon agricultural progress, an influx of money from the Empire, the stationing of troops in the area, and the establishment of a number of manufactories.[44] The town's 5,000 or so inhabitants comprised a wide range of occupations from farmers and artisans to the professional classes, especially lawyers and writers. The growth of a middle class had spawned all the accoutrements of middle-class culture, consumption and luxury: schools, a theatre, banks, clean streets and larger houses.[45] Prosecutions of traders for littering the streets with dung and rubbish signalled the town's pretensions to civility, and letters to the *Inverness Courier* urged magistrates to clamp down on a number of traditional practices, from beating drums and playing fifes on the Sabbath to the driving of horses through the narrow lanes of the town to the river to drink.[46]

In this environment, actions once accepted as customary now had the potential to be regarded as criminal, even when the consequences were slight. It was predominantly male behaviour that became the focus of attention. A street brawl involving several Inverness fleshers (butchers) in 1822 mirrored the violent confrontations reminiscent of Highland rural society: it involved several members of the same family, it was informed by revenge, it involved ritualised confrontation and the customary use of fists and iron capped boots. When James Johnstone and Samuel Macdonald began a fight with each other, Samuel's brother tried to come to his brother's aid, but was stopped by William Macdonald. William was then reproached by another flesher's servant, who said: 'You damned bugger, let him go to Johnstone'.[47] Underlying the confrontation was said to be a long-standing quarrel between James Johnstone and Samuel Macdonald.

Similarly, a mass affray between the 'trades-lads of the town and a

posse of the labourers on the Caledonian canal' in 1818 was an unwel-
come reminder of the region's unruly past. Six weeks earlier at a raffle or
lottery in a public house two of the labourers were assaulted by several
tradesmen. To gain their revenge, around sixty canal labourers marched
into town carrying bludgeons 'challenging the town lads to face them'.[48]
Only the timely intervention of a canal contractor and some constables
averted a more serious conflagration. This kind of aggressive behaviour was increasingly condemned by town officers as an affront to
civility. The emergence of a class of labourers who engaged in what
were regarded as rough pursuits such as drinking and gambling aroused
fears of disorder.[49] However, this kind of drink-fuelled altercation was
becoming increasingly common in places where large groups of men
gathered to spend their leisure time and was indicative of a new kind of
public male bravado linked to recreation. The streets of Stornoway for
instance, were often disturbed by drunken brawls which were regarded
as threats to public order; and the Glasgow burgh court frequently dealt
with the consequences of excessive alcohol consumption amongst the
city's labouring men, many of them from the Highland counties.[50] Given
the role of strong drink in fuelling confrontations in the rural counties
we should not be surprised to see it playing a similar role in Inverness.

But alongside the familiar patterns of violence was a new development: cases involving a violent response by an individual to a seemingly
insignificant or trivial transgression by another man. These urban incidents differed significantly from those in rural parts of the Highlands. In
the town environment the physical violence was often negligible; verbal
insult and perceived threats were more common as were one-on-one
confrontations. This pattern may partly be explained by the compara-
tive ease with which a wronged person could call on the restraining
forces of the law in the town, but the very nature of the altercations suggests something else was happening. Men struggling to carve out a reputation for themselves in business, trade or officialdom were sensitive to
the instability of their status and reacted in an exaggerated manner when
they perceived that fragile status being challenged. In 1804, Farquhar
McTavish found himself the victim of an assault for having 'touched the
cloathes' of a man who 'immediately ran through the street and convened a number of people' who then held McTavish by the neck cloth
and beat him.[51] A decade later in Merkinch James Beaton, a clerk, was
threatened by apprentice baker James MacPherson 'for looking at him
so steadfastly'.[52] The streets of Inverness were witness to countless small
incidents like these, which revolved around status and respect.

The sensitivities of the elite were easily triggered. Town officials were quick to take umbrage when they felt they had not been treated with the proper respect. In 1798 John Davidson, collector of commutation money for the town, pursued John Fraser for maltreatment and abuse, consisting of Fraser threatening to kick Davidson in the street. Citing Fraser's words in court – 'Damn me if I had been in the house if I would not have kicked you down the stairs and I will do so still' – Davidson regarded this 'a most improper example to set to other inhabitants liable in the payment of commutation money'.[53] In a bizarre case of an argument over the price of a fish in 1801, Sergeant Finlayson found himself in court for lashing out, having taken offence at James Gow's remark that 'he did no more know the price of a skeat (skate) than the skeat itself', and 'he Finlayson had no more sense than a brute beast and that he could not speak no more than the skeat'.[54] Following this Finlayson seized Gow by the neckcloth and struck him twice in the face. The frequency in the courts of cases such as these suggests a new kind of status anxiety amongst urban males, who treated what appear to be petty insults to their sense of self-respect and social status with an exaggerated response and resort to the courts.

Something new was happening in the crowded public spaces of Inverness. Men were not defending their honour in the traditional way; rather, they were articulating a language of respect. These were men – clerks, artisans, lowly officials – who had to work out their social place amongst other men within a new fluid urban hierarchy. They did not automatically accrue status from their membership of a clan, their social position or adherence to a set of shared values. Rather, their position had to be earned in an economic but also a social sense. The key was gaining respect from others, which had to be newly and possibly repeatedly attained. This marks a stage in what John Tosh has identified as a shift over the period 1750–1850 from 'masculinity as social reputation to masculinity as an interiorised sense of personal identity'.[55] Clearly social reputation and status were still important but these were combined with a developing sense of personal identity. What is clear is that the burghers of Inverness were beginning to internalise and impose on others a model of manhood that owed more to new standards of conduct circulated by the urban elites than to the customary behaviour of the rural hinterland.

CONCLUSIONS

The restraint of male violence was one of the key features of late eighteenth-century civilising discourse. The expressions of manhood appropriate to a society at war were being rejected as inappropriate to a society of commerce and civility. It is at the intersection between customary modes of behaviour and the new civility that we meet male-on-male interpersonal violence in the courts as the boundary between acceptable and unacceptable violence was continuously redrawn.

Customary forms of violence and restitution of honour continued to have some legitimacy in the rural Highlands until the turn of the nineteenth century and probably for longer. But by this time evidence of this kind of ritualised revenge is less weighty. The precise reasons are unclear but a combination of rural population mobility, the breaking up of clan allegiances, the creation of a rural impoverished class and migration to urban centres seem likely to have influenced male social patterns. At the same time a new model of disciplined masculinity was being applied across the region but especially in Inverness – a town striving to manage the tensions within its volatile population. Indeed, Inverness offers an insight into the new sensibilities around interpersonal violence that were to enter Highland society more generally in the following decades.

Interpersonal violence was not a hallmark of Highland masculinity, as some contemporaries would have it, and there is no suggestion here that Highland men deployed violence more frequently than men elsewhere in Scotland. But the Highland context does inform the ways in which men conducted themselves. Violence was a male resource, and a culture that maintained a place for certain forms and expressions of violence continued well into the nineteenth century. Honour – perhaps better described as respect by this period – remained at the heart of physical confrontations between men, though many incidents were also undoubtedly fuelled by alcohol and by status anxiety. In the rural Highlands this tended to be expressed in group confrontations or was a response to a long-standing grudge against a member of another family for a perceived insult towards oneself or one's kin, though the violent act itself was often played out in a recreational context. In Inverness men tended to respond to more immediate threats to their personal identity and status – an insulting word or a physical slight demanded immediate restitution. This story fits fairly neatly with the manhood-to-masculinity narrative outlined earlier and suggests that notions of Highland exceptionalism are overdrawn. By moving the focus away from the metropolitan centres and prescriptive ideals and towards actual social practice in the northern counties of Scotland, we see how male interpersonal violence provides a means by which we can discern divergent, conflicting and shifting codes of manliness in Scottish society. The evidence suggests that an essential element of the taming of the Highlands was the taming of the ordinary Highland man.

NOTES

The author would like to thank Edinburgh University Press and the Trustees of the Scottish History Society Trust for permission to publish this shortened version of the original article which appeared in *Scottish Historical Review*, 92:1 (2013), as well as the Carnegie Trust for the Universities of Scotland for supporting the initial research for this project.

1. See Stuart Carroll, *Cultures of Violence: Interpersonal Violence in Historical Perspective* (Basingstoke: Palgrave, 2007).

2. See Susan Dwyer Amussen, 'Punishment, discipline and power: the social meanings of violence in early modern society', *Journal of British Studies*, 34 (1995), pp. 1–34.

3. Robert B. Shoemaker, 'Reforming male manners: public insult and the decline of violence in London, 1660–1740', in Tim Hitchcock and Michèle Cohen (eds), *English Masculinities, 1660–1800* (London: Longman, 1999), pp. 133–50; Robert B. Shoemaker, 'Male honour and the decline of public violence in eighteenth-century London', *Social History*, 26 (2001), pp. 190–208; J. G. Barker-Benfield, *The Culture of Sensibility: Sex and Society in Eighteenth-Century Britain* (Chicago: University of Chicago Press, 1992); Michèle Cohen, *Fashioning Masculinity: National Identity and Language in the Eighteenth Century* (London: Routledge, 1996); Philip Carter, *Men and the Emergence of Polite Society, Britain 1660–1800* (Harlow: Longman, 2001).

4. Karen Harvey, 'The history of masculinity c. 1650–1850', *Journal of British Studies*, 44 (2005), pp. 296–311, at 310.

5. See Martin Macgregor and Dauvit Broun (eds), *Mìorun Mòr nan Gall, 'The Great Ill-will of the Lowlander'? Lowland Perceptions of the Highlands, Medieval and Modern* (Glasgow: Centre for Scottish & Celtic Studies, University of Glasgow, 2007).

6. See Chapters 5, 6, 7, and 8 in this collection, and also Barker-Benfield, *The Culture of Sensibility*; John Dwyer, *Virtuous Discourse: Sensibility and Community in Late Eighteenth Century Scotland* (Edinburgh: John Donald, 1987); Rosalind. J. Carr, 'The gentleman and the soldier: patriotic masculinities in eighteenth-century Scotland', *Journal of Scottish Historical Studies*, 28 (2008), pp. 102–21.

7. For the broader context of riot and protest, see Kenneth J. Logue, *Popular Disturbances in Scotland 1780–1815* (Edinburgh: John Donald, 1979); Christopher A. Whatley, *Scottish Society 1707–1830* (Manchester: Manchester University Press, 2000), pp. 142–83. On interpersonal violence as status reinforcement, see Alexandra Shepard, *Meanings of Manhood in Early Modern England* (Oxford: Oxford University Press, 2003), p. 140.

8. Sources consulted consist of all surviving papers relating to male inter-
    personal violence in the Inverness burgh court (Highland Council Archive
    [HCA], L/INV/BC, 1773–1860) and Inverness sheriff court records (HCA,
    L/INV/SC), a sample of assault cases tried before the High Court of
    Justiciary on circuit in Inverness (HCA, L/INV/HC 1729–1837); all pre-
    cognitions taken in cases of violent assault heard in the High Court in
    Inverness (National Records of Scotland [NRS], AD 14) and a sample of
    cases heard in the Inverness sheriff court before a jury (NRS, SC 29). A
    sample of cases that came before the Dingwall and Stornoway sheriff courts
    have also been scrutinised (NRS, SC 29 and SC 33). The *Inverness Courier*
    (est. 1817) carried reports of very few cases of interpersonal violence, and
    did not report on cases heard in the sheriff or burgh courts.
9. Precognitions are not commonly extant for Scottish sheriff courts (with the
    exception of Shetland).
10. The extant papers in HCA, L/INV/BC indicate the following: 1770s: 4 cases;
    1780s: 0; 1790s: 8; 1800s: 3; 1810s: 3; 1820s: 1; 1830s: 4. Numbers are cal-
    culated from the Highland Council Archive Burgh Court index, 1773–1860.
    There are no assault cases recorded in this court after the 1830s.
11. The extant papers in HCA, L/INV/SC for the period 1750–1840 indicate
    prosecutions in double figures in the 1820s and 1830s, compared with very
    small numbers in previous decades.
12. Numbers calculated from the NRS High Court of Justiciary database,
    which lists cases between 1799 and 1900, indicate 1800s: 22; 1810s: 147;
    1820s: 635; 1830s: 296; 1840s: 66; 1850s: 20; 1860s: 3; 1870s: 4; 1880s:
    9; 1890s: 12. On crime trends in general for this period, see Whatley,
    Scottish Society, pp. 286–7.
13. Women did, however, participate in significant numbers in incidences of
    collective riot and protest. See Logue, *Popular Disturbances*, pp. 199–203;
    Whatley, *Scottish Society*, pp. 197–200.
14. Allan I. Macinnes, *Clanship, Commerce and the House of Stuart 1603–
    1788* (East Linton: Tuckwell Press, 1996), p. 217.
15. Macinnes, *Clanship*; James Hunter, *The Making of the Crofting Community*
    (Edinburgh: Birlinn, 1996).
16. On the militia riots, see Logue, *Popular Disturbances*, pp. 75–115. On
    the military and the Highlands more generally, see Andrew Mackillop,
    *'More Fruitful than the Soil': Army, Empire and the Scottish Highlands,
    1715–1815* (Edinburgh: Edinburgh University Press, 2000).
17. Robert A. Dodgshon, *From Chiefs to Landlords: Social and Economic
    Change in the Western Highlands and Islands, c. 1493–1820* (Edinburgh:
    Edinburgh University Press, 1998).
18. Logue, *Popular Disturbances*, pp. 18–43, 54–74. Eric Richards, 'How tame
    were the Highlanders during the Clearances?', *Scottish Studies*, 17 (1973),
    pp. 35–50. However, there is no correlation between prosecutions for riot
    and those for interpersonal violence.

19. Hunter, *Making of the Crofting Community*, p. 12.
20. Keith M. Brown, *Bloodfeud in Scotland 1573–1625* (Edinburgh: Edinburgh University Press, 1986), p. 33.
21. Robert A. Dodgshon, '"Pretense of blude" and "place of thair dwelling": the nature of highland clans, 1500–1745', in R. A. Houston and I. D. Whyte (eds), *Scottish Society 1500–1800* (Cambridge: Cambridge University Press, 1989), p. 171. See also Allan I. Macinnes, 'Scottish Gaeldom from clanship to commercial landlordism', in Sally M. Foster, Allan I. Macinnes and Ranald MacInnes (eds), *Scottish Power Centres: From the Early Middle Ages to the Twentieth Century* (Glasgow: Cruithne, 1998), pp. 47–64.
22. T. M. Devine, 'The rise and fall of illicit whisky making in northern Scotland c. 1780–1840', *Scottish Historical Review*, 54 (1975), pp. 155–77.
23. For rules of the feud see Stephen Wilson, *Feuding, Conflict and Banditry in Nineteenth-Century Corsica* (Cambridge: Cambridge University Press, 2003), p. 197.
24. NRS, AD 14/28/285.
25. NRS, AD 14/28/285, letter from R. Fisher to sheriff substitute of Inverness, 13 June 1828.
26. See also HCA, L/INV/SC 42/12/15, 1825: a case of assault on South Uist. For other examples see NRS, AD 14/22/194; NRS, AD 14/22/139.
27. NRS, AD 14/21/131.
28. NRS, AD 14/36/107.
29. Carolyn Conley, *Melancholy Accidents: The Meaning of Violence in Post-Famine Ireland* (Lanham, 1999), pp. 2–3, 18. See also Richard McMahon, '"Do you want to pick a fight out of me, or what do you want?": homicide and personal animosity in pre-famine and famine Ireland', in Katherine D. Watson (ed.), *Assaulting the Past: Violence and Civilisation in Historical Context* (Cambridge: Cambridge University Press, 2007), pp. 222–49.
30. See Dodgshon, *Chiefs to Landlords*, pp. 87–8 and Macinnes, *Clanship*, pp. 37–46.
31. NRS, SC 29/51/3: Criminal Record 28 September 1798–7 October 1807; 27 July 1807, violent assault.
32. On the role of the kirk session see Margo Todd, *The Culture of Protestantism in Early Modern Scotland* (New Haven: Yale University Press, 2002). An examination of kirk session minutes for Highland parishes revealed only isolated cases of discipline for violent offences or disturbances.
33. NRS, CH2/966/1: Glenelg kirk session minutes, 7 November 1832, 21 November 1832.
34. See also: HCA: L/INV/SC 32/7. On disguise in ritual see Natalie Zemon Davis, 'The reasons of misrule: youth groups and charivaris in sixteenth century France', *Past and Present*, 50 (1971), pp. 41–75; Callum G. Brown, *Up-helly aa: Custom, Culture and Community in Shetland* (Manchester: Manchester University Press, 1998), pp. 114–16.

35. See, for instance, NRS, SC 29/51/1: Criminal Record 10 September 1782–7 December 1787; n.d., defendants John and William Fraser.
36. Few duels were prosecuted in the Justiciary Court 1700–1850, and just four murder cases relate to death in a duel. See Stephen Banks, *A Polite Exchange of Bullets: The Duel and the English Gentleman 1750–1850* (London: Boydell Press, 2010); Rosalind Carr, *Gender and Enlightenment Culture in Eighteenth-Century Scotland* (Edinburgh: Edinburgh University Press, 2014). On England, see Robert B. Shoemaker, 'The taming of the duel: masculinity, honour and ritual violence in London, 1660–1800', *Historical Journal*, 45 (2002), pp. 525–45.
37. NRS, SC 29/53/100: criminal processes (bundle), 6 October 1805.
38. Miller notes that this was traditionally known as the last duel in Scotland. However, see James Landale, *The Last Duel: A True Story of Death and Honour* (Edinburgh: Canongate, 2005) for the story of an 1826 duel in Kirkcaldy. Also, James Miller, *Inverness: A History* (Edinburgh: Birlinn, 2004), p. 170.
39. McKillop, '*More Fruitful than the Soil*', pp. 234–6.
40. *Inverness Courier*, 6 May 1819.
41. NRS, AD14/23/226.
42. HCA, L/INV/SC/42/6/; L/INV/BC/14/68; L/INV/BC/14/69. See also L/INV/SC/33/1–13: Miscellaneous papers re warrants of imprisonment against soldiers and deserters.
43. Carr, 'The gentleman and the soldier', pp. 120–1.
44. *Old Statistical Account*, 1791–99, vol. 9, p. 617.
45. Miller, *Inverness*, p. 167.
46. See HCA, L/INV/BC/13/146. *Inverness Courier*, 9 July 1818, 6 August 1818.
47. NRS, AD 14/22/139.
48. *Inverness Courier*, 5 March 1818.
49. See Brown, *Up-helly aa*, pp. 84–104 for similar reactions in Lerwick, Shetland.
50. Glasgow City Archives, Glasgow police court; NRS, SC 33/42/4, Stornoway sheriff court.
51. HCA, L/INV/BC/14/65.
52. HCA, L/INV/BC/14/81.
53. HCA, L/INV/BC/9/8/21.
54. HCA, L/INV/BC/14/62.
55. John Tosh, 'The old Adam and the new man: emerging themes in the history of English masculinities, 1750–1850', in Hitchcock and Cohen (eds), *English Masculinities*, pp. 217–38, at 230–2. This argument is given greater authority by evidence of recourse to the Inverness courts by citizens keen to pursue accusations of defamation and those pursuing restraining orders via the Scots law of lawburrows. For further discussion see Abrams, 'The taming of Highland masculinity', pp. 120–1.

PART II

Representations

5

Making a Manly Impression: The Image of Kingship on Scottish Royal Seals of the High Middle Ages

Cynthia J. Neville

INTRODUCTION: KINGS, MASCULINITY AND SIGILLOGRAPHIC EVIDENCE

IN A TREATISE CELEBRATING the illustrious rulers of ancient Britain the northern English historian Aelred of Rievaulx narrated the tale of an encounter between the Scottish king, Malcolm III (1057–93), and a would-be assassin. Informed of a plot to kill him, Aelred wrote, Malcolm staged a dramatic confrontation with the treacherous knight, where he fearlessly placed his life in the hands of the killer. The king demanded, however, that the knight promise to commit his abominable deed neither by resort to poison (for 'who does not know that that is womanish?'), nor by stealth at night in the royal bedchamber – for that was the way of 'adulteresses' – but rather 'like a man', that is, in open combat, with drawn sword. The chronicler had him utter his challenge with the bold words '[d]o rather what becomes a soldier; act like a man; fight me while alone with me alone, so that your betrayal, which cannot be free of perfidy, will at least be free of disgrace'.[1] Aelred's story is almost certainly fictitious, but it offers historians valuable insight into twelfth-century understandings of idealised manhood, and a useful basis from which to explore the ways in which the high medieval kings of Scots drew on contemporary British and European mores in their efforts to fashion for themselves widely accepted images of masculine authority.

In the Europe of Aelred's day the figure of the king occupied a position at the apex of several different hierarchies and a central place in a host of imagined communities. He was at once the source of all political authority in his realm, more powerful than even the greatest of his magnates; the fount of all justice in the kingdom, yet generous with his mercy; the divinely appointed protector of his clerical subjects, from the humblest clerk to the most exalted prelate. He was also husband to his queen; father to his royal children and more generally to all his people; the truest of knights; the most devout of God's servants. That the king's person embodied simultaneously the attributes of dynastic legitimacy, sovereign authority and Christian piety was the central theme of countless chronicle accounts, literary works, political treatises and artistic depictions from the late eleventh century onwards. The figure of the high medieval king stands also at the nexus of much modern scholarship. In the last decade in particular, historians of Scotland have made important contributions to a rich literature on the growth and maturation of the office of kingship in the northern realm. Their collective endeavours confirm the emergence, late in the eleventh century, of a unified kingdom ruled by a single *rex Scottorum* ('king of the Scots') and, over the course of the two hundred years that followed, the development of a concept of kingship that endowed the later medieval kings with a power and authority equal to those of any European monarch.[2]

There remains nonetheless a great deal to be written on the subject of high medieval Scottish kingship from the specific theoretical and analytical perspectives of gender. The reputations of individual rulers, like those of their English and continental counterparts, rested not merely on their ability to deploy the qualities traditionally associated with kingship – wisdom, prudence, self-mastery, clemency, military prowess – but also on their success in the active performance of masculinity.[3] This chapter offers a new reading of the ways in which twelfth- and thirteenth-century rulers gave visual expression to hegemonic notions of masculinity and maleness that were fundamental requirements of 'good' governance throughout Western Europe in the Middle Ages.[4] The source materials examined here are the images that appear on the obverse and reverse of the great seals of office with which the kings authenticated their written acts. The survival of a large number of exemplars between 1094 (the date of the first extant device) and 1283 (the date of the last known use of the seal of King Alexander III) makes it possible to trace changes in the portrayal and projection of masculine royal authority during a crucial period in the development of the Scottish polity.[5]

Waxen seals were in wide use in Europe from the late Carolingian era onwards and, in Britain, from the mid-eleventh century. They were created when a matrix (or die) of ivory or metal (gold, silver or brass) was applied to a heated waxen surface, thereby leaving an identical impression of the original. Although the term 'seal' is often used to refer to both the matrix and its replicated image, it is employed here in the latter sense. At first reserved to royal usage, seals were everywhere quickly adopted also by ecclesiastical and secular noblemen and noblewomen of all ranks (and eventually by towns and persons of modest status), simultaneously to represent the living person and to authenticate or validate an individual's written acts. Seals offer a unique kind of evidence. Their three-dimensional characteristics and the imagery with which they were impressed endow them with an artistic, cultural and historical significance quite distinct from that of other extant source materials. Sigillographic devices communicated in a language of words and symbols a series of subtly encoded messages about their owners' status and sense of self, none more forcefully than those of a king.[6] To the modern observer, they offer the opportunity to observe the process by which the high medieval Scottish kings absorbed, internalised and gave visual expression to norms of gendered identity and royal legitimacy.

The earliest extant royal seal dates from the reign of King Duncan II, who ruled briefly in 1094 (Figure 5.1).[7] Crudely and, given the circumstances under which it was created, probably hastily executed,[8] its image of an armed knight on horseback and the style of its Latin-language legend – '+SIGILL' DVNECANI DI GRA REGIS SCOTTORVM' [the seal of Duncan by grace of God king of Scots] – consciously replicated details introduced to English seals after 1066 by William the Conqueror.[9] Thus the cross that appears in the legend attested divine sanction of the office of king, while the figure of the fighting knight denoted earthly lordship and sovereign authority. The significance of such potent symbolism must have been especially attractive to a king

Figure 5.1 Seal of Duncan II, king of Scots. William Anderson, *The Scottish Nation*, volume 2 (Edinburgh: A. Fullerton, 1863), p. 84.

who had spent a good part of his youth as a political hostage at the English court and whose accession to the throne was hotly contested by a rival branch of the Scottish royal family.[10] Yet Duncan II rejected several other features of his English exemplars. Thus the artisan who made it for him used only one side of the device; for this, Duncan chose the image of a knight on horseback over the figure of the king-in-majesty that had been in use in England during the reign of Edward the Confessor (1042–66). It may be that Duncan, whose 'royal' grant actually predated his inauguration, sought to emphasise more than anything else his descent from the legitimate line of the Scottish king Malcolm III, but the personification of the manly qualities of vigour and virility inherent in the equestrian figure were surely also important. Duncan II's half-brother, rival and, from 1097, successor, Edgar, became the first of a long line of rulers to employ the imagery of the king in majesty on his great seal (Figure 5.2),[11] thereby stressing his close connection with the English royal house of pre-Conquest times through his mother and accentuating, in his choice of a visual Christological metaphor, claims to sacred rule.[12] Like Duncan II, however, Edgar used only one side of his seal, and it was not until the reign of Edgar's brother and successor, Alexander I (1107–27), that rulers began regularly to deploy images of kingship on both sides of their seals. Thereafter, sigillographic practice in the kingdom conformed closely to that of Britain and northern Europe more generally and the double-sided seal came into regular use.

Medieval seals were simultaneously 'material and conceptual entities',[13] uniquely designed to play discursive and performative roles in political and social discourse and above all to transmit strong messages about the persons whose authority they mediated and represented. Already by the late Merovingian period the practice of affixing or appending seals to royal instruments 'had become a requisite act of the behaviour of the ruler qua ruler' in Europe;[14] from the mid-eleventh century onwards in England, waxen seals imprinted with royal insignia exercised intrinsic legal agency in authenticating and validating gifts of land and privilege. A little later in that same century charter writing and seal usage expanded into Scotland, part and parcel of the growth of royal power and authority in the kingdom, of a more general process of 'anglicisation' initiated by the children and grandchildren of King Malcolm III and his English queen, Saint Margaret, and of the spread to the northern kingdom of a more generalised 'trust in writing'.[15] Alexander I and his brother and successor, David I (1124–53), enthusiastically adopted the practice of expressing the royal will in parchment and attesting their identities as donors and benefactors on the obverse and reverse of waxen seals. The proliferation of charters and other written documents in the second half of the twelfth century both reflected and contributed to a gradual routinisation of the business of royal conveyance in Scotland. While initially at least the demand for, and the production of, properly executed instruments of sasine (which documented the conveying of land) and confirmation came chiefly from beneficiaries, it is also the case that few landholders would have considered title to royal gifts capable of withstanding challenge in a court of law in the absence of written authentication and the testimony of the king's great seal.[16] By mid-century, a growing body of common law custom acknowledged the power of the words and images that appeared on those devices simultaneously to bear the image and to be the 'physical extension' of the royal will.[17]

The reign of David I also witnessed the thorough integration of the kingdom into the chivalric culture of Western Europe, and the popularisation there of the military values widely associated with that ethos: prowess in military endeavours, public gestures of loyalty to the ruling dynasty, lavishly celebrated feats of arms. The valorisation of the masculine attributes of knighthood in particular is apparent in the visual arts: in brasses, effigies, jewellery, manuscript illuminations and stained glass windows. Royal seal matrices quickly came to present a particularly promising medium upon which to inscribe compelling attestations of the rulers' embrace of masculine valour and to impart unconditional statements about the legitimacy of their dynasty. The formula used in the legend that encircled the edges of the obverse and the reverse sides of the devices was so authoritative that it remained virtually unchanged from the time of Alexander I in the twelfth century through that of Alexander III in the thirteenth.[18] The wording, unique to the kings of Scots, included a cross symbol and, after the king's name, the words 'DEO RECTORE REX SCOTTORVM' [king of Scots, under God ruling].[19] The uniformity, simplicity and clarity of the legend in turn made it possible for the artisans commissioned by the king to make full and imaginative use of the twin surfaces of the royal seal.

And employ them the kings certainly did. It is no accident that the surface space of great seals increased steadily over the twelfth and thirteenth centuries – from 6cm to 9.5cm – as successive kings abandoned the initial practice of reusing the seal imagery of their predecessors and adopted designs that made unique statements about their identity. Over the course of the two centuries between 1094 and 1283 depictions of the ruler became at once more intricate and sumptuous, with additions, on the obverse (or front side), to the details of the face and clothing of the king sitting in majesty, to the throne on which he rested and to the insignia of office that he carried. On the reverse (or back), equestrian side of the seal, the opportunities for elaboration and embellishment of the mounted knight were well-nigh limitless. The knight, his sword, shield, armour, horse and equipment: from the time of William I (1165–1214) onwards, all became small canvases upon which the rulers inscribed images of royalty, made manifest their owners' aspirations and, above all, gave visual expression to idealised visions of masculine power and authority.

THE OBVERSE OF THE GREAT SEAL

The obverse of the royal seal, attached to a document that it authenticated by a tongue or tag, was the first side of the seal visible to the reader. Edgar, Alexander I and, much later, Alexander III are the only kings depicted wearing crowns, the latter surmounted with three points (perhaps to signify the holy Trinity). The two early twelfth-century portrayals of kingship attest the dynastic claims of the children of Malcolm III and Saint Margaret; the last one gave mute voice, perhaps, to the strenuous (if fruitless) efforts of Alexander III to win papal approval of the rites of unction and coronation. Similarly, the regalia that the enthroned kings held in their hands – a sceptre in Edgar's time, and an orb thereafter – gave visual expression to legitimate governance of the kingdom. Edgar's foliated sceptre of office, symbolising his 'God-given power to govern', replicated the insignia used by Edward the Confessor (which was in turn modelled on the seals of the Ottonian emperors);[20] it was so potent a symbol that Alexander III later repeated it on his second great seal, created around 1260.[21] Between the reigns of Alexander I and Alexander III, however, the regalia of choice for inclusion on royal devices was the orb surmounted by a cross. This, too, invoked the Christological quality of princely rule, as it had done since the tenth century.[22] The sceptre and orb played a central role in the royal inauguration ceremonies and were so closely linked to the ruling Scottish dynasty that they would be carefully inventoried, seized and then carried off by Edward I on his conquest of the country in 1296.[23]

Above and beyond aspirational statements alone, however, Scottish sigillographical iconography sought to give concrete expression to the association between male authority and royal power.[24] In the careful depictions of swords on both the obverse and reverse of royal seals are inscribed the evolution of the rulers' own ideas about virility and the masculine self. Most notable was the early twelfth-century kings' abandonment, in their portrayal of royal majesty on the obverse side, of the

Figure 5.2 Seal of Edgar, king of Scots. *The Scottish Nation*, volume 2, p. 116.

sceptre in favour of a sword, the universal Western European symbol of male military prowess and, amongst kings, of sacrality and justice.[25] Its first appearance in Scottish iconography coincided with the introduction to Britain of the dubbing ceremony that transformed true knights into religiously sanctioned defenders of the church. The reception and diffusion of new ideas that in turn linked knighthood and kingly rule are readily apparent on the obverse of royal seals. Two extant devices of Edgar show him holding in his left hand a sword of state (Figure 5.2). The weapon, however, is sheathed, the king grasps it in improbable fashion high along the blade, and its pommel rests benignly on his thigh. Like the device of Duncan II, this seal has the appearance of a matrix designed above all to conform to contemporary (and especially English) exemplars. Its details speak to hasty execution, and the king failed altogether to make use of the reverse side to convey compelling statements about his right to rule.

Alexander I was more attentive to the potential of the double-sided graven matrix to communicate the connection between masculinity and authority in visual terms. He spent a good part of his reign countering the territorial and political challenges of his ambitious younger brother (and eventual heir) David and, in an effort to 'boost his prestige', attempting to give meaningful support to the papal programme for reform of the church.[26] These efforts account in part for the subtle alterations that he made to the portrayal of kingship on the obverse of his royal seal. The image devotes considerable attention to clothing, jewelled adornments and hair.[27] Here, the symbols of office have literally changed hands, with the cross-surmounted orb now in the king's left hand (where it would remain through the late thirteenth century) and, in his right, a fighting man's sword, properly gripped by its pommel. No longer resting tamely in the king's lap, this weapon is ready to be wielded. Connotations of the sword as a phallic symbol and an anthropomorphic statement of virility suggest that Alexander I was well acquainted with the idealisation of knighthood that was such an important feature of contemporary European elite culture, and that he was anxious to deploy the icons associated with it.[28] Attention to the details of weapons and symbols of kingship, moreover, allow the figure of the king in majesty to occupy a larger space on the surface of the seal: in contrast to Edgar, Alexander I is a man of action and in firm control of his realm.

That the seal of Alexander I projected an eloquent, powerful and thoroughly commanding image of kingship in majesty may explain why the two rulers who followed him, David I and Malcolm IV (1153–65), reused the same matrix, altering only the portion of the legend that identified them by name. The former's succession was hotly contested and alternative candidates for the kingship 'enjoyed significant support'.[29] David's ready adoption of his older brother's iconography represented a visual counterpart to the energetic efforts that he subsequently made to win acceptance by the political community: here, the use of identical sigillographic imagery served to reinforce continuity between the reigns. The challenges of Malcolm IV's rule were of a different sort. He came to the throne as a youth of twelve and therefore a minor; moreover, he died while still a young man at the age of twenty-four and before he had had the chance to marry. The choice of visual king-in-majesty metaphors that glossed over Malcolm's youth and depicted him instead as a fully adult fighting man accorded well with his need to forge an unbroken link with the past of his dynasty as well as with its as yet uncertain future. Malcolm's suitability to govern despite his lack of years and his sexual purity are certainly the messages encoded into an elaborate illumination painted on a royal charter dated to 1159.[30] Here, under the arches of a decorated initial letter M the young king shares equal space with his aged grandfather, David I. Tellingly, the sword of office (held in his left hand) lies in repose across his knees, in vivid contrast to the erect stance of the weapon that David holds in his fighting (right) hand. The boy's knees are crossed at the ankle, unlike David's, whose open legs and knees invite the viewer to consider his generative endowments.[31] Such a reading of the iconography associated with the rule of Malcolm IV finds some support in the initiation, around the same time, of a politically charged historiographical project, the goal of which was to fashion new and distinctive origins for the Scottish monarchy.[32]

After the accession of William I in 1165, the circumference of royal seals increased dramatically, as did the quantity and quality of the details on the image of the king-in-majesty. The thrones on which William and his two successors sit became ever more elaborate, the drapery of royal tunics more lifelike, the mantles over their shoulders more decorative; indeed, more than one scholar has remarked upon the workmanship apparent in Scottish devices of the thirteenth century.[33] Details such as these gave visual expression to the self-confidence with which first William, but especially Alexander II (1214–49) and Alexander III (1249–86), governed the kingdom. Some of the features on the obverse, moreover, communicated more than a single message. Thus, on the seals of William I and Alexander II (Figure 5.3) – and quite possibly on the first seal employed by Alexander III – the unsheathed and grooved blade of the sword held in the king's right hand extends upwards, beyond the area of the king's throne and into the space occupied by the wording of the surrounding legend.[34] William's capture and ransom by the English in 1173–4 had placed the kingdom in legal subjection to its stronger neighbour and its king in a position of submission that medieval culture closely associated with female weakness. The exaggerated size of the sword of state held in the hands of the king on his seal operated at once as a visual and metaphorical representation of the restoration of William's virility and of the reversal of the humiliation that he had endured as knight and king on the field of battle. Alexander II had different but equally pressing reasons to portray himself as something other than a king whose authority might be compromised by circumstance. Like his uncle, Malcolm IV, he succeeded to the throne as a minor. The oversized sword of state engraved onto the obverse of the royal seal accomplished a dual purpose,

Figure 5.3 Seal of Alexander II, king of Scots. James Taylor, *The Pictorial History of Scotland* (London: George Virtue, 1871), plate at front.

first, as the graphic counterpart of a vigorous programme of territorial and dynastic aggrandisement and, second, as a simple but evocative image of the young king's full capacity to govern.[35]

A host of contemporary source materials confirms that the rank and status associated with knighthood were of more than merely casual concern to the kings of Scots. Admission to the order of knighthood brought with it membership in an exclusive fellowship, recognition of which generated amongst David I and his successors an 'indecent anxiety' to pursue the honour.[36] The specific correlation between male self-fashioning and sword iconography is apparent in a comparison of an unusual small seal that the child king, Alexander III, commissioned for his personal use and the great seals of office with which he (or, until 1258, his advisors) authenticated formal deeds. On the obverse of the former the boy Alexander (who succeeded at age seven) appears wearing a crown, holding in his left hand a foliated sceptre. In his right he grasps a sword by its pommel, but this weapon is not erect: it lies passively across his knees. Just as Alexander 'could not in person dispense justice, because he was a child',[37] neither could he perform the obligations nor enjoy the privileges of knighthood which were so closely connected with the use of the weapon. Moreover, this Alexander is beardless.[38] The implications of the king's yet-to-be-achieved manhood are mutely reiterated on the reverse of the small seal where, in place of the usual equestrian figure, there appears a simple shield marked with royal insignia.

The intimate association of knightly status with manliness and legitimacy was indeed so deeply embedded in popular culture by 1249 that one royal counsellor wondered if Alexander III's inauguration as king would be valid in the absence of a dubbing ceremony; to this impudence another insisted that a king was a knight by virtue of his office.[39] Alexander III's father-in-law, Henry III of England, resolved the dilemma by granting knighthood to the young king on the occasion of his marriage in 1251.[40] The image on the obverse of the first of the great seals of state created for the king reflected the anxieties raised in 1249. Here, Alexander and the artist who crafted his seal chose to ignore the king's youth. Just as his predecessors since Edgar's time had done, Alexander proclaimed in sigillographic discourse, by means of a large erect sword, long flowing locks and a full facial beard, his twin identities as a man and the legitimate ruler of the kingdom. After January 1264 and the birth of a son to Alexander, so secure had the male line descended from Malcolm III and Saint Margaret become, and so great had the confidence in its future grown, that on the obverse of his second seal the king abandoned the sword altogether in the depiction of his majesty.[41]

THE REVERSE OF THE GREAT SEALS

Like the iconography of the king-in-majesty but of considerably more recent invention were sigillographic representations of rulers in the guise of mounted warriors on the reverse sides of their great seals. William the Conqueror was the first English ruler to use the design. Here, image and legend proudly celebrated his origins as duke (*patronus*) of Normandy; more boldly, they proclaimed his readiness to back his claim to the English throne with the force of arms.[42] In 1094, in a Scottish kingdom still unfamiliar with the social, political and economic exclusivity associated with knighthood, Duncan II recognised in the image of the warrior-king a potent and suggestive symbol of royal status and he was the first to deploy it.[43] In some contrast to the iconography of the obverse of royal seals, crowded as they were with complex and multivalent representations of kingship, the equestrian design conveyed a simpler, bolder message. From the time of Alexander I the reverse of the great seal gave visual expression to the 'essential association of man, horse and armour',[44] mutely but powerfully asserting to all and sundry that the small northern realm was closely in touch with the elite culture of Europe. The increasing sophistication of the royal writing office and a growing demand for deeds authenticated with the royal seal in turn played essential roles in disseminating this message from the setting of the royal court into the far-flung corners of the realm.

Ironically, Scottish craftsmen so thoroughly adopted the visual cues linking images of the mounted knight to idealised concepts of the male body that the artisans who designed matrices for royal patrons may eventually have found their ability to exercise artistic creativity constrained. Initially, they did little more than ensure that successive versions of the devices kept abreast of developments in military equipment and clothing styles. Thus in 1094, Duncan II appeared on horseback in stirrups and with undecorated breast leather, his mount furnished with bridle and high-cantled saddle. With its front left legs raised and hind legs bent, the horse is clearly meant to appear in motion. The king wears a knee-length chain mail hauberk of late eleventh-century style, with a conical peaked helmet that includes a nasal plate. He carries in his elevated right hand a spear topped with a gonfanon of two tails and, hanging from his left shoulder by a sling, a kite-shaped shield.[45] On Alexander I's seal the engraver has added some detail to the hauberk (now adorned with rings of chain mail over which the king wears a hooded surcoat), spurs to the king's feet, accoutrements to the royal steed and a third streamer to the pennon at the tip of the spear, but neither the overall design nor

Figure 5.4 Seal of Alexander III, king of Scots. *Pictorial History of Scotland*, plate at front.

its message about the essential qualities of the ruler's manliness has substantially changed from the days of Duncan II. In fact, so effective was the simple equestrian motif in positioning the dynasty of Malcolm III and Saint Margaret at the heart of the chivalric culture of Europe that Alexander's two successors adopted a virtually identical matrix for the reverse of their respective seals, altering it only to display their respective Christian names. The iconography of the powerful warrior-king triumphantly proclaimed David I's legitimacy to those who would challenge his right to rule. Likewise, it emphatically elided the fact of Malcolm IV's inauguration as a boy and his subsequent failure to marry and procreate, behaviour that so obviously contradicted the characteristics and expectations of kingship and masculinity amongst persons of his rank.[46]

The steady increase in the circumference and the intricacy of detail on the reverse of the great seals of William I, Alexander II and Alexander III (see Figure 5.4), reflected, on one level, the ongoing aim of artists to embed in the devices accurate renderings of military equipment and knightly accoutrements. On another level altogether they spoke to the self-confidence of the dynasty and, if more subtly, to the celebration of the sexual prowess of all three kings. Small changes to the style and position of the mounted knight's shield (from the time of William I no longer kite-shaped, but in the style known as 'heater'), to the configuration of the mailed hauberk and helmet (the latter shown with a flat top and visor beginning in the reign of Alexander II and plumed on the seal of Alexander III) to the addition of a lavishly embroidered surcoat to the royal body (beginning in 1215, with Alexander II's seal),[47] to the grooming and caparisons of that 'knightly super-phallus',[48] the warhorse, collectively accomplished the first purpose. The appearance of heraldic imagery (the lion rampant) on the royal shield of Alexander II and the elaboration of the armorial bearings on the two seals of Alexander III spoke in clear visual metaphors to the second. The privileged status that contemporary Europeans accorded the knight, so readily apparent in artistic media and literary works, found equally eloquent expression in sigillographic language, nowhere more triumphantly than in the iconography of the sword held in the royal hand.[49] On the seal of Alexander II the short, blunt weapon of William I's time is replaced by a longer, heavier, more formidable piece. Changes in the depiction of armour and equipment reflected thirteenth-century advances in military technology, of course. But the visual enhancement of the king's sword also served a crucial symbolic purpose, confirming the king as the archetype of masculine virility; likewise, his placement on horseback epitomised the ideal male form.[50] The equestrian figure on Alexander III's two great seals boldly reiterated these messages. His second device in particular is a masterpiece of the engraver's art, its details scrupulous renditions of the mounted warrior on horseback as paradigmatic man and king.[51] In 1258, after a nine-year minority, Alexander actively assumed responsibility for the governance of the realm. Despite his youth, he had successfully negotiated the major life events and 'career firsts' – marriage, fatherhood, knighthood – that contemporaries considered essential to the construction of elite male identity.[52] Thereafter, his sigillographic alter ego left scant opportunity for viewers to question his capability to exercise the duties and responsibilities of the office of king.

CONCLUSION

In the middle years of the twelfth century, the same Aelred of Rievaulx who wrote about Malcolm III's determination to perish by the sword in a fashion befitting a real man also described the chivalric reputation of Henry of Northumberland, the son of King David I. The earl, he commented, was a knight of such prowess that no one in the Scottish army resembled him; on the field of battle he was 'braver than others to pursue, keener to resist, slower to flee'.[53] Aelred's work bears eloquent witness in words to the association that contemporaries made between the characteristics of the mounted warrior and normative ideas about masculine power. The images impressed onto seals of the same period were three-dimensional representations of a similar construction of the idealised male body. As such, they raise intriguing, if perhaps unanswerable, questions about the relationship between the craftsmen who designed royal seals and the clients who commissioned them. Recent work on the material culture of high medieval Scotland has emphasised the need for scholars to be attentive to the 'language' of high-status artefacts such as jewellery, fine harnesses, display weaponry and devotional objects, and to appreciate the ways in which such goods gained currency as media through which people expressed shared values and ideals.[54] Implicit in such discussions is an understanding of the extent to which the artisans who designed high-status objects were sensitive to the aspirations of the men and women who commissioned them. Thoroughly freighted with iconography that spoke volumes about status, power and gender identity, the seals created for royal patrons offered them vehicles through which to give expression to their sense of self. It is in this light that changes to sigillographic designs are best interpreted, amongst them the enlarged sword with which William I signalled the sovereign authority of his realm despite his imprisonment at English hands, Alexander II's addition of a second tressure to the royal arms after the long awaited birth of his son in 1241 and Alexander III's choice of a bare-faced boy for the obverse of his personal device. The surface of a seal may have been small and more restricted than parchment canvases available to the painters and manuscript illuminators of the day, and the language of royal imagery less extensive than the rich chivalric vocabulary that was the stock-in-trade of contemporary chroniclers. But no less deeply embedded in the iconography were potent statements of each ruler's social and sexual identity. The messages impressed there were subtle but unambiguous. They must also have been eloquent, or the basic structure and design of royal seals would never have endured for the centuries that they did.

The use of seals of authentication and validation was never limited to members of the male elite, either in Scotland or elsewhere in Europe. Yet the equestrian seal remained the exclusive preserve of high-born secular men. The mounted horseman is not found on the seals of clerics and it was never an icon of choice for women – not even amongst women of royal dignity, who did not hesitate to deploy on their seals other symbols of royal power (orbs, crowns, sceptres).[55] The explanation for this exclusivity is simple: seal iconography reflected social reality. The hegemonic power structure of high medieval Europe allowed male clerics more circumscribed political, legal and social agency than it did kings and secular noblemen; it imposed greater restrictions still on the agency of women. When in England and Scotland seal usage spread beyond the confines of the royal court, members of the ecclesiastical hierarchy and high-status women looked to a range of different images to give graphic expression to their understanding of personhood. Amongst these groups, seals were more often than not pointed ovals on which the owner was depicted as a standing figure, fully robed. The design lent itself well to the display of symbols and icons that situated the individual within larger matrilineal and patrilineal kindreds and from the second half of the twelfth century the language of heraldry came to enjoy widespread popularity amongst landholders of all ranks and both genders.[56]

The twelfth and thirteenth centuries witnessed the evolution and growing confidence of kingship in Scotland. Indelibly associated with his fundamental role as defender of church and realm was the king's obligation to embody contemporary norms of good governance. Aelred's portrayal of Malcolm III gave eloquent expression in words to the link that the chronicler's contemporaries made between 'manly' conduct and strong rule. The intricately encoded seals that Malcolm's successors in turn appended to each of their written deeds performed a vital function as visual counterparts of those words and, ultimately, in the development and maturation of the image of Scottish kingship.

NOTES

The author wishes to acknowledge the financial support of the Social Sciences and Humanities Research Council of Canada in the research undertaken for this work.

1. Aelred of Rievaulx, 'The genealogy of the kings of the English', in Marsha L. Dutton (ed.), *Aelred of Rievaulx: The Historical Works*, trans. Jane Patricia Freeland (Kalamazoo: Cistercian Publications, 2005), pp. 116–18.

2. For the development of kingship over this period see Alice Taylor, *The Shape of the State in Medieval Scotland, 1124–1290* (Oxford: Oxford University Press, 2016); Alasdair Ross, *The Kings of Alba, c. 1000–c. 1130* (Edinburgh: John Donald, 2011); A. A. M. Duncan, *The Kingship of the Scots 842–1292* (Edinburgh: Edinburgh University Press, 2002), pp. 1–174.

3. For kingship and masculinity elsewhere, see Katherine J. Lewis, *Kingship and Masculinity in Late Medieval England* (Abingdon: Routledge, 2013), especially pp. 17–44; Christopher Fletcher, 'Manhood, kingship and the public in late medieval England', *Édad Media: Revista de Historia*, 13 (2012), pp. 123–42; John Watts, *Henry VI and the Politics of Kingship* (Cambridge: Cambridge University Press, 1996), especially pp. 20–30.

4. On medieval manifestations of hegemonic masculinity, see Lewis, *Kingship and Masculinity*, pp. 34–6; D. M. Hadley, 'Introduction', in D. M. Hadley (ed.), *Masculinity in Medieval Europe* (London: Longman, 1999), pp. 1–18; Kirsten A. Fenton, 'Ideas and ideals of secular masculinity in William of Malmsbury', *Women's History Review*, 16 (2007), pp. 755–72. Despite recent critiques, for which see R. W. Connell and James W. Messerschmidt,

'Hegemonic masculinity: rethinking the concept', *Gender & History*, 19 (2005), pp. 832–48; and John Tosh, 'Hegemonic masculinity and the history of gender', in Stefan Dudink, Karen Hagemann and John Tosh (eds), *Masculinities in Politics and War: Gendering Modern History* (Manchester: Manchester University Press, 2004), pp. 41–58, the concept remains a thoroughly appropriate paradigm for understanding medieval kingship.

5. The reference here is to both extant waxen seals and matrices known to have been created for royal patrons.

6. Peter Worm, 'From subscription to seal: the growing importance of seals as signs of authenticity in medieval royal charters', in Petra Schulte, Marco Mostert and Irene van Renswoude (eds), *Strategies of Writing: Studies on Text and Trust in the Middle Ages* (Turnhout: Brepols, 2008), pp. 63–83; Brigitte Miriam Bedos-Rezak, *When Ego was Imago: Signs of Identity in the Middle Ages* (Leiden: Brill, 2011), especially pp. 109–59.

7. For details of seals discussed here, see Walter de Gray Birch, *History of Scottish Seals from the Eleventh to the Seventeenth Century*, 2 vols (Stirling: E. Mackay, 1905–7); Henry Laing, *Descriptive Catalogue of Impressions from Ancient Scottish Seals*, 2 vols (Edinburgh: Bannatyne Club, 1850–66) and John Horne Stevenson and Marguerite Wood, *Scottish Heraldic Seals: Royal, Official, Ecclesiastical, Collegiate, Burghal, Personal*, 3 vols (Glasgow: R. Maclehose, 1940).

8. Ross, *Kings of Alba*, pp. 165–8; A. A. M. Duncan, 'Yes, the earliest Scottish charters', *Scottish Historical Review*, 78 (1999), pp. 1–38, at 3–4.

9. P. D. A. Harvey and Andrew McGuiness, *A Guide to British Medieval Seals* (Toronto: University of Toronto Press, 1996), pp. 5–6; Duncan, 'Earliest Scottish charters', pp. 11–12; Duncan, *Kingship of the Scots*, p. 4. For William the Conqueror's seal, see M. T. Clanchy, *From Memory to Written Record: England 1066–1307*, 2nd edition (Oxford: Blackwell, 1993), pp. 311–12.

10. Ross, *Kings of Alba*, pp. 159–73.

11. Laing, *Ancient Scottish Seals*, vol. 1, pp. 1–2.

12. Adrian Ailes, 'The knight's alter ego: from equestrian to armorial seal', in Noël Adams, John Cherry and James Robinson (eds), *Good Impressions: Image and Authority in Medieval Seals* (London: British Museum, 2007), pp. 8–11, at 8. For England see Clanchy, *From Memory to Written Record*, pp. 310–12; Brigitte Bedos-Rezak, *Form and Order in Medieval France: Studies in Social and Quantitative Sigillography* (Aldershot: Variorum, 1993), IV, pp. 54–66 and T. A. Heslop, 'English seals from the mid-ninth century to 1100', *Journal of the British Archaeological Association*, 133 (1980), pp. 6–7. For kingship associated with holiness and clerical masculinity, see P. H. Cullum, 'Introduction: holiness and masculinity in medieval Europe', in Cullum and Katherine J. Lewis (eds), *Holiness and Masculinity in the Middle Ages* (Cardiff: University of Wales Press, 2013), pp. 1–7,

at 4–5 and Jennifer D. Thibodeaux, 'Introduction: rethinking the medieval clergy and masculinity', in Jennifer D. Thibodeaux (ed.), *Negotiating Clerical Identities: Priests, Monks and Masculinity in the Middle Ages* (Basingstoke: Palgrave Macmillan, 2010), pp. 1–15.

13. Brigitte Miriam Bedos-Rezak, 'In search of a semiotic paradigm: the matter of sealing in medieval thought and praxis (1050–1400)', in Adams, Cherry and Robinson (eds), *Good Impressions*, pp. 1–7; see also Brigitte M. Bedos-Rezak, 'From ego to imago: mediation and agency in medieval France (1000–1250)', *Haskins Society Journal*, 14 (2005), pp. 151–73; Elizabeth A. New, *Seals and Sealing Practices* (London: British Records Association, 2010), pp. 3–8; Karl Heidecker, 'Introduction', in Karl Heidecker (ed.), *Charters and the Use of the Written Word in Medieval Society* (Turnhout: Brepols, 2000), pp. 1–12, at 11–12.

14. Bedos-Rezak, *When Ego was Imago*, p. 76.

15. Cynthia J. Neville, *Land, Law and People in Medieval Scotland* (Edinburgh: Edinburgh University Press, 2010), pp. 72–110.

16. Dauvit Broun, 'The writing of charters in Scotland and Ireland in the twelfth century', in Heidecker (ed.), *Charters and the Use of the Written Word*, pp. 113–31, at 120–4; John Reuben Davies, 'The donor and the duty of warrandice: giving and granting in Scottish charters', in Dauvit Broun (ed.), *The Reality behind Charter Diplomatic in Anglo-Norman Britain* (Glasgow: University of Glasgow, 2011), pp. 120–65.

17. Broun, 'The writing of charters', p. 155; Clanchy, *From Memory to Written Record*, pp. 312–17; Bedos-Rezak, 'In search of a semiotic paradigm', pp. 3–4.

18. On the form and function of seal legends in Europe, see Brigitte Bedos-Rezak, 'Medieval seals and the structure of chivalric society', in Howell Chickering and Thomas H. Seiler (eds), *The Study of Chivalry: Resources and Approaches* (Kalamazoo: Medieval Institute Publications, 1988), pp. 313–42, at 319; Bedos-Rezak, *When Ego was Imago*, pp. 152–3, 155.

19. Grant G. Simpson, 'Kingship in miniature: a seal of minority of Alexander III, 1249–1257', in Alexander Grant and Keith J. Stringer (eds), *Medieval Scotland: Crown, Lordship and Community* (Edinburgh: Edinburgh University Press, 1993), pp. 131–9, at 138; Duncan, *Kingship*, p. 146. G. W. S. Barrow (ed.), *The Charters of David I* (Woodbridge: Boydell Press, 1999), p. 30, regarded as 'unknown' the use of this formula, but it surely referred in coded terms to the absence from Scottish ceremonies of royal inauguration of the acts of coronation and unction until the early fourteenth century.

20. Simpson, 'Kingship in miniature', p. 138; Bedos-Rezak, *Form and Order*, I, pp. 50–5.

21. Stevenson and Wood, *Scottish Heraldic Seals*, vol. 1, p. 5; Laing, *Ancient Scottish Seals*, p. 5; Duncan, *Kingship of the Scots*, p. 137.

22. R.-H. Bautier, 'Échanges d'influences dans les chancelleries souveraines du

moyen âge, d'après les types des sceaux de majesté', *Comptes-rendus de l'Académie des Inscriptions et Belles-Lettres*, 2 (1968), pp. 192–220, at 196–9; Heslop, 'English seals', pp. 9–10.

23. A. A. M. Duncan, 'Before coronation: making a king at Scone in the thir-teenth century', in Richard Welander, David J. Breeze and Thomas Owen Clancy (eds), *The Stone of Destiny: Artefact and Icon* (Edinburgh: Society of Antiquaries of Scotland, 2003), pp. 138–67, at 155–8; J. Hunter, 'King Edward's spoliations in Scotland in A.D. 1296', *Archaeological Journal*, 13 (1856), pp. 245–55, at 245–9.

24. For this link in English kingship, see Katherine J. Lewis, 'Edmund of East Anglia, Henry VI and ideals of kingly masculinity', in Cullum and Lewis (eds), *Holiness and Masculinity*, pp. 158–73, at 158; Lewis, *Kingship and Masculinity*, pp. 1–13; W. Mark Ormrod, 'Monarchy, martyrdom and masculinity: England in the later Middle Ages', in Cullum and Lewis (eds), *Holiness and Masculinity*, pp. 174–91.

25. Maurice Keen, *Chivalry* (New Haven: Yale University Press, 1984), pp. 53, 771–7; Edward Francis Twining, *European Regalia* (London: Batsford, 1967), pp. 230, 256.

26. Ross, *Kings of Alba*, pp. 192–3, 205–98; Richard D. Oram, *Domination and Lordship: Scotland 1070–1230* (Edinburgh: Edinburgh University Press, 2011), pp. 55–64; the quotation is on p. 62.

27. See below, pp. 110, 114.

28. For the sword specifically as phallus, see Derek Neal, *The Masculine Self in Late Medieval England* (Chicago: University of Chicago Press, 2008), p. 2. A compelling assessment of the 'multivocality' of swords in late Anglo-Saxon society that has much relevance to high medieval Scotland appears in D. M. Hadley, 'Masculinity', in Jacqueline Stodnick and Renée R. Trilling (eds), *A Handbook of Anglo-Saxon Studies* (Chichester: John Wiley and Sons, 2012), pp. 115–32.

29. Oram, *Domination and Lordship*, p. 64; see also Ross, *Kings of Alba*, pp. 195–218.

30. A digital image appears at http://www.rampantscotland.com/famous/blfamdavid1.htm (last accessed 16 April 2016). King Malcolm's reputation as a virgin is reviewed in G. W. S. Barrow (ed.), *Regesta Regum Scottorum, Vol. I: The Acts of Malcolm IV King of Scots 1154–1165* (Edinburgh: Edinburgh University Press, 1960), pp. 22–3. For problems associated with a celibate and childless king, see Katherine J. Lewis, 'Becoming a virgin king: Richard II and Edward the Confessor', in Samantha J. E. Riches and Sarah Salih (eds), *Gender and Holiness: Men, Women, and Saints in Late Medieval Europe* (London: Routledge, 2002), pp. 86–100.

31. For a related discussion, see Neal, *The Masculine Self*, pp. 132–40; Vern Boullough, 'On being a male in the Middle Ages', in Clare A. Lees (ed.), *Medieval Masculinities: Regarding Men in the Middle Ages* (Minneapolis: University of Minnesota Press, 1984), pp. 31–45, at 31–4.

32. Dauvit Broun, *The Irish Identity of the Kingdom of the Scots in the Twelfth and Thirteenth Centuries* (Woodbridge: Boydell Press, 1999), p. 195.

33. See, for example, Birch, *History of Scottish Seals*, vol. 1, p. 28; Cynthia J. Neville and Grant G. Simpson (eds), *Regesta Regum Scottorum, Vol. IV, Pt 1: The Acts of Alexander III King of Scots, 1249–1286* (Edinburgh: Edinburgh University Press, 2013), pp. 31–2.

34. The swords that William and Alexander II hold extend into a space between the final V and the M in the word 'SCOTTORVM'. All extant versions of Alexander III's first seal are fragmentary.

35. On the subject of two 'new' king lists produced for Alexander II, see Dauvit Broun, 'Contemporary perspectives on Alexander II's succession: the evidence of king-lists', in Richard D. Oram (ed.), *The Reign of Alexander II, 1214–49* (Leiden: Brill, 2005), pp. 82–97. On the inappropriateness of young men (*iuvenes*) acting as fully mature men, see M. Bennett, 'Military masculinity in England and Northern France, c. 1050–c. 1225', in Hadley (ed.), *Masculinity in Medieval Europe*, pp. 73–82; Ruth Mazo Karras, *From Boys to Men: Formations of Masculinity in Late Medieval Europe* (Philadelphia: University of Pennsylvania Press, 2003), especially pp. 20–66.

36. R. R. Davies, *Domination and Conquest: The Experience of Ireland, Scotland and Wales 1100–1300* (Cambridge: Cambridge University Press, 1990), p. 51; Duncan, *Kingship of the Scots*, p. 72. Neither Edgar nor Alexander I is recorded as having been knighted, although later chroniclers wrote about them as if they had been. See Cynthia J. Neville and R. Andrew McDonald, 'Knights and knighthood in Gaelic Scotland, c. 1050–1300', *Studies in Medieval and Renaissance History*, 3rd series, 4 (2007), pp. 57–106, at 65–7.

37. Simpson, 'Kingship in miniature', pp. 136–7, with a photograph of the seal at p. 132; Neville and Simpson (eds), *Acts of Alexander III*, pp. 30–1.

38. So, too, had the young Malcolm IV been depicted in the Kelso abbey charter of 1159. For the significance of hair to masculine identity, see Joan Cadden, *The Meanings of Sex Difference in the Middle Ages: Medicine, Science and Culture* (Cambridge: Cambridge University Press, 1993), pp. 181–3; Neal, *The Masculine Self*, pp. 126–32.

39. William F. Skene (ed.), *Johannis de Fordun, Chronica gentis Scotorum*, 2 vols (Edinburgh: Edmonston and Douglas, 1871–72), vol. 1, p. 293.

40. Neville and Simpson (eds), *Acts of Alexander III*, p. 16.

41. Cynthia J. Neville, 'Preparing for kingship: Prince Alexander of Scotland, 1264–1284', in J. Nugent and E. Ewan (eds), *Children and Youth in Premodern Scotland* (Woodbridge: Boydell Press, 2015), pp. 155–72, at 155–9. From the 1260s to the end of the Middle Ages the descendants of Malcolm III and Saint Margaret abandoned the symbol of the sword of state on the obverse of their seals.

42. This side of the seal read '+ HOC NORMANNORVM WILLELMVM

NOSCE PATRONVM'; Walter de Gray Birch, *Catalogue of Seals in the Department of Manuscripts in the British Museum*, 6 vols (London: British Museum, 1887–1900), vol. 1, pp. 3–4; Heslop, 'English seals', p. 303; Robert Bartlett, *England under the Norman and Angevin Kings 1075–1225* (Oxford: Clarendon Press, 2000), p. 245. The seal set the pattern for English royal devices for centuries to come.

43. Neville and McDonald, 'Knights and knighthood', pp. 57–106.

44. Danielle Westerhof, 'Deconstructing identities on the scaffold: the execution of Hugh Despenser the Younger, 1326', *Journal of Medieval History*, 33 (2007), pp. 87–106, at 97. For the armoured knight as a 'visual construction of an idealised masculinity', see Rachel Dressler, 'Steel corpse: imaging the knight in death', in J. Murray (ed.), *Conflicted Identities and Multiple Masculinities: Men in the Medieval West* (New York: Garland Press, 1999), pp. 135–67.

45. For the association of the pennon or gonfanon with the authority to raise the army, see Bedos-Rezak, 'Medieval seals', pp. 332–3.

46. For the relationship between physical age and masculine authority, see Neal, *The Masculine Self*, pp. 16–23; Karras, *From Boys to Men*, pp. 2–66; W. M. Aird, 'Frustrated masculinity: the relationship between William the Conqueror and his eldest son', in Hadley (ed.), *Masculinity in Medieval Europe*, pp. 39–55.

47. The surcoat first appears in a seal formerly attached to a deed of Alexander II, now classed as National Records of Scotland [NRS], Melrose Charters, GD 55/174, dated 3 April 1215.

48. Neal, *The Masculine Self*, p. 227.

49. For Scotland, see Virginia Glenn, 'Thirteenth-century seals – Tayside, Fife and the wider world', *Tayside and Fife Archaeological Journal*, 5 (1999), pp. 146–62;Virginia Glenn, *Romanesque and Gothic, Decorative Metalwork and Ivory Carvings in the Museum of Scotland* (Edinburgh: Museums of Scotland, 2003), pp. 2–8; Stuart D. Campbell, 'The language of objects: material culture in medieval Scotland', in Matthew Hammond (ed.), *New Perspectives on Medieval Scotland 1093–1286* (Woodbridge, 2013), pp. 183–201.

50. See the several properties of swords valorised by the sons of Henry II in Emma Mason, 'The hero's invincible weapon: an aspect of Angevin Propaganda', in Christopher Harper-Bill and Ruth Harvey (eds), *The Ideals and Practices of Medieval Knighthood III* (Woodbridge: Boydell Press, 1990), pp. 121–37.

51. Neville and Simpson (eds.), *Acts of Alexander III*, p. 32.

52. W. M. Ormrod, 'Coming to kingship: boy kings and the passage to power in fourteenth-century England', in Nicola F. McDonald and W. M. Ormrod (eds), *Rites of Passage: Cultures of Transition in the Fourteenth Century* (Woodbridge: York Medieval Press, 2004), pp. 31–49; more generally, see Adrian Ailes, 'Powerful impressions: symbols of office and authority

on secular seals', in John Cherry and Ann Paine (eds), *Signs and Symbols: Proceedings of the 2006 Harlaxton Symposium* (Donington: Shaun Tyas, 2009), pp. 18–28, at 18.

53. Aelred of Rievaulx, 'The Battle of the Standard', in Dutton (ed.), *Aelred of Rievaulx*, p. 259.

54. Campbell, 'The language of objects', pp. 191–201.

55. See, for example, the seals of Matilda of Scotland, sister of King Edgar and wife of King Henry I of England and, later, Mary Queen of Scots (1542–67), described and illustrated in Birch, *History of Scottish Seals*, vol. 1, pp. 16–17, 68–78, 86, 179–89.

56. On women's seal designs in this context, see Susan M. Johns, *Noblewomen, Aristocracy and Power in the Twelfth-century Anglo-Norman Realm* (Manchester: Manchester University Press, 2003), pp. 122–51; Cynthia J. Neville, 'Women and land ownership in Scotland, 1150–1350', *Journal of Legal History*, 26 (2005), pp. 21–45, at 39–40.

6

Contrasting Kingly and Knightly Masculinities in Barbour's *Bruce*

Sergi Mainer

T HIS CHAPTER EXAMINES THE multiple representation, evolution and opposition of masculine constructions in John Barbour's *Bruce* (c. 1375). The text displays multi-layered visions of masculinity, favouring those that are more flexible. The two main heroes, Robert Bruce and James Douglas, represent this kind of fluid masculinity, able to adapt to the ever-changing social and political circumstances of late medieval Scotland. Their masculinity contrasts with the negative masculine models of Edward I, King of England, and Robert's brother, Edward, whose inability to evolve as a man and knight causes his downfall. After a brief historical contextualisation, the chapter will argue that the absence of proper leaders, including Robert Bruce himself, to rule the country, propitiates Edward I's successful invasion of Scotland. Second, it will examine the evolution of Robert I and James Douglas as they become the ideal king and knight respectively to liberate Scotland. Third, the lack of interactions with women will be discussed.[1] Finally, the end of the narrative will be assessed as a perfect culmination of a sovereign's life, securing progeny, peace and a profoundly Christian departure from this world.

CONTEXT

In the forty years previous to the composition of John Barbour's *Bruce*, the hostilities of the First War of Independence (1296–1328) between England and Scotland had been renewed, leading to several English victories under the rule of Edward III. David II of Scotland had been captured at the Battle of Neville's Cross (1346), although he was released in 1357, bringing the Second War of Independence to an end.[2] Robert I's military success in the first quarter of the fourteenth century was a distant memory. At a time of political instability within the realm itself, King Robert II (1316–90), who had succeeded David in 1371 but had difficulties fully establishing his authority, commissioned Barbour, archdeacon of Aberdeen, to write a romance based on the life and deeds of Robert Bruce, the king's grandfather. The verse romance was finished around 1375.[3] Robert II endeavoured to underpin his political authority, using the example of Bruce and his heroic comrades at arms as a model of the ideal relationship between a monarch and his nobles.[4]

> For auld storys yat men redys
> Representis to yaim ye dedys
> Of stalwart folk yat lywyt ar
> Rycht as yai yan in presence war.
> And certis yai suld weill have prys
> [. . .]
> As wes King Robert off Scotland
> Yat hardy wes off hart and hand,
> And gud schir Iames off Douglas
> [. . .]
> Off yaim I thynk yis buk to ma . . .[5]
> [For old stories which men read, hold up to them the deeds of brave men
>   who lived [in past times], just as if they were with us [now]. And indeed
>   those [men] should be highly esteemed . . . [Such] were King Robert of
>   Scotland, who was brave in heart and hand, and good Sir James Douglas
>   . . . I intend to make a book about them . . .] (I. 17–21, 27–9, 33)[6]

Since the Scottish monarch, his knights and foes are the main (and almost exclusive) protagonists of the narrative, the relationships between men and contrastive exemplary and failed masculine models define the core of the romance. The beginning of Book I points in that direction, stating that the narrative is written predominantly for *men*. Even if women had been part of the intended audience,[7] the exemplary characters present in the narrative are men: the kingly figure of Robert Bruce and the knightly figure of James Douglas (1286–1330), whose interactions are presented as the way in which an ideal affiliation between a king and a knight should function. However, *The Bruce* does not present masculinity as a straightforward set of attitudes, but, as in other European late medieval romances, as a complex, not always fixed set of values.[8] Barbour was aware of the multifaceted nature of masculinity: a knight's perfect incarnation of masculine values according to sociopolitical expectations is necessarily different from a king's ideal masculinity and expectations, due to their distinct roles. Knights were expected to excel in deeds of arms, in which violence was a 'mode of masculine expression'. Success in heterosexual love was also a significant feature of knightly masculinity.[9] The famous stories of Tristan and Isolde or Lancelot and Guenevere are archetypal illustrations of this.

INADEQUATE MASCULINE MODELS

Book I introduces the dispute over the succession after the deaths of King Alexander III in 1286 and of Margaret, his granddaughter and heir, in 1290. At this stage, Barbour's narrative voice already complains about the Scottish nobles' choice of Edward I as the arbiter of the succession process (I. 91–134), the two main contenders being John Balliol and Robert Bruce. Such ill judgement on the part of the nobility points to the dearth of a proper man or men to rule Scotland effectively. In Books I and II, Barbour characterises the different Scottish villains and heroes, including Robert Bruce himself, as inadequate masculine models to lead the country. In late medieval Scotland, Thomas Aquinas' *De regimine principum* (*On the Government of Rulers*) deeply influenced the ideal vision of kingship, whose main principles were also disseminated by the Declaration of Arbroath (1320).[10] For Aquinas, the archetypal Christian monarch should apply God's balance between justice and mercy on earth, that is *Rex imago Dei*:

> Therefore let the king recognise that such is the office which he undertakes, namely, that he is to be in the kingdom what the soul is in the body, and what God is in the world. If he reflect seriously upon this, a zeal for justice will be enkindled in him when he contemplates that he has been appointed to this position in place of God, to exercise judgment in his kingdom; further, he will acquire the gentleness of clemency and mildness when he considers as his own members those individuals who are subject to his rule.[11]

First, *The Bruce* purposely obscures the arguments presented by the two major factions, the Balliols and the Bruces, in the succession process (I. 41–90). As a pro-Brucean and pro-Stewart text, *The Bruce* could not openly depict the arguments deployed insofar as, according to the strict law of primogeniture, John Balliol was the rightful heir to the Scottish crown.[12] Nevertheless, Balliol's weakness (both historically and as conceptualised in the romance) incapacitated him from being the king required by Scotland. Hence, Edward I's preference for John Balliol as the king of Scots is not conceived of as being based on right but on Balliol's submission to the King of England:

> Schyr Iohn the Balleoll perfay
> Assentyt till him in all his will,

Quhar-throuch fell efter mekill ill.
[Sir John the Balliol perfectly assented to him in all his will, whereby fell
  much ill afterwards.] (I. 168–70)

Balliol's vulnerability and feebleness is further accentuated when Edward
deposes him in 1296 and takes Scotland by brute force. In Barbour's
opinion, Balliol is an inadequate kingly and manly figure, willing to
submit the country to a foreign force. He is a sombre figure, who never
even says a word.[13] This silence underlines his powerlessness, his inability to articulate the decisions a good national leader should make. In fact,
silence was considered a female virtue associated with submission and
obedience, and even more with daughters acquiescing to a father than
with grown-up women.[14] Silence metaphorically emasculates Balliol and
discredits him, both as an adult and as an effective monarch.

John Comyn, a relative and supporter of John Balliol, is constructed
as another negative masculine model, unfit to be leader of Scotland.
Barbour recounts a secret agreement between Comyn and Bruce to liberate the country from Edward I. Yet according to Barbour, this is part of
a greater scheme devised by Comyn, who informs the English king about
Bruce's 'treason'. Comyn displays the same undesirable traits as John
Balliol, favouring submitting to Edward I to become a puppet king. He
prioritises his personal ambitions over the national cause, which an ideal
monarch should support. According to Aquinas, as a monarch he should
only submit to God and not to other humans, regardless of their power.

After escaping from Edward I (II. 11–19), Robert Bruce kills Comyn
in a kirk, committing sacrilege (II. 39–48). This is as an act of vengeance for Comyn's betrayal of his agreement with Bruce. In the pseudo-
historical and mythical world of epic poetry, speedy revenge is required.
In fact, the moving forces that allow an epic narrative to progress are
revenge, treason and loyalty.[15] By way of contrast, in the more historical
setting of *The Bruce*, such an action is not available to a monarch, who
has to follow the dictates of the law. Bruce's masculinity amalgamates
traits of an epic hero (military bravery and dexterity), together with
political and legalistic concerns and courtly attributes (even if the latter
are rather more schematically mentioned than properly developed).
Hence, at this early stage of the narrative, although the hot-tempered
young Bruce could doubtless make a good Roland-like epic hero, the
responsibilities involved in the ruling of a nation require a more reflexive
and intelligent way of action: the hero's evolution through experience
will take place during the first half of the narrative.

As for the most prominent knights on Robert Bruce's side, James

Douglas stands out as the one who will incarnate a perfect symbol of masculinity. In fact, the text adopts a pro-Douglas perspective at the expense of other heroes such as Thomas Randolph, Earl of Moray.[16] At the beginning of the narrative, Douglas is associated with great knightly virtues, but when his father's lands are given to the Englishman Clifford, he does not know what to do. The lack of a guiding figure is stressed:

> For he had na thing for to dispend
> Na yar wes nane yat ever him kend
> Wald do sa mekill for him yat he
> Mycht sufficiently fundyn be . . .
> [For he had nothing for expenses, nor was there anyone who had ever
>   known him who would do so much for him that he would be sufficiently
>   looked after . . .] (I. 319–22)

At this critical moment, he leaves Scotland for Paris, where he leads a rather dissolute life in the company of unsuitable acquaintances (I. 332–5). It is precisely at this decisive stage of life, leaving home, that a knight needs to be given extensive counsel on how to confront the world.[17] The absence of a father (he had been first imprisoned, and then killed) or a substitute guiding figure makes his learning process much more difficult, to the extent that he is willing to join Edward I in return for his lands. One of the techniques used by Barbour has a similar effect: the Robert Bruce of the narrative is an amalgamation of Robert I, his father and his grandfather. Such 'deliberate confusion' creates a long-standing fictional resistance to the English.[18] As a result, Barbour's young Bruce does not have a literary father to guide him and has to learn from experience, too.

Only when the English king scorns Douglas by refusing to give him his lands back does a thirst for revenge and eagerness to recover his father's lands lead Douglas to join Bruce (II. 92–109). The main reason to join the king of Scots is personal, not national. However, as their relationship is established, it allows Douglas to progress into a more profound awareness of the community and its defence:

> Yair frendschip woux ay mar & mar,
> For he serwyt ay lelely,
> And ye toyer full wilfully
> Yat was bath worthy wycht & wys
> Rewardyt him weile his service.
> [Their friendship increased more and more all the time, because [Douglas]
>   always served loyally, and [Bruce], who was worthy, brave and wise,
>   with a good will rewarded him well [for] his service.] (II. 170–4)

The 'frendschip' between Bruce and Douglas must be understood in political terms, as the actual feudal contract of duly rewarded service as expressed in line 174. Patriarchy operates not only at the level of men's power over women in any given context but also by the authority that different groups of men exercise over other groups of men according to social hierarchies.[19] This acceptance of a new patriarchal order under the rule of the recently crowned Robert I metaphorically points to Douglas' first step to becoming an ideal knight. Nonetheless, as customary in romances, both the monarch and his knight have to experience a maturation process over the first half of the narrative to become the iconic masculinity models for the contemporary audience at the court of Robert II. At this stage Douglas is still referred to as 'Yat yheyt than wes bot litill off mycht' [who was still of little significance] (II. 241).

The characterisation of Edward Bruce, Robert's brother, is very different from that of the other heroes in the poem: his understanding and display of masculinity do not evolve. His extraordinary boldness is praised in the first half of *The Bruce* when audacious acts of heroism play a key part in the liberation of Scotland. For this reason, he is praised in Galloway, where he vanquishes a much larger English contingent (IX. 565–635). However, this useful daredevil resoluteness before the Battle of Bannockburn in 1314 is re-codified as negative after that important battle. It no longer contributes to the national cause once his brother's authority has been largely established in the whole country.

The beginning of Book XIV sets up a conflict between the two brothers that was previously absent from the narrative:

Ye erle off Carrik, schyr Eduuard,
Yat stoutar wes yan a libard
And had na will to be in pes,
Thocht yat Scotland to litill wes
Till his broyer and him alsua,
Yarfor to purpos gan he ta
Yat he off Irland wald be king.
[Sir Edward, earl of Carrik, who was stronger than a leopard and had no
   desire to live in peace, felt that Scotland was too small for both him and
   his brother; therefore, he formed a purpose that he would become king of
   Ireland.] (XIV. 1–7)

By questioning his brother's authority, Edward fails both as a knight and as a man: his measureless ambition undermines him. He only cares about his personal 'chivalric reputation',[20] doing his best to act according to social and chivalric convention all the time, as opposed to Bruce's and Douglas' more practical approach.[21] As a consequence, Edward's subsequent actions are censored whenever his conduct deviates from his brother's devotion to the collective cause.

At the same time, the narrative strategically places on him the responsibility for the later unsuccessful liberation/invasion of Ireland. Edward's supposed initiative exculpates Robert Bruce, leaving the latter's image faultless as an ideal monarch after Bannockburn. Edward Bruce's good character is lost by his lack of self-control and excessive ambition, going beyond the accepted standards of masculinity. Ironically, the historical Edward Bruce is nowadays considered an excellent military strategist of his time,[22] or at the very least his near success in the conquest of Ireland is praised.[23] The real reasons for the Scottish defeat were the small Scottish army and the volatility of the political situation in Ireland, consisting of very heterogeneous peoples, who also had their own particular relationships with the English.[24] From a gender perspective, however, *The Bruce* promotes a fluid vision of masculinity. This vision entails a set of behavioural traits, which constantly interact and negotiate with the structures surrounding society.[25] In this particular case, Edward Bruce's inability to renegotiate his role in a changing world causes his downfall. The urgency of his chivalric actions in Scotland, seeking military glory, was no longer required. More balanced and judicious reasoning was needed, such as that shown by his now mature brother.

PROWESS, VIOLENCE AND MASCULINITY

In the Battle at Methven in 1306, the first pitched battle for the newly crowned king, Bruce's forces were defeated, demonstrating that he still had a long way to go before he could become the proper leader of the country. Nevertheless, his masculine virtues as a warrior were never (and never could be) in doubt: his bravery is stressed even if he has to escape from the battlefield to save his life or avoid capture:

> He dang on and sa hardely
> Yat quha had sene him in yat fycht
> Suld hald him for a douchty knycht.
> [He attacked so determinedly and so boldly that anyone seeing him in that
>   fight would esteem him as a doughty knight.] (II. 390–2)

Subsequently, his manliness and prowess are praised after he kills three men single-handedly:

> Quhen yai of Lorne has sene ye king
> Set in hym selff sa gret helping
> And defendyt him sa manlely,

Wes nane amang yaim sa hardy
Yat durst assailʒe him mar in fycht,
Sa dred yai for his mekill mycht.
[When [the men] of Lorn saw the king give himself such great help,
  and defend himself so manfully, none of them was so bold as to dare
  attack him further in fight, they were so afraid of his great strength.]
  (III. 147–52)

Different versions of the same kind of situation, where Bruce slays three attackers, are repeated throughout the narrative before the turning point at the Battle of Bannockburn. Such anxiety to present and represent the main hero fighting 'sa manlely' and displaying so 'mekill mycht' seems designed to compensate for his inability to rule the whole land as a king should be able to do. The attributes most closely connected to assertive masculinity need to be emphasised to erase any potential signs of failed masculinity, which would be so damaging for the image of a king.

Similarly, the same narrative strategy is devised to construct the other main hero, James Douglas. As a knight and lord who has yet to recover his expropriated lands, he is a failed lord without his possessions, and, by analogy, he is also an incomplete man who cannot fulfil his social role. His willingness to submit to Edward I to recover his lands (I. 407–36) may point to Douglas' single-minded drive to recover his property to feel complete. As a result, the taking of his family's castle, popularly known as the 'Douglas' Lardner', is depicted as one of the most graphic and bloody episodes in *The Bruce*. The concept of chivalry fades away, whereas the cruellest revenge is exacted and never questioned:

And ye presoneris yat he had tane
Rycht yar-in gert he heid ilkane,
Syne off ye townnys ye hedis outstrak.
A foule melle yar gane he mak,
For meile & malt & blud & wyne
Rane all to-gidder in a mellyne
Yat was wnsemly for to se.
[[Then] he had the prisoners whom he had taken beheaded there every
  one; then he struck the heads off the barrels [of wine]. He made a foul
  concoction there, for meal and malt and blood and wine all ran together
  into a mush that was disgusting to see.] (V. 401–7)

As with Bruce's outnumbered fights, Douglas' use of extreme violence in the first half of the romance endeavours to compensate for the still unaccomplished icon of the hero as an ideal knight and man. At the same time, it banishes any hint of potential emasculation. The exhibition of the decapitated heads in the town articulates the need for the public performance of masculinity. Some of the masculinity that has been stripped from him is now regained. Barbour deploys the same narrative and thematic technique to enhance the two main heroes' masculine virtues at a time when their authority as king and lord could not be completely exercised.

MARGINALISATION OF COURTLINESS

As I have argued elsewhere, since the ideology of the poem conditions the representation of courtliness, the conception of masculinity is equally affected.[26] The martially centred narrative and national political discourse revolve around masculine values in the world of politics and warfare. For this reason, courtliness is marginalised and re-codified within the national tenets. The small number of female characters means there are only a few courtly interchanges between ladies and knights: courtly action is sketched rather than properly developed. As discussed earlier, masculinity is primarily grounded upon the display of prowess and bravery in conflicts with other men whereas the complementary courtly values appear only either nominally or in the few conversations with women.

A typical illustration of Barbour's conceptualisation of courtliness is the treatment of Bruce's second wife, Elizabeth de Burgh, whose name is never mentioned; she is just referred to as 'the queen'. She becomes a type, rather than an actual character who can evolve or to whom the audience can relate. After the defeat at Methven, she joins Bruce in Aberdeen:

> Yarfor yai went till Aberdeyne
> Quhar Nele ye Bruys come & ye queyn
> And oyir ladyis fayr and farand
> Ilkane for luff off yar husband
> Yat for leyle luff and leawte
> Wald partenerys off yar paynys be.
> [So they went to Aberdeen, where Neil the Bruce and the queen with other
>   fair comely ladies [came], each for love of their husbands, a true love and
>   loyalty, wanting to share their sufferings.] (II. 515–20)

As opposed to archetypal *romans courtois*, in which the psychological tribulations, sorrows and joys of love are depicted,[27] in *The Bruce* this is reduced to a mere reference: 'for luff off yar husband'. The reader/listener must accept the narrator's words at face value even though an actual display of those feelings is not present. As a consequence, the subsequent 'leyle luff' seems to imply loyalty, not because of the bond of matrimony, but to the national cause. The courtly is necessarily redefined according to the political discourse to conform to the poem's national purpose.

Bruce's few appearances in chivalrous scenes conform to this practical vision of courtliness. The portrayal of lady helpers typical of *romans courtois* is reimagined in functional terms: they do not simply offer shelter to the warrior but also provide useful information and men to join Bruce's national cause.[28] The conversations between the Scottish monarch and these female characters still retain the courtly rhetoric and motifs of the *romans courtois*. In Book VII, Bruce asks for shelter in a lady's house, presenting himself as a mysterious knight:

> 'A trawailland man, dame,' said he,
> 'Yat trawaillys her throw ye contre.'
> ['A travelling man, lady,' said he, 'who journeys here through the country.']
>   (VII. 243–4)

While the presence of an enigmatic knight errant is reminiscent of the *roman courtois* tradition, the political overtones are inescapable: Bruce needs to keep his real identity secret in case this lady is on the English side. Formally, her reply captures the same courtly tone:

> Ye king said, 'Gud dame, quhat is he
> Yat gerris ʒou haiff sik specialte
> To men yat trawaillis?' 'Schyr, perfay,'
> Quod the gud-wyff, 'I sall ʒou say,
> Ye king Robert ye Bruys is he,
> Yat is rycht lord off yis countre.'
> [. . .]
> Scho said, 'It may na wys be swa.
> Ik haiff twa sonnys wycht & hardy,
> Yai sall becum ʒour men in hy.'
> [The king said, 'Good lady, who is he who makes you have such feeling for men who travel?' 'Sir,' said the good-wife, 'I'll tell you: good King Robert the Bruce is [the man] who is rightful lord of this country' . . . She said, 'it can't be like that. I have two sons, strong and hardy; they shall become your men at once.'] (VII. 247–52; 264–6)

The political and the courtly intermingle. Aware that by the late fourteenth century, epic and romance had borrowed motifs from each other,[29] Barbour knew that his royal masculine model could not be reduced to the values espoused in epic poetry. However, he ingeniously re-codified the courtly discourse to suit his dynastic/national tenets.

The manners of a courtly dialogue are applied to a much more political context. The lady's aid goes beyond offering Bruce shelter: instead she articulates the ideology of the romance and offers her sons to fight by the king's side. The displacement and relocation of courtliness serves a series of purposes: (1) it demonstrates the king's sophistication and command of rhetoric beyond inspiring his men on the battlefield, contributing to his image of kingly perfection; (2) the poet/author avoids the potential artificiality of over-embellished language because of the pragmatic approach he takes to describing the Wars of Independence, maintaining the same tone all through the text; and (3) it establishes the rhetorical and thematic bases that future Scots romances such as *The Wallace* and the Arthurian and Alexander romance would follow (and also transform) up to the mid-sixteenth century.[30]

The case of the knightly masculine archetype, Sir James Douglas, is more extreme. Even in his early characterisation in *The Bruce*, his image could not be further removed from that of an archetypal courtly knight such as Lancelot. Barbour makes it clear that Douglas' appearance is not so appealing:

> Bot he wes nocht sa fayr yat we
> Suld spek gretly off his beaute.
> In wysage wes he sumdeill gray
>   And had blak har as ic hard say,
> Bot off lymmys he wes weill maid
>   With banys gret & schuldrys braid,
>   His body wes weyll maid and lenȝe . . .
> [But he was not so good-looking that we should say much of his beauty.
>   His face was somewhat pale, and, as I heard it, he had black hair, but he
>   was well made in his limbs, with strong bones and broad shoulders. His
>   body was well made and lean . . .] (I. 381–7)

The rather half mocking, half ironic tone used to portray Douglas' physical looks possibly denotes the narrator's detachment from and transformation of courtly motifs. In his functional construction of courtliness, beauty is but secondary. Indeed, what defines Douglas' appearance as positive is the disposition of his body insofar as it looks perfectly built for combat. The description subsequently concentrates on his personality, in which his courtliness is vaguely implied:

> Quhen he wes blyth he wes lufly
> And meyk and sweyt in cumpany . . .
> [When he was in good spirits he was delightful, and meek and sweet in
>   company . . .] (I. 389–90)

The audience must accept the veracity of these two lines since his courtesy is never actually shown. In case there remained any doubts about the most important features that delineate Douglas as a man and knight, the sentence beginning with an illuminating 'but' returns to the central characteristic of his personality:

> Bot quha in battaill mycht him se,
> All oyir contenance had he.
> [But if you saw him in battle, he had quite another look [to him].](I. 391–2)

Hence, instead of being compared to a *roman courtois* hero, he is likened to Hector of Troy both in appearance and manly behaviour (I. 395–406). The main two heroes and masculine prototypes of kingship and knighthood are anchored in the masculine world of warfare and politics, in which their more feminine attributes are either adapted to or conform to the ideological discourse or mentioned only in passing, so as not to interfere with the main narrative.

Revealingly, as opposed to the rarity of social interchanges between men and women, the bonds and relationships between men in the homosocial world of *The Bruce* demonstrate much stronger links and feelings than those with women. In contrast with most frequently antagonistic knightly knights in romances, *The Bruce* proposes what Tison Pugh has called a homosocial 'cooperative model of heroic masculinity'.[31] After the defeat at Methven, when the Earl of Lennox joins Bruce, the Scottish monarch him greets cheerfully and 'kyssyt him [Lennox] in gret daynte' [kissed [the earl] with great pleasure] (III. 505). They end up weeping together. These lines show much more emotion and affection than any encounter between Bruce and a lady, including his unnamed wife. Nevertheless, the narrator straightaway underlines the nature of their tears so that they cannot be mistaken for those of women, which would call into question the hero's manliness and masculinity:

> Yocht I say yat yai gret sothly
> It wes na greting propyrly,
> For I trow traistly yat gretyng
> Cummys to men for mysliking,
> And yat nane may but angyr gret
> Bot it be wemen, yat can wet
> Yair chekys quhen-euer yaim list with teris,
> Ye-quheyir weill oft yaim na thing deris,
> [Although I say that they wept, truthfully it wasn't real crying, because I
>   firmly believe that weeping comes to men with misgiving, and that no one
>   can cry without grief, except women who can wet their cheeks with tears

whenever they like, even though very often nothing is hurting them,]
(III. 513–20)

These rather unfortunate comments disclose the fear of emasculation
and try to delimit clearly defined boundaries between what a man and
what a woman should be. On the one hand, in the late Middle Ages
tears were regarded as 'fine and honourable'[32] and some authors associated female weeping with that of the Virgin Mary, which signified positive virtues such a truth and compassion.[33] On the other hand, female
weeping could also be regarded as a subtle form of women's power,
such as those of a mother in biblical texts, which could help to save her
son.[34] Barbour seems to align himself with this more ambiguous use of
tears with his misogynistic comment.

In the realm of courtliness, one of the central themes that bring women
(or at least noblewomen) to the core of the narrative, is *fin'amors* (courtly
love).[35] In verse *romans courtois*, it traditionally operates as the axis that
allows the main male character to progress and develop in the realm of
courtliness. The knight in love must demonstrate both his devotion to
his beloved, and his dexterity and bravery in the battlefield to attain the
lady's heart. However, in *The Bruce*, the moving force for Bruce and
his comrades at arms is not their personal pursuit of *fin'amors* and their
integration into feudal society. Instead, the destiny of the whole nation
replaces love: the collective takes precedence over the personal. As a
consequence, the references to *fin'amors* and its psychological features
are scarce, only featuring as the necessary courtly counterpart to the
epic traits, which contribute to the overall construction of the heroes as
full men. For example, the descriptions of Bruce's well-known historical extramarital affairs are intentionally devoid of courtly rhetoric. The
narrative and ideological role of these very functional *fin'amants* is also
re-codified within the national discourse:

> Throw wemen yat he [Bruce] wyth wald play
> Yat wald tell all yat yai mycht her . . .
> [From women with whom he was sleeping, who would tell all that they
>   heard . . .] (V. 544–5)

The reference to their sexual games is almost incidental, since what really
matters is their more active role as the monarch's informants in Barbour's
conception of a whole nation fighting together for its emancipation.[36]

In fact, the one love relationship that can be catalogued as *fin'amors*
involves an English knight and his beloved. After Douglas' recovery of
Castle Douglas from the English, the men discover that one of the dead
enemies, Sir John Webton, carries a love letter from an English lady,

in which she promised to give him 'Hyr amowris and hyr drouery' [her love and her service] (VIII. 498) if he succeeded in defending the stronghold against Douglas. Such a heroic enterprise traditionally makes courtly and knightly action converge in *romans courtois*. In this way, the courtly and the knightly depend on each other and both discourses are balanced. In *The Bruce*, however, the displacement and reinterpretation of the *militia et amor* topos questions excessively idealistic behaviour in warfare. At the same time, it establishes an imbalance between the epic and the courtly narratives. The unsuccessful outcome of Webton's love pact implicitly discredits *fin'amors* and the disproportionally sophisticated rhetorical and ritualistic world surrounding it. The creation of masculine models will therefore concentrate on characteristics that would be potentially valid on the battlefield and in the realms of kingship and politics, at the expense of courtly action and rhetoric. Robert Bruce and James Douglas are constructed as ideal but not idealistic models, men whom members of the Scottish court and nobility could follow beyond the world of literary production.

BEYOND MASCULINITY

In the poem, Bruce recognises that the deployment of guerrilla tactics is necessary to confront the much larger and better prepared English army.[37] The Battle of Loudon Hill, the first pitched battle between both armies after Methven, marks a sea-change in the War of Independence. The Scottish victory also contributes to Bruce's evolution inasmuch as his demeanour matches that of a king, as seen in both political treatises and manuals of chivalry.[38] In this way, the ideal model of kingly masculinity finally emerges. At Bannockburn, his aggressiveness as a warrior operates as the perfect preamble to the battle when he famously kills Sir Henry Bohun with an axe, riding a small palfrey (a lightweight horse) as opposed to the Englishman's larger horse (XII. 25–86). Bruce makes the required public display of his masculinity and leadership, and his physical prowess remains uncontested. It is a metaphor for the battle as a whole, where the outnumbered and poorly equipped Scots defeat a larger and better equipped English army. From then on, masculinity and kingship are (re)presented as inseparable, a triumph of masculine Scottishness over masculine Englishness. It becomes the national heteronormative patriarchal ideal of power and dominance.[39] Close to the end of the work, the physical and active Bruce gives way to a mature king, corresponding to his ageing. After a conspiracy against him is led by William II, Lord of Soules, and David, Lord of Brechin, they are both put to trial, where they are condemned to be hanged (XIX. 68). As opposed to the young Bruce, who angrily killed Comyn at the Greyfriars Church, the now mature king follows the dictates of law, reinforcing both his image as an ideal king and the functioning of the Scottish judicial system. Such construction of kingship and masculinity reinforces the existing structures of power in Scotland, defining them as ideal.

Book XX is designed as the perfect ending both for the romance and for the main heroes' departure from this world: a truce with England is reached and the marriage and coronation of Bruce's son, David, allegorically convey the continuation of Scotland's future prosperity (even if historically, things turned out rather differently). After having settled everything, Bruce is now prepared to die in the most dignified manner. At this stage, Barbour needs to change the tone and negotiate between Bruce, the king and warrior, and Bruce the penitent Christian, who must find his way to heaven. Hence, the intermingling of the epic and the hagiographic narrative transforms the warrior into the saint. Barbour's constant reconstruction of masculinity reveals once again the fluidity of the concept, which needs to be reassessed on a regular basis and adapted to the ever-changing surrounding circumstances.

The best manner to reconcile the epic and the hagiographic narratives is by deploying the crusading motif, which merges knightly and religious elements. Even if the historical Robert Bruce had the intention of going on a crusade during his lifetime, possibly to atone for the killing of Comyn, the circumstances of the War of Independence prevented him from doing so.[40] At this juncture, the political and geographical axes of the romance drastically change: the political becomes spiritual and the action moves to Castile. At the king's request, after his death his heart is removed from his chest and taken by Douglas on Crusade when he goes to fight the Moslem army in the Iberian Peninsula.[41] Hence, Bruce's last battle and display of his masculinity are symbolic rather than physical. Now he is emblematically transformed into a Christological figure, inasmuch as he rises from the dead. Finally, the king of Scots accomplishes the longed-for holy enterprise of intervening in a crusade. His involvement in the battle fulfils two main narrative objectives: (1) it is Bruce's gate to enter heaven, and (2) it contrasts with Edward I's unhistorical desertion of the crusades to invade Scotland in Book I.[42] The narrative now establishes the structural parameters of divinity: 'the temporality and devilish "sleness" of the English king are thus contrasted with the holy death and resurrective journey of his Scottish counterpart'.[43] Barbour's *Bruce* adds another layer of significance to the traditional pious death of late medieval sovereigns and to the construction of their masculinity. It is not only a king leaving his mutable human body behind, renouncing the characteristic features of his masculinity to attain salvation; instead, Bruce is able to rise from the dead and 'fight' a final atoning battle against the enemies of the faith as a Christological icon. Even after leaving his human body behind, he manages allegorically to keep the masculine virtues of a warrior.

Moreover, the always active and ruthless Douglas has a similarly redemptive death. After being chosen to take Bruce's heart to fight the Saracens in Spain, he dies in the same heroic fashion in which he has lived: he tries his best to rescue a Scottish knight surrounded by enemies when heavily outnumbered:

> Sum off yer lord Douglas men,
> Yar yar lord ded has fundyn yen
> ʒeid weill ner woud for dule & wa,
> Lang quhill our him yai sorrowit sua
> And syne with gret dule hame him bar.
> [Some of the lord Douglas' men, who had found their lord dead there,
>   nearly went mad from grief and sorrow. They grieved like that over him
>   for a long while and then carried him back with great lamentation.]
> (XX. 491–5)

The homosocial tears, expressing great sorrow for Douglas' death, reappear but are now relocated in the context of the holy enterprise. The next two lines bring together both heroes when:

> Ye kingis hart haiff yai fundyn yar
> And yat hame with yaim haf yai tane . . .
> [They have found the king's heart here, and taken it with them . . .] (XX.
>   496–7)

Insofar as the main reason for the existence of the Order of Chivalry was to defend the Christian faith amongst chaos, the two main characters transcend the human in their last military mission: the unification of the knightly, kingly and religious discourses redefine masculinity in the realm of the sacred. As happens in saints' lives, both protagonists can be seen as leaving their gender/masculinity behind by departing from the human world, for they need to renounce their human bodies to embrace heaven with their souls.

CONCLUSION

Masculinities in *The Bruce* are represented as dynamic, fluid and adaptable, depending both on the position of a given man in society and on changes in the political situation of the country. The evolution (or lack thereof) of the characters' masculinity responds to their capacity to adjust to the demands that new circumstances pose. Those who manage to evolve and understand their role in society according to their hierarchical position triumph in the end, Robert Bruce as a king and James Douglas as a knight. By contrast, those who either are unable to progress, such as Edward Bruce, or do not comply with their role in society, such as the tyrannical King of England, Edward I, are bound to fail.

The two main characters' masculinities are designed in parallel, following an Aristotelian-based progression from youth to maturity as recodified along Christian parameters. The characterisation of impulsive, hot-blooded young men hinders them from liberating Scotland at the beginning of the romance. The lack of a guiding figure forces them to learn from experience. In the case of Douglas, his father is imprisoned and killed, whereas the amalgamation of three generations of Bruces as Robert I leaves the hero without a father. Their maturation process and evolving masculinity are delineated mainly through their prowess on the battlefield and, in Bruce's case, his more mature political decisions. In Barbour's *Bruce*, little room is left for courtliness, which is reduced to a minimum: its deployment contributes to the image of the heroes as complete men, but its non-idealistic depiction points to the kind of practical masculinity that the romance puts forward – masculine models that the noblemen at Robert II's court could actually follow. The necessary Christian turn at the end of the narrative reimagines both heroes having a pious death, which metaphorically guarantees their entrance into heaven. The demise of their bodies and human attributes can be interpreted as the spiritual *erasure* of gender in the Other World.

NOTES

1. In the French *roman courtois*, the interactions between knights and ladies were at the heart of the narrative, where the narratives of love and action interwove.
2. Steve Boardman, '"That nobill eldrys gret bounte": *The Bruce* and early Stewart Scotland', in Steve Boardman and Susan Fordan (eds), *Barbour's Bruce and its Cultural Contexts: Politics, Chivalry and Literature in Late Medieval Scotland* (Cambridge: D. S. Brewer, 2015) pp. 191–212, at 192–3.
3. The genre of *The Bruce* has been widely analysed. Recently Susan Fordan has referred to it as both history and romance, 'A nation of knights? Chivalry and the community of the realm in Barbour's *Bruce*', in Boardman

and Fordan (eds), *Barbour's Bruce and its Cultural Contexts*, pp. 137–48, at 138. Chris Given-Wilson labels *The Bruce* as a 'chivalric biography', 'Chivalric biography and medieval life-writing', in ibid. pp. 101–17, at 105.

4. R. D. S. Jack and P. A. T. Rozendaal (eds), *The Mercat Anthology of Early Scottish Literature, 1375–1707* (Edinburgh: Mercat Press, 1997), p. 2; Boardman, '*The Bruce* and early Stewart Scotland', p. 197.

5. John Barbour, *The Bruce*, Matthew P. McDiarmid and J. A. C. Stevenson (eds) (Edinburgh: Scottish Text Society, 1981–5).

6. All translations are taken from John Barbour, *The Bruce*, A. A. M. Duncan (ed. and trans.) (Edinburgh: Canongate Classics, 1997).

7. Rhiannon Purdie claims that the target audience of the romance consisted of nobles and courtiers directly affected by the events narrated in *The Bruce*, 'Medieval romance and the generic frictions of Barbour's *Bruce*', in Boardman and Fordan (eds), *Barbour's Bruce and its Cultural Contexts*, pp. 51–74, at 72.

8. Helen Phillips, 'Rites of passage in French and English romances', in Nicola F. McDonald and W. M. Ormrod (eds), *Rites of Passage: Cultures of Transition in the Fourteenth Century* (York: York Medieval Press, 2004), pp. 83–108, at 102.

9. Ruth Mazo Karras, *From Boys to Men: Formations of Masculinity in Late Medieval Europe* (Philadelphia: University of Pennsylvania Press, 2003), pp. 21, 25.

10. Edward J. Cowan, 'Identity, freedom and the Declaration of Arbroath', in Dauvit Broun, Richard J. Finlay and Michael Lynch (eds), *Image and Identity: The Making and Remaking of Scotland through the Ages* (East Linton: John Donald, 1998), pp. 38–68, at 57.

11. Thomas Aquinas, *On Kingship* (Toronto: Pontifical Institute of Mediaeval Studies, 1946), p. 95.

12. R. J. Goldstein, *The Matter of Scotland: Historical Narrative in Medieval Scotland* (Lincoln, NE: University of Nebraska Press, 1993), p. 155.

13. Ibid. p. 154.

14. Rachel E. Moss, *Fatherhood and its Representations in Middle English Texts* (Cambridge: Cambridge University Press, 2013), p. 113.

15. In medieval Scottish literature, a perfect example is the anonymous *Buik of Alexander* (c. 1438), a translation of two episodes of the late twelfth-century Old French *Roman d'Alexandre*.

16. Steve Boardman and Susan Fordan, 'Introduction', in Boardman and Fordan (eds), *Barbour's Bruce and its Cultural Contexts*, pp. 1–31, at 7.

17. Helen Cooper, 'Good advice on leaving home in the romances', in P. J. P. Goldberg and Felicity Riddy (eds), *Youth in the Middle Ages* (York: York Medieval Press, 2004), pp. 101–21, at 101.

18. A. M. Kinghorn, 'Scottish historiography in the XIVth century: a new introduction to Barbour's *Bruce*', *Studies in Scottish Literature*, 6 (1968–9), pp. 131–45, at 141.

19. Michael Kaufman, 'Men, feminism, and men's contradictory experiences of power', in Harry Brod and Michael Kaufman (eds), *Theorizing Masculinities* (Thousand Oaks, CA: SAGE Publications, 1994), pp. 141–62, at 145.

20. Purdie, 'Medieval romance and the generic frictions', p. 69.

21. Sonja Cameron, 'Chivalry and warfare in Barbour's *Bruce*', in Matthew Strickland (ed.), *Armies, Chivalry and Warfare in Medieval Britain and France* (Stamford: Paul Watkins, 1998), pp. 13–29, at 21.

22. Robin Frame, *Ireland and Britain, 1170–1450* (London: Hambledon, 1998), p. 75.

23. Colm McNamee, *The Wars of the Bruces: Scotland, England and Ireland 1306–1328* (East Linton: Tuckwell Press, 1997), p. 198.

24. Frame, *Ireland and Britain*, p. 84.

25. Kaufman, 'Men, feminism, and men's contradictory experiences', p. 147.

26. Sergi Mainer, *The Scottish Romance Tradition c. 1375–c. 1550: Nation, Chivalry and Knighthood* (Amsterdam: Rodopi, 2010), pp. 169–75.

27. The most famous illustration of this is probably Lancelot in Chrétien de Troyes' *Chevalier de la Charrette*.

28. Even if they have a more prominent role than in *The Bruce*, this functional role of women is also present in *The Wallace*. See Inge Milfull, 'War and truce: women in *The Wallace*', in Sarah Dunnigan, C. Marie Harker and Evelyn S. Newlyn (eds), *Woman and The Feminine in Medieval and Early Modern Scottish Writing* (Basingstoke: Palgrave, 2004), pp. 19–30.

29. Sarah Kay, *The Chansons de Geste in the Age of Romance: Political Fictions* (Oxford: Clarendon Press, 1995), pp. 4–5.

30. Mainer, *Scottish Romance Tradition*, p. 262.

31. Tyson Pugh, *Sexuality and its Queer Discontents in Middle English Literature* (Basingstoke: Palgrave Macmillan, 2008), p. 102.

32. Johan Huizinga, *The Waning of the Middle Ages* (London: Penguin, 1990), p. 6.

33. Katherine Goodland, *Female Mourning and Tragedy in Medieval and Renaissance English Drama* (Aldershot and Burlington: Ashgate, 2006), p. 32.

34. Nancy A. Jones, 'By woman's tears redeemed: female lament in Saint Augustine's *Confessions* and the correspondence of Abelard and Heloise', in Barbara K. Gold, Paul Allen Miller and Charles Platter (eds), *Sex and Gender in Medieval and Renaissance Texts: The Latin Tradition* (Albany: State University of New York Press, 1997), pp. 15–39, at 15–16.

35. I prefer to use the original Occitan term, *fin'amors*, as opposed to its English (mis)translation as 'courtly love' because the original keeps the extramarital transgressive nature of its beginning in troubadour poetry as a kind of love that could even challenge *caritas*, the love of God. Its later evolution in *romans courtois*, however, could also lead to marriage.

36. Bernice W. Kliman, 'The idea of chivalry in Barbour's *Bruce*', *Medieval Studies*, 35 (1973), pp. 477–508, at 480.

37. Barbour justifies the use of this unchivalrous tactic by the king, by using Bruce's nephew, Thomas Randolph, Earl of Moray, to question such military strategy, which is then validated by the urgency of the Wars of Independence (Mainer, *Scottish Romance Tradition*, pp. 162–3). See also Purdie, 'Medieval romance and the generic frictions', pp. 69–70.

38. In his *Buke of the Governaunce of Princis*, Gilbert Hay claims: 'Tharfore suld na realms be gevin in governaunce to nane bot to thame that war fulfillit of vertues to governe the peple, and namely into justice' (Gilbert of the Haye, *Gilbert of the Haye's Prose Manuscripts*, J. H. Stevenson (ed.), 2 vols (Edinburgh: Scottish Text Society, 1901–14), II. 145. Although this quotation does not refer specifically to a king's conduct on the battlefield, a king should show his capability to defend and govern his people. A proper pitched battle is the perfect environment to demonstrate his leadership and ability to protect his subjects.

39. Arthur Flannigan-Saint-Aubin, 'The male body and literary metaphors for masculinity', in Brod and Kaufman (eds), *Theorizing Masculinities*, pp. 239–58, at 241.

40. Joachim Schwend, 'Religion and religiosity in *The Bruce*', in Dietrich Strauss and Horst W. Drescher (eds), *Scottish Language and Literature* (Frankfurt: Peter Lang, 1986), pp. 207–16, at 208.

41. George Eyre-Todd relates the finding of what was supposed to be Bruce's grave in the Abbey Church of Dunfermline in the early years of the nineteenth century. Once the skeleton had been unearthed, witnesses related that its breastbone had been sawn through. John Barbour, *The Bruce*, George Eyre-Todd (trans.) (Edinburgh: Mercat Press, 1996), p. 358 [note].

42. In Book I, Edward I leaves an unhistorical crusade to be the arbiter of the Scottish succession (I. 137–40). Barbour invents this episode to discredit the English king as a Christian monarch.

43. R. D. S. Jack, '"A! Fredome is a noble thing": Christian hermeneutics and Barbour's *Bruce*', *Scottish Studies Review*, 1 (2000), pp. 26–38, at 34.

7

Negotiating Independence:
Manliness and Begging Letters in Late Eighteenth- and Early Nineteenth-Century Scotland

Katie Barclay

To THE MODERN READER, begging appears an unmanly act. The association of modern manliness, and indeed the modern individual, with independence, self-sufficiency, 'breadwinning' or 'provision', and equality and fraternity locates the dependency of the beggar in unmasculine, even feminine, territory. Relying on another, the beggar is placed as unable to help himself, affirming his 'lack' and his subordinate place in the social hierarchy. Such a positioning of the self is challenging for modern historians who, as individuals, resist dependency, seeing it as a threat to autonomous selfhood. While feminist and postmodernist scholars challenge such discourses of autonomy, celebrating the benefits of embracing the other to our sense of identity and to understanding historical selves, we still find it difficult to apply such analysis to deeply hierarchical relationships, where one self appears so vulnerable, so reliant on the benevolence – the exercise of power – of the powerful. As feminists, we resist the implication that dependency (so closely tied to femininity) is 'negative', that reliance on the other makes us less; yet we seem drawn to place more emphasis on agency, on resistance, on negotiation, than on the ways in which dependency shapes the self.[1]

Reflecting this, the history of beggars has not viewed them as entirely helpless. Begging has been located amongst a range of strategies that men and women used to make ends meet, to survive in times of economic downturn, or to further their families' social mobility.[2] As Tim Hitchcock notes, begging in the eighteenth century was an acknowledged social practice that located beggars within the community and endowed them with particular rights.[3] In this framework, begging was less a form of debasement of the self than a method of negotiation within particular power structures.

Understanding begging as a social practice is useful for a study of early modern and modernising Britain, where social and political equality was far from the idealised social structure. By the late eighteenth century, there was growing emphasis on individual character and independence as the basis of economic and political rights, supported by a tolerance of the socially mobile and the spread of democratic ideals. Yet this should not be overstated. Allegiance to hierarchical social structure and belief in its importance to social stability was mainstream.[4] The fulfilment of paternal responsibility towards the less fortunate remained a key evidence of patriarchal manhood, and the right to bestow patronage endured as a central privilege and benefit of landownership, political power, wealth and particular occupational and civil service roles.[5]

While understandings of social order, and masculinity in relation to social order, underwent reformulation, there remained considerable space for begging in late eighteenth- and early nineteenth-century Britain, especially when conceived broadly to embrace not only the requests of the very poor but those seeking patrons to find them work, positions in the military, apprenticeships for children, and similar.[6] Here 'beggar' incorporated not only those who sought alms on the street or at doors, but also those making petitions for patronage and charity from individuals and institutions.

Individual charity and patronage was particularly important in Scotland, where the poor relief system was less institutionalised than in England. While parishes had a legal obligation to support the poor, the definition of the poor, levels of support, and who was expected to pay the bill remained contentious issues across the eighteenth century.[7] Until the mid-nineteenth century, poor relief was commonly funded by voluntary and charitable payments, rather than regular taxation.[8] Begging on the street – particularly by vagrants, or those without parish residence – was criminalised and discouraged by early policing. At times of economic downturn or poor harvest, this system was particularly problematic as demand for relief exceeded available funds. During such periods, the poor were given permission to beg in the streets of their own parishes, while the charitable and voluntary nature of the system encouraged personal approaches to landowners and other wealthy individuals to intervene with aid for the needy. Such frameworks for charitable giving and patronage reinforced traditional power structures well into the nineteenth century, requiring both patrons and beggars to invest in a particular form of social hierarchy. As R. A. Houston notes, charitable social relationships were played out in begging letters, where Scottish petitioners were less likely to use the language of rights than their English counterparts.[9] While it was a system that placed those asking in a subordinate role, patronage operated reciprocally to vest power in the patron, reinforcing the mutually beneficial nature of the relationship.

Given this, how men constructed their 'self' in the begging letter raises interesting questions. In an English context, Alannah Tomkins demonstrates how devastating the disability brought by illness and injury could be to male paupers' sense of masculinity, and charts the traces of psychological distress they displayed in the letters that they wrote to poor boards. Yet illness also provided a language to justify their need and to defend against their failure as providers and so as men.[10] Joanne Bailey notes the importance of provisioning to male and female identity in English pauper letters (challenging the notion that this was an exclusively masculine ideal for the labouring classes), as well as how they drew on a language of sensibility to locate themselves as loving, nurturing parents.[11] While these men were unable to achieve economic independence, affectionate fatherhood provided another outlet for the display and performance of masculine identity.

These studies provide insights into how men articulated their manliness in particular contexts, but both focus on how men resisted being labelled 'unmanly' through their 'positive' or defensive articulations of themselves as men and as fathers. Such discussions disentangle particular components of men's begging practices as articulations of masculinity within an act that is either explicitly or implicitly assumed to be unmanly. Part of this may be due to a tension that lies between masculine ideals (sometimes articulated as models of hegemonic masculinity) versus male behaviours and social practices that do not or cannot conform to the ideal.[12] Yet no society has a single 'ideal' for masculine behaviour, with models influenced by social class, religion and sexuality as well as personal choice. In hierarchical societies, it makes little sense for masculinity to be patterned on one form of values or behaviours, given that broader social expectations relied on people 'knowing their place' and performing to that place, through behaviour, dress and other forms of consumption, education and social values.

It is more helpful to think about masculinity in terms of performance or social practice, where all male behaviour becomes implicated in the construction of masculinity – although not all performances may be perceived, either by the actor himself or those around him, as successful.[13] Such an approach encourages an exploration of not only behaviours that are perceived as 'positive' assertions of maleness, but also those that challenge hegemonic ideals, opening up insights into the multiple and complex ways that men construct their sense of self and allowing reflection on, and re-articulation of, the 'ideal'. It allows for a more sensitive rendering of power relations between men and between men and women, with its focus on the operation of power not just at the level of representation, but in everyday life.

This chapter explores begging as an arena for the performance of manly identity with a particular focus on men's use of the language of deference and gratitude in their requests for aid from other men. As is discussed below, such performances required the use of rhetorical strategies that explicitly recognised the hierarchical social relationship between those giving and those receiving help. The chapter reassesses this language and explores its implications for the masculine identities of both writer and recipient. It places a particular emphasis on the word 'gratitude', as a key emotional concept used to articulate and perform a particular mode of masculinity. This is not to say that 'gratitude' did not appear in letters written to or received by women negotiating a patronage relationship, but it appears that gender played an important role in how writers constructed their claims for help.[14]

THE 'BEGGING' LETTER

A historiography of the pauper begging letter is now well established in an English context. Historians have demonstrated the utility of such letters not only as evidence for the operation of poor relief, but as a source for poor people's general experiences, including those of unemployment, ill health, medical practices, disability and family relationships.[15] Aware of the paucity of sources for the voices of the poor, they have been keen to explore a source that is at least written by or for them, rather than about them. Yet historians of the poor have been more anxious than most historians of the letter in trying to disentangle the rhetoric of the begging form from the 'authentic' feelings and experiences of the poor themselves – a concern heightened by the fact that a number of these letters were written by scribes, whether literate family members or officials. It is now almost ubiquitous to begin a work using such sources with a disclaimer that we can only access the 'mediated voices of the poor', or more optimistically that 'a few pauper letters raise issues of "authorship"', or even 'rhetorical elements must not be regarded in any way interfering with their "true" substantive message', a focus that has placed considerable emphasis on the analysis of form.[16]

Thus we know that it was typical of pauper letters to poor relief overseers to combine some variety of polite and deferent entreaties for help from those in authority, with specific details of illness or circumstances, veiled threats to return home or to become a greater burden on the parish, assertions of moral or legal rights to relief, and promises not to bother the recipient in the future.[17] It is also evident that rhetorical strategies were shaped by gender, age and region, and that people shared successful strategies with each other to improve their success rates.[18] Given that many of the claims made in these letters were investigated by benefactors and their agents, it is also clear that what was stated about their circumstances was largely true and that some groups regularly had successful outcomes.[19]

These findings situate this branch of the historiography easily within the latest work on letter writing as a historical source, which emphasises the genre rules that guide its form and the ways that writers were educated to use them.[20] Yet while this has implications for the 'authenticity' of voice within any letter, historians of the letter (rather than the poor) are less concerned with the role of form in mediating experience. Rather than viewing this as a question of 'authenticity', letter writing is located as a social practice. The letter is not (and could never be) the free expression of the soul, but a performance that is shaped by the context in which the letter is written, the genre rules that inform writing in that context, as well as the writer's relationship with the reader. It becomes a space to construct identity, whether that is as a man, a father, a provider or a beggar; that construction always involves more than one person, with identity informed by the reader, wider society, and, where appropriate, those that aid in writing the letter.[21]

Most of the literature on begging letters draws on the papers that survive for English poor relief boards or charitable institutions.[22] A notable exception is Houston's *Peasant Petitions* that compares petitions from tenants to their landlords across the United Kingdom. His work provides a comprehensive introduction to this source and its uses in the making of rural class relationships. This chapter similarly uses letters written to private individuals, mostly Scottish landowners or other wealthy elites, by those seeking various forms of help, from alms to more sophisticated forms of patronage, between c. 1760 and 1830. They survive in estate papers, collated either in separate files as collections of petitions and begging letters, or interspersed amongst general correspondence.[23] It is apparent that some individuals, perhaps a considerable number of the Scottish elite, were regularly sent requests for help and treated them seriously as part of the responsibility that went with their social role.[24] Landowners typically received letters from those that lived on their estates and in nearby towns, urban dwellers from the local poor. Both received letters from those with whom they had previous relationships, such as merchants, servants and political clients, as well as random requests from across Britain – a group that were often viewed suspiciously as 'professional beggars' or 'frauds'.[25] While these categories could include kin, this chapter focuses on relationships where fulfilling familial obligation was not the primary mode of persuasion used by the writer.

Letters asking for help were written by a range of social groups, including paupers, the elderly and ill, tenants, merchants and other middling people. What they had in common was their need for patronage from the elite, who often filed their letters together – how social distinctions played out in letter writing will be explored below. As the letters were written between named individuals, rather than from the poor to social institutions, writers needed to take account of the identity of the recipient and to create or rejuvenate a personal relationship with her or him. This was particularly notable in Scotland, where Houston observes that references to a personal service relationship between petitioners and landlords was a distinctive petitioning strategy.[26]

I REST YOUR HUMBLE AND OBEDIENT SERVANT

Begging letters to the Scottish elite generally took two forms: the official petition and the personal letter. By the late eighteenth century, both genres had established rules that determined structure and content, and which were taught widely in school and through the circulation of formal conduct books.[27] The petition was a widely used form, where individuals or groups sought aid or intervention from the powerful. Political petitioning was a key form of democratic engagement for the disenfranchised, acknowledged as a legitimate form of expressing political opinion.[28] Personal petitions were more narrowly conceived, usually desiring intervention for individuals, whether that was a reprieve from a criminal sentence or aid for a starving family. Yet they can be situated with formal political petitioning, both in adopting the same structure and in acting as a commentary on contemporary affairs.

Structurally, the petition differed from a letter in that the opening was usually centred on the page (rather than set to the left), addressing the full name and title of the patron, and introducing the petitioner. Finlay McDiarmid opened his, 'To the Right Honble the Earl of Breadalbane The Representation and Petition of Finlay McDiarmid, late Servant & Now Cottar in Murlagan beg of Glenlochy'.[29] This was followed by 'Humbly Sheweth', usually set alone, and sometimes in the margin, with a space above and beneath. The petition then followed, normally but not always in the third person. At times, the petition was written by a scribe, who sometimes made observations on the case; at others, the petition moves between the first and third person, suggestive of the tensions of telling a personal narrative in this form. Generally, the document introduced the petitioner's circumstances and need, and the relationship to the patron (and why they are the appropriate patron), before proposing the desired solution. Petitions concluded with the phrase 'he will forever pray &c'.[30]

Personal letters were similar and some adopted the structure of the petition within the frame of a letter. Letters written to men typically began 'Dear Sir', unless another title was required due to rank, such as 'My Lord Duke'. People used the expected form taught within conduct manuals for formal letter writing.[31] Internally, letters varied more than petitions, depending on the relationship between the writer and reader. Where there were few existing ties, personal letters resembled petitions in content and structure. Where a previous relationship existed, there might be references to past or ongoing conversations, the well-being of mutual friends and acquaintances, business, and the sharing of local news or gossip. Unlike petitions, letters were written in the first person. Authors usually finished with some version of 'I remain your grace's most dutifull and very humble servant', 'your lords most obedient and very humble servant', 'your obligd Humble Servant'.[32]

Formal addresses and subscriptions were not mere formalities, but, as argued elsewhere, actively shaped the dynamics of the relationship between reader and writer.[33] Petitions were generally written by people in desperate circumstances, who needed basic aid to survive, whether that was food, money or accommodation (typically in the form of rent relief). They had little to offer the recipient other than prayers in return for their charity, and the signature 'he will forever pray &c' acknowledged that (at least at that time) they could not even provide the service offered by the 'humble servant'. The petitioning format formalised their requests for help, while the use of the third person distanced their claims from personal requests, giving them weight as 'truthful' or 'factual'. This was often reinforced by character references from local notables, kirk elders or poor law officials.[34] In petitioning, the poor claimed the authority that the petition held within the British polity, demanding the reader take it seriously. Not all petitions were granted. Yet if archival practices can be used as evidence of their significance, the Scottish elites, or their representatives, like those south of the border, gave serious consideration to such requests, often citing the reasons for refusal briefly on the petition and in some cases sending factors to investigate claims.[35] It appears that petitions, and so petitioners, could not simply be ignored.

The offer to pray is worth commenting on further. As Houston notes, prayer involved both bodily posture and a 'submissive heart'; it was a form of aspiration and an expression of thanks that transformed 'political dependence into the humility of religious reverence'.[36] Within a Catholic context, such prayers had active utility in speeding the movement of the dead from purgatory to heaven, or, for the living, in reducing their time in purgatory later. Prayer was an act of charity towards the dead and viewed as a reciprocal exchange between the praying poor and the patron, although benefits to the latter accrued in the afterlife. Protestants rejected purgatory and with it prayers for the dead, although the latter continued in practice.[37] Prayers offered by the poor in this context were for the continued well-being and success of the patron and his family in the present; prayer was intended to ensure the continuing social order.

In offers to pray was an implicit, and sometimes explicit, acknowledgement of a commitment on the behalf of the petitioner to remain in their subordinate role. John Campbell of Edramucky finished his: 'May it please your Lordship to take the promises in consideration and order the Petitioner such Relieff and assistance as to your Lordship shall appear reasonable, and he will forever pray &c'.[38] Although perhaps unintentional, this run on sentence suggested that Campbell's prayers were the reward for the Earl of Breadalbane's 'Relieff and assistance'. Alexander Loutit noted: 'It shall ever be my study and care, to continue deserving of your humane patronage, and in duty bound I shale for ever pray'.[39] Loutit's prayers arose from a duty that patronage bound him within. Without such patronage, there was no such duty. By locating this social relationship within a religious context, writers placed their call for aid within a Christian framework where the rich man was rewarded for charity through God's mercy, giving moral weight to the duties that bound men together.

Personal letters were also written by the poorest in society and could contain promises to pray for patrons. William Sinclair concluded his letter 'may god kepe your honer long well and may he allwais find his faver'.[40] Yet the formal subscription of 'I rest your humble and obedient servant', which was the expected closing for such letters, suggested a slightly different dynamic. As a subscription, it was used widely in a great range of relationships, from business partners to siblings to strangers requesting help. Its broad usage has led to it being dismissed as little more than polite rhetoric, 'artifice, flattery and deference'.[41] The range of people that described themselves as 'humble servants' cautions against reading this subscription as entirely sycophantic.

The service relationship was not limited to master and servant, but was an expected component of all 'friendships', where 'friend' incorporated a broad range of social ties.[42] The use of 'servant' was a simple acknowledgement that affective social relationships – whether between spouses, kin, business partners or wider friends – incorporated practical, often economic, duties or 'services'. The adjective 'humble' reflected the esteem, real or pretended, in which the writer held the recipient. 'Humble' held two meanings – one was 'low; not high; not great' and was generally used to refer to the poor. The other meaning, the first meaning in Johnson's dictionary, was 'not proud; modest; not arrogant' and was a key Christian virtue.[43] Christian humility required people to 'esteem others better than yourself', to show love and charity for neighbours, to show appropriate sociability.[44] It required an 'act of submission' of the self in its displacement of pride and selfishness, but it was not expected to undermine social relationships, rather to impress people with their duties and responsibilities towards their fellow man. This meaning was reinforced when coupled with the word 'servant', which suggested the shared Christian community of God's servants.[45] 'Humble servants' embedded themselves within a complex set of social relationships that demanded the mutual fulfilment of duties, charity and care, according to social position.

When those writing begging letters used this subscription, they were declaring themselves part of this broader affective community, not effacing the self in any simple way. That the poor interpreted their relationships with the elite in this way was also evident in references to charity and service within the body of the letter. A common rhetorical strategy used by men and women was to locate their appeal for help as a request for charity, and to emphasise the spiritual and temporal benefits of charity to the patron as well as the poor. This often incorporated significant flattery of the patron, reminding him of his duty to be charitable. The observation of the poor widow Elizabeth Glas to the Duke of Buccleuch that 'constantly hearing that your exalted noble character is blessed with every humane generous feeling has emboldened me to venture to lay my situation before your grace' was not dissimilar to the recent medical graduate P. MacDermott's comment that:

> I was reading in the newspapers some pleasing anecdotes of your generosity so well becoming the heir of a splendid fortune, therefore I am led to hope that my request will be graciously considered by the representative of the noble House of Buccleuch, the members of which have always been high-minded and generous.[46]

Or indeed from the university student Charles Clark's 'knowing that your Grace is the Patron of that which is generous liberal and good and being a distinguished nobleman of Scotland'.[47]

John Campbell felt assured that the Earl of Breadlbane would 'in your well known humanity, deem him a proper object of commiserations and charity', while Dr William Sinclair of Lochend was challenged about his generosity when Donald Ogg angrily wrote: 'I rely [sic] thought that there was more Charity in your heart till now.'[48] Patrons were reminded of their reputation for 'generosity', 'humanity' and 'charity', as well as that of their kin, locating their charitableness within a range of activities that provided glory and status to the broader family and themselves. Charity brought reciprocal benefits to both parties.

Charitable behaviour did not just enhance the giver's reputation amongst the poor, but provided real spiritual and temporal benefits that were refracted along gendered lines. A number of women called upon their patrons to 'take up the Cause of the widow and the father-less now as at other times', tying this biblical command closely to a spiritual blessing.[49] Joan Robertson wrote to the Duke of Buccleuch 'May the blissings of god even be with you for your former kindness to me – your Nobel graces will have the widow and the fathelas bliss-ing'.[50] Isobel Grant was more effusive in writing to a female patron, observing that:

> And as I am not in a Capacity to Retaillerate your Good offices. I hope the almighty who is a husband to the widow & father to the fatherless will . . . concluding with not only my best wishes and my blessing . . .; May it be Gods will to prosper all of you well your undertakings and that he may go pleas'd to send your honourable Ladyship such an Honourable Fortune, as you deserve and your Petitioner shall ever pray.[51]

Women, especially widows, recognising either the reality or the cultural expectation that they would not be in a position to repay charity were much more likely to locate the benefits of answering their requests in spiritual terms – a strategy that also allowed them to draw on their cul-tural capital as 'deserving poor'.

In contrast, men sidelined discussions of God's blessings. Men who were very poor, and particularly the elderly, usually avoided the topic of repayment, beyond their formal acknowledgement to pray. Younger men and those seeking patronage for work or similar, were more likely to acknowledge explicitly that this 'humble servant' meant to dem-onstrate their service. The wright George Home, when seeking to go into business, hoped that his namesake, George Home of Wedderburn, would give him £50, which 'if complied with will entail upon me the most lasting obligation to you for such a great favour'.[52] W. Lindley explicitly observed:

> if your Humanity could *for the last* assist me it would render me happy and something may turn out as put me in a way to return your Goodness. I am awar my Lord Humanity may be ill aid [paid?] But depend it will not be so by me for my Heart Bleeds within me to be troublesome.[53]

While unable to specify how they would return their patron's charity, both men sought to stress that this request would create a reciprocally beneficial relationship.

For a number of men and particularly those from a slightly higher social background, demonstrating their sense of obligation was considered to be an important aspect of 'gratitude'. Ruth Perry notes that in the late eighteenth century, literary representations of charity, at least, focused more on the giver than the recipient. It is the 'inner life' of the generous 'that is supposed to interest the reader, not that of the recently relieved poor. *Their* hyperbolic gratitude is taken for granted; gratitude is presumed to be a less interesting emotion than the exquisite feelings of the giver.'[54] This might explain why charitable patrons were so often located as generous heroes, but, as Houston notes, it underestimates the importance placed on gratitude within wider society, particularly as a mode for ensuring social order. The Irish landlord Richard Warburton observed that 'gratitude will oblidge tenants ye more to honour and esteeme their landlord'.[55]

In an eighteenth-century context, gratitude was understood less in terms of feeling than action. Samuel Johnson defined gratitude as, first, 'duty to benefactors' and second, 'desire to return benefits'.[56] By 1835, James Barclay's dictionary placed more emphasis on feeling, with duty as a secondary meaning: 'a virtue, consisting in a due sense and outward acknowledgement of a benefit received, together with a readiness to return the same, or the like. Duty to a benefactor'.[57] The emphasis on 'duty' tied gratitude into social relationships. Duty was not just an obligation to which men were bound (Johnson's first definition), but the 'obedience and submission due to parents, governours, or superiors; loyalty', and an 'act of reverence and respect'.[58] Gratitude was a social emotional practice that combined the desire to fulfil reciprocal obligations with appropriate awareness of the social relationship between benefactor and recipient and was marked by a suitable emotional display and behaviour. Like the begging letter itself, which combined the identities of both writer and reader, it was an act that created a hierarchical social bond, and emphasised the mutual benefits of that connection.

Because of these semantic connotations, gratitude was an emotion that acted as an offering in an exchange relationship. William Campbell was 'mortified' to learn that his thanks to a patron for procuring his son a job in the excise had not been transmitted to him. Defending himself, he wrote:

> I am truly concerned at what you state regarding my want of gratitude ..., I immediately, as in duty bound, wrote a letter of thanks to you, and begged of you the additional favour as above stated, for I abhor, and detest Ingratitude in whomsoever it is found.[59]

He emphasised his awareness of gratitude as a 'duty' to be fulfilled, and its social importance in its own right. On his son receiving a commission in the army, James Wingate observed:

> my feelings I cannot suppress, the only recompense which I can or ever may have it in my power to offer, is gratitude, but if at any future period, I can be of the least use to your Lordship or any of your family, I shall esteem it an honour to be of the smallest service.[60]

Wingate offered gratitude as 'recompense', a form of compensation for patronage, in addition to his offer of future service. For both men, gratitude was articulated as a useful commodity on its own, not only due to the future promise of service that it implied.

At least in part, the utility of gratitude was due to its commitment to social hierarchies. P. MacDermott argued the reciprocal benefits of gratitude explicitly in his letter:

> I am but an humble individual as a young physician, I flatter myself that I possess talents to raise me to some eminence in my profession, and hope it will yet be in my power to testify my gratitude to your Grace in a suitable manner.[61]

MacDermott notes that his expected future prominence in his profession would allow him to make a return of service, but also that he would 'testify my gratitude', a particularly evocative phrase, implying not only that he would prove his gratitude through reciprocal return but act as witness to his patron's benevolence – a beacon for the patronage relationship. In this, gratitude reinforced social hierarchies, but like prayer and humble service, it emphasised that the patronage relationship did not only flow in one direction.

OF MANLINESS AND GRATITUDE: CONCLUSION

While the deferent structure of the begging letter has so often been dismissed as strategy or as a layer that detracts from the 'authentic' self of the beggar, the letter structure reflected and created the relationship between patron and client. It demarcated a social world that relied on people knowing their place in a hierarchical order and so asked men to perform different social roles in relation to each other, and to display such roles in their writing. Yet while reinforcing traditional social structures, the begging letter also emphasised the importance of reciprocity. Humble servants provided service whether they were members of the social elite or the poorest peasant, because it was a duty of charitable Christians and because it reinforced the power of the giver. Beggars knew this and utilised a language of gratitude that reflected the mutuality of their relationship, aware and possibly hoping that they too could be called on to perform their part in an exchange relationship.

For the very poorest and for many women, with little possibility of offering a practical fulfilment of the obligations created by charity, duty could be fulfilled through prayer for patrons – an action that provided a service in the form of seeking a spiritual blessing, but also enforced their acknowledgement of the current social order. In so doing, the democratic potential of the petition, which provided the petitioner with the authority of the British political tradition, was held in check, enforcing the duties and social place of both patron and client. Other men could attempt to fulfil their obligation in practical ways; in doing so, they positioned themselves as holding greater social power than the very poor, while also promising to uphold the current system of social order.

Given this, analyses of the begging letter that distinguish manly activities from unmanly dependence miss the nuances of how social dependency informed structures of masculinity. Acknowledging one's social position in a hierarchical system was not a denial of self, but a recognition of self within a sociable community. Gratitude provided poor men with a language to assert their own role within the social order, to acknowledge the benefits that such an order accrued to the social elite, and which they ensured through their cooperation within that system – it allowed them to highlight that dependency operated in both directions. While this was also true for women, the gendered performance of gratitude provided men with more space to demonstrate this quality and consequently with greater levels of social authority than those who did not have this opportunity. Yet through their prayers, this was a system where even the very poor had a place.

NOTES

This research was funded by the Australian Research Council DE140100111.

1. Alison Mackinnon, 'Fantasizing the family: women, families and the quest for an individual self', *Women's History Review*, 15 (2006), pp. 663–75; Sal Renshaw, *The Subject of Love: Hélène Cixous and the Feminine Divine* (Manchester: Manchester University Press, 2009); Gilles Deleuze, *Difference and Repetition* (London: Continuum, 1994).
2. Tim Hitchcock, 'Locating beggars on the streets of eighteenth-century London', in Kim Kippen and Lori Woods (eds), *Worth and Repute: Valuing Gender in Late Medieval and Early Modern Europe: Essays in Honour of Barbara Todd* (Toronto: University of Toronto, 2011), pp. 73–92; M. J. D. Roberts, 'Reshaping the gift relationship: the London Mendicity Society and the suppression of begging in England, 1818–1869', *International Review of Social History*, 36 (1991), pp. 201–31.
3. Tim Hitchcock, 'Begging on the streets of eighteenth-century London', *Journal of British Studies*, 44 (2005), pp. 478–98.
4. Matthew McCormack, *The Independent Man: Citizenship and Gender Politics in Georgian England* (Manchester: Manchester University Press, 2005); Katie Barclay, 'Manly magistrates and citizenship in an Irish town: Carlow, 1820–1840', in Krista Cowman, Nina Koefoed and Åsa Karlsson Sjögren (eds), *Gender in Urban Europe: Sites of Political Activity and Citizenship, 1750–1900* (London: Routledge, 2014), pp. 58–72.
5. Trev Lynn Broughton, 'Promoting a life: patronage, masculinity and Philip Meadows Taylor's *The Story of My Life*', in David Amigoni (ed.), *Life Writing and Victorian Culture* (Aldershot: Ashgate 2006), pp. 105–21; Alison Duncan, 'Patronage and presentations of the self: a late eighteenth-century correspondence' (unpublished master's dissertation, University of Edinburgh, 2008); Ellen Gill, '"Children of the service": paternalism, patronage and friendship in the Georgian navy', *Journal for Maritime Research*, 15:2 (2013), pp. 149–65.
6. For masculinity and social order in Scotland, see Lynn Abrams, 'The taming of Highland masculinity: interpersonal violence and shifting codes of manhood, c. 1760–1840', *Scottish Historical Review*, 92 (2013), pp. 100–22 and Chapter 4 in this collection; Rosalind Carr, *Gender and Enlightenment Culture in Eighteenth-Century Scotland* (Edinburgh: Edinburgh University Press, 2014); Susan Broomhall and David Barrie, 'Changing of the guard: governance, policing, masculinity and class in the Porteous affair and Walter Scott's Heart of Midlothian', *Parergon*, 28:1 (2011), pp. 65–90; Anna Clark, *The Struggle for the Breeches: Gender and the Making of the British Working Class* (Berkeley: University of California Press, 1995).
7. Rosalind Mitchison, *The Old Poor Law in Scotland: The Experience of Poverty, 1574–1845* (Edinburgh: Edinburgh University Press, 2000).

8. Ibid. pp. 158–9.

9. R. A. Houston, *Peasant Petitions: Social Relations and Economic Life on Landed Estates, 1600–1850* (Basingstoke: Palgrave Macmillan, 2014), p. 182.

10. Alannah Tomkins, '"Labouring on a bed of sickness": the material and rhetorical deployment of ill health in male pauper letters', in Andreas Gestrich, Elizabeth Hurren and Steven King (eds), *Poverty and Sickness in Modern Europe: Narratives of the Sick Poor, 1780–1938* (London: Continuum, 2012), pp. 51–68.

11. Joanne Bailey, '"Think wot a mother must feel": parenting in English pauper letters', *Family & Community History*, 13:1 (2010), pp. 5–19.

12. Raewyn Connell, 'Hegemonic masculinity: rethinking the concept', *Gender & Society*, 19 (2005), pp. 829–59; Leslie McCall, 'The complexity of intersectionality', in Davina Cooper (ed.), *Intersectionality and Beyond: Law, Power and the Politics of Location* (Oxon: Routledge-Cavendish, 2009), pp. 49–76.

13. Judith Butler, 'Gender as performance', in Peter Osborne (ed.), *A Critical Sense: Interviews with Intellectuals* (London: Routledge, 1996), pp. 111–12; Chris Brickell, 'Masculinities, performativity, and subversion: a sociological reappraisal', *Men and Masculinities*, 8 (2005), pp. 24–43.

14. Works on female patronage include: Rosalind Carr, 'Women, land and power: a case for continuity', in Katie Barclay and Deborah Simonton (eds), *Women in Eighteenth-Century Scotland: Public, Intellectual and Private Lives* (Farnham: Ashgate, 2013), pp. 193–210; Sharon Kettering, 'The patronage power of early modern French noblewomen', *Historical Journal*, 32:4 (1989), pp. 817–41.

15. Gestrich, Hurren and King (eds), *Poverty and Sickness*; Alannah Tomkins, '"I mak bould to wrigt": first-person narratives in the history of poverty in England, c. 1750–1900', *History Compass*, 9:5 (2011), pp. 365–73; Peter Jones, '"I cannot keep my place without being deascent": pauper letters, parish clothing and pragmatism in the south of England, 1750–1830', *Rural History*, 20:1 (2009), pp. 31–49; K. D. M. Snell, 'Belonging and community: understandings of "home" and "friends" among the English poor, 1750–1850', *Economic History Review*, 65:1 (2012), pp. 1–25; Thomas Sokoll (ed.), *Essex Pauper Letters 1731–1837* (Oxford: Oxford University Press for the British Academy, 2001); Thomas Sokoll, 'Writing for relief: rhetoric in English pauper letters, 1800–1834', in Andreas Gestrich, Steven King and Lutz Raphael (eds), *Being Poor in Modern Europe: Historical Perspectives 1800–1940* (Oxford: Peter Lang, 2006), pp. 91–112; Tim Hitchock, Peter King and Pamela Sharpe (eds), *Chronicling Poverty: The Voices and Strategies of the English Poor, 1640–1840* (Basingstoke: Macmillan, 1997).

16. Andreas Gestrich, Elizabeth Hurren and Steven King, 'Narratives of poverty and sickness in Europe 1780–1938: sources, methods and experiences', in

Gestrich, Hurren and King (eds), *Poverty and Sickness*, pp. 1–33, at 13; Snell, 'Belonging and community', p. 2; Sokoll, 'Writing for relief', p. 108.

17. 'Sokoll, 'Writing for relief'.

18. Steven King, 'Regional patterns in the experiences and treatment of the sick poor, 1800–1840: rights, obligations and duties in the rhetoric of paupers', *Family & Community History*, 10:1 (2007), pp. 61–75.

19. 'Sokoll, 'Writing for relief', p. 106.

20. For example, Martyn Lyons, 'Love letters and writing practices: on *ecritures intimes* in the nineteenth century', *Journal of Family History*, 24 (1999), pp. 232–39; C. Brant, *Eighteenth-Century Letters and British Culture* (Basingstoke: Palgrave Macmillan, 2006); Susan Whyman, *The Pen and the People: English Letter Writers, 1660–1800* (Oxford: Oxford University Press, 2009).

21. Mireille Bossis and Karen McPherson, 'Methodological journeys through correspondences', *Yale French Studies*, 71 (1986), pp. 63–75; Katie Barclay, *Love, Intimacy and Power: Marriage and Patriarchy in Scotland: 1650–1850* (Manchester: Manchester University Press, 2011), pp. 28–30. For discussion of another type of letter, see Chapter 8 by Lynn Abrams in this collection.

22. Notable exceptions are Peter Wessel Hansen, 'Grief, sickness and emotions in the narratives of the shamefaced poor in late eighteenth-century Copenhagen', in Gestrich, Hurren and King (eds), *Poverty and Sickness*, pp. 35–50 and Donna T. Andrew, '*Noblesse oblige*: female charity in an age of sentiment', in John Brewer and Susan Staves (eds), *Early Modern Conceptions of Property* (London: Routledge, 1995), pp. 275–300.

23. These papers are held by the National Records of Scotland [NRS], Edinburgh.

24. Andrews, '*Noblesse oblige*', p. 276.

25. See for example, NRS, Papers of the Montague-Douglas-Scott Family, Dukes of Buccleuch, GD224/588/1/13 Begging Letter Department, Mendicity Office, London to Duke of Buccleuch, 25 March 1828, describing one petitioner as 'wholly undeserving', having 'supported herself for many years by writing begging letters'.

26. Houston, *Peasant Petitions*, pp. 184–5.

27. Whyman, *Pen and the People*, pp. 19–38.

28. David Zaret, *Origins of Democratic Culture: Printing, Petitions and the Public Sphere in Early Modern England* (Princeton: Princeton University Press, 2000).

29. NRS, Breadalbane Muniments, GD112/11/8/16/36, Finlay McDiarmid to Earl of Breadalbane, 26 July 1826.

30. Houston, *Peasant Petitions*, pp. 97–103.

31. Ibid. pp. 94–6.

32. NRS, GD224/588/1/9, John Williamson to Duke of Buccleuch, 2 October 1828; GD112/74/23/10-11, James Wingate to Earl of Breadalbane, 16

November 1811; GD136/524/56, Papers of the Sinclair Family of Freswick, Caithness, John Crear to William Sinclair of Freswick, 24 September 1836.

33. Barclay, *Love, Intimacy and Power*, p. 105.

34. For example, NRS, GD224/588/1/8, George Simmonds to Duke of Buccleuch, 18 September 1828; GD112/11/8/16/36.

35. For example, NRS, GD112/11/8/16/36; GD224/588/1/8; GD224/588/1/32, James Brackenridge to Duke of Buccleuch, 1829; Donna Andrew, '"To the charitable and the humane": appeals for assistance in the eighteenth-century London press', in Hugh Cunningham and Joanna Innes (eds), *Charity, Philanthropy and Reform: From the 1690s to 1850* (Basingstoke: Macmillan Press, 1998), pp. 87–107, at 91–5.

36. Houston, *Peasant Petitions*, p. 98.

37. For an extended discussion, see Ralph Houlbrooke, *Death, Religion and the Family in England, 1480–1750* (Oxford: Clarendon Press, 1998).

38. NRS, GD112/11/1/6/65, John Campbell to Earl of Breadalbane, September 1788.

39. NRS, GD136/524/204 Alexander Loutit to William Sinclair of Freswick, October 1820.

40. NRS, GD136/524/394 William Sinclair to William Sinclair of Freswick [c. 1824–6].

41. Whyman, *Pen and the People*, p. 22.

42. Naomi Tadmor, 'The concept of the household-family in eighteenth-century England', *Past and Present*, 151 (1996), pp. 111–40.

43. Samuel Johnson, *A Dictionary of the English Language* (Dublin: W. G. Jones, 1768), unpaginated, see 'humble'.

44. Gardiner Spring, *Essays on the Distinguishing Traits of Christian Character* (Boston: Samuel Armstrong, 1819), p. 116.

45. Houston, *Peasant Petitions*, p. 103.

46. NRS, GD224/588/1/17, Elizabeth Glas to Duke of Buccleuch, 24 October 1828; GD224/588/1/3, P. MacDermott to Duke of Buccleuch, 28 July 1828.

47. NRS, GD224/588/1/6, Charles Clark to Duke of Buccleuch, September 1828.

48. NRS, GD112/11/1/6/65; GD136/435/241, Donald Ogg to Dr William Sinclair of Lochend, 21 August 1794.

49. NRS, GD136/524/43, Margaret Campbell to William Sinclair of Freswick [c. 1816–38].

50. NRS, GD224/588/1/14, Joan Robertson to Duke of Buccleuch, 5 December 1828.

51. NRS, Seafield Papers, GD248/371/4/32, Isobel Grant to 'Miss Grant' [c. 1762–88].

52. NRS, Home of Wedderburn, GD267/12/1, George Home to George Home of Wedderburn, 12 April 1817.

53. NRS, GD112/74/23/15–16, W. Lindley to Earl of Breadalbane, 23 November 1811.
54. Ruth Perry, 'Home economics: representations of poverty in eighteenth-century fiction', in Paula R. Backscheider and Catherine Ingrassia (eds), *A Companion to the Eighteenth-Century English Novel and Culture* (Oxford: Blackwell Publishing, 2009), pp. 441–58, at 449.
55. Houston, *Peasant Petitions*, p. 131.
56. Johnson, *Dictionary*, unpaginated, see 'gratitude'.
57. James Barclay, *Barclay's New Universal English Dictionary* (London: H. Fisher, R. Fisher, & P. Jackson, 1835), p. 433.
58. Johnson, *Dictionary*, unpaginated, see 'duty'.
59. NRS, GD136/524/45 William Campbell to William Sinclair of Freswick, 12 November 1830.
60. NRS, GD112/74/23/10–11.
61. NRS, GD224/588/1/3.

8

A Wartime Family Romance:
Narratives of Masculinity and Intimacy during
World War Two

Lynn Abrams

> Though I haven't written to you for so many days you have been constantly
> in my thoughts. I suspect you must hold a bond on my heart. I miss you I
> think most in the evenings – the Trinidad scene is so colourful & beautiful
> in the late afternoon & early evening light that I yearn to have you by me to
> share the joy of it. Yes, I have to admit that Trinidad can be very beautiful
> – but it needs a 'whole' man to appreciate it – and I'm not a 'whole' when
> I am away from you.[1]

IN DECEMBER 1944, SIX months into his period of military service in
the Caribbean, George Johnstone Brown made his feelings for his wife
explicit. Only with her could he find emotional satisfaction and fulfilment. Wartime service represented an interruption to their life together,
a necessary, dutiful but irritating interlude before they could resume
their married love affair. In this chapter a neglected facet of Scottish
men's sense of self is under scrutiny. Emotional openness, vulnerability,
affection, devotion, romantic love and desire – these are not qualities
commonly identified in the accounts of masculinity in Scotland in the
twentieth century, a history populated by the so-called hard men of the
shipyards and coalmines, the heavy drinkers, the gang members of city
streets and the political heroes, some of whom appear elsewhere in this
book.[2] Historians have tended to portray work, and the leisure activities contingent upon that work, as the key to masculine identity despite
evidence that romantic love and its expression in the couple relationship was a key characteristic of the modern age.[3] The emotional turn
that is shifting historical attention and interpretation away from publicly articulated standards and cultural discourses towards subjectivity
is beginning to recast the historical landscape and has the potential to
complicate and expand understandings of male identities. By recover-
ing articulations of selfhood and emotion, by bringing 'subjectivity and

emotion back into view', historians have begun to write an alternative history of men and masculinity that privileges subjectivity and the self.[4] Using George Brown's sixteen-month epistolary relationship with his wife, this chapter interrogates facets of modern Scottish manhood – emotional literacy and the embrace of intimacy – that rarely find expression outwith the privacy of the one-to-one relationship, and therefore seldom find their way into historical interpretations.

Intimacy in its modern incarnation has been described by Anthony Giddens as a 'pure relationship' based on trust, privileged knowledge and equality, and contingent upon the process of self-reflexivity or an ongoing project of self-construction played out through the practice of disclosure.[5] This model of 'disclosure intimacy' is located in late twentieth-century Western societies coinciding with the late modern project of the self, the striving for self-exploration and an historical moment of relative affluence and economic and political stability.[6] In this conceptualisation, intimacy is a process of connectedness incorporating both emotional and physical disclosure in a relationship that has surpassed mere romantic love and has become a project of mutual self-idealisation. In the case of George Brown we can observe an earlier manifestation of modern intimacy in the context of wartime and absence through the medium of the letter. This chapter shows how male self-narration and disclosure could be liberated by the 'freedom' of wartime; how being positioned within a liminal space – separated from combat but also from everyday life, enveloped within a total institution (the armed forces), thereby at liberty to reflect on himself and forced to sustain his relationships in writing – enabled George Brown to fashion a reflexive self through a narrative of intimacy that predates current interpretations of when this kind of relationship emerged. George Brown encapsulates the modern masculine self who imagined himself in a 'pure relationship' based on commitment and mutuality.[7]

The emotional and intimate lives of men in the past have been rather more impervious to investigation than those of women, in part because the gendered norms of behaviour and opportunities for the expression of affection (as opposed to anger or aggression) were often more limited for men. Even in the twentieth century, when the ideals of emotional restraint were beginning to be questioned in the wake of World War One, when so many men had evidently failed to live up to the tenets of 'manliness' expected of them, it is difficult to chart the ways in which men began to act and think differently.[8] Historians have recently argued that, beginning in the 1920s, the emotional landscape began to alter with mutuality (the privileging of affective relationships founded on mutual

affection and sexual pleasure) superseding hierarchical, patriarchal relationship models.[9] Marriage, according to Claire Langhamer, increasingly
came to offer 'a dynamic emotional connection' and she suggests that
by the 1940s a 'revolution in the value attached to emotional intimacy'
was underway.[10] After World War Two this revolution was almost
complete; self-fulfilment, at least in one's emotional life, was prioritised
over self-restraint, albeit within the heterosexual familial relationship.[11]
Moreover, the interwar years had offered young people far greater freedoms in their social relations; in the 1920s and 1930s romance, leisure,
consumption and youth became 'increasingly entwined', producing a
climate of 'emancipating emotions'.[12] Hollywood films in particular
offered romance narratives, glamour and the language of eroticism as
well as a model of conjugality that 'fused romance, material security,
and self-development'.[13] And although the models of masculinity that
dominated in popular film narratives rarely strayed from those of bread-
winner, soldier and stalwart of the nation, nonetheless the discourses of
heterosexual love and romance offered a space for the romantic hero
too, a man who was comfortable expressing his feelings for the opposite
sex.[14]

DISCLOSING THE SELF

George Brown grew up in this climate of more relaxed social mores and
acceptable public intimacy in interwar Clydebank, a town in the west
of Scotland dominated by shipbuilding and light engineering but close
enough to Glasgow for there to be a range of masculine archetypes on
offer. George took advantage of the opportunities open to clever young
men. Born in 1911 to William Brown, a machinist at the Clydebank
Singer factory, and Annie Johnstone, whose family hailed from the
Hebridean island of Tiree, George was brought up in an environment that valued books and learning. He excelled at school and won a
Glasgow University bursary to read History and English. Athletic as well
as academically bright, he played for Scotland's amateur football team
Queen's Park. Upon graduation in 1935 he trained as a teacher and then
worked as a community organiser in Blantyre, a Lanarkshire mining
town. After war service he joined the Scottish Education Department as
a civil servant, becoming an HMI (Her Majesty's Inspector) responsible
for the post-war implementation of policy on sport, recreation and community facilities. On his retirement in 1976 he was awarded an OBE.

George married Margaret Seaforth Sinclair (known to her family
as Seaforth) on 12 September 1939, six years after they began seeing

Figure 8.1 George Johnstone Brown and Seaforth Sinclair Brown on their wedding day, 12 September 1939. Brown family collection.

one another (see Figure 8.1). Their son Ian was born in October 1940. When George enlisted in 1940 they had only been husband and wife for a matter of months and their married life had been spent living with her mother in Clydebank. His service in the Royal Artillery took him to anti-aircraft postings in Wester Ross, Shetland and Cromarty so until he was posted overseas the couple were able to see one another on a fairly regular basis during his home leave. Seaforth had been forced to move out of Clydebank following the bomb damage to the Sinclair family home during the Clydebank Blitz in 1941 whereupon she, Ian and her mother decamped first to Dumfriesshire and then to Leeds to lodge with her married sister. Relations in that house were fraught however, and eventually in 1944 Seaforth purchased a cottage near Hawick in the Scottish Borders, which was to become the couple's first home together when George was demobbed in 1945.

In May 1944, George was posted to the Headquarters of the South Caribbean area in Port of Spain, Trinidad as Staff Captain and rapidly rose up the ranks, ending the war with the honorary rank of Major. This was a safe posting, thousands of miles from the conflict zones, for which he and his new wife were thankful. But their separation necessitated a deluge of correspondence between them as a means of maintaining and sustaining their relationship across the miles. He wrote on average twice a week, she sometimes two or three times, and the letters allow us to reconstruct the psyche of a man caught between duty to his country, love for his wife and his desire to start family life.[15] Self-expression came most naturally through the written word for George and he used the correspondence to talk to himself as well as to his wife, in the process sustaining a relationship through a constant disclosure of his inner thoughts and feelings – what has been described as an 'intimacy of the self' rather than an 'intimacy of the body'.[16]

George Brown is the father-in-law I never met. His trove of letters, kept within the family since his death in 1991, form part of a large collection consisting of photographs of his time in Trinidad as well as family snaps, miscellaneous letters, character references, university lecture notes, speeches to various voluntary organisations, snatches of creative writing and other personal ephemera, all of which paint a portrait of a complex man for whom the conduct of intimacy was not incompatible with other facets of his character such as a sense of duty, responsibility and fair play. The letters to Seaforth are in some ways distinct from the rest of the personal papers in their emotional bravery and narrative confidence but at the same time they also bring into sharper focus many of the elements of George's character, giving the reader a rounded picture of the man – or at least the man he constructed in narrative form.[17] George's letters, although conforming in many ways to letter-writing conventions, are literary performances of the self, designed to inform, amuse, maintain contact, reassure and sustain intimacy or connectedness. In wartime, letters came to bear an enormous burden of significance and were pored over, read and re-read, their very presence symbolising, in paper and ink, the physical reality of the letter writer.[18] The flimsy airmail was a physical link with the writer, standing in for the body of the one who was missed. 'Well my darling I can't tell you how much better I feel as a result of getting your letters', he wrote shortly after his arrival in the Caribbean; 'they reduce the distance between us to a miraculous degree. I shall look forward to the rest with keen anticipation' (13 June 1944). It was common for writers to number letters in order to keep track of a correspondence that was disrupted by the vagaries of the wartime postal service, and individuals obsessed about the sending and receipt of letters and parcels, perhaps because the letter had to stand for so much. George and Seaforth were no exception. A lull in the arrival of airmails on either side could be interpreted as lack of commitment to the relationship.[19] In August 1944 George was doing his best to keep up:

> Your 29th to hand, dated 1 Aug; also your 28th a day or so ago. So I am really quite up to date. Unfortunately you do not seem to be receiving mine so regularly or so swiftly, and your last letter was a trifle plaintive. I'm awfully sorry, darling, because I'm well aware what it means to go without letters. I do try to keep them flowing but it is difficult. (12 August 1944)

Letters are a potent form of communication, often containing what would not be spoken aloud. In such circumstances personal letters have to do a lot of work: they take the place of everyday practices from banal chit-chat to acts of physical intimacy. Written 'in the moment', they often reveal everyday routines and bear the signs of the stop-and-start nature of daily life. George often returned to a letter several times over a day or two before mailing it. Similarly, Seaforth included her husband in the matter-of-fact stuff of daily life on the home front: 'That was Mr Kirk at the door with some lettuce. Jean is in bed so I had to see him. He is still as charming as ever' (9 July 1944). People wrote even when they had nothing to say in order to maintain a kind of everyday-ness. This was more evident in Seaforth's letters to George. Lacking the relative excitement and novelty of a Caribbean posting she often struggled to find anything of note to tell him from her hum-drum days: news of family and friends, updates on Ian and reports of visits to the cinema or theatre. For George and Seaforth, who had been married just a few years and had not had the opportunity to establish the routine of married life in their own home, let alone get used to being a family unit with their baby son, correspondence had to carry a great deal of weight: it conveyed information, offered advice, facilitated joint decisions, provided emotional and material support, maintained morale, and not least, maintained and sustained intimacy. The majority of George's letters contained all of these elements, common themes being his sporting and amateur dramatics exploits, observations on Trinidadian life, enquiries regarding matters at home, observations on the course of the war, and a good dose of advice to Seaforth on all matters from her choice of reading material to their son's upbringing in addition to providing emotional sustenance.

George's prose style was fluent, literary, confident and creative, exhibiting his university education and his love of literature while, at the same time, revelatory of his inner feelings. Each letter, even when composed in a hurry, was crafted to speak only to his wife. By means of jokes, false modesty, intimations of weakness (and superior judgement), the imparting of information, judgements on world affairs and not least, a willingness to put his heart on his sleeve and tell his wife how much he missed, loved and desired her, George maintained a level of intimate contact with Seaforth, whether he was writing about everyday affairs or the passion he felt for her. George Brown expressed his manhood in a modern reflexive way that permitted the unbridled expression of emotion, a practice shaped by his exposure to a range of influences before the war, from the romantic tropes of popular culture (especially film and music), the literature he loved to read, side by side with an active leisure culture incorporating plenty of opportunities for young men and women to spend time with one another. The war and George's position as a member of the colonial military merely provided the backdrop for a correspondence; the letters themselves were one place where the war did not need to be spoken about apart from as the context for everyday life or as a melodrama on notable occasions such as D-Day. Personal letters written by servicemen in times of war operate as devices to maintain a semblance of normality, to sustain relationships and to maintain a presence at home by engaging in a conversation about everyday occurrences that were happening without them. And it was overwhelmingly in this domestic context that George constructed his masculine self, not in the more hyper-masculine environment of military life (albeit a softer version experienced in the tropics).

George's letters to his wife constitute an intimate space, a place where they could speak privately about anything and that was, for the most part, separate from the war. George did not assume the mentality of the soldier when he wrote home; that was reserved for his military duties, which he fulfilled with exemplary diligence. Rather, he projected a self-deprecating persona that downplayed his fitness for soldiering, and projected himself as a good citizen, the domestic, conservative and fundamentally decent man, the man who, in public at least, was rather emotionally reserved with a stiff-upper-lip approach to adversity and who subscribed to the code of fair play, of decency, of moderation. This was a restrained, domestic manhood, encapsulated in the attributes of good humour, decency and stoicism, suited to the new model of conjugal mutuality.

The George Brown who wrote to his wife from his quarters in the British military compound in Port of Spain was not entirely comfortable in his new position as part of the colonial service. He rather assiduously and self-consciously cultivated an anti-heroic persona, representing himself as the victim of circumstance. The identity of the imperial

soldier hero was not a comfortable uniform. As a Scotsman more used
to the damp, chilly climate of the west coast than the heat of the tropics,
and with fair skin prone to sunburn, he was ill-equipped for the ener-
vating conditions he experienced in Trinidad. In his very first letter he
established a tone that he maintained throughout:

> Like the cautious old war horse you know, I am slowly digesting the set-up
> & not attempting over-night resolutions. The climate of course is a bit hard
> on one so gross & flabby; yet I am surprised to find it less exacting than at
> Miami. Perhaps later on I shall manage a quiet game of tennis but I fear
> soccer must be passed by. Just now a walk is strenuous enough exercise.
> (2 May 1944)

This was a man who had embraced sport and physical recreation in
his youth. One of his first jobs after university was as organiser of
the Blantyre Community Service Club, where he developed community
classes in keep fit, country dancing and football. And in Trinidad he participated regularly in many sports – football, tennis, cricket and swim-
ming in the ocean. George was a fit and trim thirty-three-year-old. But
he downplayed his physicality, preferring to joke about his inability to
cope with insect bites, the heat that left him feeling like a 'wet weekend'
and the sun, which was not providing the desired tan.

Neither was the identity of imperial man one that he embraced even
though he succeeded in his military colonial role, being swiftly promoted, and clearly able to rub along with the long-standing colonial set
up in this British imperial outpost.[20] He poked gentle fun at his role in
'empire building' (16 May 1944) and although tireless in fulfilling his
duty in attending the round of social events, fetes and cocktail parties
that were part and parcel of the colonial scene, he was always careful
to position himself at the edges of such occasions which oiled the imperial machine: 'Tonight I have to appear at the Sgts Mess Dance which
is quite a big affair'; he wrote on 30 June 1944. 'You will appreciate
from past experience that I look on it more as a duty than a pleasure.'
As an educated and engaged citizen, George did take an interest in the
colonial context in which he found himself. He offers glimpses of his
engagement with the social problems affecting Trinidad and he was well
aware of the fragility of British colonial power. But as for the war – it
was happening without him. He was conscious of the fact that his wife
and son were closer to hostilities than he was and that he was a very
distant observer of the momentous final stages. 'All this social chit-chat
must sound unreal at a time when events of such great moment to the
world are unfolding', he wrote on 10 June 1944, just after D-Day:

Figure 8.2 British Army Garrison, Trinidad, 1944. George Brown, front row, fourth from left. Brown family collection.

> You must forgive me; it is not because I am by nature frivolous but rather that circumstances make me so impotent – impotent even to say anything of value about the matter which looms largest in all our minds today. I know you must feel secretly glad that I am out of it, but though I am no fire-eater I cannot but think that after four years' service I should be nearer to the front. (10 June 1944)

For George Brown then, wartime service was not an opportunity for him to test or exhibit his manliness or at least not in the sense of performing physical prowess or bravery. His tendency to poke fun at his 'flabby' body, prone to sunburn, was possibly one way of deflecting a sublimated anxiety about his role in the war now he was in a safe posting; but more likely it was also a means of maintaining an easy and normal relationship with his wife. References to the war postings of family and friends, some of whom were closer to the action in Europe, served to emphasise that he was just 'frigging around' 'empire building' – the latter always in inverted commas. In this sense George's correspondence offers an anti-heroic narrative of the British soldier's involvement in the war, a story likely very common but rarely portrayed in the various representations of that war in popular culture and, until now, in histories of World War Two.[21] For George, the war – or at least this posting – was not a defining experience, a rite of passage or an adventurous interlude between university and real life. It was an inconvenience that separated him from his wife and young son, delaying his transition from bachelor to husband and father and to committed and useful citizen. His letters to Seaforth then, are substitutes for the married life he had envisaged. They stand in for the disclosures of self that serve to bind couples together, and he uses the correspondence to articulate a selfhood defined by the expression of deeply felt emotions and a commitment to marriage and family life founded on love, albeit imagined in somewhat conventionally gendered ways with George as provider and protector. This, though, was a modern masculinity worked through and expressed in writing rather than in practice owing to the exigencies of war and long-term absence. It is the unusual circumstances that forced George to expose himself emotionally as a means of sustaining the relationship with his young wife and son. Paradoxically, the experience of military discipline – the rules and regulations, the conformity and hierarchy and the predominantly male company – and the twist of fate that saw him stationed so far away in a place of relative security gave him the freedom to express himself with greater openness than might have been the case in normal circumstances.

CONJUGAL INTIMACY

It was a rare letter from George that did not contain some emotional investment in his relationship with his wife. He was unwavering in his efforts to persuade Seaforth of his deep love and admiration for her. He did this in a variety of ways and, it appears, without holding back his emotions albeit never losing control. It is has been said of World War One that letter-writing conventions were inadequate for establishing intimacy, forcing inexperienced letter writers to create their own forms and styles better suited to the feelings they wished to express.[22] George, however, was never lost for words, often making literary allusions, digging deep into his reservoir of education (with Robert Burns a favourite) and presumably drawing on language and sentiment popularised in novels and film.[23] He never employed what he would have regarded as crude or smutty language, rather making allusions to feelings and memories that for him – and presumably for her – evoked their carefree and intimate times together. On 12 September 1944, their wedding anniversary, George was in fine form:

My own Dear Seaforth

Having written that date I feel inadequate to do justice to the thoughts & feelings it prompts in me. There was a time when I imagined there lurked within my gross substance a spark of the poetic fire . . .; when I felt urged on occasion to express in rhythmic language the surge of some spiritual or sensory experience. Alas, the pedestrian routine of Army life seems to have stamped out any vestige of the divine fire. Yet I can still feel, deeply though mutely. And today, casting back as I inevitably do over the years of our association & especially over the last five years I start such a shoal of tender & passionate memories that coherent thought or speech is impossible. I can feel your presence so near to me that chill shivers & fevers chase one another along my veins & round my brain. Yet do not imagine that physical hunger is the dominant factor in my present psychological state. Far from it; rather it is a tender respect & admiration for the one who, although so obviously created for love and graceful, comfortable living, has faced & so cheerfully endured the trials & deprivations that war has imposed on you. That, I'm sorry to say, probably sounds pompous to you. But I think you will guess what I'm driving at; that I take off my hat to the most loyal & courageous wife any man was ever blessed with – as well as taking off ....
to the most seductive, alluring, responsive & completely satisfying mistress any man ever climbed into bed with!

Seaforth's response – 'Thanks for your lovely wedding anniversary letter. Though it was late in coming I enjoyed every bit of it' (28 September 1944) – like her writing generally, did not rise to the same literary heights as that of her devoted husband, and one suspects that she may have been somewhat overwhelmed by George's expansive expression of his love and desire for her. She was certainly less well educated and well-read than he – when she mentioned a novel she was reading, her husband's response indicated an intellectual gap between them:

> you told me of being engaged on something by Daphne du Maurier which is no doubt interesting & diverting. But you want to peg away at something more solid; something to give you background – the classics of English literature, history & the like. I know that sounds a bit pedantic, but it's really sound advice. (12 August 1944)

He could be a little pompous, as he freely admitted, but for him the letter was an ideal conduit for his deepest emotions. As someone who enjoyed literature and writing, for him the letter form was not a constraint but offered a freedom to express himself in a way that may not have been so evident in other contexts. He wrote on New Year's Eve 1944:

> Have I told you recently that I adore you? That your beauty, charm and freshness can intoxicate me over four thousand miles of sea? That I know I

have found in you a jewel beyond price – a companion who never bores, a mistress who never satiates, a courageous and loyal wife? If I haven't I should have – it's all true. (31 December 1944)

It is impossible to know if George was prone to articulating similar feelings in words face-to-face with his wife, but in the privacy of his tropical paradise he was not inhibited in expressing his physical and emotional desire for her: 'Well, my dear, that must be all for tonight. Are you still enticingly lovely at night when you sit up in bed in a revealing negligee & with a misleadingly innocent & virginal look? I'm sure you are – and the thought of it does things to me!' (12 October 1944).

Sustaining intimacy across the miles took more than literary flourishes though. Those who could draw on a long history together had a rich resource of memories of happy occasions that could be mined to withstand the strain of absence and to maintain a common narrative of togetherness. Not long after he arrived in Trinidad that togetherness was conjured up to transport them both back to their courtship days in Glasgow:

A quiet Sunday evening which makes me think of other happier Sunday evenings. I've just been outside looking at the new moon, decently draped in a negligee of clouds and posed, as in a Pleasure Cruise Poster, over a rotund saman tree ... My thoughts are of the Old Smiddy and Peel Glen, of the avenue of trees on the track from the gamekeeper's house (I've forgotten his name) down to the ford above the Bluebell Woods, of the Boulevard and the roads & tracks around Garscadden, Westerton, Hardgate and the outskirts of Bearsden. With those names what a flood of memories flows! 'Do you remember an inn, Miranda?' (25 June 1944)

Shared experiences and in-jokes – the reference to an Hillaire Belloc poem allegedly presented to a Scottish Miranda must have been recognisable to Seaforth – served to reduce the distance between them and to strengthen their shared bonds. In August 1944 he adopted a similar device, skilfully weaving together war news with a memorable trip to Paris in 1937, ending with a French flourish that brought the story back to the intense feelings they had for one another:

I wonder if you listened to Radio Newsreel tonight; it contained two recorded reports from BBC men in Paris. The first was given from under the Arc de Triomphe & painted the scene on the Champs Elysée; the other came from the Place de la Concorde, of which we had a snap taken I think by Connell at the World Exhibition. I was guilty of a bit of nostalgic reminiscence (you needn't feel embarrassed – it was purely mental not verbal!) There was a little para in the newspaper today which showed that fighting was going on around the École Militaire in Montparnasse, and of course I fell to thinking of a little hotel on the Boul' Mich & the restaurant in the Rue Saint Jacques where they could produce the most excellent champagne. I hope the place is not being destroyed; unlike many others. I have a warm affection for France & look forward to taking you back to revisit our former haunts & breathe again the exciting air of Paris. Pour la Guerre perhaps not so bon, but pour l'amour – mais oui, mais oui! (26 August 1944)

Spoken out loud such sentiments might have sounded a little comical or rehearsed but the letter offered George a space in which he could articulate his feelings safely and privately. He could be confident that only his wife would read these sentiments and would recognise (and respond to) the signals.

In April 1945 after almost a year apart, he embarked upon what he termed a 'private cavalcade' of memorable moments of their twelve-year relationship, taking in holidays, trips to London and Paris, the Blitz, the birth of their son and much more besides, finishing at the beginning – in Glasgow:

We're getting on now -- 1935. I am still attending classes at Varsity: we visit Connell: sit on the Kings Gallery: go to gild dances and functions: I walk you home from night school.

1934 and I . . . who to the horror of your family calls for you at 10:30 pm to go for a walk. We managed a flick on Saturday evening: you watch me play football and tennis. You see me graduate and we steal a moment together in the English class library of which I am librarian. And surely it was in 1933–12 years ago that it all began with a walk on which time stood still for us. (21 April 1945)

Yet it seems that for all of George's efforts to maintain the intimate narrative of togetherness and connectedness, Seaforth had some anxiety about their future reunion (or perhaps this was a device of her own designed to encourage him to maintain his romantic entreaties), prompting George to resort to rare comedic coarseness albeit quoting his favourite writer: 'Whatever makes you think that will feel strange when we meet? Didn't I ever read you Burns' letter about his reconciliation with Jean Armour? "There's no conciliator like weely waly . . ." pardon me if that shocks your maidenly modesty' (30 April 1945). Alternatively Seaforth was perhaps responding to a characteristic of the lengthy correspondence – that it takes on a life of its own, whereby the writer creates a persona that can only exist on the page.[24] The relationship between the couple that preceded the absence becomes something static; it is superseded by the epistolic relationship, which in many respects is a simulacrum, separate from the real relationship and yet standing in for it. In George's view the war had 'strengthened, tempered and enriched' their relationship, and his literary eloquence was employed to achieve this (24 August 1945). Seaforth was certainly more restrained in expressing her feelings, though no less adoring of her husband, and of course in his absence she was coping with the everyday irritations of wartime while bringing up a young son. Her own letters were far more down to earth and grounded in everyday matters: the tensions in the Leeds household, the frustrations of rationing, Ian's health, and her endeavours to secure a home she could call her own.

In September 1944 Seaforth purchased a house in the Scottish Borders after enduring the trials and tribulations of living in Leeds with her sister for long enough. The purchase of the cottage, named 'Frostleyburn', was a turning point in George's correspondence and in his conception of their married life together. Until this point George and Seaforth had not really had the opportunity to make the transition from a courting couple to a family; their relationship was in stasis, unable to move on because of the war, despite the birth of their son. But now George could begin to really envisage life after the war's end and imagine himself and his family in a home of their own. Thereafter George badgered Seaforth for information about the house:

> Now, darling, how is the home building getting on? What extra furnishings have you managed to pick up? Are you really liking it? Got enough lamps etc? God, what a lot there is that I want to know! Come on, my dear, give me more details. You won't bore me no matter how minute they are. (10 November 1944)

He was anxious to know everything about the house and its surroundings:

> The sort of things I want to know is – the height of the house level above the road; the area around the house & especially the distance from the house to the top of the river-bank; the size of the enclosed garden; whether the area around is grassed. Do tell me more, my dear; it all helps to construct the picture in my mind. (29 January 1945)

He began to imagine himself there, completing the image of family life and his place within it: 'Of course I realise that a pair of male slippers under your bed would solve all difficulties! (or is that just vanity?)', and began to start thinking about his future employment – 'I have been thinking about our policy after the war, and my present inclination is to return to teaching. If I do, why shouldn't I do it in Hawick?' (31 March 1945).

From this point on, George began to envisage himself as the family man, ensconced in the domestic environment and providing for his wife and son, a 'family-orientated masculinity', as Laura King has termed this identity.[25] Now he could inhabit and perform the persona of husband and father as well as lover. Historians of twentieth-century masculinity have cautioned that we should recognise that the embrace of domestic masculinity was always balanced by 'fantasies of the energetic life and homosocial camaraderie of the adventure hero'.[26] While this may have been the case in literary and filmic representations and men themselves may have found escape from their conjugal role in adventure stories and, in the post-war era, in war films that romanticised male escapades, the attraction of the companionate marriage and the 'sober responsibilities of the male breadwinner, patient father, and considerate husband', should not be underestimated.[27] For many servicemen, like George, the war had not been an opportunity to put their adventure fantasies into practice. Rather it was an interregnum when, certainly, they developed homosocial friendships framed by wartime exigencies but at the same time, it delayed their establishing their own families. The strategies conveyed in writing designed to establish and sustain intimacy – the self-revelation, the disclosure of knowledge, emotions and desires – had reached their natural end point and needed to be practised for real.

DISTANT FATHERHOOD

One of the consequences of his efforts to sustain intimacy with his wife is that Ian sits apart somewhat from them as a couple in George's correspondence. George's relationship with his son had been characterised by 'dramatic entries and swift exits', an experience shared by so many men in wartime (12 October 1944). It was difficult for him to develop a persona as a father in absentia, especially when his son was still so young.[28] In the absence of everyday contact he had to imagine his son's development: 'There must also be big changes in Ian since I saw him – now almost a year ago. So if you can possibly do it, take some pictures for me – and don't forget a view of the house' he wrote in January 1945. Seaforth updated him regularly on Ian's progress though usually only in the most general terms:

> Ian is full of health and strength. Everywhere I take him people admire him. Though he has grown quite a lot in height: his shoulders are still broad and he has lost no weight. In his summer suit he weighs exactly 3 stones and he is as firm as a rock. He is interested in everything about him and asks all sorts of questions. (19 July 1944)

Understandably perhaps, George did not quite know how to build his relationship with his son but he had clear ideas about his own role as a father: it was to educate and amuse. He began a collection of stamps and of butterflies for Ian, both of which he regarded as 'a great stimulant to geographical interest', and he regularly advised Seaforth on Ian's education. When he received a letter from Ian in his own hand (Ian was just four years old) George responded: 'Today I received your letter and Ian's both dated 9th July. Ian's shows great improvement on his first attempt; quite mature in fact! ... Keep encouraging him & he will soon be producing the real thing.' (21 July 1944) Just a month later, after he and Seaforth had exchanged thoughts on their son's education, George again urged his wife to stimulate their son's development:

> Make him write letters to me & send his drawings – and demand a higher standard every time. Encourage his appreciation of worth-while things – books, flowers, animals, etc & stimulate his interest in the things of everyday life. But don't let me lecture. I can be an awful bore. (4 August 1944)

George's attempts to maintain contact with his son and to develop a relationship with him were heartfelt and genuine but understandably Ian could not be included in the 'pure relationship' that George cultivated with his wife. Occasionally he wrote to Ian and did as much as he could in the circumstances to engender a relationship with him. He was delighted when Seaforth informed him of Ian's interest in football, a sport that George played at a high level. As a proponent of sport as a vector of improvement and as a transmitter of the values he believed in – fair play, effort, the amateur spirit – he was pleased that Ian was following in his own footsteps: 'You will appreciate that I am highly delighted by Ian's interest in football. Not only is it a source of much enjoyment, but properly handled is a wonderful character builder' (5 October 1944).

The value of a rounded education was central to George's world view. He had benefited from it himself and clearly had strong views on how it should be imparted. He instructed Seaforth to ensure his son was reading the right literature and made the best of his absence overseas:

> The news you give me about Ian's progress delights me. It may be that my journeyings in foreign parts will be a good thing for him, by giving him the necessary interest in broader horizons. Have you introduced him to Columbus yet? ... You might get the material for a serial bed time story from the novel on Columbus by Sabatini (A copy came from the Book Club). (23 January 1945)

The relationship George imagined with Ian was an affective one, albeit tempered by a more traditional understanding of his role – as educator in the conventional sense as well as in life. 'Please don't encourage Ian to weep over little disappointments like the non-arrival of sweets', he advised Seaforth, 'otherwise he is going to be ill-fitted to meet the shocks that he is bound to meet in life. Don't imagine from that that I'm being hard; but facts are chiels that winna ding' (12 February 1945).[29] In June 1945 he wrote a letter printed in capitals for five-year-old Ian to read for himself. 'It should not be very long now until I am home and then we shall have some good fun together', he wrote, finishing with a characteristic P.S. 'Your Uncle John has come home from Africa. Can you still point on the globe to where he lived?' (11 June 1945) In his absence, George played the role of the caring and involved father, just one element of the imagined family life he yearned to return to. But until he was back in the bosom of his family the intimacy he maintained with his wife through letters was something real that could be conjured up in words whereas the relationship with his son was still undeveloped, characterised by attempts to find points of contact – football, stamp collecting – which he could only imagine might become the locus of a father–son relationship when he returned home.

CONCLUDING THOUGHTS

George Brown's correspondence reveals a masculine self caught between the duties of war and the desire for a sustaining and fulfilling family life. While he was 'frigging about' in this 'theatre of operations', part of him wanted nothing more than to put his 'feet on the mantelpiece & who knows, perhaps you on my knee'. In his mind's eye he had created an image of home with his adored Seaforth and his young son, an environment in which he could perform a 'family-orientated masculinity' that encompassed both romantic, conjugal love and the protective and educational role he envisaged as a father. In the latter years of the war he had effectively become a bureaucrat in uniform, yet George's alter ego as a man of letters enabled him, through his correspondence, to perform a manhood that encompassed elements of the anti-heroic masculinity of the interwar years with the new emotional masculinity of the post-war era. In his service role George was able to practise his commitment to fair play, good citizenship and public service while serving His Majesty's Forces in the Caribbean, and these were principles that he maintained throughout his life as he made the transition to civilian life, finding a satisfying role in the Scottish Education Department. Here, responsible for the next thirty years for the development of sports and recreation facilities in Scottish communities, he was able to harness his sense of responsibility to something he really believed in.

In November 1945 George finally received his demobilisation papers and was cleared to sail for home. 'I fear you are going to have a full time job looking after me for quite a time' he wrote in his last letter from Trinidad.

> I shall have to be molly coddled and protected against the weather: you will have to soothe me when I become impatient with the difficulties of civilian life; and you will have to lead me through the maze of coupon purchasing, registration and form filling which is the civilian's lot. There's much more you will have to do but I know there is no purpose in telling the complete & perfect wife what they are. My dear it's too wonderful to believe that very soon you are going to take over as my Commanding Officer! (2 November 1945)

But having invested so much in sustaining his emotional relationship with Seaforth, he was only to enjoy a short time with her. Seaforth died of a long-standing heart condition in 1948. Yet the letters stand as testimony to a new kind of man, forged in circumstances that permitted alternative models of manhood to be imagined and displayed. George's letters to his wife allowed him to play with styles of manliness that were in flux in this period. Removed from normal constraints of everyday life, and forced to assume a literary persona, George Brown exhibited a modern masculinity that was in touch with his feelings though never out of control, committed to a mutually sustaining emotional and sexual partnership and to being an engaged and loving father to his son. In letters, rather than in real life, George encapsulated a modern masculine self that Scottish men were to practise in the post-war decades.

NOTES

1. George Brown to Seaforth Brown, 3 December 1944. Correspondence in private possession of the Brown family.
2. For example, Andrew Davies, 'Street gangs, crime and policing in Glasgow during the 1930s: the case of the Beehive Boys', *Social History*, 23 (1998), pp. 251–67; Arthur McIvor and Ronnie Johnston, 'Dangerous work, hard men and broken bodies: masculinity in the Clydeside heavy industries, c. 1930–1970s', *Labour History Review*, 69:2 (2004), pp. 135–51; Daniel Wight, *Workers Not Wasters. Masculine Respectability, Consumption and Unemployment in Central Scotland: A Community Study* (Edinburgh: Edinburgh University Press, 1993).

3. Claire Langhamer, 'Afterword', in Alana Harris and Timothy Willem Jones (eds), *Love and Romance in Britain, 1918–1970* (Basingstoke: Palgrave, 2015), pp. 245–52.

4. Michael Roper, 'Slipping out of view: subjectivity and emotion in gender history', *History Workshop Journal*, 59:1 (2005), pp. 57–72.

5. Anthony Giddens, *The Transformation of Intimacy: Sexuality, Love and Eroticism in Modern Societies* (Cambridge: Polity, 1992), p. 58.

6. Lynn Jamieson, *Intimacy. Personal Relationships in Modern Societies* (Cambridge: Polity, 1998), pp. 1, 37–41.

7. Jamieson, *Intimacy*, p. 136.

8. See Michael Roper, 'Between manliness and masculinity: the "war generation" and the psychology of fear in Britain, 1914–1950', *Journal of British Studies*, 44:2 (2005), pp. 343–62.

9. Marcus Collins, *Modern Love. An Intimate History of Men and Women in the Twentieth Century* (London: Atlantic Books, 2003), p. 5.

10. Claire Langhamer, *The English in Love: The Intimate Story of an Emotional Revolution* (Oxford: Oxford University Press, 2013), pp. 6–9.

11. Langhamer, *English in Love*, p. 24.

12. Claire Langhamer, 'Love and courtship in mid-twentieth century England', *Historical Journal*, 50:1 (2007), pp. 173–96; Melanie Tebbutt, *Being Boys: Youth, Leisure and Identity in the Inter-War Years* (Manchester: Manchester University Press, 2012), p. 169.

13. Langhamer, 'Love and courtship', p. 179; Tebbutt, *Being Boys*, pp. 152–61.

14. Christine Grandy, *Heroes and Happy Endings: Class, Gender and Nation in Popular Film and Fiction in Interwar Britain* (Manchester: Manchester University Press, 2014); Stephen Brooke, '"A certain amount of mush": love, romance, celluloid and wax in the mid-twentieth century', in Harris and Willem Jones (eds), *Love and Romance*, pp. 81–99, at 85–6.

15. The letters that survive – around a hundred – amount to all of his letters sent to Seaforth between May 1944 and November 1945; only a small selection of Seaforth's letters have survived (May–November 1944), presumably those George brought home from Trinidad. I am grateful to Deborah Hackett who transcribed them for me.

16. Jamieson, *Intimacy*, p. 1.

17. For the wider context of George Brown's association with sport in his civil service career see Callum G. Brown, 'Sport and the Scottish Office in the twentieth century: the promotion of a social and gender policy', *European Sports History Review*, 1 (1999), pp. 183–202. See also Angela Bartie and Alistair Fraser's chapter in this volume for a discussion of Glasgow gangs. George, in his HMI role, was involved in the provision of a youth project in Easterhouse following the visit of Frankie Vaughan.

18. Liz Stanley, 'The epistolarium: on theorizing letters and correspondences', *Auto/Biography*, 12 (2004), pp. 201–35, at 208–9.

19. See Christa Hämmerle, '"You let a weeping woman call you home?" Private

correspondences during the First World War in Austria and Germany', in Rebecca Earle (ed.), *Epistolary Selves: Letters and Letter Writers 1600–1945* (Aldershot: Ashgate, 1999), pp. 152–82, at 158–9.

20. On imperial masculinity, a concept more relevant to World War One, see John Mackenzie, 'The imperial pioneer and hunter and the British masculine stereotype in late Victorian and Edwardian times', in J. A. Mangan and James Walvin (eds), *Manliness and Morality: Middle-Class Masculinity in Britain and America, 1800–1940* (Manchester: Manchester University Press, 1987), pp. 176–98.

21. Penny Summerfield and Corinna Peniston-Bird, *Contesting Home Defence: Men, Women and the Home Guard in the Second World War* (Manchester: Manchester University Press, 2007).

22. Michael Roper, *The Secret Battle: Emotional Survival in the Great War* (Manchester: Manchester University Press, 2009), p. 55.

23. Kate Hunter, 'More than an archive of war: intimacy and manliness in the letters of a Great War soldier to the woman he loved, 1915–1919', *Gender & History*, 25:2 (2013), pp. 339–354, argues that 'words to describe love eluded Great War correspondents', p. 344.

24. Stanley, 'Epistolarium', p. 213.

25. Laura King, 'Hidden fathers? The significance of fatherhood in mid-twentieth-century Britain', *Contemporary British History*, 26:1 (2012), pp. 25–46, at 27.

26. Martin Francis, 'The domestication of the male? Recent research on nineteenth- and twentieth-century British masculinity', *Historical Journal*, 45:3 (2002), pp. 637–52, at 643.

27. Francis, 'Domestication of the male', p. 644.

28. Lynn Abrams, '"There was nobody like my Daddy": Fathers, the family and the marginalisation of men in modern Scotland', *Scottish Historical Review*, 78:2 (1999), pp. 219–42. More generally see Laura King, *Family Men: Fatherhood and Masculinity in Britain, 1914–1960* (Oxford: Oxford University Press, 2015).

29. This quotation from Robert Burns translates as 'Facts are fellows that cannot be disputed'.

PART III

Lived Experiences

9

Social Control and Masculinity in Early Modern Scotland: Expectations and Behaviour in a Lowland Parish

Harriet Cornell

IN EARLY MODERN SCOTLAND, the religious doctrine of Calvinism permeated everyday life through the regulation of personal behaviour. From the Reformation in 1560 until the turn of the nineteenth century, Scotland's network of church courts – the kirk sessions – policed the manners and morals of their parish congregations, punishing purse and person in the name of a godly society.[1] The kirk sessions operated with and alongside a sophisticated network of secular courts at local level. Individuals were also governed by codes of honour, shame and reputation, like their contemporaries on the European continent. Recorded detail from ecclesiastical and secular court cases involving neighbourhood disputes, the supernatural, violence, gossip, slander and sexual misconduct, have proved a valuable source for the historical investigation of ordinary folk and the ways in which their everyday lives were shaped by the values and strictures of reformed religion.

In a society where church and state championed marriage and the godly household, this meant that divisions were drawn not just between the sexes but also within them. The existence of a gendered double standard when it came to regulating popular behaviour has long been debated, but real divisions existed amongst men of different ages, economic power and status. This chapter will draw on the experiences and representations of some individual men and boys in the legal process to examine the workings of patriarchy and masculinity during the early modern period. It will show how social status, economic power, and age combined to inform and influence the experience of authority within these two paradigms.

While the history of Scotland's Reformation has been well documented, the study of ordinary folk has only received attention in recent decades.[2] Furthermore, historians have tended to focus on the actions of the kirk sessions when investigating the implications of Reformation for popular behaviour, thanks in part to the wealth of qualitative detail contained in these records. Rosalind Mitchison and Leah Leneman were early pioneers of such historical investigation, concluding that the experience of the official regulation of behaviour in both rural and urban areas was dependent on gender and social status up until around 1780.[3] Their research initiated a new debate over what was the popular experience of kirk session discipline, and specifically if all Scots were subject to the policing of morals and manners equally and evenly, in accordance with the *First Book of Discipline*.[4] Margo Todd concluded that this was indeed the case – but the homogeneity argument has since been challenged by evidence that geography, social rank, and gender did exert influence over the implementation of the state's disciplinary agenda.[5] Indeed, while both men and women may have been fined equally for their misbehaviour by Scotland's kirk sessions, their reduced ability to pay put women at an intrinsic disadvantage.[6]

English and continental scholarship has been quick to identify the web-like operation of early modern judicial systems where secular and ecclesiastical courts worked in tandem to regulate, control and influence the behaviour of local people.[7] The same might be said for Scotland where ecclesiastical authorities were not acting in isolation but as a part of an integrated justice system that was not just operational, but sophisticated at the local level.[8] In this chapter, that integrated secular and ecclesiastical system is under the spotlight in respect of the ways in which men's behaviour was subject to kirk discipline and the broader judicial system across the life course. It argues that not only did different men experience social control in different ways depending on their rank, but that experience also changed over the course of the individual man's lifecycle.

The focus is East Lothian in the east of the country. Formerly known as the sheriffdom or constabulary of Haddingtonshire, East Lothian incorporates the urban centres of Haddington and North Berwick and their large landward portions, as well as rural settlements such as Pencaitland and Saltoun.[9] By the early seventeenth century this region was bureaucratically well developed. It contained the presbyteries of Haddington and Dunbar, with their kirk sessions and sheriff and burgh courts that headed up the local secular legal system. The authority and legitimacy of these courts extended from the tolbooths in Haddington and North Berwick into rural county parishes, thanks to a network of shared officials, shared business and shared punishment rituals.[10] This was possible in part because of a common, unifying religious belief that extended from central government to the most local of legal institutions, the two complementing and reinforcing a common set of moral and religious principles.[11] It was through this local judicial network that sexual relationships, personal conduct and the governance of the household were subjected to state regulation under the guise of establishing (and later maintaining) a godly society.[12] But this was not entirely a top-down process of social control whereby judicial mechanisms exerted authority; rather it relied upon informal and acculturated models of behaviour enforced within the community as well as upon the community.

Although established, legitimate state institutions can exert control over local populations by defining and limiting popular behaviour through judicial mechanisms, opportunities remain for ordinary people to negotiate and contest this formal power dynamic. Social theorists including Georg Simmel have argued that formal social control can often be reliant on the loyalties and shared obligations that individuals subscribe to as members of neighbourhoods. These community relationships then result in a collective identity that informally checks the behaviour of individual members.[13] In early modern societies this informal social control occurred at the most local level, providing an additional context to the exertions of state and religion, as well as a marked degree of variability that blurs the defining line between the formal and informal. The helpfulness of distinguishing between 'sin' and 'crime' is negligible (associated with the religious and secular justice systems respectively), and Falconer's study of Aberdeen demonstrates this by elucidating the role ordinary people played in navigating the parameters of behaviour, and then policing popular adherence within those accepted definitions.[14] As a result, social control during this period was much more than a religious aim of Reformers that was enforced through simple religious doctrine by those in official positions of power.[15]

Social control depended on ordinary folk upholding broad godly standards of behaviour that were accepted as normative within their communities. It is within this context that ordinary people navigated their daily lives in East Lothian while the secular and ecclesiastical authorities regulated their behaviour and movements.[16] Local courts enjoyed established, locally acquired, popular legitimacy. Whether this was achieved because of broad agreement with doctrinal principles, popular fear or common apathy is not clear, but some combination is most likely.[17] If the Reformers were not popular in Haddington, they were not dismissed as a laughing stock and the Calvinist drive for ecclesiastical discipline became a reality throughout the shire. Any reservations may have been offset by the appealing nature of some of the

services these bodies provided within the atmosphere of social solidarity
that small, pre-industrial societies enjoyed.[18] As a result, state authority
and power helped construct parameters of acceptable and ideal behaviour for ordinary men and women that drew on established patriarchies
and gendered ideals. Prosecutions involving relationships between men
and women, including extramarital sex, dominated kirk session business, and the language of acceptable, godly personal conduct became
pervasive too in the secular courts. Violations of the established sense
of order were interpreted as offences against a community bonded by
shared experience, understandings, and beliefs.[19]

This legal interpretation of social control was exerted formally
through the court system, but also informally by neighbours within
their communities. Ordinary folk reported transgressions and perceived
wrongs to their kirk sessions for redress and participated in punishments
meted out by both ecclesiastical and secular authorities. By recognising
that patriarchy was at the centre of godly household and realm, historians can adopt new analytical approaches towards the regulation of the
behaviour of individuals and communities in early modern Scotland.
In doing so there is acknowledgement that being a man or a woman
was not a binary category operating in isolation from other important
factors.

These communities were hierarchical, and bargaining power
depended on social rank, age, and economic power. Alongside gender,
these factors influenced the decisions taken by kirk sessions and the
regulation of criminal behaviour by the secular authorities. As a result,
a degree of geographical variation must also be acknowledged, despite
not being a central focus of this chapter. Although parameters of acceptable behaviour were both flexible to the reality of everyday life, and
were also variable over the course of the lifecycle, there were limits. The
young male domestic servant, newly arrived in an East Lothian parish,
had less socio-economic agency than the established male burgess for
example.

The Reformation quest to establish godly societies throughout
Europe can be traced in the litigiousness of those ordinary people who
were affected by it. Women and the poor found themselves in the historical record in significant numbers, and historians have evaluated the
existence of a gendered 'double standard' in prosecutions, including
those in Scotland's kirk sessions between 1560 and 1780. But, as in
France, Germany and England, parish communities were patriarchal
societies whose complex social hierarchies were stratified by more than
just gender. The salience of age and socio-economic status broadens

analysis of the operation of formal and informal social control, and for the purposes of this chapter facilitates a more nuanced understanding of the ways in which men encountered and engaged with the experience of kirk discipline and the broader judicial authority of the state across the lifecycle.

The concept of patriarchy has been rehabilitated recently as an analytical term that offers the opportunity to broaden understandings of authority, especially within interpersonal relationships.[20] Where Scottish scholarship has tended to focus on the female experience of patriarchal power in the ecclesiastical courts, a focus on men's encounters with the legal system more broadly offers an analytical opportunity that allows for a complementary examination of different masculinities as they were performed over the lifecycle and represented through the eyes of the secular and kirk authorities. For men, patriarchal authority was contingent upon age, life stage, and social status and its associated economic power. For example, in Tyninghame, a rural parish on the eastern coast of East Lothian, surviving records show that 224 men and 148 women were punished by its kirk session between 1615 and 1640 – a total of nearly 400 individuals.[21] If we move beyond the obvious gender disparity, the detail contained in these records offers rich evidence of contemporary attitudes towards different men, and the complicated relationship between patriarchy, masculinity, and manhood.

Evidence from East Lothian points to a working model of the early modern household centred on the interdependence of gender, age and economic contribution. Household heads had responsibilities towards other household members, who in turn had obligations to obey their superiors but these reciprocal responsibilities were cut across by other factors.[22] The case of John Airth, a parishioner from Tyninghame whose life can be charted through the session records between 1616 and 1629, is illustrative of how popular expectations of this man altered over the period and how status and rank continued to affect his experience of authority and participation in local governance. There are two narratives to Airth's story, which hinged around his marriage in December 1618. The first involves a series of sexual indiscretions, and the second charts a youthful flirtation with physical violence. Rather than a simple micro-history, the two parts of this case study work to challenge the notion that men's experience of discipline and authority in early modern Scotland was in any way homogeneous, and illustrates the importance of male socio-economic status in negotiating that dyad in a local setting.

John Airth's interaction with his local judicial system can be contextualised and illuminated by the broader business of East Lothian's courts. Haddington's burgh and sheriff courts enjoyed the most far-reaching jurisdiction of the local court network, and included hosting local justice courts when they were convened to try capital crimes including witchcraft.[23] Each of these courts operated within defined legal parameters and rules. And yet, as in the neighbouring kirk sessions, negotiation took place. Mitigating and inflammatory behaviour influenced punishments – as did socio-economic status. A hierarchy was in operation, and different men at different stages of their lives interacted with these institutions in different ways. For some, negotiation was simply out of reach due to lack of wealth; for others, office-holders negotiated on their behalf. Thus men's position in the socio-economic pecking order interacted with notions of the ideal household and associated connotations of patriarchy, masculinity and manhood.

Between 1616 and 1627, John Airth appeared before the session on which his father, Thomas, served as an elder, to answer at least five different charges ranging from fornication to acts of physical violence. He appeared in the minutes for the first time on 28 April 1616 when:

> Jhone Airthe sone to Thomas Airthe in Tyninghame and Jonet Watsone servitrix to the said Thomas Airthe being suspect of fornication and being warnit lawfullie callit on compeirit first the said Jonet and accusit of fornication confessit hir falt with the said Jhone Airthe. Jhone Airthe also callit compeirit and accusit of fornication with the said Jonet Watsone confest the same, being rebuikit heavily having fallin in ane elderis house.[24]

Thomas Airth's patriarchal authority within his own household had been flouted by his son and servant. As Elizabeth Foyster has observed for England, 'it was deeply insulting to men to suggest that they had lost control over their households'.[25] The couple were ordered to separate immediately and Thomas Airth reacted quickly to the outcome of the case in order to restore his personal authority and standing, promising 'to remove the said Jonet out of his hous this day, quhilk [which] he did'. John Airth and Jonet Watson were both ordered 'to sitt 3 several sabbothis on the pillar [of repentance] and to pay according to the act', which was a twenty-shilling fine.[26] Order was restored to the Airth household for a period of over eighteen months, but Jonet Watson would not be the last of Thomas Airth's servants to fall for his son's charms. On 28 December 1617:

> Marion Nisbett being sumond lawfullie callit on and accusit of fornication with Jhone Airthe confessed hir offence being rebuikit and admonished earnestlie to repentance she was ordainit presentlie to separate and to remove fra Thomas Airthis hous quhair Jhone Airthe was resident.[27]

John Airth did not appear before the session until 4 January 1618, when he confessed his fault and 'being vehementlie rebuikit and earnestlie exhortit to repentance being his second fall and also in his fatheris hous quha was ane elder'.[28] Although the session minutes do not record any direct questioning of Thomas Airth's household governance, that his house was the locus of his son's sexual infidelities was seen by the session as relevant to the circumstances of the case. For those actions in his father's house, Airth was sentenced to sit on the pillar (or stool) of repentance for six Sundays' worth of public penance during divine service, and was ordered to pay a forty-shilling fine. Their illegitimate son, Thomas, was baptised after the afternoon sermon on 12 April.[29] Although not indicated in the records, this suggests that their illicit relationship had been ongoing for some time but, as with many fornication prosecutions, pregnancy provided the necessary proof for the ecclesiastical authorities to proceed against the couple with any hope of success.[30]

The following November, Airth put his name forward to be proclaimed in marriage to Margaret Neilson, also from Tyninghame, and they were married a few weeks later on 22 December 1618.[31] They had only been married for four months when a new sexual scandal arose. On 14 March 1619:

Marin Traill compeirit and being demandit if she was with bairne [child] answerit that she was with bairne, being demandit to quhom she answerit to Jhone Airthe sone to Thomas Airthe in Tyninghame, being demandit if she had led [laid] with any uther men but Jhone Airthe answerit that she had to do with na uther bot him onlie.[32]

Three years earlier in 1615, Traill appears in the kirk record as a married woman with a legitimate son. George Borthwick was baptised without his father, William Borthwick, being present.[33] So Traill had been a Tyninghame resident for at least four years – she was no stranger to the parish, but she was a woman with an unfavourable reputation. Session members believed that many in the parish thought her 'to be ane woman of na gude', and any accusations made by her were handled with caution.[34] It was a reputation that Airth possessed enough knowledge of to exploit when he was called to answer the fornication charge, and 'being demandit if he had carnal deal with Marin Traill denyit and affirmit that he wald not be the father to hir bairn because he thocht hir ane woman of evill carradge and had to do with uther men'. When asked by the session to name some of these 'uther men', Airth refused and Traill was called back to reaffirm her allegations – which she did, in vehement fashion. When threatened with an appearance before the presbytery, she retorted 'that albeit they should call her befor any judicatorie she wald never say utherwayis because she had already confessit the treuthe', adding that the fornication was committed 'on ane Sonday at even at the west end of hir moteris yaird about twentie dayis or ane moneth before Mertimes [Martinmas] last bypast'.[35] To the session it was emerging as a complicated case, with reputations on both sides. There were many things to consider: first as the session noted, it was not certain whether Marion Traill's husband was dead; it was not clear whether John Airth had relations with Marion (he denied it), and John Airth despite now being a married man had 'fallin twys in fornication befor with twa sev-erall women'.[36] Airth had fallen into 'dangerous passions', with previous extramarital liaisons with women affecting his reputation and status as an 'honourable man'.[37] The session therefore adjourned the case until it had received advice from the presbytery on how to proceed.

On 21 March 1619, both parties appeared again before the session. Traill had appeared before the presbytery when summoned and had stuck to her story, but Airth had not and so the presbytery ordained him to be tried again before the session with the prospect of having to give a public declaration of his innocence. With this prospect in mind:

> Jhone Airthe ... confessit that he had ance to do with hir as she deponit about aucht or fourteine dayis efter Michaelmess last bypast and if the bairn come to that recking that he sald be father to the said bairn.[38]

This was before Airth's marriage, but Traill had not been able to prove that her husband, William Borthwick, was dead and offered the session no elaboration of the circumstances. Borthwick had not been present at the baptism of his son in 1615, but no reason had been given. Proof of his demise was, of course, a necessity if the charges should be dealt with as fornication rather than adultery. She was given twenty days in which to produce a testimonial of his death – and so the scandal of Airth's trilapse in fornication was to prove to be a prolonged affair. The first testimonial she produced, on 2 May 1619 from Borthwick's last known whereabouts in Leith, was thought 'not altogidder sufficient warrand to cleir hir from the cryme of adulterie', and she was ordered to bring another that had been signed by a minister or bailie within fifteen days.[39]

On 16 May 1619 Tyninghame's minister, John Lauder, reported that Airth had been to see him, eager to speed up the process of proving Traill's widowhood and thereby ensuring that he satisfy the kirk as a trilapsed fornicator, not an adulterer, by any method within his means. This personal intervention by Airth, using his own contacts and resources, would prove to be central to the case. Lauder reported that

Airth had sent a man, John Nisbett, to Leith with a view to obtaining better certification of Borthwick's death. There he happened upon one William Jackson, son to a Tyninghame man called Patrick Jackson, who testified that sometime fellow parishioner Borthwick 'was departit this lyfe being hangit at Linlithgow and declairit to him bothe the place and caus of his execution', which he put in writing to both Airth and the minister.[40] But it was not until 29 August, after more than three months of paper-chasing in West Lothian, that the session agreed that Airth 'had producit some testimonialis quhilk were provable evidentis of the deathe of the said Marin Traillis husband'.[41]

In the meantime, on 27 June, Traill had sat on the stool of repentance and started to satisfy the impatient kirk as an adulteress.[42] As a woman without the socio-economic status of her one-time sexual partner, after initial questioning she had been omitted from the process of establishing her husband's fate entirely. If Airth had been in a similar situation, as a low-status male parishioner perhaps in service himself and lacking the connections needed for his intervention to the minister, it follows that his fate would have been sealed in similar fashion.

The post-Reformation kirk sessions may have been lauded as a sophisticated network of authority capable of pursuing and tracing individuals, but in this case the system failed to elicit the answers that the Tyninghame session needed. The secular and ecclesiastical authorities from nearby localities did not share information readily – perhaps because they were simply unable to due to the incongruous or incomplete nature of their recordkeeping. Airth's fornication case with Marion Traill lasted five months after his confession, largely due to the problems that he encountered in acquiring the necessary information. This was despite Airth evidently having money and influence at his disposal – both of which he used and would probably be beyond the resources of most contemporary women and many men. He met personally with the minister on 16 May 1619 to offer his help in drawing the case to a swift close, and could employ a man and horse to travel to Leith to investigate accordingly.[43]

Airth's personal endeavours there revealed a location and a jurisdiction that could be contacted by the minister – a turning point in the case. On 23 May 1619, probably frustrated by his lack of progress and with this information in hand, Airth asked the minister personally to write to the session of Linlithgow to enquire if they had any information on Borthwick's death.[44] In fact, the Tyninghame authorities had no better success; significant delays persisted in Linlithgow while the burgh authorities there tried to ascertain if William Borthwick had indeed been executed by them. An extract from the relevant records would have sufficed: in his capacity as minister, John Lauder is noted to have written 'to caus the towne clerk to seik unto the process anent the execution' in Linlithgow.[45] The delays in locating and obtaining an extracted process of an execution says something about the piecemeal state of early modern record keeping by Scotland's secular courts, not just their oft-berated kirk counterparts.[46] This was so even when the case in question was purported to be a capital one resulting in execution.

Although a time-consuming and costly process for Airth, that he was not on the pillar of repentance with Marion Traill giving public satisfaction for adultery proved motivation enough. While Traill was still performing public penance as an adulteress, 'Jhone Airthe compeirit befor the session desiring baptism to his bairn, seing he had usit diligence in getting testimoniallis quhilk [which] wer as he alledgit sufficient testimoniallis being certain evidentis of the deathe of Marin Trailis husband'.[47] The session had previously stated otherwise, yet Airth had credit enough with his friends and neighbours to be able to find caution that he too would start his penance as an adulterer, but only if he was unable to prove otherwise. His socio-economic power – which reflected positively on his reputation – had bought him time, and his illegitimate daughter was baptised on 20 July.

The couple were spared the requisite twenty-six Sundays on the stool just over one month later, thanks to Airth's continuing endeavours in Linlithgow, and resumed their penance before the congregation as fornicators – drawing their narrative together to a close. But sufficient doubt had been cast in the minds of the session members, so this was under the condition that Airth consign £5 10 shillings that he would satisfy as an adulterer or pay a further £40 if it should be later proved that Borthwick was alive. Airth must have been in possession of ready cash, and in relatively large sums, because he paid the £5 10 shillings immediately.[48] Traill had already sat three Sundays on the stool, completing the prescribed penance for a first fornication, therefore the session received her back into the fold of the congregation on 19 September 1619, after she had paid a 10 shilling penalty. As a known member of the community, Traill found caution to satisfy as an adulteress should it be discovered that she was still married at the time of her fornication. This was in the form of George Shortus, the session elder, who had presented her other son, George, for baptism in 1615. But she was not ordered to pay the £5 10 shillings that Airth had been, nor given the option to pay £40 instead.[49] Perhaps in Traill's case, the session realised that delivering such sums to them would not be possible, and so they were removed from the available options – an example of 'according to rank' in practice and the greater financial resources that adult males generally enjoyed.

John Airth's sexual failings seem to have ended with this third and final fornication and the birth of his second illegitimate child. After August 1619, he does not appear in the minutes again on any similar charges. All three of those fornications had taken place before his own marriage, after which he became the head of a household, no longer a member of someone else's. As in early modern England, this independence marked a new stage in the lifecycle of manhood, with a new set of responsibilities to correspond with the skills of self-government and restraint that were readily prescribed as ideals.[50]

Indeed, a second, parallel narrative of John Airth's behaviour had been winding through the Tyninghame session minutes during 1617, twenty months before he would marry Margaret Neilson and appear to adopt and conform to a new set of patriarchal expectations. Alongside answering for the moral laxity he showed by seducing his father's servants and a third woman shortly before he was due to be married, Airth's appearances before the session had extended into displays of overt masculinity of the kind that Alexandra Shepard classifies as having 'existed in tension with patriarchal principles of order'.[51]

On 16 March 1617 the minister reported to the elders that he had informed the presbytery of a great disturbance that had taken place within Dunbar parish on the night of 9 March, which included men from Tyninghame who 'drew swords and quhingers [small dagger-like knives] and raist the pepill of the towne' as 'they notoriouslie brak the sabboth' after copious amounts of drinking.[52] John Airth was amongst the group and was duly summoned to appear before the Dunbar kirk session to answer the charges of aggravated Sabbath breach. This he eventually did. He satisfied the Dunbar session in accordance with the presbytery on 13 April 1617, in the same manner as Robert Sinclair and Robert Young had done before him, 'by cuming befor the blissing befor the pulpit publicklie and sitting downe on their kneis, confessit their falt and cravat mercy according to the order and payit the penaltie of sabboth breakeris'.[53] On 22 June 1617, Airth was back before the Tyninghame session where:

> the minister shew to the elderis present how that the last sabbothe about the sun setting John Airthe sone to Thomas Airthe in Tyninghame had abused Alexander Davidson and his man also in the said Alexander Davidsone his hous efter drinking by schorning [scorning] him and thretतening farther by

manacing to stryk him and that he struik Robert Shortus the said Alexander his man.[54]

Elizabeth Foyster argues that 'being able to defend one's honour with one's fists was important'.[55] Although with a whinger rather than fists, Airth's actions here illustrate the similar tensions that existed for Scottish men, caught between demonstrating and defending their manhood by standing up to anyone perceived to have done them ill, and a peaceful, ordered existence within a patriarchal household and community. When the session reconvened one week later, witnesses to the attack were called, shedding some light on the background to the outburst in line with this analysis. Four witnesses deponed that Airth had wanted Davidson to sell him ale, but Davidson refused. The witnesses saw Airth react to the slight, and Davidson then move to defend himself:

> Jhone Airthe raiss up and said he shall put ane quhinger throuch baith his cheikis bot as yit drew not ane quhinger for the rest held him. Alexander Davidson seing this drew his quhinger first apparentlie to defend himself quhilk maid the said Jhone Airthe to be the mair intensed against him quhairupon he drew his quhinger and manacit the said Alexander Davidson thretning to stryk him.[56]

Whether a show of manly strength for the benefit of his companions or an assertive, masculine reaction against the insult of being refused service, it was unusual for such a case to come before the kirk sessions. Instances of violence were heard much more commonly in either the burgh or sheriff courts. The session evidently thought the same and, deciding that the case was beyond their judicial remit, referred it 'to the civil magistrat'. No further record exists past this referral, nor details as to which 'civil magistrat' they had in mind – the bailies, a baron court or the sheriff court. The session did, however, order both men to pay a fine and perform public repentance on their knees, while the minister emphasised to the congregation that John Airth was in the greater wrong having started the altercation in the first place. The session also drew Airth's father back into its dealings with his son when the minister had to ask Thomas Airth to use his patriarchal authority to chase his son's unpaid penalty so that he could be received by the congregation, having performed adequate penance.[57] Father–son relationships were recognised as having influence long past childhood, and patriarchal authority and its established hierarchies had a key role to play in safeguarding the good behaviour and spiritual salvation of the community.

After these cases of violence and the fornication with Marion Traill, John Airth disappears from the session minutes entirely until 1626 and his actions in the intervening ten years are unknown. It is possible that his actions before 1617 were similar to those of the hot-headed, lusty young Cambridge men examined by Shepard, and that Airth had since managed to tame his temper and sexual appetite to embrace the role of being a father within marriage and the head of a patriarchal household, which held the ideals of thrift, order and self-control at its centre.[58]

On 28 November 1619, Airth was one of three male witnesses at the baptism of the illegitimate daughter of John Davie, grieve (overseer) to Lady Bass.[59] Two legitimate children of his own shortly followed.[60] But, on 7 January 1626 the session noted that there was 'some suspicion of fornication betwixt Andrew Fay servand to Jhone Airthe and Bessie Lairmonth in Skugall'.[61] Airth's position was beginning to resemble his father's a decade before. The minutes then cease from February 1626 until March 1627; but the first entry when they resume on 18 March reads:

> The minister desyrit Thomas to adverteise Jhone Airthe his sone to tak heid if Bessie Wallace reportit to Jhone Airthis and was seing Robert Skugall servand to Jhone Airthe [who] was suspect in fornication with the said Bessie Wallace, and if they so servit togidder they sald be callit befor the session againe.[62]

Airth may have tamed his own sinful ways but now the governance of his household was in question as he embarked on a new phase as a patriarchal householder. The moral lapse of another of his servants, within his own house, had called his own adult masculinity into question. Established norms dictated that the patriarchal householder was to have oversight of those in their charge. This included the responsibility to control their behaviour, and a responsibility for that behaviour when it was found wanting.[63] When John Airth found himself in this position, the session cast a role for his father once more in the unfolding situation. Although his son no longer lived with him, Thomas Airth's paternal position still included advisory responsibilities, which could be both judged and used by the session at this stage of the younger Airth's lifecycle.

One month later and Thomas Airth would no longer have to impart such official messages to his son: at the meeting of the session on 22 April 1627, the clerk noted that 'Alexander Cunnyhame, George Lawder and Jhone Airthe nominat to be elderis'.[64] Airth was accepted to the same post that his father still held and was still serving as an elder in 1629.[65] He had acknowledged and accounted for his previous behaviour and had graduated to the formal position of an office-holder, responsible for the oversight of the behaviour of others beyond his own household. That he does not appear again at the sharp end of the session's business is lasting evidence of this. That he had accounted for his previous behaviour had made these developments possible. The kirk was able to welcome Airth into an official role, his socio-economic status allowing him to follow his father's lead because he had been absolved of all his youthful sins and was aware of any new personal challenges that his servants may have had in store for him as their employer and master – the dominant male householder.

John Airth's behaviour over a thirteen-year period had, on occasion, led the session to solicit the intervention of others in positions of authority. The civil authorities were one of those approached, but it is the role the session cast for his father over the course of thirteen years that highlights the relationship between different (and sometimes competing) masculinities that existed within an established patriarchal society with enduring father–son bonds. Both Thomas and John Airth had their authority as householders questioned at different points in their lives, and Thomas Airth found himself called upon to use his paternal authority to get his son to pay an outstanding fine and to keep him abreast of session business that involved him personally. In fact, the kirk session often used the position of male householders to assist and enable the drive to regulate personal and popular behaviour, to the extent that such demands could be expected by men at this adult stage of their lives. And with this expectation there came the possibility of failure.

In 1639, a Sabbath breach in the parish of Saltoun saw its kirk session react strongly against perceived failings of patriarchal male householders. On 20 October 1639, a group of eight 'boyes quho trublit the kirk in the tyme of divine service [were] ordained to be wairnit'. When none of the eight appeared before the session the following week, the session ordered that:

> the master sould bring their servantis, the parentis their childrein and quhipp them in fais of saisson upon Fryday nix. And incais of contempt the masteris and parentis to underly the censur of the session.[66]

The clerk made no record of the prescribed ordeal, but neither the boys nor their corresponding authority figures appear again in the minutes. Troublesome male youths were evidently a problem that autumn in Saltoun – at the next recorded meeting on 3 November, the session ordained 'to wairn some other boyes that troublit the kirk', and listed a further seventeen names.[67] It is not clear what happened to this group because this entry is the only record of their misbehaviour; but the treatment of the former group warrants consideration in its own right.

These boys had been called to appear before the session and had not obeyed, therefore the session ordered that the consequence of their original fault should be a public display of masculine, household authority in action. The group are referred to as 'boyes' in the minutes. Some were in service or apprenticeships and had 'masteris', while others were living at home under the authority of their 'parentis'. Beating younger members of any household would not have been a joyful task for the majority of authority figures, even in the seventeenth century. The session felt it necessary to warn these authority figures – these patriarchs, examples of a dominant masculinity – of the consequences they would face should they not appear to administer the whipping. The shaming nature of this punishment was twofold. First, the boys would be punished for their unruly behaviour. Secondly, those who were responsible for them at home were to be humiliated for not controlling their household in allowing the original behaviour to take place, and then for allowing the boys not to appear before the session when cited. The resulting public display would serve to demonstrate to fellow parishioners what happens when household authority was not being upheld to the kirk's standards. In such situations, the session would be forced to step in to re-establish that authority for all to see, and to the shame of all involved.

Failing as a dominant male householder was not to be tolerated. But, in this case, it is perhaps not entirely clear whether the Saltoun session was working to enforce established ideals regarding masculinity, authority and control, or imposing its own ideals on the domestic setting. It is not known what the boys' parents or masters thought of their misbehaviour. It is not known whether they thought that it was a matter that could be dealt with at home without outside intervention, or if they accepted that the boys were individuals with individual responsibility for their actions on the Sabbath, and should therefore be dealt with by the kirk. But what is clear is that it was unacceptable to flout the accepted norms of ideal behaviour for your station in hierarchical parish society.

While this was a responsibility for adult male householders that held some risk if not fulfilled, the socio-economic power of such men did also work to afford them some protection from the judicial power of the local secular authorities. In Haddington burgh court on 7 September 1615, John Simpson younger, John Wilkie, and John Thomson appeared, all three having been apprehended and warded on certain points of theft. All were notaries – educated, literate men. Simpson was himself a burgess and, alongside Wilkie, had represented Alexander Sinclair, a Haddington indweller, as procurator in the prosecution of John Bartholomew's children for theft on 5 March 1611.[68] All stood accused of stealing three young goslings from George Thomson's stables, 'under clude of nyt'. Of the three men, only Thomson was convicted and was sentenced to 'remaine in waird for the space of four dayis heirefter and to pay twentie pundis of penaltie for his offence'.[69]

On 1 February 1623 Thomas Wauchope ('alledging him to be borne in Mersingtoun') was prosecuted for stealing corn from a barnyard in Clerkington. He was banished, with the promise that he would be scourged through the streets and branded on the shoulder without further trial should he return.[70] For John Thomson, a professional man and burgh resident, four days' imprisonment in the relative privacy of the tolbooth and the payment of a hefty fine was seen to suffice for being convicted of a like offence of stealing moveable property. But there is no record of punishments for theft being defined by central government according to the social status of the thief in question, nor exemptions being allowed on such grounds.[71] What 'type' of man you were – economically vulnerable, or a professional, long-standing burgh resident – was not taken into account by the law itself.

And yet what 'type' of man you were did have bearing on the extent of punishment deemed appropriate by Haddingtonshire's secular courts. It also affected the ability to secure caution to appear in court or to pay a fine, much like a modern-day bail bond. If a man lacked the means and social standing to form personal relationships with other individual men with enough socio-economic power to stand surety for their behaviour, then it was a quick route to appearing on the stool of repentance, being warded in the tolbooth, banished, or worse.[72] Indeed, John Airth managed to use his socio-economic position as surety to delay his public penance for fornication with Marion Traill, and Traill herself managed to secure caution because she was a local resident with existing relationships with those in formal positions of power. Men who did not enjoy similar personal relationships found themselves unable to do likewise.[73]

East Lothian between 1610 and 1640 was a patriarchal society, with the patriarchal household at the centre of each parish community. Patriarchy in this period did not simply encompass gender differences, but the importance of rank – a hierarchy present within households and families and within the broader community – as conferred by socio-economic status and seniority, and the associated agency both afforded. Such conditions served to exclude many ordinary women from the bargaining process, but they also drew divisions between men – including those appearing before secular burgh authorities.

As popular expectations of men changed over the course of the life-cycle, the personal experience of authority varied within East Lothian on a parish-by-parish basis, and could even vary within a parish depending on the matter in hand. The experiences of John Airth illustrate this well, as he responded to allegations of sexual misadventure and violent conduct before transitioning to the roles of husband, householder and office-holder. Airth's position within established patriarchal structures was redefined over thirteen years, and the agency afforded to him by his rank and wealth allowed him to navigate changing expectations after conforming to institutional, judicial norms by submitting to offering penance for his previous sins.

Rather than reflecting an urban–rural divide in the experience of social control, this group of East Lothian men suggests the truly local-ised nature of governance during this period. Local men in official positions of authority were making local decisions that often differed from those of their neighbours. Similarly, the experience of prosecution by the Haddington burgh authorities and sheriff court were not always divorced from matters of status. The ability to pay fines, find sufficient caution and, occasionally, punishment itself was experienced according to rank as part of established patriarchal hierarchy.

Parishes in lowland Scotland can, and should, be cited alongside contemporaneous examples from early modern France, Germany, and England. Different men were treated in different ways for similar contraventions. Their socio-economic status and age affected their treatment, partly because those in power thought it should, either because of situational realities or pervasive normative hierarchies. The boy, the young man, the servant, the householder – all were part of an overarching socio-economic hierarchy with associated expectations. These expectations were subscribed to by church, state, and – crucially – ordinary people. There was no homogeneous blanket of state authority, but the setting and regulation of behavioural standards in a godly society was structured along patriarchal lines.

NOTES

1. The most recent survey is Margo Todd, *The Culture of Protestantism in Early Modern Scotland* (New Haven: Yale University Press, 2002).
2. For example Robert Fenwick, 'Locating Scotland's ordinary folk, among the lesser known sources for social and family history research, c. 1630–c. 1790'

(unpublished doctoral thesis, University of Edinburgh, 2006); Margaret Sanderson, *Ayrshire and the Reformation: People and Change 1490–1600* (East Linton: Tuckwell Press, 1997); Julian Goodare, 'Scotland', in R. W. Scribner, Roy Porter and Mikuláš Teich (eds), *Reformation in National Context* (Cambridge: Cambridge University Press, 1994), pp. 95–110; Michael Lynch, *Edinburgh and the Reformation* (Edinburgh: John Donald, 1981).

3. Leah Leneman and Rosalind Mitchison, *Sin in the City: Sexuality and Social Control in Urban Scotland, 1660–1780* (Edinburgh: Scottish Cultural Press, 1998), p. 86. See also Rosalind Mitchison and Leah Leneman, *Girls in Trouble: Sexuality and Social Control in Rural Scotland* (Edinburgh: Scottish Cultural Press, 1998).

4. James K. Cameron (ed.), *The First Book of Discipline* (Edinburgh: Saint Andrew Press, 1972), pp. 165–79.

5. Todd, *Culture of Protestantism*, pp. 266, 403, 405–7; Michael F. Graham, *The Uses of Reform: 'Godly Discipline' and Popular Behaviour in Scotland and Beyond, 1560–1610* (Leiden: Brill, 1996), pp. 148, 267–8, 279, 289; 'Women and the church courts in Reformation-era Scotland', in Elizabeth Ewan and Maureen M. Meikle (eds), *Women in Scotland c. 1100–c. 1750* (East Linton: Tuckwell Press, 1999), pp. 187–98, at 195–6; Harriet Cornell, 'Gender, sex, and social control: East Lothian, 1610–1640', (unpublished doctoral thesis, University of Edinburgh, 2012).

6. Gordon DesBrisay, 'Twisted by definition: women under Godly discipline in seventeenth-century Scottish towns', in Yvonne Brown and Rona Ferguson (eds), *Twisted Sisters: Women, Crime and Deviance in Scotland since 1400* (East Linton: Tuckwell Press, 2002), pp. 137–55, at 141–2.

7. For early modern England, pioneered and advocated by Martin Ingram in *Church Courts, Sex and Marriage in England, 1570–1640* (Cambridge: Cambridge University Press, 1987), p. xi.

8. Julian Goodare, *The Government of Scotland, 1560–1625* (Oxford: Oxford University Press, 2004), especially chapters 8 and 9; Stephen T. Davies, 'The courts and the Scottish legal system, 1600–1747: the case of Stirlingshire crime and the law', in V. A. C. Gatrell, Bruce Lenman and Geoffrey Parker (eds), *Crime and the Law: The Social History of Crime in Western Europe since 1500* (London: Europa Publications, 1980), pp. 120–54.

9. Cornell, 'Gender, sex and social control', pp. 21–3.

10. On shared office-holding and punishment rituals, see ibid. chapters 2 and 3.

11. Graham, *Uses of Reform*, pp. 75, 90–1, 213.

12. Establishing a 'godlie societie' was a central aim of the 1560 Reformation, as outlined in *The First Book of Discipline*. See Cameron (ed.), *The First Book of Discipline*; and James Kirk (ed.), *The Second Book of Discipline* (Edinburgh: Saint Andrew Press, 1980).

13. James J. Chriss, *Social Control: An Introduction* (Cambridge: Polity, 2007), pp. 109–17.

14. J. R. D. Falconer, *Crime and Community in Reformation Scotland: Negotiating Power in a Burgh Society* (London: Pickering & Chatto, 2013).

15. M. Spufford, 'Puritanism and social control?', in Anthony Fletcher and John Stevenson (eds), *Order and Disorder in Early Modern England* (Cambridge: Cambridge University Press, 1987), pp. 41–57.

16. Explored fully in Cornell, 'Gender, sex, and social control', especially pp. 123–4, 198–200.

17. John McCallum, *Reforming the Scottish Parish: The Reformation in Fife, 1560–1640* (Farnham: Ashgate, 2010), p. 228; Graeme Murdock, *Beyond Calvin: The Intellectual, Political and Cultural World of Europe's Reformed Churches, c. 1540–1620* (Basingstoke: Palgrave Macmillan, 2004), pp. 100–1.

18. Todd, *Culture of Protestantism*, chapters 5 and 6; Chriss, *Social Control*, pp. 17–21.

19. See also Falconer, *Crime and Community*, pp. 23–44.

20. For example see Katie Barclay, *Love, Intimacy and Power: Marriage and Patriarchy in Scotland, 1650–1850* (Manchester, Manchester University Press, 2011).

21. Cornell, 'Gender, sex and social control', p. 98.

22. Wally Seccombe, 'Patriarchy stabilized: the construction of the male bread-winner wage norm in nineteenth-century Britain', *Social History*, 11:1 (1986), pp. 53–76, at 59.

23. For a detailed analysis of the East Lothian court network, see Cornell, 'Gender, sex and social control', chapters 2 and 3.

24. Tyninghame Kirk Session Minutes, National Records of Scotland [NRS], CH2/359/1, f. 5.

25. Elizabeth A. Foyster, *Manhood in Early Modern England: Honour, Sex and Marriage* (London: Longman, 1999), p. 87.

26. NRS, CH2/359/1, f. 5.

27. NRS, CH2/359/1, f. 17.

28. NRS, CH2/359/1, f. 17.

29. NRS, CH2/359/1, f. 18.

30. Cornell, 'Gender, sex, and social control', pp. 160–3.

31. NRS, CH2/359/1, ff. 22–3.

32. NRS, CH2/359/1, f. 24.

33. NRS, CH2/359/1, f. 2.

34. NRS, CH2/359/1, f. 24.

35. NRS, CH2/359/1, f. 25.

36. NRS, CH2/359/1, f. 25.

37. Foyster, *Manhood in Early Modern England*, pp. 55–8.

38. NRS, CH2/359/1, ff. 25–6.

39. NRS, CH2/359/1, f. 26.

40. NRS, CH2/359/1, f. 27.
41. NRS, CH2/359/1, f. 30.
42. NRS, CH2/359/1, f. 28.
43. NRS, CH2/359/1, f. 27.
44. NRS, CH2/359/1, f. 27.
45. NRS, CH2/359/1, f. 27.
46. This helps to verify and possibly extend the caution suggested by Michael Graham when employing quantitative analytical methods to such records. See: Graham, *Uses of Reform*, pp. 75, 90–1.
47. NRS, CH2/359/1, f. 29.
48. NRS, CH2/359/1, f. 30.
49. NRS, CH2/359/1, f. 31.
50. Alexandra Shepard, *Meanings of Manhood in Early Modern England* (Oxford: Oxford University Press, 2003), pp. 23–37.
51. Ibid. p. 128.
52. NRS, CH2/359/1, f. 11.
53. NRS, CH2/359/1, f. 11.
54. NRS, CH2/359/1, f. 13.
55. Foyster, *Manhood in Early Modern England*, p. 177.
56. NRS, CH2/359/1, f. 13.
57. NRS, CH2/359/1, ff. 13, 14.
58. Shepard, *Meanings of Manhood*, pp. 93–113.
59. NRS, CH2/359/1, f. 32.
60. NRS, CH2/359/1, ff. 34, 45.
61. NRS, CH2/359/1, f. 54.
62. NRS, CH2/359/1, f. 56.
63. Julie Hardwick, *The Practice of Patriarchy: Gender and the Politics of Household Authority in Early Modern France* (University Park: Pennsylvania State University Press, 1998), x.
64. NRS, CH2/359/1, f. 56.
65. On 22 February 1629, John Airth is referred to in the minutes as collecting and consigning the penalty of James Anderson to the poor box. NRS, CH2/359/1, f. 60.
66. NRS, Saltoun Kirk Session Minutes, CH2/322/1, f. 14.
67. NRS, CH2/322/1, f. 14.
68. NRS, B30/10/9, ff. 32–3.
69. NRS, B30/10/9, f. 230.
70. NRS, B30/10/10, f. 252.
71. Sir James Balfour of Pittendreich, *Practicks*, 12 vols, T. Thomson and C. Innes (eds) (Edinburgh, 1814–75), pp. 521–9.
72. For example, see the case of George Baillie in North Berwick, NRS OPR 713/1 f. 143.
73. For example, see the case of James Gullane in Haddington, NRS, SC40/7/18, f. 163.

10

A 'Polite and Commercial People'? Masculinity and Economic Violence in Scotland, 1700–60

Tawny Paul

VIOLENCE IS OFTEN GIVEN a central place in accounts of male behaviour and identity in early modern Britain. The majority of violent crime was carried out by and against men, and violent behaviour served a variety of social functions related to gender identity.[1] Violence was a resource that could be used by men of all social ranks across the lifecycle and in a variety of private and public contexts to assert status and to defend their honour. It was, therefore, one of the main props of patriarchy. For young men, violence was a component of coming of age and a means of demonstrating physical courage and strength, and it remained a tool of patriarchal power throughout men's lifecycles.[2] Those who became independent heads of households (though achievement of this status was by no means universal) were expected to exert control over their dependents. Aggressive language and physical punishments could help them to maintain superior positions over women and servants. For those in subordinate positions, violence could be a means of claiming agency and resisting authority.[3]

According to standard narratives, violent masculinity was tamed in the eighteenth century.[4] Though its timing and reach in Scotland is debated, a 'civilising process' occurred here as throughout Europe.[5] Conduct literature advocated the replacement of an outdated honour culture with new codes of politeness that emphasised self-restraint and problematised male aggression and the legal system was increasingly used to enforce new codes of male behaviour. Respectable men were expected to turn to legal mechanisms rather than to their fists or their swords to resolve disputes. Alongside the law, modernisation narratives afford commerce a central role in the acculturation of new codes of male behaviour. Indeed, Adam Smith's final phase of civilisation was 'commercial society'.[6] Modern commercial culture required new

behavioural ideals and these ideals were adhered to, especially by an
'upwardly mobile, modestly middle class'.[7] For middling men, commer-
cialism refined and polished individual passions and manners, and came
to define new forms of prudential masculinity.[8]

This chapter contends that the relationship between masculinity,
economy and interpersonal violence in eighteenth-century Scotland was
more complicated than the linear narrative of 'civilisation' suggests.
Commerce was not merely an agent in the civilising process; rather,
masculine violence and commerce reinforced one another. Indeed, violence played a functional role within the commercial sphere where it
supported claims to masculine gender identity. Economic violence, as
defined by contemporaries and by more recent social theory, took a
number of forms. First, while violence is often defined as a physical,
harmful act, physical abuse was not the only form of violence carried out
by men in eighteenth-century Scotland. Contemporaries understood that
violence occurred on a spectrum, from words or 'verbal violence' at one
end, encompassing threats and harassment, to physical aggression and
actual bodily harm at the other. There was an overlapping zone between
physical and verbal violence structured around notions of honour.[9] This
range of violent acts was carried out by men as part of interpersonal economic relationships, related to negotiations over economic rights, power
and reputation. Second, violence was understood as being directed not
only at persons, but objects as well. Malicious and violent damage
towards property was one of the major concerns of the Scottish police
courts from the late eighteenth century, related to middle-class concerns
over wealth.[10] Finally, social theory makes clear that violence does not
have to be physical at all. It can be symbolic, social and emotional. As
such, economic acts can themselves be considered forms of violence
by impinging upon individual agency and autonomy, serving as tools
of coercion and repression. Relations of credit and debt, a ubiquitous
feature of the early modern economy, have been described as a form of
'gentle violence'. Pierre Bourdieu considered credit to be an 'attack' on
the freedom of debtors because it established control and created the
obligation to reciprocate, much like a gift.[11]

The following discussion explores the intersections between masculinity, interpersonal violence and commerce in Edinburgh and its envi-
rons, focusing on the years 1700 to 1760, a period when the city was
undergoing significant economic and cultural improvements preceding
the building of the New Town. This 'improvement' extended to the
self, and should have had a significant impact on men's public, commercial behaviour. In what follows, two forms of economic violence

are discussed: a spectrum of psychological and physical acts of violence, carried out within a commercial sphere, and economic actions interpreted as forms of violence. These individual acts of violence intersected with gender in suggestive ways, serving individual claims to commercial masculinity. Because masculine identities were intricately bound up with issues of social rank, the chapter focuses specifically on the violent exchanges that took place between middling men who, we assume, should have been influenced by the dictates of polite society.

The middling sort included a broad swathe of society, from wealthy merchants and civic authorities to more humble tradesmen and craftsmen, whose claims to independent status were fragile and competitive.[12] Examples of violent behaviour emerge from three main bodies of civil court records: Tolbooth prison records, cases of defamation and small debt litigation.[13] Unlike records of violent crime, these sources do not provide an account of changing levels of violence over time. However, they do provide an opportunity to attend to the forms and meanings of violence, as well as to acts that might have been considered routine or legitimate rather than violations of socially or legally acceptable behaviour.[14] The content of such exchanges, as they emerge in court records, suggests that for middling individuals, violence served as a competitive tool, a resource in negotiations over honour, reputation and authority, and a means of claiming the 'patriarchal dividends' of social status, power and privilege.[15] Economic violence was therefore not only the property of the 'crowd', used to defend customary rights and a symptom of class antagonisms, but was deployed interpersonally by a range of different men including those of the middle ranks of society.[16]

PHYSICAL VIOLENCE IN EDINBURGH

In the eighteenth century, Edinburgh was a town undergoing major economic, social and structural change. After the Union of 1707, it became a deposed capital and lost significant political power. However, it remained a provincial capital that fulfilled a range of functions, acting as a legal, financial, cultural and intellectual centre, and its physical environment provided the backdrop for polite society.[17] An active participant in Britain's provincial 'urban renaissance', Edinburgh society was characterised by large numbers of professionals as well as members of the gentry and aristocracy who were attracted to the city's cultural resources.[18] It was arguably eighteenth-century Scotland's most 'polite' town, and its population of middling men should have been significantly influenced by new codes of civility and sensibility, though as Rosalind

Carr suggests, polite and enlightened thought was not necessarily intolerant of violence.[19] Like cities elsewhere, the urban environment served as a space for new masculinities to be made.[20] Increasing layers of civic governance created opportunities for middling social advancement through office holding, but also became venues for competition and conflict over property, rank and power.

Economic violence within this urban context was a particularly male activity. The overwhelming majority of violent acts discussed in the courts involved male perpetrators and victims. In instances of public insult and ruined credit that were accompanied by physical violence or threats of violence (brought before the town's consistory court), men accounted for sixty-two per cent of victims and sixty-six per cent of transgressors. In acts of imprisonment for debt, which might be considered forms of judicial violence (discussed below), men constituted eighty-nine per cent of creditors and ninety-one per cent of imprisoned debtors. Furthermore, this was violence waged primarily *between* men. Though violence could be used as a means of asserting dominance over women, most legal disputes involved conflicts between individuals of the same gender.[21] These figures do not suggest that women in Scotland did not engage in violence, a subject that has been investigated elsewhere, but rather that violence seemed to occupy a central position in men's economic disputes.[22]

Physical violence appeared in a number of commercial contexts. One of its foremost functions was to defend masculine honour.[23] Honour held a significant place in the economy because of the system of credit. Due to shortages of coin, volatile trade cycles, and irregular incomes, most day-to-day economic transactions took place by using credit. Credit was based upon trust and assessments of individual credibility and worth were based largely upon a person's social reputation.[24] Slights to a man's honour, therefore, could have significant financial consequences by ruining individual credit. It was often expected that men would respond to slights upon their credit by resorting to violence, and failure to do so could be interpreted as a sign of weakness or affirmation of an insult. Middling men might respond violently to actions that threatened their reputation for independence or which questioned their control over the economic activities of their households, both features of ideal patriarchal masculinity.[25] When in 1762 Matthew Bell, a court officer designated as an 'indweller' in the legal records, came to the house of Thomas Small with a warrant to seize ale that had not been brewed by licence, Small 'said that if any came to seize ale out of his house he would putt a pair of bullets through his head and if that would not do he would make a sword do it'. When Bell returned a second time, Small 'graspt him and swore that he would be the butch of any man that would offer to break up his door and take away his ale under cloud of night'. At the time, Small had an iron mattock in his hand and aimed some strokes at Bell with his fists.[26] For Small, violence was a form of defence against another man's attempt to regulate his household activities or to take household items, thus threatening his patriarchal status. His response might also have served to question Bell's authority within the system of civic governance, a system that, by strictly regulating activities such as brewing, limited Small's access to a livelihood and to independent status.

Particular forms of disciplinary violence were used by men over their inferiors as a way of reminding them of their subordinate status.[27] Acts of disciplinary violence, when mimicked in public by men who were not in relationships of dependency, could serve as a means of humiliation and competition in which one man symbolically asserted authority over another through symbolic violence. After William Durham, a servant, insulted and threatened the reputation of the dyer Alexander Hepburn by calling him a liar, Hepburn came to Durham's house, and 'on the stair without the house where the defender was standing, did lash him with his whip several times'.[28] Whipping, a punishment normally reserved for household discipline and the correction of criminals, served to debase Durham and remind others of his lower rank. For Hepburn, violence was a tool that helped to discredit Durham's defamatory words while restoring his own honour.

Patriarchal discipline and control extended not only to the household, but to business and property as well. Perceived infringements upon a man's property or business interests could easily lead to violent confrontations. In 1756, when one man grazed his cattle on another's land, the property owner 'insulted alltackt [attacked] and beat him'.[29] In 1760, Adam Robieson, tacksman of a paper mill at Gifford, physically assaulted Robert Laing, saying that Laing enticed away the people who furnished him with rags by offering them a higher price.[30] Violence or threats of violence tended to occur especially within disputes over property. For men, a violent blow was an action that asserted dominance or ownership over physical property. In 1699, when Alexander Cunningham came across the servant of Thomas Semphill carrying a bundle of whins [gorse] that he believed had been cut from his own land, Cunningham 'offered to stryke him and took the whime [whins] off his back and carried the same away with him'. Angry with Cunningham's disciplining of his servant and the implications that an accusation of theft had for the honour of his household, Semphill responded with an act of physical violence.[31]

While the confrontation between Semphill and Cunningham exemplifies the use of violence to defend rights, it also shows that individual acts of violence were subject to competing interpretations and could be understood within differing definitions of middling masculinity. While a man's right to defend his property, his home and his dependents was accepted and to some extent expected under codes of honour, acts of violence were also framed and understood within masculine ideals of self-control. Aggression could be perceived not as an assertion of rights, but rather as a failure to master control over one's emotions and impulses, or a failure to assert reason.[32] Because a man's ability to rule over his own body, desires and passions was a precondition of his authority to rule over others, such loss of control undermined his claims to patriarchal status.[33] These competing interpretations of violence became part of the rhetorical strategy of the courtroom. Thus men's violent behaviour was sometimes framed as 'passionate' or 'furious' as a means of discrediting or dishonouring opponents in the courtroom.[34] So, while Semphill framed his actions as an assertion of rights, Cunningham framed them as a loss of control, describing how Semphill responded with thoughtless emotional impulse, and 'took up a pair of branks lying at his foot and ran *furiously* to strick the defender'.[35] Beyond these contradictions, there were many aspects of middling masculinity that the violence discussed in the courtroom left out. While violent acts were discussed as defending or discrediting claims to honour, patriarchy and power, they seemed to bear little relation to more varied forms of masculine identity, including economic management, fatherhood, or domestic emotion.[36] This serves as a reminder that, as recent studies of domestic violence suggest, changing conceptions of masculinity and societal beliefs could have limited impact on the justice system and subsequently on courtroom discussion.[37]

A range of men resorted to economic violence, complicating any simple relationship between violence, masculinity and patriarchy. Violent acts and gestures formed part of the masculine 'toolbox' both for those in positions of power, and for men who could not lay claim to independent status or household and civic authority. Violence could therefore be used both to assert governance and power and also to receive, accept, avoid, undermine or reject it.[38] Violent acts were thus directed at officers and civic officials within the context of economic disputes, rejecting their authority to seize property or carry out court orders within bankruptcy disputes. Violent gestures might include snatching or tearing up legal orders. In 1735, when the writer [lawyer] John Din came to the house of James Wright, a staymaker, with papers demanding payment of a debt, Wright 'violently snatched them away from him and immediately run away with them into another room without paying the money'.[39] In 1768, when George Milne came to David Seton's house, threatening him with a legal instrument related to a debt case, Seton 'tore the same in pieces and threw it on the floor, and afterwards in a rage gathered it up and threw it out the window into the street'.[40]

Violence in the face of legal action often involved the debasement of the official carrying out regulation or seizure in order to question his authority. When James Thom, collector for the taxmen of the Light of May came to the shipmaster Thomas Pillans to collect his dues, threatening to seize the ship if Pillans did not pay, Pillans insulted Thom, saying 'You are but weak', to which Thom answered 'Whither he was weak or strong, that he behoved to do by the strength of others'.[41] When John Gant, a soldier, came to the house of a local stabler with a court officer to seize a horse, he was 'without giving the lest offence most barberously attacked' by the stabler and 'beat to the effusion of [his] Blood and [his] cloth Tore and Hatt interely lost in the scuffell'.[42] Striking off or destroying a man's hat was a common symbolic form of defiance, and in the context of property seizure, it served as a refusal to accept the official's authority over a debtor's property.

In addition to negotiations with civic authorities, violent acts were part of the negotiation of power within household and employment relationships, serving as a tool for dependents to claim economic rights. In the context of labour relations, men used aggression and violence to assert their rights to opportunities for work and access to wages. In August 1762, when John Mitchell, a tenant from outside of Edinburgh, hired five shearers at the West Port to cut down corn, a group of shearers who felt that they had a right to the work used violent action to assert their labour rights. One labourer, Laughlin McIntosh, 'came up to the complainer attacked him and called him damned scoundrel, and swore he would knowck him down if he did not give him their hooks'. The others then came to the complainer's farm and demanded their wages. The action was considered a violation and brought to court as a breach of the peace, but shows how violence could be used as a tool to enforce rights to a contract.[43]

Whether in public, domestic, or labour contexts, the violent acts carried out by men could be highly meaningful and symbolic. Though codes of civility and self-control provided alternative rhetorical frameworks for understanding violence, and some individual acts were no doubt motivated by mindless aggression, interpreting acts of violence as mere examples of untamed emotions fails to recognise that many acts had precise meanings that conformed to patterns in their form of expression. Men drew on a repertoire of gestures and postures intended to humiliate, debase and extend verbal insults.[44] Physical actions often involved gestures directed at the head or face, aimed particularly at denying another man his bodily autonomy.[45] Tweaking the nose of another man, or tearing off his hat or wig, was a symbolic act of exposure and humiliation. For example, in 1703, in the context of a dispute over a business deal that had fallen through between Patrick Cowan and Joseph Sheill, Sheill, upon encountering Cowan in a house, 'fell upon the persuer and base him took him by the throat, took off his hat and whig and threw them on the ground and tramped upon them'.[46]

Uplifted hands or weapons often accompanied insults in order to assert dominance. In a dispute over the quality of a peruke sold by Alexander Campbell, peruke maker, to George Campbell, George, 'in a bold and impertinent manner with his kean [cane] in his hand uplifted', accused Alexander of being a cheat and selling him a peruke 'which was not worth half the money he took for it'.[47] Similarly, in a public dispute between the ministers Andrew Kerr and George Oswald, Oswald insulted Kerr while 'lifting up his hand and staff over the complainer's head'.[48] In such disputes between individuals of competitive social status, violence served as a means of claiming superiority, even if it was only threatened and never carried out. Here, physical violence, threats of physical violence and words were conflated as means of claiming dominance and asserting power.

The threat or infliction of physical harm upon one man by another had multiple and layered meanings within an economic context. However, violence was not always physical. As a central feature of masculinity, aggression persisted throughout the eighteenth century, both in rhetoric and lived experience.[49] It had a central role to play in eighteenth-century credit relations. While the system of credit, based upon trust, has been described as a social system engendering positive social relations and encouraging reciprocity and neighbourliness, there was plenty of room for aggression, especially at the moment when a debtor defaulted.[50] In Edinburgh, aggressive language emerged as a regular feature in cases of disputed debts, failed payments and contract negotiations. For example, in a dispute over a payment for smith work, the mason Thomas Smith complained that one of his customers, Robert Lauder, 'paid nobody who wrought to him'. Smith threatened that he 'would do all he could to stop and hinder masons and other tradesmen from working to him' and furthermore that 'no person should possess his houses and that he would endeavour to keep them from tennents'.[51] Smith used his status and power within the trading community to back up a threat intended to entice payment from Lauder. Threats to ruin another man's honour or fortune were another tactic used within economic disputes. In 1738, John Mitchell, a merchant in North Leith, in an altercation over the payment of customs duties with a sailor, 'threateaned to send letters to every port he knew the complainer went and inform his acquaintances what kind of a man he was'.[52] In 1735, John Alexander, a maltman, in the context of a dispute over the price of meal with Alexander Smith, threatened that he would have '[Smith] and Leith Milns ruined in a short time'.[53] Such threatening and aggressive tactics, especially within an economy where economic ruin was a very real and persistent threat, could ultimately lead to incidents of physical violence. When James Brotherstons, a harness maker in the Canongate, threatened to expose Adam Boig, author of the *Edinburgh Courant*, for refusing to place his advertisement in the paper, an argument resulted in which 'both parties took instruments', in an honour-based physical contest.[54] In none of these examples did the commercial context provide a setting that 'tamed' men's aggressive qualities, demanding polite and civilised behaviour. Rather, commerce created conflicts that might be resolved through violence, and in some cases the economy provided the very means by which aggression could be carried out.

THE VIOLENCE OF LAW

The spectrum of violent acts employed by men included not only physical and socially aggressive actions, but also sanctioned or routine acts in which violence could remain hidden in the legal record. Use of the legal system itself could constitute an act of aggression. As legal theorists recognise, law and violence have a contradictory relationship. The law intends to disrupt and prevent violence. The Scottish law of lawburrows, for example, was a means of restraining a potential violent act. However, the law can itself constitute a kind of violence, as a 'restraint or violation imposed by somebody on somebody against their will'.[55] In some eighteenth-century circles, aggressive litigation was perceived as a legitimate tool within the negotiation of economic contracts. Contemporary trade manuals even advocated aggressive legal tactics within credit relationships. Daniel Defoe wrote in 1729 that 'the security of the tradesman's trusting his neighbour is the power he has by law to *enforce* his payment'.[56]

The line between enforcement and coercion, however, was thin. Contemporaries understood that legal action could go too far and litigation was sometimes framed using a language of violence. One English pamphlet warned readers against doing business in Scotland because 'there a spirit of litigation frequently operates with such violence that expence is disregarded when victory is the consequence'.[57] In 1742, the merchant Robert Wilson described himself as 'being attacked' by litigation carried out against him.[58] Because interpersonal credit was so ubiquitous, cases of debt, by far the most common type of court case and a form of litigation that was relatively easy and inexpensive to instigate, provided a means for parties to further a variety of economic and non-economic disputes. Buying up coercive debts was a way for men to establish power over one another. In 1739, Archibald Thomson brought a case of scandal to the consistory court, claiming that his opponents 'dayly used their utmost to ruin his credit by purchasing and buying up his debts, torturing and tormenting him with groundless lawsutes, by all which the defenders are guilty of abuse against the complainer'.[59] Here, indebtedness coupled with legal force was itself an act of symbolic violence, though there was no physical contact between protagonists.

One of the most ubiquitous forms of legal economic violence in Scotland was the debtors' prison. Under Scottish law, if a debtor could not or refused to pay, a creditor could choose between a range of recourses. After taking the debt to court to establish its validity, he or she could initiate a lengthy court process to gain access to the debtor's effects. Alternatively, the creditor could choose to take the debtor's body through imprisonment. Creditors thus had the legal ability to seize both the debtors' property as well as their bodies as a form of collateral for economic obligations. Though facilitated by the legal system, imprisonment for debt was an action imposed interpersonally by creditors upon their debtors. Once a debt was proven in court, the creditor hired a messenger to carry out the arrest and pay the jailor a fee to have the debtor incarcerated. In Edinburgh, debtors were confined in the Tolbooth, a building located on the High Street that served as a space of incarceration for both criminals and debtors.

Imprisonment as a legitimate legal action can be considered a form of violence. Prison denied debtors bodily autonomy and many were subjected to physical hardship. Unlike in England, where debtors' prisons were 'porous' and afforded their inmates some degree of autonomy, the Scottish law of *squalor carceris* stipulated that debtors be actively denied fresh air as a way of coercing them into paying their debts.[60] The law deliberately subjected debtors to close confinement and uncomfortable conditions. The prison contained two open rooms where male debtors were confined. Debtors were furnished only with a straw mattress, a blanket and two rugs for which they had to pay.[61] Debtor petitions frequently complained of ill health and poor conditions. Some complained of inadequate nourishment. David Henderson petitioned in 1738 that 'I have been thrie or four days that I have never tasted meett'.[62]

Imprisonment was an act that ruined men's reputations, signalling to the community that a debtor was either broke or recalcitrant. For middling men, the damage to reputation could be particularly gendered. Incarceration harmed male credit by depriving men of the ability to fulfil patriarchal and civic responsibilities while confined. Deprivation of these hard-earned roles could mean a loss of status. Charles Cock lost the ability both to support his family and to fill a position of authority he had earned within the Incorporation of Hammermen. Petitioning the bailie court, he framed his circumstances as a deprivation of 'liberty' and begged to be released 'that he may be useful to his family, and in his own sphere as some service to that society of which he is a member'.[63]

Imprisonment was not the most effective or rational means of collecting a debt. Periods of incarceration lessened rather than facilitated debtors' chances of improving their financial situations. Debtors had to pay to keep themselves fed, and no employment was permitted while a person was held in prison.[64] Debtors claimed that imprisonment caused them to neglect business and lose income, and worried that they would never recover financially.[65] As their predicaments worsened, so did the chances of paying off their creditors. Imprisonment only rarely resulted in satisfaction for the creditor. Furthermore, it could be financially costly to creditors. If the court determined that a debtor was too poor to aliment himself, creditors were expected to pay maintenance fees. In 1780, John Meldrum, a merchant, paid 10s to aliment his prisoner for a debt of £8 Scots (12s 4d sterling).[66] Compounded with legal fees, the costs of imprisoning a debtor could easily amount to a significant proportion of the debt being pursued. Contemporaries seemed well aware of these pitfalls, and that there was little material gain to be expected from imprisoning one's debtors. As an eighteenth-century proverb stated, 'prison pays no debts'.[67]

The prison was therefore not so much a rational tool for extracting payment from debtors, but must rather be considered a constituent part of an economic culture of honour, in which aggression carried out by creditors was part of men's competitive interaction. Because credit was based on social trust, failure to pay could be interpreted as a social transgression, an insult, or a breach of a promise. Responding with appropriate force was a point of honour, rather than a transgression. Indeed, as Robert Shoemaker has suggested, in the eighteenth century 'men were expected to assert their independence by resorting to violence when their honesty or authority was challenged'.[68] In using the prison, aggression could serve as a signifier of social identity and as a means of confirming gender identity.

As elsewhere, the uses and perceptions of male violence were highly influenced by social status.[69] The majority of instances of imprisonment were carried out by and against men of competitive middling status. Very few men of the high and low ends of the social spectrum (gentlemen and labourers) spent time in prison or were responsible for imprisoning their debtors. The majority of cases involved artisans, tradesmen and merchants. These men were both highly competitive and extremely vulnerable, faced with conditions that could encourage aggressive behaviour. As the power of trade incorporations changed and waned across the century, craftsmen found themselves engaged in demarcation disputes and their business interests more exposed.[70] Political disputes between craftsmen and merchants punctuated the period as these groups vied for civic authority within the town.[71] While Edinburgh's growing economy offered opportunities for middling success, tradesmen were also vulnerable to frequent crises and a fluctuating economy.[72]

Within such a competitive environment, use of the legal system could be a means for men to claim power and authority. Imprisonment, like the duel, was a means of conferring horizontal honour, or asserting honour between relative equals.[73] Despite the knowledge that prison probably would not pay, many creditors chose to keep their debtors in prison at their own expense. As long as the creditor was willing to continue paying, the debtor could theoretically be kept in prison indefinitely. The subjection of debtors to the threat of perpetual confinement, balanced by pardoning debts and consenting to their liberation, echoed the system of terror and mercy within England's penal code.[74] By giving creditors an extraordinary amount of discretion over their debtors' bodily autonomy, the law enabled creditors to use debt as a means of establishing structures of paternalism and deference. The debtors' prison became an instrument to establish authority and social distinction. Though the justice of this system was questionable, its use by and against relative equals may have contributed to societal acceptance of imprisonment, where other forms of aggression towards those considered 'vulnerable' were not tolerated.[75] As incidents of 'public' violence and punishment became less tolerable, they were superseded by a more acceptable form of violence that was cloaked within a 'rational', legal framework.

To some extent, men who used imprisonment as a tool had to be concerned about their own reputations. Within the credit economy, creditors were expected to act charitably and kindly towards their debtors.[76] Inflicting vengeful and unnecessary harm on a debtor could injure a creditor's own reputation, but aggression towards those who were deemed to have acted unethically was a fairly safe strategy. Many of the men subjected to imprisonment were accused of having acted dishonestly within an economy that continued to be conceptualised in explicitly moral and social terms. Despite Smithian notions of economic individualism, previous studies suggest that individual credibility and worth were based upon social reputation and character throughout the eighteenth century.[77] Creditors argued that their debtors deserved imprisonment because they had acted dishonestly. For example, the creditor of the imprisoned candlemaker John Johnston claimed that Johnston had acted 'contrary to all faith and just dealing', having concealed his goods rather than paying his just debts.[78] Many of the people imprisoned were incarcerated several times. James Somervaile, a goldsmith, was incarcerated by Charles Bruce, a glazier, for a debt of four pounds outstanding for several years. The same month, he was incarcerated by Antony Murray, his late servant, for not paying him twelve shillings. Persecuting creditors therefore were not always acting independently, but in tandem with others and in the interests of a wider community. Through the act of punishing transgressors through imprisonment, creditors could establish a claim as stakeholders in the maintenance of the commercial order. Behavioural regulation was an entrée to urban governance, and disciplinary violence had a functional role in confirming social hierarchies.[79] As Alexandra Shepard suggests, 'in devaluing the status of offenders through physical correction, regulatory officials and household heads reiterated their own power and authority'.[80]

In their aggressive actions towards debtors, middling creditors also had to consider the changing image of violence, at least in conduct literature, which framed overly aggressive behaviour as unbecoming to respectable men.[81] While polite dictates against aggression would seem to problematise the use of the prison, in fact use of this legal mechanism accorded with rhetorical codes of restraint, control and emotional mastery. Imprisonment in Scotland involved a slow legal process that required careful calculation and consideration. Debtors attempted to discredit their creditors by describing their actions as 'unmerciful', 'inhuman', and motivated by emotional impulses such as passion or rage. Legal commentators, however, applauded the Scottish system for its unemotional content. According to the legal theorist George Joseph

Bell, the very slowness and carefulness of the legal process meant that incarceration was in itself 'a measure of constraint'.[82] This controlled and legitimate form of violence, committed through the legal system, could appear civilised.

The legally sanctioned and rational violence of the prison allowed men to use debt coercively, even within disputes that were not primarily 'economic'. The economic sphere became a venue where individuals could carry out vengeance related to disputes emerging from a wider social context. Here, the law emerged as a form 'indistinguishable from revenge'.[83] Debtors were the only class of prisoner for whom prison was inflicted as a punishment. Others were held in prison while awaiting trial, and if found guilty, could be subjected to a variety of punishments. Though shaming continued to play an important role within Scottish criminal and police courts, in the eighteenth century, church and civil courts gradually replaced a number of traditional shaming punishments, including whipping and public recantation before the Kirk, with the imposition of fines due to victims as a form of reparation.[84] Victims could then use unpaid fines (a form of debt) to inflict imprisonment upon their adversaries. For example, in 1734, William Watson, a mason at Bristo, had another mason John Overwhyte imprisoned for non-payment of a fine that was awarded after Overwhyte publicly called Watson a villain and 'beggarly dog'.[85] In 1736, James Shearer, a wigmaker who was engaged in a trade demarcation dispute with his former servant, Alexander Finney, accused Finney of stealing his customers, shaving their heads and selling wigs. After pursuing a case before the Dean of Guild, in which Finney was fined, Shearer was able to have the servant imprisoned for non-payment of the debt.[86] Thus while punishments appear to have been 'modernised' and 'economised' by authorities in some legal settings, individuals found ways to use the legal system to impose punishments that were more traditionally shaming and physical in nature. The economic sphere, through a system of debt intertwined with judicial violence, facilitated this resistance to modernisation.

CONCLUSION

Violence played a functional role within eighteenth-century Scottish commerce. In an economy that was structured around notions of honour and that involved frequent interaction between men who were socially competitive and financially vulnerable, violence and aggression served a number of important functions. Violence was a tool that men used to defend their honour and independence, to establish or assert authority and power, and to compete with others. Acts of violence took a number of forms. They could involve physical incidents, but in order to fully account for the role that violence played in the economic sphere, we must be attentive to a range of behaviours including words, aggression, the use of litigation and the imprisonment of debtors. While some of these behaviours violated social norms, others, especially the use of legal institutions, were acceptable and befitting a civilised society. Economic violence was not only a tool used by the masses to claim economic rights as part of food riots; it was a tool employed by a range of men to claim diverse rights and to negotiate their relationships with others.

This Scottish case study suggests that modifications to narratives of commercial modernisation, politeness and the decline of violence are necessary. First, the commercial sphere was not a sphere where men were 'mild and sociable'. In contrast to advice literature, which advocated grace, control and 'dextrous management' of words and actions, examples of lived experience that emerge from court records suggest a rather different economic culture. Aggression was a constituent and acceptable form of economic behaviour in the eighteenth century, and it helped men shape and assert their gender identities. Second, violence did not disappear. For men, it remained a functional and meaningful form of action. In accounting for change, violence might be more accurately characterised as having been displaced or repackaged, rather than simply declining.[87] New forms of legally sanctioned violence emerged that were not necessarily at odds with notions of civility and self-restraint. As Gerd Schwerhoff has suggested, interpersonal violence is not merely a product of uncontrolled emotion and spontaneous action. Therefore, the rise of civility and polite forms of emotional control do not necessary lead to a decline of violence, but rather a reshaping of the types of violence considered acceptable.[88] The extent to which the Scottish case is unique within a British or European context remains unclear. However, records emerging from the Scottish legal setting provide unique and experience-based forms of evidence that suggest the need for modification of broader narratives, and the need to examine the gendered meanings of violence in new and different contexts. The use of violence within economic settings is one of these.

NOTES

1. J. A. Sharpe, *Crime in Seventeenth-Century England: A County Study* (Cambridge: Cambridge University Press, 1983), pp. 117–18, 124; Susan Dwyer Amussen, 'Punishment, discipline and power: the social meanings

of violence in early modern England', *Journal of British Studies*, 34 (1995), pp. 1–34.

2. Robert Shoemaker, *The London Mob: Violence and Disorder in Eighteenth-Century England* (London: Hambledon Continuum, 2004), p. 167.

3. Elizabeth A. Foyster, *Manhood in Early Modern England: Honour, Sex and Marriage* (London: Longman, 1999), pp. 4–5; Alexandra Shepard, *Meanings of Manhood in Early Modern England* (Oxford: Oxford University Press, 2003), p. 128; John Tosh, *A Man's Place: Masculinity and the Middle-Class Home in Victorian England* (New Haven: Yale University Press, 1999), p. 3.

4. See Robert Shoemaker, 'Male honour and the decline of public violence in eighteenth-century London', *Social History*, 26 (2001), pp. 190–208; G. J. Barker-Benfield, *The Culture of Sensibility: Sex and Society in Eighteenth-Century Britain* (Chicago: University of Chicago Press, 1992), especially Chapter 2; Michèle Cohen, *Fashioning Masculinity: National Identity and Language in the Eighteenth Century* (London: Routledge, 1996); Philip Carter, *Men and the Emergence of Polite Society, Britain 1660–1800* (Harlow: Longman, 2001).

5. Lynn Abrams, 'The taming of Highland masculinity: interpersonal violence and shifting codes of manhood, c. 1760–1840', *Scottish Historical Review*, 92 (2013), pp. 100–22 and Chapter 4 in this collection; John Dwyer, *Virtuous Discourse: Sensibility and Community in Late Eighteenth-Century Scotland* (Edinburgh: John Donald, 1987).

6. Adam Smith, *An Inquiry into the Nature and Causes of the Wealth of Nations: Book 1* (London: W. Strahan, 1776).

7. Paul Langford, *A Polite and Commercial People: England 1727–1783* (Oxford: Oxford University Press, 1992), p. 316.

8. J. G. A. Pocock, *Virtues, Commerce, and History: Essays on Political Thought and History, Chiefly in the Eighteenth Century* (Cambridge: Cambridge University Press, 1985), p. 49; John Smail, 'Coming of age in trade: masculinity and commerce in eighteenth-century England', in Margaret Jacob and Catherine Secretan (eds), *The Self Perception of Early Modern Capitalists* (New York: Palgrave, 2008), pp. 229–52, at 239.

9. Gerd Schwerhoff, 'Criminalized violence and the process of civilisation: a reappraisal', *Crime, Histoire et Sociétés*, 6 (2002), pp. 103–26.

10. David G. Barrie and Susan Broomhall (eds), *Police Courts in Nineteenth-Century Scotland, Volume 2: Boundaries, Behaviours and Bodies* (Farnham: Ashgate, 2014), pp. 21–7.

11. Pierre Bourdieu, *Outline of a Theory of Practice* (Cambridge: Cambridge University Press, 1977), p. 193, quoted in Margot Finn, *The Character of Credit: Personal Debt in English Culture, 1740–1914* (Cambridge: Cambridge University Press, 2003), p. 10.

12. For accounts of the middling sort in Britain, see H. R. French, *The Middle Sort of People in Provincial England, 1600–1750* (Oxford: Oxford

University Press, 2007); Jonathan Barry and Christopher Brooks (eds), *The Middling Sort of People: Culture, Society and Politics in England, 1500–1800* (Basingstoke: Macmillan, 1994); Stana Nenadic, 'The rise of the urban middle class', in T. M. Devine and Rosalind Mitchison (eds), *People and Society in Scotland, I: 1760–1830* (Edinburgh: John Donald, 1988), pp. 109–26.

13. National Records of Scotland [NRS], Edinburgh Tolbooth Warding and Liberation Books, HH11; NRS, Edinburgh Commissary Court Processes, CC8/6; Edinburgh City Archives [ECA], Bailie Court Processes [BCP].

14. Alexandra Shepard, 'Violence and civility in early modern Europe', *Historical Journal*, 49:2 (2006), pp. 593–603.

15. R. W. Connell, *Gender* (Cambridge: Polity Press, 2002).

16. E. P. Thompson, 'The moral economy of the English crowd in the eighteenth century', *Past and Present*, 50 (1971), pp. 76–136.

17. A. J. Youngson, *The Making of Classical Edinburgh, 1750–1840* (Edinburgh: Edinburgh University Press, 1988).

18. Peter Borsay, *The English Urban Renaissance: Culture and Society in the Provincial Town, 1660–1770* (Oxford: Clarendon Press, 1989); Stana Nenadic, 'Middle-rank consumers and domestic culture in Edinburgh and Glasgow 1720–1840', *Past and Present*, 145:1 (1994), pp. 122–56, at 126.

19. Rosalind Carr, *Gender and Enlightenment Culture in Eighteenth-Century Scotland* (Edinburgh: Edinburgh University Press, 2014), pp. 142–74.

20. Susan Broomhall and Jacqueline Van Gent (eds), *Governing Masculinities in the Early Modern Period: Regulating Selves and Others* (Farnham: Ashgate, 2011), p. 6.

21. Imprisonment figures are based upon samples taken of all prisoners incarcerated in 1720, 1730, 1740, 1750, 1760. NRS, Tolbooth Warding and Liberation Books, HH11/11–26. Slander figures are based upon all cases brought before the Edinburgh Consistory Court, 1700–1760. NRS, CC8/6/86–383.

22. Anne-Marie Kilday, *Women and Violent Crime in Enlightenment Scotland* (Woodbridge: Boydell Press, 2007).

23. Shoemaker, *London Mob*, p. 154.

24. Craig Muldrew, *The Economy of Obligation: The Culture of Credit and Social Relations in Early Modern England* (Basingstoke: Macmillan, 1998), pp. 123–8, 148.

25. Foyster, *Manhood in Early Modern England*, p. 65.

26. NRS, HH11/26, 30 June 1762.

27. Shepard, *Meanings of Manhood*, p. 159.

28. NRS, CC8/6/197.

29. NRS, CC8/6/361.

30. NRS, CC8/6/379.

31. NRS, CC8/6/85.

32. Elizabeth Foyster, 'Boys will be boys? Manhood and aggression, 1660–

1800', in Tim Hitchcock and Michèle Cohen (eds), *English Masculinities, 1660–1800* (London: Longman, 1999), pp. 151–66, at 162.

33. Broomhall and Van Gent (eds), *Governing Masculinities*, pp. 7, 11.
34. K. Tawny Paul, 'Credit, reputation, and masculinity in British urban commerce: Edinburgh c. 1710–1770', *Economic History Review*, 66:1 (2013), pp. 226–48, at 242.
35. My emphasis. NRS, CC8/6/85.
36. Karen Harvey, *The Little Republic: Masculinity and Domestic Authority in Eighteenth-Century Britain* (Oxford: Oxford University Press, 2012).
37. Annmarie Hughes, 'The "non-criminal" class: wife-beating in Scotland, c. 1850–1949', *Crime, Histoire et Sociétés*, 14:2 (2010), pp. 31–54; Joanna McEwan, 'Attitudes towards male authority and domestic violence in eighteenth-century London courts', in Broomhall and Van Gent (eds), *Governing Masculinities*, pp. 247–62, at 250.
38. E. J. Kent, 'Raiding the patriarch's toolbox: reading masculine governance in cases of male witchcraft, 1592–1692', in Broomhall and Van Gent (eds), *Governing Masculinities*, pp. 173–88, at 174.
39. NRS, CC8/6/268.
40. NRS, H11/28, 12 July 1768.
41. NRS, CC8/6/296.
42. NRS, HH 11/22, 31 January 1746.
43. NRS, HH11/26, 20 August 1762.
44. Shepard, *Meanings of Manhood*, p. 144.
45. For a fuller discussion of the importance of bodily autonomy to notions of masculine honour, see Carr, *Gender and Enlightenment Culture*, pp. 162–74.
46. NRS, CC8/6/110.
47. NRS, CC8/6/156.
48. NRS, CC8/6/164.
49. Jenny Skipp, 'Violence, aggression and masculinity during the eighteenth century: a review', *Cultural and Social History*, 4:4 (2007), pp. 567–73, at 567.
50. Muldrew, *Economy of Obligation*, pp. 123–5.
51. NRS, CC8/6/374.
52. NRS, CC8/6/278.
53. NRS, CC8/6/264.
54. NRS, CC8/6/148.
55. Christoph Menke, 'Law and violence', *Law and Literature*, 22:1 (2010), pp. 1–17, at 1–2.
56. My emphasis. Daniel Defoe, *Some Objections Humbly Offered to the Consideration of the Hon. House of Commons, Relating to the Present Intended Relief of Prisoners* (London, 1729), p. 20.
57. A. Grant, *The Progress and Practice of a Modern Attorney; Exhibiting the Conduct of Thousands Towards Millions! To Which are Added, the*

Different Stages of a Law Suit, and Attendant Costs ... (London, 1795), p. 78.

58. NRS, CC8/6/300.

59. NRS, CC8/6/276.

60. Joanna Innes, 'The King's Bench prison in the later eighteenth century: law, authority and order in a London debtors' prison', in John Brewer and John Styles (eds), *An Ungovernable People: The English and Their Law in the Seventeenth and Eighteenth Centuries* (London: Rutgers University Press, 1980), pp. 250–98, at 275; John Erskine, *The Principles of the Law of Scotland: In the Order of Sir George Mackenzie's Institutions of That Law* (Edinburgh, 1783).

61. James Neild, *State of the Prisons in England, Scotland and Wales, Not For the Debtor Only, But For Felons Also, and Other Less Criminal Offenders* (London, 1812), p. 188.

62. ECA, Petition of David Henderson, September 1738, Box 285, Bundle 40.

63. NRS, Court of Session Papers, CS271/14459.

64. Neild, *State of the Prisons*, p. 189.

65. ECA, Petition of David Balfour, 17 July 1711, BCP, Box 285, Bundle 40.

66. NRS, HH11/30, 24 February 1780.

67. Quoted in Innes, 'King's Bench', p. 255.

68. Shoemaker, *London Mob*, pp. 154, 164–6.

69. Barrie and Broomhall (eds), *Police Courts*, p. 44.

70. R. A. Houston, *Social Change in the Age of Enlightenment: Edinburgh, 1660–1760* (Oxford: Clarendon Press, 1994), pp. 366–71.

71. R. A. Houston, 'Popular politics in the reign of George II: the Edinburgh cordiners', *Scottish Historical Review*, 72 (1993), pp. 167–89.

72. R. A. Houston, 'The economy of Edinburgh, 1694–1763: the evidence of the common good', in S. J. Connolly, R. A. Houston, and R. J. Morris (eds), *Conflict, Identity and Economic Development: Ireland and Scotland, 1600–1939* (Preston: Carnegie Publishing, 1995), pp. 45–63.

73. Markku Peltonen, *The Duel in Early Modern England: Civility, Politeness and Honour* (Cambridge: Cambridge University Press, 2006), p. 286.

74. Douglas Hay, 'Property, authority and the criminal law', in Douglas Hay, Peter Linebaugh, John G. Rule, E. P. Thompson and Cal Winslow (eds), *Albion's Fatal Tree: Crime and Society in Eighteenth-Century England* (London: Allen Lane/Penguin, 1975), pp. 17–64.

75. Barrie and Broomhall (eds), *Police Courts*, pp. 37, 46–7.

76. Muldrew, *Economy of Obligation*, p. 160.

77. Paul, 'Credit, reputation, and masculinity', p. 243; Finn, *Character of Credit*.

78. ECA, BCP, Petition of John Johnston, 8 December 1750.

79. David G. Barrie and Susan Broomhall, 'Policing bodies in urban Scotland, 1780–1850', in Broomhall and Van Gent (eds), *Governing Masculinities*, pp. 263–82, at 263.

80. Shepard, *Meanings of Manhood*, p. 139.
81. Foyster, 'Boys will be boys?', p. 162.
82. George Joseph Bell, *Commentaries on the Laws of Scotland, and on the Principles of Mercantile Jurisprudence: Considered in Relation to Bankruptcy, Competitions of Creditors and Imprisonment for Debt* (Edinburgh, 1810), p. 578.
83. Menke, 'Law and violence', p. 12.
84. Leah Leneman, 'Defamation in Scotland, 1750–1800', *Continuity and Change*, 15 (2000), pp. 209–34, at 229. For the continuing importance of shaming, see David Nash and Anne-Marie Kilday (eds), *Cultures of Shame: Exploring Crime and Morality in Britain, 1600–1900* (Basingstoke: Palgrave Macmillan, 2010); Barrie and Broomhall (eds), *Police Courts*, pp. 458–72.
85. NRS, HH11/18, 18 October 1734.
86. ECA, Dean of Guild Extracted Processes 1736, Box 49.
87. Shepard, 'Violence and civility', p. 594.
88. Schwerhoff, 'Criminalized violence', pp. 103–26.

11

Music Hall, 'Mashers' and the 'Unco Guid': Competing Masculinities in Victorian Glasgow

Tanya Cheadle

O N A WINTER'S NIGHT in 1875, in Glasgow's insalubrious Saltmarket district in the city's East End, two separate female acts began a two-week run at the Whitebait music hall. First to perform was the Francis Parisian Ballet Troupe, a four-girl dance act performing their can-can for the first time in Scotland. Next were the Sisters Ridgway, a pair of female dancers and duettists making their debut appearance of the season.[1] These two 'turns' were to precipitate a media furore that filled the columns of Scotland's newspapers for a month and prompted a number of the city's influential male citizens to launch a vigorous campaign against the immorality of music hall. Indeed, according to one outraged observer, 'A dance of Satyrs and Bacchantes', with words and actions arranged by the notorious female Restoration playwright Aphra Behn, would probably have caused less offence.[2]

Like all scandals, it provides an exceptionally useful starting point for historical investigation. Prompted by the transgression of a perceived borderline of acceptable social behaviour, it produced a proliferation of evidence detailing the multifaceted views of nineteenth-century Glasgow's 'fractured, heterogeneous public sphere'.[3] Yet an analysis of the articles and letters from the variously appalled, defensive and bemused inhabitants of the city, suggests more than just another middle-class attempt at the embourgeoisement of a working-class leisure form, an increasingly common occurrence from the 1870s and already noted and debated in the historiography.[4] Instead, the scandal caused by the acts at the Whitebait indicates the existence in Victorian Glasgow of an intra-gender competition, in which three conceptualisations of masculinity vied for cultural dominance, each asserting the right to define the meaning, and therefore ultimately the management, of the city's music halls.

The first masculine identity was that performed by the 'men of standing and influence' responsible for launching the morality crusade.[5] Comprising wealthy industrialists, school board officers and presidents of Sunday school unions, boys' clubs and young men's religious societies, they belonged to the 'unco guid', a Scots phrase meaning literally 'extremely good' and used to refer, often derisively, to the resolutely respectable and morally rigorous members of Scotland's middle classes. The second rendering of masculinity was that exhibited by the male consumers of music hall, a large number of whom were upper working-class clerks, warehousemen and shop-workers, known colloquially as 'mashers'. Identifiable by their ostentatious clothes, overt consumption of tobacco and alcohol, and unabashed appreciation of music halls' more risqué performances, they were a primary focus of the moralisers' concern, who were convinced that a 'vast number' of them were nightly putting their moral and physical health at risk.[6] The third and final masculine constituency to enter the fray were the bourgeois hedonists and libertarians. As Mike Huggins has demonstrated, not all middle-class men wished to 'join the temperance movement . . . [or] keep themselves morally distinct from the lower orders', and a significant number rejected normative codes of respectability and restraint, instead seeking out the myriad of morally ambiguous pleasures perennially on offer in Scotland's public houses, racecourses and music halls.[7]

An analysis of the power play between these three masculine identities is suggestive in three distinct yet interrelated ways. First, it indicates that unrespectable middle-class men possessed an influence in nineteenth-century Glasgow hitherto underappreciated in the historical literature. Victorian Scotland is commonly depicted as a place in which the 'unco guid' successfully upheld a pervasive and entrenched Presbyterian religiosity, with Protestant moral values permeating the public consciousness.[8] Yet the evidence from the 1875 music hall scandal reveals the existence of a space for the expression of alternative forms of hedonistic, frivolous and irreligious masculinity. Secondly and relatedly, it highlights the importance of considering resistant and alternative masculine identities in their own right, and not solely in relation to a hegemonic norm. As Alexandra Shepard has asserted in her critique of R. W. Connell's work, 'it is important to recognise the plurality of masculinities, many of which existed in tension with each other and with patriarchal concepts which were themselves varied and muddled', a view substantiated by a consideration of the 'mashers', the 'unco guid' and the middle-class hedonists of Glasgow.[9] Finally, the scandal provides a notable example of historical change being effected from within the gender system, of how 'gender has been a constitutive part of wider processes of historical transition'.[10] According to Peter Bailey, despite the increasing efforts of moral purity campaigners intent on proscribing vulgar material in music halls, the use of sexual innuendo and crude repartee persisted, forming part of a popular discourse of 'knowingness', described by one 1883 observer as 'an unwritten language of vulgarity and obscenity known to music-hall audiences, in which vile things can be said that appear perfectly inoffensive in King's English'. It is contended here that this preservation of 'the essential circuitry of music-hall's performative relationship' was the outcome as much of a gendered as a class-inflected contest for control.[11]

The chapter begins with a narrative of events as they unfolded in Glasgow in the early months of 1875. This includes an attempt to determine the exact nature of what initially took place on stage at the Whitebait, information withheld by the 'unco guid', who believed 'the publication of such would be an outrage upon public decency'.[12] It then examines in detail the arguments of the male morality crusaders, a discourse centring around the allegedly pernicious influence that deviant, working-class female sexuality had on the minds, bodies and morals of working- and middle-class men. The final section dissects the gendered contest between the three masculine identities, arguing that the clash ultimately resulted in the formation of a cross-class alliance, albeit tentative and provisional, between the upper working-class 'mashers' and the middle-class hedonists, in defence of men's privileged access to heterosexual sex and female bodies.

A SCANDAL UNFOLDS

On 8 February 1875, an advertisement in the *North British Daily Mail* announced the 'Immense Attraction' of the 'Powerful Company' on stage that week at the Whitebait in Glasgow. At the top of the bill was the Francis Parisian Ballet Troupe with 'The Mountaineer', a 'Grand Musical and Terpsichorean Entertainment', followed by a song and dance routine by the Sisters Ridgway. The remainder of the night's entertainment consisted of a pair of duettists, a serio-comic, who sang and told jokes, and a black-face 'Negro Comedian'.[13]

After the first night, rumours began to spread of the particularly 'spicy' nature of the entertainment, and large numbers of the city's young men began flocking to the music hall to catch the acts.[14] Almost immediately, a number of concerned parties sought to intervene. Among the first was John Burns, a wealthy Glaswegian shipping magnate soon to become chairman of steamship company the Cunard Line. He was also married with five children and an active Episcopalian who fulfilled a number of public roles, including Justice of the Peace for Renfrewshire.[15] He was in fact already acquainted with some of the 'worst haunts' of Glasgow, having been an active participant in what has been identified by Seth Koven as the widespread Victorian phenomenon of 'slumming it'.[16] In the previous year he had spent a 'wild night' amongst the city's poor, writing up his reflections for the Scottish periodical *Good Words*.[17] Burns now tasked himself with investigating the rumours of indecent music-hall performances. Accompanied by two directors of the City Mission and a member of the Glasgow School Board, he conducted a thorough 'tour of inspection'.[18] He subsequently instigated a private meeting of 'the most influential [male] citizens of Glasgow' who petitioned the Lord Provost, requesting his immediate consideration of 'the flagrant and serious evils' currently being perpetuated in Glasgow's music halls.[19]

Next to visit the Whitebait was the theatre critic of the *Mail*. He too was shocked by the 'thoroughly objectionable and immoral tendency of the entertainment', the newspaper neatly identifying the cause and effect – degraded female performers and their influence on vulnerable young men – that would come to dominate much of the debate:

> It [the performance] was of so gross a nature as to leave us in doubt which to pity most, the miserable condition of the women who were engaged in it, or the vicious effect on the minds, habits and tastes of the frequenters who could gloat over such an exhibition. The saddest thing connected with the affair is that the audience attracted by it were chiefly shop and warehouse lads and young clerks.[20]

At some point during the second week of 'spicy' performances, the police intervened, Glasgow's Chief Constable, Alexander McCall, sending a notice to the Whitebait, presumably demanding that the manager clean up the acts.[21] By the time the *Mail*'s theatre critic returned on Saturday, the performances had been 'so greatly modified as to be comparatively unobjectionable' and by the following Monday, the Whitebait's newspaper advertisement had been subtly altered; the Francis Parisian Ballet Troupe would now perform their '*refined* Terpsichorean Entertainments and *chaste* Dances, every evening'.[22] By this point however, the press had sensed a larger story, both the *Mail* and the more liberal *Glasgow Herald* publishing lengthy editorials on the matter. The *Mail* came out in full support of the morality campaigners, underlining their right to judge on such matters by referring to them as 'men of standing and influence' and describing Burns in particular as 'thoroughgoing in all he undertakes'.[23] The solution to the problem, the newspaper argued, was for the authorities to 'force respectability' on the music halls through an implementation of the existing Police Act (1866), under which 'indecent behaviour' in places of public entertainment could be punished with a £10 fine or sixty days' imprisonment. The *Herald* was more circumspect, stating it wanted to see the case against the halls framed 'in language a good deal more precise'.[24] While admitting that many public forms of entertainment had become more indecent, the newspaper included legitimate theatre in its criticism and was generally more sympathetic to the forty or fifty thousand working men who, it estimated, regularly attended music halls in Glasgow, arguing that 'they find these places, with their alleged vulgarity and indecency, very much to their taste'. The solution, the *Herald* believed, could never lie with the police. The Police Act would require common sergeants to exercise constant discretion 'between the decent and the indecent, the modest and the repulsive', which would by consequence turn them into 'tyrants of morals'.[25]

When the day of the public meeting with the Lord Provost arrived, the momentum was such that the two hundred men who turned up with Burns could not be accommodated in the original venue and even the larger room was 'crowded to the doors'.[26] Despite a total of six speeches, each much applauded, the distinguished gentlemen limited their addresses to the generally ruinous consequences of music hall, with no specific description of the offences committed, Burns arguing that 'the publication of such would be an outrage upon public decency'.[27]

So how do we ascertain what took place on stage at Glasgow's Whitebait music hall? Fortunately, there are testimonies from others who witnessed some of the scandalous performances, albeit after they had been censored. The first were two policemen, who under McCall's orders, made two separate visits to the city's music halls. With hindsight however, their investigative approach was lamentably circuitous. On their first excursion, Superintendent Brown and Lieutenant Andrew visited two other halls before arriving at the Whitebait, by which time the Francis Parisian Ballet Troupe had left the stage. They did manage to catch the Sisters Ridgway however, and duly described how the two women went through 'a variation of tomfoolery, by taking hold of each other, throwing their legs up towards the roof of the Hall, and dancing something in the "Can-Can" style', Helen dressed as a 'woman' and Rose dressed as a 'man', in pantomime tights and leotard.[28]

Two elements of the performance appeared to cause them anxiety. First, they noted that Rose's costume and dancing were deliberately designed to reveal the contours of her body:

Rose wears a dress which consists of a flashy blue silk body with light trim-
ming and skin tights disclosing the form of her legs and thighs up to the hips,
in fact the skirt scarcely comes down to the private parts but is quite modest
as far as the upper part of the body is concerned. She appears to be a model
in figure and in her performance she throws up her legs in such a manner as
to cause an impression on the minds of her audience that it is done for the
purpose of showing off her figure to the best possible advantage, and gains
great applause. In my opinion her conduct is very unbecoming of her sex.

Indeed, the police subsequently contacted a music-hall chairman for
clarification on exactly what type of underwear female music-hall performers were supposed to wear, Harry Harcourt from Brown's Royal
Music Hall obliging with an illustration of knee-length, puffed 'coloured
under Draws' [sic], which the Sisters Ridgway had clearly omitted to put
on.[29] Furthermore, as Paul Maloney has noted, the policemen appear
to have been disconcerted by the gender manipulation enacted by the
'sisters', taking pains in their report to stress that both the 'male' Rose
and the 'female' Helen were lodging respectably with their mother in
Stockwell Street.[30] However, while the policemen were clearly critical of
'females degrading themselves in such unbecoming performances', their
report makes it clear that they believed the questionable nature of such
entertainment was by no means a recent phenomenon. Similar costumes
had been worn and dances performed for many years, in their opinion,
and not just in music halls but by ballet dancers and columbines in pan-
tomimes and circuses, entertainment forms that constituted a routine
Christmas treat for vast numbers of middle-class children.[31]

When Lieutenant Andrew returned to the halls at the beginning of
March, he again missed the performance by the Ballet Troupe, although
the manager of the Whitebait was good enough to assure him that their
act was restricted to Highland dancing, an innocuous style in comparison to the far more risqué can-can. The policeman did, however, find
the four dancers in the green room, 'seated round a table along with a
few fast young men with liquor before them', and noted that when they
left, at 10.45 p.m., the young men followed just a few minutes later.
Regarding the acts on stage at the other halls he visited, Andrew was
adamant they contained nothing remotely objectionable, reserving his
most effusive praise for the Britannia, where he found 'All the arrangements in Connection with this Hall . . . as near perfection as possible'.[32]
Indeed, contrary to the *Herald*'s impression of the 'common sergeant of
police' being transformed into a tyrant by the burden of making moral
judgements, Lieutenant Andrew seemed rather to have enjoyed his evening's work.[33]

Another witness to the controversial acts at the Whitebait was a correspondent to the *Herald* who signed himself 'H. le D.'.[34] Clearly a connoisseur, he boasted that he had attended 'nearly every music hall in England and America, as well as the French café *chantants*, and the lager-beer saloons and gartens of the Dutch and Germans'. He had been following the unfolding controversy with interest and had determined to go to one of the city's 'naughty realms of harmony' to judge for himself. Yet despite setting out from his home in the fashionable west end of the city with the deliberate intension of having his 'nerves unstrung' and his 'better nature degraded', 'H. le D.' found the Sisters Ridgway disappointingly tame, describing them as:

> two poor, miserable-looking creatures, who strutted about the stage, one dressed as a boy, the other as a girl and sang duets which had neither spirit nor wit to recommend them to the public. Whatever might have been before, and I believe the only fault was in wearing skin-tights, there was nothing approaching indecency this evening either in their songs or their actions.[35]

When the infamous Francis Parisian Ballet Troupe arrived on stage, they were greeted enthusiastically by a 'multitude of loudly-dressed shopmen', who filled the boxes on either side of the stage and who 'smiled, jeered and giggled at them, with a combination of facial expression difficult to describe, but caused by the mixture of too much bad drink and tobacco on brains and constitutions never of the strongest, but rather the reverse'. 'H. le D.', however, who, if he is to be believed, had enjoyed a singularly broad experience of music hall, was again left unmoved, dismissing the act as 'simply a can-can of the most modest form, danced by two skinny girls and a fat one, who tried to sing a song'.

It should be remembered that by the time both the two policemen and 'H. le D.' visited the Whitebait, McCall had already censored the performances. What was initially both so enticing and so shocking must therefore remain a matter of conjecture. Yet whether the transgression had involved a scandalously immodest can-can or the wearing of flesh-coloured tights, when the Lord Provost tried to claim to the assembled petitioners that as the 'exhibition' had now been discontinued, the matter had been satisfactorily concluded, he was met with a barrage of hostility. The issue, declared Burns, to loud applause, had by no means been resolved. In fact, things were 'as bad as ever'.[36] For Burns and his morally conservative supporters, music hall's immorality had never been confined to one or two acts, but instead pervaded the whole entertainment form. They had long thought the halls were doing 'grievous harm to the people', and the scandal had merely provided them with a forum in which to air their opinions. Their discourse in the profusion of letters and articles to the press reveals a convergence of concerns around the operation of an insidious cause and effect – the impact watching female music-hall performers had on the 'minds, habits and tastes' of the city's vulnerable young men.[37]

THE DISCOURSE OF THE 'UNCO GUID'

At the root of much of music hall's licentiousness, according to the discourse of Burns and his supporters, lay the impact the sexualised bodies of female music-hall performers had on the male audience members. The outfits of the women were repeatedly described as unacceptably revealing, one scandalised correspondent in the *Mail* referring to 'half nude' women on stage wearing 'next to no costume at all'.[38] While actual skin was at all times concealed by 'fleshling' tights and leotards, ballet dancers and burlesques artistes were nonetheless criticised for wearing costumes that accentuated parts of their bodies deemed sexually arousing. According to contemporary women's fashion, the lower body was to remain hidden in voluminous swathes of fabric and, as a consequence of this, their legs, buttocks and genitals were heavily fetishised, with one contemporary writer recalling the erotic charge engendered by the relative undress of a principal 'boy' during a childhood visit to the pantomime:

> Amble-bosomed, small-waisted and with thighs – oh such thighs! – thighs that shone and glittered in the different coloured silk tights in which she continually appeared. How she stood about the stage, proud and dominant, smacking those rounded limbs with a riding crop![39]

Music-hall women were thus defined, in the eyes of their middle-class critics, purely by their sexuality, the only function of their bodies to inflame 'the worse passions and lusts' of their male audience.[40] Like prostitutes, it was a service they provided in exchange for money, selling their souls, according to one letter, 'for a little gain'.[41] The hideous impropriety of this Faustian pact reached its apotheosis in the thrusting, repetitive high kicks of the can-can, performed by acts such as the Sisters Ridgway and the Francis Parisian Ballet Troupe, with calls for even the music accompanying the dance to be banned, so insidiously suggestive was it considered.[42]

   The corrupting influence of witnessing semi-naked dancers performing their assorted melange of 'leg business' was further compounded by the obscene sexual wordplay engaged in by other acts. The most notorious culprits were serio-comics, of whom female professionals, according to one source, existed in roughly equal numbers in Scotland to men.[43] Often, it was not necessarily their songs that were explicitly sexual, although these too could certainly be risqué. Marie Loftus, arguably Scotland's biggest female home-grown music-hall star, used material that skirted the boundaries of respectability, the weekly periodical *Quiz* commenting: 'As for her songs! They are difficult to write about. A man in the pit last night said he thought some of them were "no verra proper". But he was a bigot.'[44] By 1875, managers had begun to insist that lyrics be submitted prior to a performer's engagement, but what was far harder to police were the spontaneous gestures, the seemingly impromptu banter, the 'patter', which was often highly scripted. It was here, correctly surmised one of Burns' men, that the greatest threat to impropriety lay.[45]

One of the most common and effective comic devices in such exchanges was sexual innuendo. It allowed performers to avoid the explicitly crude vocabulary that might have resulted in disciplinary action from the management, by re-signifying everyday language. Seemingly innocent phrases were given a second, hidden meaning relating to sexual anatomy or activities, the decoding of which required a degree of competence on the part of the audience. When the correspondent 'Truth', for example, heard a female comic recite 'an apparently aimless, pointless story', which nevertheless had the audience convulsed with laughter, it was only through his realisation that she was using music-hall slang for 'certain indecent acts' that he was able to get the joke and 'laughed too'.[46] His sense of select inclusion in the performance was his reward for being 'in the know', and is an example of what Bailey has termed 'knowingness', a popular discourse that no doubt played a significant role in the casual interactions of working- and middle-class young men, and involved an implicit rejection of moral and religious prescription in favour of what Bailey has called 'the business and enjoyment of living', with sex looming particularly large in this 'business and enjoyment'.[47]

The potent site in music halls where this sexual discourse was translated into reality, according to the 'unco guid', was the green room, where artistes sat in evening dress during and after the show and were bought drinks by audience members. Indeed, according to one horrified 'Eye-Witness', the female performers were compelled to wait there by a clause in their contract, effectively institutionalising the link between performed and lived sexual promiscuity.[48] Whether such contractual obligations existed remains uncorroborated, and the theatrical press were certainly critical of more extreme examples of such arrangements in European halls. However, even the sympathetic Lieutenant Andrew was suspicious of ballet dancers drinking with 'fast young men' and where it would lead, while the tone of 'Eye-Witness' was of unreserved horror, as he observed groups of men and boys hanging around, dangerously close to the dressing rooms (sites with even more transgressive potency), waiting to secure introductions via waiters to 'notorious' singers and dancers.

A CROSS-CLASS ALLIANCE OF 'MASHERS' AND HEDONISTS

Music-hall women, along with prostitutes, actresses and mill girls, had been visible as figures of sexual deviance in Glasgow prior to the 1870s. The question therefore follows, why the 'unco guid' chose this specific historical moment to turn their disciplinary gaze upon the female performers. Clearly, the scandal occurred within a wider context of increasing bourgeois scrutiny of music halls and other loci of working-class leisure in cities and towns across Britain. However, the morality campaigners in this instance were exclusively male, as well as middle class, suggesting a gendered as well as a class imperative.

One answer could be that John Burns and his cohort felt their masculinity to be under threat. According to R. W. Connell, men in possession of hegemonic masculinity, arguably in this period the 'unco guid', were implicated in a constant battle to protect their masculine-derived wealth and status, or patriarchal dividend, from those disadvantaged by their assumption of power.[49] One sector of society with a perennial interest in challenging masculine authority was feminist women, and there is a case to be made that during the 1870s, conservative Scottish men may have felt threatened by campaigns such as that led by Sophia Jex-Blake to secure medical training for herself and her female colleagues at Edinburgh University.

However, challenges to hegemonic masculinity's legitimacy can also come from other men, those in possession of subordinate, complicit or marginalised masculinity. During the morality campaign, a group of men emerged who were clearly situated in an inferior social position to the 'unco guid': the young, unmarried, upper working-class men who formed a substantial proportion of music-hall audiences and who referred to themselves as 'mashers'. Often employed as clerks, warehousemen and apprentices, they nonetheless wished to transcend the limitations of their cultural and social backgrounds. Their stratagem was to reimagine themselves as counterfeit 'gents' or 'swells', by adopting the 'hyper-masculine leisure habits of a super-annuated aristocracy'.[50]

Also known as 'dudes', 'toffs' and 'Johnnies', the 'masher' or 'swell' was an archetype with a complex heritage. First appearing in the 1830s and 1840s as an imitation of the upper-class dandy, by the 1870s it had become 'increasingly institutionalised as a self-sufficient and indigenously authentic style' amongst working-class men, an identity validated and disseminated through popular music-hall characters such as 'Champagne Charlie'.[51] Such identities, according to Judith Walkowitz, 'served as a compensatory fantasy for a troubled working-class masculinity', which had become increasingly unstable through a decline in apprenticeships, a too-close association with the female domestic sphere, and a lack of adequate paternal breadwinning role models.[52] For the 'mashers' of 1870s Glasgow, this 'compensatory fantasy' consisted of dressing extravagantly, socialising with friends on Buchanan Street, smoking, drinking and attending 'spicy' music-hall performances with male friends and colleagues. Here, they were able to gain valuable masculine validation by demonstrating their sexual prowess in front of their peers, either through their objectification of the female performers or through their laughter as they 'got' the crude punchlines of the jokes. For those seeking to translate this sexual transaction into more tangible illicit pleasures, assignations could be made with female artistes in the green room, or in some music halls, with the prostitutes who circulated in the auditorium. Despite or perhaps because of such behaviour, such men were a target for middle-class condescension, in 1893 the Glasgow author John Hammerton dismissing them with undisguised disdain:

> A masher is a thing that would
> Be a young lady if he could,
> But since he can't does all he can
> To let you know he's not a man.

and asking,

> What good is ever done by these silly youths, who think they are men because they can 'stand drinks', smoke a penny cigar, play billiards, and ogle the girls who have the misfortune to pass them on the street? I repeat: What is their use on the face of this planet of ours? I have never been able to discover.[53]

However, the 'mashers' were not the only group of men threatening the masculine status of the 'unco guid' during this period. Another constituency exhibiting a comparable set of normative masculine attributes were Scotland's middle-class hedonists or libertarians. As Huggins has argued, the ideology of respectability was by no means universally accepted as a lived code of values across the middle classes.[54] Significant numbers of middle-class men, at certain points in their lifecycle, within particular occupational groupings or in specific locations, chose to spend their leisure time in disreputable and sometimes debauched pursuits. For the young medical student, the commercial traveller or the bohemian artist or writer, rigid codes of respectability were unlikely to hold significant sway, while the liminal spaces of the seaside resort, the music hall, the gentleman's club and the upmarket betting room, provided large numbers of bourgeois men with safe, secluded, homosocial settings in which to misbehave.

During the 1875 scandal, the errant sons of Glasgow's middle classes emerged as frequent music-hall patrons, a letter from an 'old professional' claiming a significant proportion of audiences were composed of 'members of the families of many in the west end terraces', a view substantiated by a 'working man', critical of the 'idle sons of the middle and upper classes' who frequented such 'dens' and whose money was 'more plentiful than their brains'.[55] For such men, a visit to a music hall represented a 'spree', an exciting, occasional and tacitly sanctioned excursion into an illicit world, the writer John Jay Bell recollecting how his visit to the Scotia as a young man left him feeling 'as desperately wicked as only seventeen can feel'.[56]

Yet there was also a coterie of older, middle-class men who visited the halls. During the scandal, they entered into a brief, cross-class alliance with the working-class 'mashers', marshalling their superior social capital and economic means to publicly defend their shared hedonistic lifestyle, articulating their position in *The Bailie*, a weekly satirical journal describing itself as 'a Tory of the old-school'.[57] It was scathing towards 'respectable Glasgow', ridiculing the 'disagreeable prigs' who eschewed the pleasures of music halls, smoking, and fashionable dress for Shakespeare, dark colours and the Young Men's Christian Association.[58] In its column, 'What Folk are Saying', it accused the 'unco guid' of hypocrisy, claiming that visiting music halls 'in search of improprieties' had become a fashionable pursuit, with wives left bemused 'why the Pater thereof should desert the fireside to gape at "these hussies", and listen to the chimes at midnight'.[59] Even the letters generated by the scandal were portrayed as providing a degree of titillation, the *Bailie* asserting that 'next to turning-up at a music hall yourself, the best (or worst) thing is the reading of a spicy moral letter descriptive of its improprieties'.[60] Highlighting the often overblown rhetoric employed by the 'unco guid', it satirised their gloomy predictions of the fatal consequences awaiting 'Young Glasgow' if they continued their visits to the halls:

Why will ye tae thae Saloons gang,
Whaur ocht that's richt is driven wrang,
And whaur 'Auld Saunny's' working thrang
    Tae get a grip,
And ye wha worhip Comic Sang
    Shall feel his nip . . .

. . . Tak' tent, sma' evils grow tae greater,
Sae change ere it be ony later,
Or like that puir commercial crater
    Wha wadna heed,
Ye'll find it's no a laughin' matter
    Tae drap doun deid.[61]

In addition, the *Bailie* presented an alternative portrait of the morality campaigner John Burns. While the *Mail* had described him as an 'unimpeachable' man of 'standing and influence', to the editors of *Bailie* he was an egocentric meddler in the city's politics and a corrupt manipulator of the press, using scare tactics and pay-offs, in the form of 'free passes' and invitations to garden parties, to ensure any inappropriate articles were 'burked' or censored.[62]

The attitude towards music hall of the allied middle-class hedonists and 'mashers' was clearly directly oppositional to that of the 'unco guid'. One correspondent articulated this succinctly when he wrote that 'Seduction has many ways of being looked at, the extremes being society's way and the music hall way'.[63] During the morality campaign, these two positions asserted the validity of their contrasting interpretations and with it their authority to decide on the halls' management. As indicated earlier, one way of understanding this masculine power struggle might be to consider the hegemonic masculinity of the 'unco guid' to be under threat from the marginalised masculinity of the hedonists and 'mashers'. Yet on closer examination such masculine identities defy neat categorisation and are hard to position within Connell's schema. While the 'unco guid' were clearly powerful, respected patriarchs, Burns being a successful, wealthy married businessman with five children, the hedonists were arguably their social equals, while also exhibiting the hyper-masculine quality of sexual virility. Furthermore, the contest was not over patriarchal dividends, but rather over which version of masculinity should have cultural authority. It might therefore be more useful to follow Shepard's suggestions for the early modern context, to recast the dominant patriarchal mode as normative rather than hegemonic and to acknowledge that there were 'deliberate countercodes of resistance adopted in flagrant rejection of patriarchal imperatives', which existed in a complex relationship with patriarchal norms.[64]

CONCLUSION

In the Victorian intra-gender contest over music hall, it was the libertarian attitudes of the male hedonists and 'mashers' that triumphed. While the social standing of Burns and his men enabled them to petition the local government and mobilise a section of the Scottish press, the moralists were ultimately to be disappointed. They left the meeting with the Lord Provost, 'with the uncomfortable feeling that they had not received the encouragement which they had hoped for', echoing the fate of similar campaigns in London, where the local magistrates tended to side with the commercial interests of music-hall managers.[65] Less than two months later, the Whitebait lost its alcohol licence, but music hall generally in Glasgow continued to thrive, so that by 1914 the city boasted eighteen halls (in comparison with only six legitimate theatres), including several large and ornate 'Palaces of Variety', built in the more fashionable city centre.[66] As their managers were only too aware, sex sold to a significant number of working- and middle-class men, its consumption a key marker of their masculinity. Termed 'parasexuality' by Peter Bailey, its careful deployment in the sanctioned and contained spaces of late Victorian and Edwardian music halls, pubs and bars, enabled 'a new breed of capitalist cultural managers' to make rising profits from the commodification of women's bodies.[67]

The 'unco guid' are often represented as sounding the key-note of Scottish moral values, in a society in which, according to Callum Brown, a pervasive, discursive Christianity held sway until the late 1950s.[68] Yet as Huggins notes, '*active* middle-class moralists and social reformers were always a small, albeit highly vociferous minority'.[69] The evidence from the scandal suggests that from the 1870s, other renderings of masculinity gained significant purchase in Scottish society. According to Connell, hegemonic masculinity is merely the 'currently accepted' strategy of social organisation, and 'when conditions for the defence of patriarchy change, the basis for the dominance of a particular masculinity are eroded'.[70] Whether we consider the masculinity of the 'unco guid' to be hegemonic or normative, changing social and cultural conditions meant that its dominance was never assured. While an alternative, more hedonistic set of masculine values based on men's innate, active, sexuality had existed throughout the nineteenth century, the new leisure spaces of the late Victorian period provided increasing opportunities for such values to find expression and validation.

The ultimate losers however, were the female performers. While their voices have not been heard in this chapter, due in part to paucity of evidence, contrary to the discourse of the 'unco guid', they clearly did not embark upon a career in music hall because of sexually depraved natures or a taste for finery. Instead, when faced with limited employment opportunities, performing the can-can or risqué songs in front of drunken male clerks and students was an attractive alternative to the tedium and long hours of factory work or domestic labour. Yet their career choice had numerous disadvantages. While some male performers perceived their sexual allure as an unfair advantage, one disgruntled comic singer complaining 'I wish I had been a serio-comic lady with a well made form and a good pair of legs', this ignored the real costs involved.[71] There is evidence that sexual harassment was endemic, with young girls particularly at risk. For example, in 1886 'Roving Jack', the gossip columnist for Glasgow's main theatrical trade paper, reported that an 'Old Party connected with the law' had been spotted repeatedly propositioning young performers, Jack commenting 'I am told he don't care about them being anything above eighteen'.[72] Furthermore, in an industry in which women were valued primarily for their youth and beauty, the career of an artiste was often short, while music hall's reputation for immorality compromised any attempt at respectability. In John Davidson's 1884 poem, set in a Glasgow music hall, the character Mary-Jane Macpherson awaits her fiancé's reaction to her new profession with ill-disguised trepidation:

> He thinks I'm a governess still,
>   But I'm sure that he'll pardon my choice;
> I make more, and rest when I'm ill,
>   And it's only the sale of my voice.[73]

Yet we should avoid portraying such women as wholly without agency. While undeniably disadvantaged by class and gender, there is evidence that female performers were nonetheless able to exercise a modicum of power at a local level. In an apocryphal story told by 'Roving Jack', when 'John the Toff' attempted to make a conquest of a particular 'dazzling donah' by buying her several rounds of drinks, his efforts were swiftly curtailed with the arrival of her husband, whereon 'she hurriedly bids the dude good-bye, with a merry twinkle in her eye, which means "Old boy, you've been fairly had . . ."'[74] During the

Victorian period, Scotland's music-hall women were the objects of the unwanted attentions of 'mashers', middle-class hedonists and moral crusaders. It is good to think, therefore, that on some occasions at least, they had the last laugh.

NOTES

1. Advertisement, 'Whitebait Concert Rooms', *North British Daily Mail* (hereafter *Mail*), 8 February 1875, p. 1.
2. 'Music Hall Morality', *Mail*, 5 March 1875, p. 4.
3. Judith R. Walkowitz, *City of Dreadful Delight: Narratives of Sexual Danger in Late-Victorian London* (Chicago: University of Chicago Press, 1992), p. 80.
4. See for example Gareth Stedman Jones, 'Working-class culture and working-class politics in London, 1870–1900: notes on the remaking of the working class', *Journal of Social History*, 7:4 (1974), pp. 460–508; Penelope Summerfield, 'The Effingham Arms and the Empire: deliberate selection in the evolution of music hall in London', in E. and A. Yeo (eds), *Popular Culture and Class Conflict 1590–1914* (Sussex: Harvester, 1981), pp. 216–21; Peter Bailey, 'Conspiracies of meaning: music hall and the knowingness of popular culture', *Past and Present*, 144 (1994), pp. 138–70; Susan Pennybacker, '"It was not what she said but the way in which she said it": the London County Council and the music halls', in Peter Bailey (ed.), *Music Hall: The Business of Pleasure* (Milton Keynes: Open University Press, 1986), pp. 118–40.
5. *Mail*, 26 February 1875, p. 4.
6. 'The morality of the city: important deputation to the magistrates', *Mail*, 2 March 1875, p. 4.
7. Mike J. Huggins, 'More sinful pleasures? Leisure, respectability and the male middle classes in Victorian England', *Journal of Social History*, 33:3 (2000), pp. 585–600, at 586.
8. See for example, T. C. Smout, 'Churchgoing', in *A Century of the Scottish People, 1830–1950* (London: Fontana, 1987), pp. 181–208 and Callum Brown, 'Piety and progress', in *Religion and Society in Scotland Since 1707* (Edinburgh: Edinburgh University Press, 1997), pp. 1–12. Brown does state however, that 'the discourse on the puritan Scot has sat alongside, though often estranged from, the discourse on the dissolute Scot', and in other work details how post-1800 religious discourse became effectively re-gendered, with Scots men increasingly considered 'the major religious and social problem of the nation'. See 'Religion', in Lynn Abrams, Eleanor Gordon, Deborah Simonton and Eileen Janes Yeo (eds), *Gender in Scottish History since 1700* (Edinburgh: Edinburgh University Press, 2006), pp. 84–110, at 100.
9. Alexandra Shepard, 'From anxious patriarchs to refined gentlemen?

Manhood in Britain, c. 1500–1700', *Journal of British Studies*, 44:2 (2005), pp. 281–95, at 292.

10. Alexandra Shepard and Garthine Walker, 'Gender, change and periodisation', *Gender & History*, 20:3 (2008), pp. 453–62, at 456.

11. Peter Bailey, 'Conspiracies of meaning: music hall and the knowingness of popular culture,' *Past and Present*, 144 (1994), pp. 138–70, at 156; F. Freeman, *Weekly Despatch*, 4 February 1883, cited in Bailey, 'Conspiracies of meaning', p. 158.

12. 'The morality of the city', *Mail*, 2 March 1875, p. 4.

13. Advertisement, 'Whitebait Concert Rooms', *Mail*, 8 February 1875, p. 1.

14. Ibid.

15. Anthony Slaven, 'Burns, John, first Baron Inverclyde (1829–1901)', *Oxford Dictionary of National Biography* (Oxford University Press, 2004; online edition, January 2006) http://www.oxforddnb.com.ezproxy.lib.gla.ac.uk/view/article/48614 (last accessed 7 March 2016).

16. Seth Koven, *Slumming: Sexual and Social Politics in Victorian London* (Princeton: Princeton University Press, 2004).

17. John Burns, 'A wild night', Rev. Donald Macleod (ed.), *Good Words*, vol. 15 (London: Daldy, Isbister, 1874), pp. 211–16.

18. 'The morality of the city', *Mail*, 26 February 1875, p. 4.

19. 'The morality of the city', *Mail*, 25 February 1875, p. 4; 'Memorial from various Citizens of Glasgow to the Lord Provost and Magistrates, 24 February 1875', Glasgow City Archives, SR 22/62/1.

20. 'A night in a Glasgow music hall', *Mail*, 22 February 1875, p. 4.

21. 'The morality of the city', *Mail*, 2 March 1875, p. 4.

22. My emphasis. 'A night in a Glasgow music hall', *Mail*, 22 February 1875, p. 4; advertisement for 'Whitebait Concert Rooms', *Mail*, 22 February 1875, p. 1.

23. 'The morality of the city', *Mail*, 26 February 1875, p. 4.

24. *Glasgow Herald*, 26 February 1875, p. 4.

25. Ibid.

26. 'The morality of the city', *Mail*, 2 March 1875, p. 4.

27. The key protagonists instead insisted on relaying the details of the risqué music hall performances to the Lord Provost in a private meeting, to which the press clearly did not have access.

28. 'Report of Visits to Music Halls on 27 Feb 1875' from Superintendent Brown to Captain McCall, Chief Constable, dated 1 March 1875, Glasgow City Archives, SR 22/62/1.

29. Letter from Harry Harcourt, Director and Chairman of Brown's Royal Music Hall, to Captain McCall, 3 March 1875, Glasgow City Archives, SR22/62/1.

30. Paul Maloney, *Scotland and the Music Hall, 1850–1914* (Manchester: Manchester University Press, 2003), p. 144.

31. 'Report of Visits to Music Halls on 27 Feb 1875' from Superintendent Brown to Captain McCall, Chief Constable, dated 1 March 1875, Glasgow City Archives, SR 22/62/1.
32. Report 'Visit to Music Halls, 8 March 1875' from Lieutenant Andrew to Captain McCall, Chief Constable, dated 9 March 1875, Glasgow City Archives, SR22/62/1.
33. *Glasgow Herald*, 26 February 1875, p. 4.
34. Letter signed 'H. le D.', *Glasgow Herald*, 11 March 1875, p. 7.
35. Ibid.
36. 'The morality of the city', *Mail*, 2 March 1875, p. 4.
37. 'A night in a Glasgow music hall', *Mail*, 22 February 1875, p. 4.
38. Letter signed 'Vindex', *Mail*, 27 February 1875, p. 4.
39. E. H. Shepard, *Drawn From Memory* (London, 1957), cited in Martha Vicinus, 'Turn-of-the-century male impersonation: rewriting the romance plot', in Andrew H. Miller and James Eil Adams (eds), *Sexualities in Victorian Britain* (Bloomington: Indiana University Press, 1996), pp. 187–213, at 189.
40. Letter 'Confessions of a singing saloon habitué', *Glasgow Herald*, 6 March 1875, p. 3.
41. Letter signed 'Q', *Mail*, 24 February 1875, p. 4.
42. Letter from Harry Harcourt, Director and Chairman of Brown's Royal Music Hall, to Captain McCall, dated 3 March 1875, Glasgow City Archives, SR 22/62/1.
43. 'An Old Professional', in a letter written to the *Mail*, stated that there were 273 professional female serio-comics in Scotland, compared to 303 male comics. *Mail*, 13 March 1875, p. 5.
44. 'Series of character sketches, no. 49. Marie Loftus', *Quiz*, 15 November 1894, p. 16.
45. 'The morality of the city', *Mail*, 2 March 1875, p. 4. That spontaneous 'patter' was perceived as a problem can also be seen in the 'Rules for Artistes' at Brown's Royal Music Hall, which state 'No Artiste allowed to address the audience, under any circumstances, without permission of the Director', Glasgow City Archives, SR 22/62/1.
46. Letter 'Confessions of a singing saloon habitué', *Glasgow Herald*, 6 March 1875, p. 3.
47. Bailey, 'Conspiracies of meaning', p. 155.
48. Letter signed 'Eye-Witness', *Mail*, 8 March 1875, p. 4.
49. R. W. Connell, *Masculinities*, 2nd edition (Cambridge: Polity Press, 2005), p. 82.
50. Walkowitz, *City of Dreadful Delight*, p. 44.
51. Peter Bailey, 'Ally Sloper's half-holiday: comic art in the 1880s,' *History Workshop Journal*, 16 (1983), pp. 4–31, quoted in Walkowitz, *City of Dreadful Delight*, p. 43.
52. Walkowitz, *City of Dreadful Delight*, p. 44.

53. J. A. Hammerton, *Sketches from Glasgow* (Glasgow: John Menzies, 1893), p. 123.
54. Huggins, 'More sinful pleasures?', pp. 585–6.
55. Letters signed 'An Old Professional' and 'W. R.', *Mail*, 13 March and 27 February 1875.
56. J. J. Bell, *I Remember* (Edinburgh: Porpoise Press, 1932), p. 131.
57. *The Bailie*, 28 January 1990, p. 11.
58. 'Resolutions for the New Year', *The Bailie*, 1 January 1873, p. 7.
59. 'What folk are saying', *The Bailie*, 3 March 1875, p. 7.
60. 'What folk are saying', *The Bailie*, 10 March 1875, p. 5.
61. *The Bailie*, 10 March 1875, p. 3.
62. 'What folk are saying', *The Bailie*, 3 March 1875, p. 7 and 10 March 1875, p. 5.
63. Letter 'Confessions of a singing saloon habitué', *Glasgow Herald*, 6 March 1875, p. 4.
64. Alexandra Shepard, 'From anxious patriarchs to refined gentlemen?', p. 291.
65. 'The morality of the city', *Mail*, 2 March 1875; Tracy C. Davis, 'The moral sense of the majorities: indecency and vigilance in late Victorian music halls', *Popular Music*, 10:1 (1991), pp. 39–52, at 40.
66. *Mail*, 24 April 1875, p. 4: Maloney, *Scotland and the Music Hall*, p. 57.
67. Peter Bailey, 'Parasexuality and glamour: the Victorian barmaid as cultural prototype', *Gender and History*, 2:2 (1900), pp. 148–72, at 149.
68. Callum G. Brown, *The Death of Christian Britain: Understanding Secularisation, 1800–2000* (London: Routledge, 2001).
69. His emphasis. Huggins, 'More sinful pleasures?', p. 586.
70. Connell, *Masculinities*, p. 77.
71. 'Notes by Roving Jack, an old stager', *Professional and Authors' Journal*, 16 April 1887.
72. 'Notes by Roving Jack', 9 January, 13 March, 15 May and 2 October 1886.
73. John Davidson, *In a Music Hall and Other Poems* (London: Ward and Downey, 1891), p. 2.
74. 'Notes by Roving Jack', 25 September 1886.

12

'That Class of Men': Effeminacy, Sodomy and Failed Masculinities in Inter- and Post-War Scotland

Jeffrey Meek

MUCH OF THE WRITING about twentieth-century Scottish masculinities has focused upon the changing definitions of 'manliness' and its links to social, economic and domestic shifts, which have resulted in a renegotiation of men's roles.[1] Yet despite considerable scholarship focusing on the emergence of queer masculinities in England during the interwar period, there is a paucity of research from a Scottish perspective. The notion that a solid, inflexible form of Scottish masculinity has existed relatively unchanged has rightly been challenged, but largely from a heterosexual position. Just where are Scotland's queer masculinities? This chapter will demonstrate that deviant, subversive and oppositional forms of masculinity did exist in twentieth-century Scotland, with the interwar period featuring centrally in the history of queer men and queer masculinities.

The emergence of the resolute British male has its links to Empire, where a culture of 'otherness' disassociated the British man from his effeminate subordinates in the colonies. Empire-driven masculinities also shunned expressive sexuality, viewing it as a dangerous threat to order and control and likely, if unrestrained, to lead to dangerous and deviant behaviours.[2] The concept of the British soldier in World War One was built upon Edwardian notions of masculinity, which promoted self-control, emotional restraint and physical toughness.[3] The inability of some men to adhere to these principles, as a result of either mental trauma or a failure to reassert their place within the breadwinner family model, led to considerable concerns over the shape of British manhood.[4] Further, the queer man had come to represent an unacceptable version of masculinity, both deviant and dangerous. Noel Pemberton Billing, publisher, aviator and Member of Parliament, infamously saw within the homosexual the potential for perfidiousness,

through his claim in *The Imperialist* magazine that Germany was infil-
trating British society through the use of male and female homosexuals
during World War One.[5] German spies had allegedly formed intimate
relationships with British subjects with the intention of blackmailing
them for sensitive information.[6] The homosexual was just a nudge
away from treachery. Despite concerns during the late Victorian and
Edwardian periods about gender transgressions, recruitment of soldiers for World War One had paid little attention to effeminacy or
queerness.[7] This was due to, first, the absence of a coherent discourse
of same-sex desire, which failed to conceptualise an identifiable queer
personage and, secondly, the belief that military training would be
effective in 'physically and mentally [moulding most men] into an effective combatant'.[8]

During the first third of the twentieth century there were a number of
trials in Scotland concerning sex between men, predominantly relating
to the commission or the attempted commission of sodomy. Although
legal records are not particularly effective in assessing attitudes towards
same-sex desire, they do demonstrate that by the interwar period male
prostitution was causing concern to Scottish legal authorities and social
commentators. However, such revelations received little media coverage;
neither did a spate of blackmail cases involving male prostitutes.[9] Such
were the concerns over the sheer numbers of blackmail cases in Glasgow
during the 1920s that questions were asked in the House of Commons
regarding measures to ensure the anonymity of the defendants in such
cases and the impact upon the moral character of the young should
such cases eventually find their way into the printed media.[10] Scotland
had historically lacked a media-amplified 'queer panic', which had been
evident in England for some time, most obviously in the 1889 Cleveland
Street Scandal in London in which working-class youths consorted with
upper-class men and the 1895 trial of Oscar Wilde. These cases 'became
vehicles for the continuation of the aggressive middle-class morality
that sought to define the national character'.[11] Investigations into male
prostitution rings uncovered evidence that even within solid, working-
class communities, same-sex desire and male prostitution appeared to be
thriving. George Buchanan, MP for the Glasgow Gorbals constituency,
was unnerved by such revelations, and seemed genuinely perplexed that
such men existed amongst Glasgow folk:

> They were without dress, or any male attire, but with tight fitting jackets;
> and all that; with their hands finely chiselled – far more finely chiselled than,
> say, the hands of my wife; who called each other by female names, used the
> scents common to women, and even painted . . . [12]

Rather than a critique of Mrs Buchanan's cuticles, Buchanan was tapping into emerging concerns over a 'class of men' that was becoming more and more visible – to the authorities at least – and heightened concerns over the longer-term impact that such men would have upon Scottish morals and Scottish masculinity.[13] This class of men was failing to adhere to the constituents of Scottish working-class masculinity, which involved hard physical labour, involvement in a fraternal work and leisure culture, and financial and moral support of his family.[14] This specific interest in the manner by which men carried and adorned themselves with products originally aimed at the image-conscious female is also evident in a number of homosexual offence prosecutions in Scotland, and points to a dominant construct of masculinity that was as much about outward appearance and mannerisms as it was about any inherent sexuality.

The subject of police surveillance on a September evening in Glasgow in 1928 was one of the men George Buchanan referred to in his speech three years previously. His name was William Paton and he was considered the leader of Glasgow's 'whitehats', a relatively organised subculture of queer male prostitutes, operating in and around Glasgow city centre. Paton toured Glasgow city centre, including St Enoch and Central stations, searching for customers whom he would then escort to the backroom of his mother's fish restaurant. While working, Paton went by the name 'Liz Paton' which, to the authorities, was an indication of his subversive nature.[15]

On that evening the police, acting on a tip-off, followed Paton around the city centre and watched him as a he spoke to one man before they walked off arm in arm, apparently on 'very affectionate terms'.[16] Their route took them back to the fish restaurant in McAlpine Street, off the Broomielaw. Three police officers positioned themselves at an external window, and when the officers were sure that the act of sodomy was being committed they entered the premises. Paton refused an order to get dressed and was conveyed to the local police office wearing only his shirt. The police officers had collected some evidence at the scene: a bed-roll, scented powder, a lipstick, Cutex paste polish, and a box of boracic ointment. One of the arresting officers stated that 'the cosmetics are such as are commonly used by male prostitutes. Paton's face was painted and powdered.'[17] The focus upon personal items owned by Paton is telling. Such items had no bearing on whether the crime of sodomy had been attempted or committed, and their identification mirrors events in England during this period, when independently innocuous objects coupled with their owner suggested an effeminised male body: a criminal 'type'.[18]

Men such as Paton, and his 'whitehat' associates, presented the authorities with an easily identifiable sexual and gender transgressor. These men were easy to label, manifesting physical symptoms of their sexual deviance. The trial notes also focus on the utterances of Paton, his use of sexual language, his feminine manner: he teased his companion and offered advice on his performance: 'Oh darling, I do love you, I think you are wonderful, let me play with you'; 'You are hot stuff'; 'Go on sweetheart, put it in'; 'You are not getting it right'.[19] The reporting of the verbal exchanges in these cases stands in contrast to other sodomy cases not involving male prostitutes where much less attention is devoted to the words said, as if the acts were committed in relative silence.

Paton was found guilty of sodomy and was sentenced to three years' penal servitude at Glasgow High Court.[20] Curiously there is no mention of a trial for his client, William McCluskey. The precognition papers state that the twenty-eight-year-old had recently been discharged from the Royal Artillery. He had no previous convictions and was considered by the court to possess a good character. The apparent failure to prosecute McCluskey was an unusual occurrence as in most prior cases both parties were prosecuted and received similar sentences. Within the trial papers very little is said about the discharged soldier, his 'good character' and his clean record appear almost as reassurances that his masculinity was unblemished by this aberration. Indeed, young working-class men in London saw the opportunity to have sexual relations with effeminate homosexuals as an acceptable form of sexual release that did not detract in any way from their masculinity.[21] McCluskey, it appears, was free to return to his 'straight' life, unblemished by this flirtation with queerness. The notion that male and female same-sex desire was the result, not of an inherent pre-disposition but of moral excess, appears to have been a relatively popular idea during the interwar and post-war periods. Writing in the *Aberdeen Evening Express* in November 1953, Lady Cynthia Colville, a social worker and Justice of the Peace, lamented the growth of 'self-indulgence' and the lack of inhibition and self-control, which she viewed as a causal factor in the rise of homosexuality amongst men and women. Colville's view was that diminished feelings of responsibility had led to a belief that 'sexual relations of all kinds outside of marriage are natural, interesting, and show a fine spirit of manly (or womanly) independence and freedom'.[22]

Yet the male prostitute was an altogether different phenomenon. Cases from the mid- to late nineteenth century were predominantly viewed as instances of 'errors of judgement' or occurred after imbibing strong liquor.[23] The focus of the police involved in such prosecutions, and of the courts, was upon the act of sodomy rather than the type of men involved. The legal records consistently make reference in such cases to 'unnatural carnal connection', 'the act of sodomy', or 'abominable practices'. These men were not viewed as being 'habitually addicted to passive paederasty', as one Highland police surgeon remarked in 1914,[24] but were deemed to have engaged in a form of 'unrestrained heterosexual lust', a sure sign of heterosexual moral excess.[25]

The McCluskey case demonstrates that respectability might have shielded some men from accusations of sexual deviance. It was not unusual for men accused of engaging in sexual acts with other men to foreground within their criminal defence their respectability and good character, a process that further alienated those men who failed, or refused, to conform to sexual mores, or masculine ideals.[26] Indeed, Joan Tumblety, in the context of France, suggests that the emergence of the stigmatised effeminate queer male played a part in helping to endorse 'an exaggerated version of the inter-war era's preference for muscular masculinity'.[27]

Prior to World War One normative concepts of masculinity had been challenged by men and women who refused to comply passively with gendered roles.[28] Yet World War One was to provide exponents of normative masculinity an opportunity to reaffirm such a concept. The fighting man was to become a salient exemplar of a certain model of masculinity, embodying aggression, courage and strength, an idealised form of manhood which had implications for men far beyond the military arena.[29] 'The man as warrior' became central to the British concept of masculinity during World War One,[30] however, the war and its aftermath impacted significantly on men's ability to perform this form of masculinity in the domestic realm. The post-war economic depression and associated high levels of unemployment undermined the traditional model of the family.[31] Physically and mentally disfigured former soldiers found the stifling rhetoric of interwar masculinity difficult to internalise with its emphasis on physical and mental order, and led, as Joanna Bourke has argued, to a partial redefinition of masculinity that viewed such imperfections not as failures but as representations of heroic martyrdom, albeit somewhat temporarily.[32]

By the late 1920s the Glasgow police were actively collecting detailed information on queer males, mostly prostitutes, which was contained within photograph books issued to the city's night detectives. By the early 1930s the collection of descriptions and photographs of Glasgow's 'whitehats' comprised around a dozen individuals and listed their *modi operandi*, and notes on their appearance and associations.[33] Notably, the descriptions also listed their 'professional' names which, although demonstrating some imagination, further underlined their otherness and their descent into gender subversion: 'Happy Fanny Fields', 'Florence Ramsay', 'Eadie Healy', 'Ella Shields', and 'Maria Santoye', amongst others.[34]

In January 1930, John Rae, another 'whitehat', was arrested at a lodging house in McAlpine Street when he accompanied a client back to a rented cubicle, a stone's throw from the Paton's fish restaurant. Rae was thirty-seven, single and had been an orderly at Bellahouston Hospital. He was a known male prostitute whose 'professional' name was 'Daisy James'. Rae had spent time as a patient in both Gartloch Asylum and Stoneyettes Hospital as a result of his 'defective will power' and problematic behaviour.[35] The police were informed when the lodging house attendant became suspicious, alerted by Rae's feminine appearance and voice, as the two men hurried towards their bed for the night. After the men's apprehension Dr Gilbert Garvey from Duke Street Prison was called to examine Rae and found him to be 'a person of unsound mind' who required 'care and control'. Dr Ivy McKenzie described Rae's general manner as being 'soft and childish' and his behaviour 'silly and fatuous', he was 'simple and facile' and was 'defective in intelligence and will power'.[36] Despite his informal profession as a prostitute Rae was described as having the intellect of a small boy. Rae never faced trial due to being declared 'unfit' due to insanity;[37] his informal occupation resulting in his psychiatric competency being questioned. Men not described as effeminate in trial records did not have to submit to psychiatric scrutiny, which is further evidence that this class of man was viewed differently to those who engaged, casually, in same-sex sexual acts. Notably, the male prostitutes involved in these Scottish cases were, without exception, the passive actors in the sexual act, which has symbolised submission and effeminacy.[38]

However, Glasgow was not alone in hosting a subculture of sexual and gender transgression, Edinburgh was also viewed by some as a hotbed of unnatural vice. William Merrilees, then a detective inspector and head of vice in the city, endeavoured in the 1930s 'to wage wholesale war on . . . perverts and their associates'.[39] According to Merrilees, those who engaged in homosexual acts (he was writing in the 1960s when such terms were in common use) fell into two categories: the effeminate 'poof', 'bitch' or 'pansy', or the male prostitute/blackmailer.[40] Merrilees also asserted that Edinburgh 'poofs' often took female names, frequently appropriated from female celebrities of the period. 'Tallulah Bankhead',

'Myrna Loy', 'Countess Betsy', 'Gloria', 'Godiva', and 'Princess this and that' featured in the roll call of aliases. Merrilees himself was not averse to 'going native', affecting a lisp and peculiar walk, cruising Calton Hill, or visiting the Russian Baths (where he beat two men who propositioned him) in order to observe Edinburgh's homosexual subculture.[41]

Merrilees did not hide his disgust at the activities of queer men in Edinburgh and he directed particular scorn at the perceived effeminacy of the men he encountered. On undertaking a raid on a brothel in the city he was horrified to find men there 'dressed in brassieres, and knickers, with toenails and fingernails painted, using all types of cosmetics, and adopting female names'.[42] For Merrilees, sex between men was only one aspect of this distinct criminal underworld; his focus was also upon the gender transgressions of these feminine men, and their degradations. Take for example, his collection of evidence: personal items, including gold cigarette lighters, makeup and letters, especially those which included references to femininity, which he described as being of a disgusting nature – 'He says I'm his girl', 'From your loving sister', 'He calls me Blondie', and so on.[43]

Merrilees had been involved in the Edinburgh Kosmo Club investigation in 1933, an attempt to crack down on female prostitution in the city,[44] and within a year he was investigating Maximes Dance Hall for male prostitution and homosexual offences, which resulted in a couple of prosecutions. This case involved soldiers from the nearby barracks, tempted by the charms of effeminate male prostitutes, and men of wealth from Edinburgh who lavished upon them money and gifts. The owner of the dance hall and his 'accomplice' received lengthy sentences but the soldiers escaped prosecution; they had simply been going along with it all to see what they could get out of it, or at least that was Merrilees' interpretation.[45] There were almost a hundred cases relating to sodomy heard at Scottish high courts between 1885 and 1930, and ten per cent involved members of the armed forces.[46] Again, the soldier represented a form of normative masculinity that appeared beyond reproach, even when individuals entered the subversive arena of same-sex desire. The fact that these soldiers were able to emerge from their involvement with prostitutes and queer men of means relatively untainted points towards a form of masculinity impervious to deviance; certain parallels exist with men from the brigade of guards in London whose bodies' position of 'domination' enabled them to enact their masculinity with both male and female sexual partners without submitting to an effeminised queer identity.[47] This appears to be the case for the Edinburgh soldiers whose involvement with queer men was dismissed as transitory and fuelled by material temptations.

What these cases demonstrate is that there were heightened concerns in the interwar period in Scotland about the emergence, or at least the visibility, of men who engaged in both gender transgressions and sexual transgressions. Such men were a double-barrelled assault on Scottish manhood, occupying the nexus of gender and deviance. What is also evident is that despite the terms homosexuality and heterosexuality being introduced into Scottish discourse by the early twentieth century, the regulatory power of the sexual binaries had yet to be realised.[48] Thus discourses of same-sex desire were mired in discussions of gender transgression and the excesses of 'normal' sexuality.

QUEER SCOTTISH MEN, EFFEMINACY AND HOMOSEXUALITY

It was not until the 1950s that queer men were described in popular discourse as homosexual, the binary opposite of normative heterosexuality.[49] Such an assertion posits that by the post-World War Two period the choice of sexual partners defined sexuality and overtook interwar concepts of the queer man as effeminate, weak and emotional.[50] The publication in 1957 of the Report of the Departmental Committee on Homosexual Offences and Prostitution (known as the Wolfenden Report) enabled a wider appreciation of the 'problem' of male homosexuality, and reflected reformist principles concerning the law and morality.[51] The report was published after considerable discussion and deliberation by the appointed committee into whether the legal proscriptions against homosexual sex were fit for purpose. In the end the committee determined that sex between adult males in private should be decriminalised (this did not occur in England and Wales until 1967 and 1980 in Scotland).[52]

Despite the report enabling a slightly more liberal discourse of homosexuality, the popular press, particularly in England, still engaged in demonising rhetoric, focusing on the insidious threat to morality that homosexuals posed, and continuing to conceive male homosexuality as centred on effeminacy and moral weakness.[53] Within Scotland, the central discussion regarding the findings of the report was heavily influenced by the thoughts of James Adair – the most prominent Scot on the committee and fierce critic of legal reform – and the strong objections of Scotland's Protestant churches, each perceiving decriminalisation as providing a gateway to further moral degradations.[54]

Yet while Scottish legislators may have restrained themselves from belittling homosexual men as mincing effeminates, the implications of decades of demonising rhetoric problematised homosexual Scottish men's relationship with masculinity. While a visible queer presence within major Scottish cities emerged during the interwar period, questions remain as to whether the links between same-sex desire and gender transgression dissipated as understandings of same-sex desire developed during the second half of the twentieth century. Yet according to views expressed in a series of interviews with self-identifying Scottish gay and bisexual men in 2007–8 who had experience of life in post-war Scotland, the model of effeminacy continued to create considerable identity anxieties. The alleged declining visibility of 'camp' men after World War Two, which was the result of greater scrutiny from legal and social quarters, led homosexual men to distinguish between sexuality and gender.[55] This had the potential of marginalising those men who fully engaged with a 'queer' identity that embodied gender transgression. In the narratives of Scottish queer men who matured during the 1940s, 1950s and 1960s, the issues of masculinity, heterosexuality and public representation still resonated.

Colin (b. 1945) reflected upon the perceived threat that an effeminate university acquaintance posed for his own burgeoning non-heterosexual identity:

> I remember a guy at university with me, probably the year under me and he was from sort of like a middle-class English background and he was in the sort of student drama society and he was very, very camp . . . There were other people I knew at university who were nasty, manipulative, megalomaniacs, all kinds of things but there wouldn't have been the stigma associated with being as there was with him . . . I had a friend who did speak to him . . . and I thought, 'Why's he doing this?!' This friend was about the same level of sexual development as I was, struggling with his own homosexuality, em, and I just thought, 'He's making a fool of himself'.[56]

Colin's experience demonstrated that he was fearful that by associating with this 'camp' man, this would attract scrutiny regarding his own sexuality. Esther Newton suggests that the desire not to associate with such men is related to the fear of stigmatisation: 'the overt homosexual is accused of a more degrading crime, that of being "too nellie", that is roughly, "too effeminate" . . . In effect, I will not associate with you because you are too stigmatized'.[57]

A stigma was associated with homosexual men who did not conform to an assumed masculine role, or to what R. W. Connell determined as hegemonic masculinity.[58] According to Connell homosexual men are subordinated to heterosexual men through a wide range of practices, including legal proscription, intimidation and violence.[59] The effeminate man fails to embody cultural practices associated with heterosexual masculinity, which leads heterosexual men to develop an antagonism towards men who choose not, or fail, to conform.[60] The stigmatisation suffered by homosexual men is not simply exogenous but also exists internally. Internalised homophobia has been described by Gregory Herek as a psychological conflict between what an individual thinks they should be (heterosexual) and their actual sexual preferences (homosexual).[61] This internalised homophobia was not simply about the individual but could have implications for homosexual men who did not meet dominant cultural expectations of heterosexual masculinity.

Harry (b. 1950) remained in the 'closet' for much of his early adult life, only coming out in the late 1980s, a decision informed by the homophobic hostility that surrounded him during his early life in Glasgow. The exogenous homophobia Harry experienced during the 1960s and early 1970s arguably led to a form of internalised homophobia:

> the main word [used to describe homosexual men] seemed to be 'poof', 'poofter', that seemed to be the word really when I was in 'macho' circles and if anybody saw somebody that looked a wee bit, well, effeminate or spoke rather oddly, we used to say, 'poof' . . . I suppose there was a time in my life when I thought an effeminate homosexual was basically what a gay man represented and I . . . didn't feel effeminate; I didn't prance about or mince about . . . I still don't feel at ease with an effeminate gay man. That's just the way it is. There was a time that I used to feel guilty about that but not anymore, live and let live, I don't have to cross that barrier and join an effeminate gay man, my choice. My choice is just to stay with butch gay men, if I ever meet them.[62]

Harry's discomfort with the 'obvious' homosexuals he encountered taps into the pattern of disassociation that emerged in the post-war period which saw many homosexual men retreat from the flamboyant and gender-subversive identities that seemed to typify queer urban life during the interwar period. His ability to act 'normally', to perform a version of masculinity acceptable to his peers, protected him from suspicion. This tactic only failed when his sexuality was revealed and caused a breakdown in his relationships with his male heterosexual friends owing to their discomfort with his version of homosexual masculinity, which aped a heterosexual version. This discomfort is echoed in the recollections of Brian (b. 1936) who, during his twenties, wished to avoid a certain type of queer identity: 'I think what I didn't want to be at a fairly early age was a bit "obvious" . . . flamboyant . . . a homosexual "type"'.[63] Historian Richard Hornsey describes a 'more modern form of homosexuality' as developing as a counter-culture to the more public gender-transgressive representations in interwar London.[64] Typically, this was experienced by middle-class homosexuals as an oppositional movement that embodied discretion, monogamy and domestic propriety.[65] This rejection of gender subversion was an attempt to reassert these men's masculine conformity; it was rooted within heterosexual masculinity.

There is further evidence that such counter-culture communities existed in Glasgow during the post-war period. Alastair (b. 1948) recalled his transition from working-class boy trawling the Glasgow queer scene to immersion within a distinctly more discreet and genteel middle-class environment, which forsook public flamboyancy for evenings at the theatre and private functions: 'I was taken to the opera and I was taken to the theatre but that was sort of passive consumption as I was actually then in the network of people, you know, performers and directors and all that sort of thing.'[66] Brian (b. 1936) similarly forsook immersion in the developing queer scene in Glasgow for middle-class conformity, as he feared that engaging with this scene, and with those who 'advertised' their sexuality, would lead to his own sexuality being revealed to family, peers and other heterosexual acquaintances.[67]

Sean's (b. 1955) recollections from working in the shipyards in Glasgow during the 1970s offer an indication that the effeminate homosexual was not perceived as a threat to the heterosexual male as he did not challenge heterosexual men's self-concepts:

> People in the yerds could only accept somebody like that [a homosexual] if ye were very camp and . . . if you were like a joke or a caricature, they could live wi' that but whit they couldnae live wi' was somebody talkin' the same way, cursin' the same way, actin' the same way. That is like a big major no-no.[68]

In effect, a form of masculinity very different to the cliché of the hard-working, laddish culture of the shipyard did not force those workers to adjust their own concept of masculinity. In these terms the homosexual male was still perceived as effeminate and separate; an incursion into a working-class masculine environment by an otherwise indistinguishable homosexual was viewed as much more challenging – hence explaining why Sean never 'came out' while working in the shipyard. This accords somewhat with Harry's experience in that he was rejected by his heterosexual peers when his homosexuality was revealed, despite sharing many of the supposed outward signifiers of heterosexual masculinity: working hard, supporting his family and enjoying a fraternal work

culture. What this suggests is that even by the 1970s, this narrow interpretation of masculinity and heterosexuality appeared co-joined, but
also points to competing interpretations of homosexuality.

Yet despite a shift in the ways in which men who were attracted to
other men were conceptualised, this emergent homonormativity, which
reflected many homosexual men's desire to express a form of masculinity not associated with effeminacy, sat alongside an acknowledgement
of difference. Robert (b.1937) was ambivalent about this over-simplistic
binary: 'men who presumably [were] gay but who [behaved] in a very
outgoing way. . . effeminate or even a bit camp . . . that always kind of
amazes me . . . I kind of admire that, there is a clarity about that . . .'[69]
For Robert the post-war effeminate homosexual was not a figure of
scorn, to be dismissed as unrepresentative of modern concepts of the
masculine homosexual. He was, in fact, asserting *his* right to exist, *his*
right to challenge gender binaries, *his* right to pleasure.[70] With regard
to urban Scotland, the shift from a queer identity, which challenged and
threatened versions of heterosexuality, is evident during the post-war
period when gay and bisexual men actively sought to distinguish themselves from a highly punished and discredited identity. Events such as
the publication of the Wolfenden Report introduced some to the concept
of the distinct male homosexual personage identified not by appearance
or manner but by their attraction to people of the same sex. Yet what
is apparent is that the concept of the gender-subversive queer man from
interwar society still resonated amongst some homosexual Scots, but
was, by this time, deemed largely an aberration. Thus despite a solid-
state, inflexible form of Scottish masculinity failing to exist unmolested
across time and space, some Scottish homosexual men still desired to 'fit
in' with a loose model of masculinity that did not obviously challenge
and did not obviously subvert.

CONCLUSION

The emergence of a distinct and subversive queer, male effeminate identity during the interwar period had implications for the state of Scottish
masculinity, but it also helped to reassure 'heterosexual' men of their own
normalcy. The subversive queer man helped to define the 'heterosexual'
by presenting an 'other'; a divergent and deviant form of manhood that
flirted publicly with accepted norms of masculinity and femininity.[71] Yet
concepts of gender normalcy were never rigid and inflexible; men could
engage in same-sex activity with other men without challenging their
own self-concepts or indeed the attitudes of the authorities, such as in

the case involving Edinburgh soldiers, prostitution and Maximes Dance Hall. Having a previously 'good character' could also protect non-queer men from being labelled as sexual deviants and gender transgressors, which suggested that for legal authorities sex between men could be a transitory episode, and highlighted the attitude that confirmed sexual deviants had an almost infectious sexual proclivity.

The manner in which male prostitutes were treated by the police suggests that the twin terrors of sodomy and effeminacy, with suggested blackmail thrown into the pot, marked these men out for special treatment. Their deviance was inscribed upon their body and character in an indelible way. While effeminate homosexuals were still attracting considerable derision in 1950s and 1960s Scotland, they were assisting 'heterosexual' and 'homosexual' men to define their own masculinity. Much more threatening to some heterosexual men were homosexual men who were performing a version of masculinity similar to their own. What this demonstrates is that masculinities within interwar and post-war contexts were flexible, contested and constantly adjusted to cope with perceived threats to a rather vague yet powerful concept: male heterosexual normalcy.

It is also clear that in post-war Scotland competing concepts of homosexuality existed. The apparently dominant concept amongst my interviewees was that homosexuals were not necessarily effeminate, and that effeminacy was to be shunned in favour of a homosexual masculinity that conformed to heterosexual masculinity and encouraged self-restraint and self-control. The emergence of a sexuality binary, which supposedly disentangled sexuality from gender performance, did not act as liberation but created another form of constraint. The effeminate queer man, once representative of same-sex desire in interwar Scotland, was now viewed as a discreditable homosexual, and further constrained personal expression and any form of liberty from constructed models of gender.

NOTES

1. For example see: Hilary Young, 'Being a man: everyday masculinities', in Lynn Abrams and Callum Brown (eds), *A History of Everyday Life in Twentieth Century Scotland* (Edinburgh: Edinburgh University Press, 2009), pp. 131–52; Gabriel Koureas, *Memory, Masculinity and National Identity in British Visual Culture, 1914–1930: A Study of 'Unconquerable Manhood'* (Aldershot: Ashgate, 2007).
2. Philippa Levine, 'Sexuality, gender, and empire', in Philippa Levine (ed.),

Gender and Empire (Oxford: Oxford University Press, 2004), pp. 134–55, at 134.

3. Michael Roper, 'Between manliness and masculinity: the "war generation" and the psychology of fear in Britain, 1914–50', *Journal of British Studies*, 44 (2005), pp. 343–62, at 347.

4. Tracey Loughran, 'A crisis of masculinity? Re-writing the history of shell-shock and gender in First World War Britain', *History Compass*, 9 (2013), pp. 727–38.

5. Florence Tamagne, *A History of Homosexuality in Europe, Volume I & II: Berlin, London, Paris, 1919–1939* (New York: Algora, 2006), pp. 20–1.

6. 'The libel sensation: Maud Allen case, Lower Court proceedings', *Marlborough Express*, 7 June 1918, p. 4; see also, Deborah Cohler, *Citizen, Invert, Queer: Lesbianism and War in Early Twentieth-Century Britain* (Minneapolis: University of Minnesota Press, 2010), and 'Sapphism and sedition: producing female homosexuality in Great War Britain', *Journal of the History of Sexuality*, 16 (2007), pp. 68–94; Jodie Medd, 'The cult of the clitoris: anatomy of a national scandal', *Modernism/Modernity*, 9 (2002), pp. 21–49.

7. Emma Vickers, *Queen and Country: Same-Sex Desire in the British Armed Forces, 1939–45* (Manchester: Manchester University Press, 2013), pp. 26–7.

8. Ibid. pp. 26–7.

9. William Merrilees, *The Short Arm of the Law* (London: John Long, 1966), p. 115.

10. Hansard, House of Commons [HC] 181, 10 March 1925, cols 1269–73.

11. Morris B. Kaplan, 'Who's afraid of John Saul? Urban culture and the politics of desire in late Victorian London', *GLQ: A Journal of Lesbian and Gay Studies*, 5 (1999), pp. 267–314, at 293.

12. Hansard, HC 181, 10 March 1925, cols 1269–70.

13. Hansard, HC 181, cols 1269–70.

14. Annmarie Hughes, *Gender and Political Identities in Scotland, 1919–1939* (Edinburgh: Edinburgh University Press, 2010), p. 3; R. Johnston and A. McIvor, 'Dangerous work, hard men, and broken bodies: masculinity in the Clydeside heavy industries, c. 1930–1970', *Labour History Review*, 69 (2004), pp. 135–51.

15. National Records of Scotland [NRS], Trial and Precognition Records, AD15/28/84.

16. NRS, Trial and Precognition Records, AD15/28/84.

17. Ibid.

18. Matt Houlbrook, 'The man with the powderpuff in interwar London', *Historical Journal*, 50 (2007), pp. 145–71, at 146–7.

19. NRS, Trial and Precognition Records, AD15/28/84.

20. NRS, Trial and Precognition Records, JC14/40.

21. Richard Hornsey, *The Spiv and the Architect: Unruly Life in Postwar*

London (Minneapolis: University of Minnesota Press, 2010), pp. 7–8; Matt Houlbrook, *Queer London: Perils and Pleasures in the Sexual Metropolis, 1918-57* (Chicago: University of Chicago Press, 2005), pp. 167–77.

22. Lady Cynthia Colville, 'Young people and the moral challenge', *Aberdeen Evening Express*, 24 November 1953, p. 3.

23. Jeffrey Meek, *Queer Voices in Post-War Scotland: Male Homosexuality, Religion and Society* (Basingstoke: Palgrave Macmillan, 2015), pp. 13–22.

24. NRS, Trial and Precognition Records, AD15/14/117.

25. Charles Upchurch, *Before Wilde: Sex Between Men in Britain's Age of Reform* (Berkeley: University of California Press, 2009), p. 193.

26. Upchurch, *Before Wilde*, p. 194.

27. Joan Tumblety, *Remaking the Male Body: Masculinity and the Uses of Physical Culture in Interwar and Vichy France* (Oxford: Oxford University Press, 2012), p. 55.

28. George Mosse, *The Image of Man* (Oxford: Oxford University Press, 1996), p. 78.

29. Graham Dawson, *Soldier Heroes: British Adventure, Empire, and the Imagining of Masculinities* (London: Routledge, 1994), p. 1.

30. Mosse, *The Image of Man*, p. 110.

31. Young, 'Being a man', pp. 131–2.

32. Joanna Bourke, *Dismembering the Male: Men's Bodies, Britain and the Great War* (Chicago: University of Chicago Press, 1996), p. 56.

33. Glasgow City Archives [GCA], SR22/63/20, Photograph album of convicts with notes on each (c. 1930).

34. GCA, SR22/63/20.

35. NRS, Trial and Precognition Records, AD15/30/59.

36. Ibid.

37. Ibid.

38. Matt Houlbrook, 'Soldier heroes and rent boys: homosex, masculinities, and Britishness in the Brigade of Guards, circa 1900–1960', *Journal of British Studies*, 42 (2003), pp. 351–88, at 360.

39. William Merrilees, *The Short Arm of the Law* (London: John Long, 1966), p. 118.

40. Ibid. p. 116.

41. Ibid. p. 119.

42. Ibid. p. 117.

43. Ibid. p. 118.

44. Louise Settle, 'The Kosmo Club case: clandestine prostitution during the interwar period', *Twentieth Century British History*, 25 (2014), pp. 562–84.

45. Merrilees, *The Short Arm of the Law*, p. 121.

46. Jeffrey Meek, 'The legal and social construction of the sodomite in Scotland, 1885 to 1930' (unpublished master's dissertation, University of Glasgow, 2006), pp. 78–81.

47. Houlbrook, 'Soldier heroes and rent boys', p. 360.
48. See for example: 'The German scandals: the decision of the court, Herr Harden acquitted', *Aberdeen Journal*, 30 October 1907, p. 5; 'Berlin scandal', *Dundee Courier*, 30 October 1907, p. 5.
49. Houlbrook, *Queer London*, p. 164.
50. Matt Houlbrook, '"Lady Austin's camp boys": constituting the queer subject in 1930s London', *Gender & History*, 14 (2002), pp. 31–61, at 50.
51. Matthew Waites, *The Age of Consent: Young People, Sexuality and Citizenship* (Basingstoke: Palgrave Macmillan, 2005), p. 96.
52. Home Office Scottish Home Department, *Report of the Committee on Homosexual Offences and Prostitution* (London: Her Majesty's Stationary Office, 1957).
53. Terry Sanderson, *Mediawatch: The Treatment of Male and Female Homosexuality in the British Media* (London: Cassell, 1995), p. 8.
54. For a full discussion of these factors see: Meek, *Queer Voices*, pp. 39–52.
55. Houlbrook, *Queer London*, pp. 164–65.
56. Interview with 'Colin', 20 September 2007.
57. Esther Newton, 'The queens', in P. Nardi and B. Schneider (eds), *Social Perspectives in Lesbian and Gay Studies: A Reader* (London: Routledge, 1998), pp. 38–50, at 40.
58. See: R. W. Connell, *Masculinities*, 2nd edition (Cambridge: Polity Press, 2005).
59. Connell, *Masculinities*, p. 78.
60. Mike Donaldson, 'What is hegemonic masculinity?', *Theory and Society*, 22:5 (1993), p. 643–57, at 648.
61. Gregory M. Herek, 'Beyond "homophobia": thinking about sexual prejudice and stigma in the twenty-first century', *Sexuality Research and Social Policy*, 1 (2004), pp. 6–24, at 19.
62. Interview with Harry, 2 April 2007.
63. Interview with Brian, 25 June 2007.
64. Hornsey, *The Spiv and the Architect*, pp. 8–10.
65. Ibid. p. 8.
66. Interview with Alastair, 16 May 2007.
67. Interview with Brian.
68. Interview with Sean, 3 August 2007.
69. Interview with Robert, 1 August 2007.
70. Stephen Garton, *Histories of Sexuality: Antiquity to Sexual Revolution* (London: Equinox, 2004), pp. 215–16.
71. Connell, *Masculinities*, p. 81.

13

Speaking to the 'Hard Men': Masculinities, Violence and Youth Gangs in Glasgow, c. 1965–75

Angela Bartie and Alistair Fraser

GLASGOW HAS LONG HAD a reputation as a 'hard city' with a particularly masculine image.[1] While this image of rugged masculinities was forged in the context of working-class labour amid the potent mixture of industrialism, migration and urbanisation that founded modern Glasgow, it has also often been associated with social problems such as male interpersonal violence, ill health and high mortality. In cultural representations, these forms of masculinity are frequently combined in the figure of the 'hard man' or 'gemmie', a working-class figure who displays an attitude of fearlessness, of violent defiance, and of fighting his corner against all odds.[2] Nowhere is this manifestation of Glasgow masculinity more apparent than in representations of the youth 'gang'. From H. Kingsley Long's rewriting of Alexander McArthur's Gorbals notebooks as *No Mean City* (1935), through to Peter Mullan's semi-autobiographical film *NEDS: Non-Educated Delinquents* (2010), images of Glaswegian masculinity have been interwoven with images of the gang, oscillating between fact and fiction, past and present. As the historian Andrew Davies has pointed out, *No Mean City* 'cemented' Glasgow's reputation as the gang city of Britain, while the ghost of its main protagonist, the fictional 'Razor King' Johnnie Stark, arguably continues to haunt it.[3] Like the 'urban legends' that surround Glasgow youth gangs more generally, depictions of the city frequently collapse representation and reality.[4]

This chapter seeks to unite historical and sociological perspectives in excavating the lived experiences of everyday masculinities and violence that lie behind this persistent image, while interrogating popular representations of the 'hard city'. Investigating the historical relationship between gangs and masculinities in Glasgow has the potential to illuminate understandings not only of this specific context, but the contingent relationships between history, culture and geography in the patterning of Scottish masculinities more broadly. From a sociological perspective, engaging with historical analyses can go beyond broad-based theories of social reproduction to more grounded representations of the subjective experiences and narratives of situated masculine actors. As such, this chapter seeks to contribute to both a historical and sociological framing of the persistence and development of specific forms of masculinities in Scotland by combining micro-level narratives of everyday life with sociological theorisations of gender, masculinities and social reproduction.

Drawing on oral history interviews conducted in 2010–11 with individuals involved in violent territorialism in the 1960s and 1970s – specifically through street-based 'gangs' of young men – we contrast popular representations of the Glasgow 'hard man' with the lived experiences of those living and working in the city at that time. Focusing specifically on Easterhouse, a major post-war housing scheme in the east end of Glasgow, we highlight the prominence of 'the street' in narrative accounts of masculine identity-formation for young working-class men and link this to the specific social, cultural and economic composition of the locale. We argue that such 'street' masculinities should be understood in historical context, recognising the influence of local cultures of machismo on the persistence of certain forms of masculine identity. As Linda McDowell has pointed out, masculinities are more than personal characteristics – they are 'collective social practices'.[5] The particular social and cultural context is crucial to our understanding of how gang masculinities – and masculinities in general – are formed in the city and surrounding area.[6]

THE HARD MAN IN THE MEAN CITY

Groups of young men engaging in territorial violence have been reported by the press in Glasgow since the 1880s, from the peak of the city's industrial productivity, and throughout the twentieth century.[7] Sometimes the same gang names have recurred consistently; for example, the Baltic Fleet, from Baltic Street, Dalmarnock, in Glasgow's East End, were first reported in 1916 and remain listed on Strathclyde Police intelligence databases to this day.[8] Gangs have evolved into more organised criminal units in times of economic hardship, while at others, such as wartime, they have fallen away.[9] Throughout this time, gangs have been reported in working-class communities marked by a lack of amenities, frequently accompanied by high levels of overcrowding and high populations of young people. However, although gangs have a long lineage, the issue has only become the subject of popular outrage and political attention at particular historical moments, with certain periods producing more interest and publicity than others. Gangs were rarely mentioned in the public discourse between the interwar period and the mid-1960s. Even a national survey of crime carried out in 1964 made no mention of the phenomenon.[10] While gang activity may have continued, it was only in the mid-1960s that the issue re-emerged as a 'focal point for a host of economic, social and cultural anxieties'.[11]

From mid-1965, a groundswell of news reports on gangs and violence appeared, and an increasing amount of police, government and public attention became focused on the issue. Comparisons were inevitably made with the razor gangs of the 1920s and 1930s, with Glasgow seen once again in terms of the No Mean City image of hard men and violence – although it was argued that the young gangs of the 1960s were more dangerous than their interwar predecessors because they used knives instead of razors (causing real injury rather than disfigurement) and involved innocent bystanders in their altercations.[12] Figures pointing to alarming rises in violence, and the possession of offensive weapons and crime more generally, were regularly reported in the press. Many incidents involving more than two people were presented as 'gang' skirmishes and those involved denounced as thugs, hooligans and gangsters. Glasgow was, in the words of one journalist in 1968, 'exhibited to the world as the most lawless city in Britain where fear-ridden citizens are under constant menace by gangs of young thugs'.[13]

Much attention focused on the new post-war housing estates, built to try and relieve Glasgow's chronic housing problems, but particularly on Easterhouse, a large peripheral housing scheme that was formally opened in 1956 and contained nearly nine thousand houses and around fifty thousand people by the mid-1960s. By this point, it was also becoming a focus of press attention and public concern about gangs and violence amongst young people.[14] In 1968, at the height of renewed concerns over youth gangs in Glasgow, the popular entertainer Frankie Vaughan swooped into the area in a blaze of publicity. Meeting with gang leaders from the local Drummy, Pak, Rebels and Toi gangs, Vaughan promised to help them to organise a youth centre in exchange for their promise to end their violence. In February 1969, Vaughan's intervention culminated in the opening of the Easterhouse Project, a youth club run by and for young people in the area with the support of a board of trustees, which included local politicians, representatives of the police in Glasgow, and Vaughan himself.[15]

But despite this high-profile attention, by spring 1968, there was increasing acknowledgement in both the press and in political circles that concern about youth gangs, offensive weapons and violent crime in Glasgow was 'out of all proportion' to the threat. Press coverage had increased, as had demands for more powers of arrest for the police and more punitive responses to those caught with offensive weapons; at the same time, figures for assaults and the use of offensive weapons had declined. By 1968, it was clear that this concern had become unfairly focused on Easterhouse, as a range of evidence showed that gang violence and offensive weapon use was actually a bigger problem in *older* housing areas in the city.[16] The ghost of Johnnie Stark had returned, and Glasgow was once again seen as a hard and violent gang-ridden city.

SPEAKING TO THE 'HARD MEN'

This period was a particularly formative one in the consolidation of the popular image of the 'hard man'. Yet, despite an extensive literature on moral panics over youth, the voices of these so-called 'folk devils' have remained curiously absent.[17] We wanted to interrogate popular representations of Easterhouse by examining the intersections between these representations and the lived experiences of young people in the area.[18] Oral history interviews are a way of exploring experiences and perceptions of youth, deviancy and crime in a way that goes beyond 'official' accounts. We were particularly keen to explore the continuities and changes in forms of masculinity between past and present, particularly as Glasgow – and Easterhouse – have retained their reputations as prominent centres of gang violence in Britain.

We were fortunate in being given permission to reanalyse an important collection of previously unpublished research notes and analyses.[19] Gail Armstrong and Mary Wilson, two sociologists who conducted research with young people and youth workers involved in the Easterhouse Project during the 1960s, assisted in identifying other interviewees. Armstrong still had a cache of transcripts from sixteen interviews she had undertaken in 1969–70 with a range of young people, many of whom had been involved in the Drummy gang (named after Drumlanrig Avenue). These were examined alongside new interviews we undertook (sixteen in all) with individuals reflecting back on their involvement in youth gangs, as well as with a number of people who interacted or worked with youth. These included a social worker, a police officer, a local Church of Scotland minister (who ran monthly dances in his church hall to try and divert young people from gang activity) and youth workers in the Easterhouse Project.

The present chapter draws upon all of these interviews, but attention is largely focused on the experiences of one individual, Danny McCall (pseudonym). Armstrong interviewed Danny in 1969, when he was eighteen and involved in the Drummy gang. We conducted a follow-up interview with him in the summer of 2011. By then, Danny was approaching the age of sixty, working as a manager for a well-known UK firm, and lived with his wife in a commuter town outside Glasgow. This allowed us to compare his perspectives on Easterhouse and youth gangs then, when he was very much involved in a youth gang and now, reflecting back on his youth as he approaches retirement age.

Despite the appearance of much academic work exploring gangs in recent years, 'there remains a dearth of research that explores the understandings, experiences and social meanings of "gangs" for children and young people', particularly in relation to the construction of gender norms and identities.[20] Oral history offers a means of exploring subjective identities, and is therefore ideally suited to exploring the meanings associated with gang involvement. In oral history, the relationship and interactions between discourse and subjectivity have the power to shape individual memories, meaning that the discourses that circulate about masculinities (and femininities) in any given time or place have the power to influence personal narratives and subjectivities.[21] The concept of the 'cultural circuit' – the way that personal narratives can be informed and influenced by public legends – comes into play in Danny's interview, as public discourses about the Glasgow 'hard man' and the violent city play out in his narrative of growing up in Easterhouse.[22] A number of historians have successfully utilised oral history to explore aspects of masculinities in twentieth-century Scotland.[23] This chapter is the first to use oral history interviews to explore masculinities as articulated and performed in the 'gang' in Scotland.

GROWING UP: LEISURE, CLASS AND HABITUS

In making connections between continuities in masculinity over time, it is important to recognise that masculinities are not simply forms of individual practice, but are constituted by unique configurations of history, culture, and gendered relations. Local cultures of machismo, for example, intersect with much broader processes of economic and socio-spatial exclusion. The 'gang' is part of the fabric of the community in which it exists, and conceptions of masculinity in youth gangs are influenced and shaped by those of the wider community and society in which the 'gang members' live. Andrew Davies has noted that being in a gang was a way in which young men strived to embody the working-class ideal of the hard man that suffused their local culture and society. The gang, therefore, *reproduced* rather than diverged from these local expectations about male identity and behaviour.[24]

Pierre Bourdieu's concept of 'habitus' is helpful here. Habitus refers to the set of durable character dispositions that all individuals carry with them in daily life. These dispositions are both intellectual and physical, and frequently operate at a *pre*-conscious level.[25] While each human interaction is different, each individual's approach is, in fact, structured by his or her habitual range of responses, learned during childhood.[26] As Bourdieu has argued, 'masculinity is stitched into the habitus' – and in this way, habitus is both 'gendered and gendering'.[27] In the process of socialisation, gendered attitudes and beliefs are also imprinted, forming a 'layer of embodied experience that is not immediately amenable to self-fashioning'.[28] Individuals sharing a particular social, economic and cultural space may also share deep-seated traits and characteristics that operate at a pre-conscious level. These 'unconscious schemata' are an imprint of 'particular social conditions and conditionings' – structural determinants such as social class, gender or ethnicity – which 'are shared by people subjected to similar experiences even as each person has a unique individual variant of the common matrix'.[29]

A key site in which a gendered habitus has been constituted for young people is the street. The street has long been significant in working-class popular culture, particularly in those urban centres in which overcrowding is a problem. In Glasgow street-based leisure took on an increasingly important role in the period following industrialisation.[30] Despite the proliferation of new entertainment venues in the early twentieth century (for example, cinemas and dance halls), working-class leisure remained largely focused around the local neighbourhood well into the mid-twentieth century. By the 1960s, Glasgow was undertaking a major programme of slum clearance and redirecting large swathes of its population to the new post-war housing schemes in order to tackle the enormous problem of overcrowding. In these newly built schemes, street-based leisure remained the norm, despite the fact that – for most families – overcrowding had become a thing of the past.

Easterhouse was marked by a severe lack of amenities. Even by 1970, it still had 'no public toilets, no public washhouse, no banks, no cinema, no theatre, no public dance hall, no internal transport system, no community centre, no cafés or restaurants and no shopping centre', one pub and very few shops.[31] Half of the population was under the age of twenty-one and, with few resources or amenities, large numbers of young people congregated on street corners and in public spaces.[32] Established territorial loyalties from working-class communities like the Gorbals, from which many people in Easterhouse moved, became fragmented. The result was for 'residents of all ages to identify with their own neighbourhood, rather than with the Easterhouse area, the most explicit expression of which has been the "territory-based gang"'.[33] In this context, gang fighting became, for some, a form of street-based entertainment, which partly grew out of earlier area-based friendships and group games.

A number of observers have commented upon the form that gang fights took. In Armstrong's interviews, young people emphasised the 'entertainment value' that the boys said they gained from planning large-scale 'battles' with 'gangs' from other areas, mainly as a way of 'letting off steam'. The first Secretary of the Easterhouse Project, Graham Noble, wrote that he was:

> struck by the amount of sheer energy and high dramatic skill which goes into a battle ... Display counts for a great deal. There is much running about, striking postures, and brandishing weapons ... Little groups make short charges and then retreat. There is much shouting of slogans incorporating the gang name – 'Toi Rule', 'Drummy Kill', and so on.[34]

One of our contemporary interviewees had lived in the Gorbals in the 1950s, an area associated with gang violence in the 1920s and 1930s (and the setting for *No Mean City*), before moving to Easterhouse around the age of ten. He recalled:

> Even as a very small child I could stand in a close mouth and see and perceive what was happening in the gang activity, and that was that [when] one crowd were chasing another crowd, most of them didn't ever actually want to catch up, it was almost like a game. But ... if you were unfortunate enough to catch up with somebody you've got to be seen to be doing something.[35]

The combination of 'crowds' and 'games' mentioned here denote an overlap with another popular spectator sport in Glasgow: football, which was certainly significant in Easterhouse.[36] When asked about what he did during his leisure time, Danny answered, 'our leisure activities just was, pure and simply you played football down the pitches and that was it.'[37] Clear overlaps between gangs – so-called 'young teams' – and football 'teams' can be discerned in this context. In the context of few amenities or resources, both represented an inexpensive, temporary, street-based release from boredom that 'fit' with the masculine habitus of many of the young men in the area. Indeed, gang fights often grew out of football, as one Easterhouse interviewee recalled:

> It was through playing football that it all started. Used to hang about the corner after the game ... If anyone got dug-up [usually a *verbal* provocation], you'd all go down; that was classed as a 'gang fight'.[38]

When asked if there were any casualties, the interviewee responded:

> No, there were no weapons, knives and that; just sticks to bash them over the head. Used to ... [laughs] ... used to be great y'know, everybody used to know each other, say you knew him from school [the person on the other side] or something, used to go 'How's it going?' an' that, but you'd still fling bricks at him! ... We just let off steam that's all it was. It was better than playing football.[39]

There are a number of historical continuities to be seen between Easterhouse and older working-class communities in Glasgow. We can see these in relation to street-based play, for example, and the lack of amenities that contributed to territorial identity – in the form of gangs – amongst a number of young people. Fighting was seen as an exciting break from the norm, and as a form of leisure for many young men. Pearl Jephcott, in her study of youth leisure in 1960s Scotland (two of her three case study areas were in Glasgow), describes such fights as 'a pleasurable break in an otherwise tame existence'.[40] These parallels suggest a pattern of street-based socialisation in the context of limited opportunities, in which gang conflicts emerge as an opportunity for excitement that both reflects and sustains a form of 'hard' masculinity revolving around loyalty, sport and violence. For the boys in Armstrong and Wilson's study, this was learned and deeply rooted, an aspect of habitus that had been imprinted and developed over time.

BEING A 'GEMMIE'

One of the images most closely associated with gangs and masculinities in Glasgow, both past and present, is that of the 'gemmie'. In his study of youth gangs in 1960s Glasgow, James Patrick describes 'a gemmie' as 'someone who is prepared to fight, whatever the odds, even if defeat or physical punishment is inevitable'.[41] In a similar way, for the writer William McIlvanney, 'standing up for yourself, sometimes against improbable odds, became a Glaswegian convention'.[42] Despite recent challenges to this model of masculinities in cultural representations of Glasgow, the practice of 'being a gemmie' has remained important.[43] As Fraser's recent study of Langview (pseudonym) shows in the east end of Glasgow, there are distinct continuities to be seen between industrial and contemporary masculinities in the city, the crucial difference being that the connection between 'hard' labour and 'hard' street masculinities has been severed in the context of post-industrialism. For the young men in Fraser's study, while 'being a gemmie' gained them prestige within the local context, it served to further alienate the group from employment in a service economy that demands subservience and obedience.[44]

The formation of 'gemmie' masculinities has clear links with the history of working-class labour in Scotland, in particular the potent mixture of industrialism, migration, and urbanisation that founded modern Glasgow. In the Clydeside heavy industries, for example, 'working-class masculinities were nurtured in the tough street culture of the neighbour-hood'. Young boys would play risky games, such as the 'big sui' (sui being short for 'suicide'), jumping gaps between washhouses in the back of tenement flats with those who succeeded being 'instantly assured of hero status.'[45] Risk-taking has been closely associated with the forma-tion of this manifestation of 'gemmie' masculinity, and in childhood it has often taken the form of dares and increasingly dangerous tests of bravado.[46] This can be seen in the context of the street-corner gang, still prevalent in post-war British cities – in these adolescent male groups, 'masculinity was demonstrated through toughness and the ability to take risks, whilst the quest for excitement shaped the selection of activities'.[47]

The image of the Glasgow 'hard man' was formed between the heavy labour of industry and the street-based environments for young men growing up in the same communities. As in Britain more broadly, 'the concept of the "fighter" as a measure of masculinity remained within many post-war working-class neighbourhoods, where the emphasis was on "toughness" within urban street culture in order to stand up to "bullies"'.[48] This continued to be the case, even after de-industrialisation began and the connection between work and street life was eroded. In his contemporary study of crime and masculinities in Sunderland on Tyne and Wear, another industrial and then post-industrial city, Simon Winlow has shown how violence has remained an important part of masculine identity for many working-class men, and argued that the 'conspicuous use of violence' was a 'major deviant activity that was worthy of cultural recognition by working-class males in the modern industrial era.'[49]

In Glasgow, a similar pattern of continuity and change is evident. This process relates to the part that fighting plays in boyhood and ado-lescence. For some of our participants, fighting – and more specifically standing up for yourself – was normalised and seen as a necessary part of learning to be a man. As Elizabeth Stanko argues, 'learning how to manage other boys' violence is a key lesson when growing up male'; boys, and later men, 'learn how to negotiate physical danger, largely in the company of other men.'[50] When we interviewed Danny, he spoke of the importance of standing up for yourself and how his father had communicated this to him:

> ... in those days you were, if you come up and got a doing as a kid yer dad gave you a choice. You either get back doon and get in again or he woulda gied ye a doin', so that was pretty much the, the culture then.

In Danny's narrative, learning to 'stand up for yourself' was therefore an expected element from a young age, from his father but also through peer pressure from local boys. Physical violence was still part of parental discipline, but was also communicated through corporal punishment in schools – Danny referred to getting the belt in school for even simple things like dropping your pencil during a lesson.[51]

The streets that Danny walked were coded as masculine, the domain of those with the ability to handle themselves, and contrasted with the private – and less risky – space of the family home. Street-based, 'gemmie' masculinities were therefore contrasted with 'safe', indoor spaces; Eileen Yeo puts it nicely when she describes the street as 'the stage-set for performing masculinity'.[52] This distinction also highlights issues of hierarchy within the context of gender. As Michael Roper and John Tosh have pointed out, 'understanding gender in relational terms is important because dominant or 'hegemonic' masculinities function by asserting their superiority over the "other"'.[53] The 'street', in this context, was where local forms of 'tough' masculinity were embedded. Asked about whether those involved in gangs wore colours to identify themselves, Danny answered:

> You never had colours. You would know them. But if they were walking about, if there was two guys, three guys walking about they were in the gang because sensible ones would be good sitting in doing their studying and all that or whatever, you know. If they were out walking about you knew they were in a gang ... [54]

Simply walking about in public signified that you were 'fair game'. To Danny, and other young men, being out in the public space of the street with one or more other males was enough to signify gang membership; in contrast, being in the more feminised space of the family home 'studying and all that or whatever' was seen as the less masculine 'other'. The binary gender divide is used to define 'real' masculinity in contrast to perceived deviations from the 'norm', which are labelled as weak, feminine behaviour.[55] This is what sociologist Connell refers to as 'subordinated masculinities'; masculinities are not just relational in terms of how they contrast with – and are influenced and shaped by – *femininities*, but also how they sit in relation to other forms of male attitudes and behaviours.[56]

When asked to talk about Easterhouse at the start of the interview, Danny recounted a narrative infused with themes of risk, 'gemmie' masculinities, and street-based adventure. He began by telling us about how it was like an 'adventure playground' or big 'play park' before recounting an incident that occurred when he was out riding his bike at the age of twelve:

> I think the first instance I had problems with gangs was I got shot in the head once with an air rifle. I was on my bike at the time and I must say it was a cracking shot because I was pedalling at the time, you know [laughter], so it was a good shot, and it kind of a hit me right in the temple and knocked me right off my bike. And needless to say obviously there was an altercation. I chased him, you know. And, [pause] and, eh, I found in these days you had to stand up, if you just accepted it then you woulda just got more of that type of thing. So I think probably you had to earn your reputation very early on in the sense of, if they'd seen you were what we called gemme enough to stand up to them, you know, and, and you could handle yourself then you'd get more and more accepted into it and you wouldnae get that kind of thing . . . [57]

For Danny, of central importance to masculine identity, whether in play or fighting, was the ability to stand up for yourself and to be able to handle yourself – in other words, to be 'gemme'. This reflected the prevailing culture in the Clydeside area.[58] In order to secure respect from his peers, as well as those both younger and older, 'you had to quickly learn how to fight, how to handle yourself, that way you got a bit of respect and they left you alone if they seen you could.'[59] While this form of 'gemmie' masculinity was undoubtedly prized and often strived for in Danny's narrative, it was far from exclusive to the area or, indeed, to the territorial gang. The notions of honour and reputation – usually demonstrated through fighting prowess – have been associated with masculine status for many centuries, as this collection demonstrates. But, we must ask, how do these expectations, attributes and behaviours change over time, for individuals as well as places?

GANG IDENTITY AND THE LIFE COURSE

While several recent publications have pointed to the 'intergenerational' nature of gang identity in Glasgow, few studies have explored these apparent continuities empirically.[60] A benefit of our longitudinal data is the ability to examine the way in which violence, masculinities and gang identity alter and reconfigure over the life course. Danny, once a 'gemmie' on the streets of Easterhouse, is now a businessman, indicating that gangs – and masculinities – must be understood not only in historical context, but also through subjective, narrative-based inquiry. At the same time, it is important to attend to the *processes* through which specific configurations of masculinities are learned and embodied by successive generations.

Criminologists have drawn attention to the ways in which gang identification changes during the life course.[61] For children and young teenagers, gang identification may represent a form of youthful experimentation rather than a commitment to a criminal lifestyle. The sociologist Elijah Anderson, in his study of violent street culture in Philadelphia, describes how the 'code of the street' is learned and internalised: 'by the age of ten, children . . . are mingling on the neighbourhood streets and figuring out their identities. Here they try out roles and scripts in a process that challenges their talent and prior socialisation.'[62] For some, gang identities become a more fixed aspect of identity, fusing violent masculinities and local reputation with group status and area attachment. For others, following similar processes as those involved in more general patterns of desistance from crime, gang identities are simply grown out of.[63] While some young people successfully 'grow out' of gangs – transitioning to alternative sources of identity – for others the reputations gained through gang fighting are not straightforward to live down.

For Danny, the role of street-based age hierarchies was important in shaping younger boys' perceptions and understandings of what it was to be a man. Armstrong, in her 1969 interview, asked Danny about the existence of younger gangs in Easterhouse:

> Aye, there's the Toddler, all the younger lads . . . There's no many of them but, they're all just [smiles] wee crooks, y'know. Just wee thiefs an' that, . . . A lot of wee weans but, y'know, you kid on with them. They come up an' just [indistinct], a lot of wee weans, but. But that's them starting out, wait 'till we see them, they'll just be the same routine. They just hear the older ones at it, so they start I suppose.[64]

We asked Danny about whether there was an older Drummy gang that he was aware of as *he* was growing up. He responded positively, talking about his older peers as having 'earned their badges' and gained respect through their ability to fight as well as, in many cases, having served time in prison. He also noted the importance to him of showing them that he, too, could handle himself with them and thus gain *their* respect. This pattern of age-based hierarchies was also identified by Fraser, in his contemporary research in Langview.

The role of peers is critical in the formation and transmission of masculine identity. Asked whether there was any sort of formal initiation for joining a gang, Danny answered:

> I don't think, you were just basically became friends with them. But I mean obviously if, if, them as friends became in an altercation you had to back 'em up you couldnae run away from it or shy from it.[65]

For Danny, being involved in gangs and fighting was just something you were expected to do. Gang activities involved:

> Bravado and things like that just to get a bit of respect and a name for yourself so that you could be left alone probably, that's what I did it for, you know, I really just, em [pause] you had to do it, you had to do it because, as I say, to go to yer work in the morning, to come home at night, to go into town, to come home at night, you would always come across it so if you didn't you would have just lived in fear.[66]

The repetition here of Danny saying that you 'had to' do these things – be tough, be able to stand up for yourself – to prove yourself as a man underlines the masculine attributes and behaviours that were prized in Easterhouse in the late 1960s. These overlap with forms of masculinity that more widely pervaded working-class culture, both within the city and further afield. For many young men, the territorial gang was the medium through which they developed their masculine identities – but not the only one. Young men like Danny were also sons, who lived in family homes, attended school and work, and might also be brothers, boyfriends and so on. All of these influenced and shaped their sense of self, and their understanding of what it was to be a man. As gender is, of course, relational, we need to explore gender identities in young men in relation to those of young women, and masculinities in relation to femininities – thus far, most historical work on youth gangs has focused almost exclusively on young men.[67]

The importance of being able to handle oneself without recourse to weapons, of standing one's ground, and of being loyal to one's friends and backing them up in any altercation pervaded Danny's narrative, and many of the other interviews that we have examined. As we have noted, these qualities are not restricted to the gang, or to Glasgow, nor are they found only in twentieth-century forms of masculinity. Lynn Abrams has argued that similar characteristics were prized amongst Highland men in the eighteenth century.[68] Danny's contemporary narrative contained similar themes of friendship, loyalty and masculinity in discussing conflicts he had encountered as an adult. The imprint of a youthful masculine habitus, for Danny, remained visible in his adult self. Ultimately, Danny was able to successfully grow up through gangs and then to transition out of them. In his early twenties, he made an active decision to move away from Easterhouse, as he feared 'something would happen' and he would end up in jail. He got married, bought a little house in another part of the east end of Glasgow, and began his adult working life. This was no simple transition, however. Danny noted that, despite being away from Easterhouse and no longer actively part of any gang, Glasgow was 'rife' with the fight culture associated with youth gangs:

> I mean if you went to the pub in the town there was guys from Maryhill Fleet, there was guys from the Calton Tongs . . . so you had the same scenario, you had to stand up to them as well otherwise you would have got a sore face, you know, and you just had to gain your respect all over again . . . [69]

Although his youthful 'hard man' identity was placed in the past during our interview, it is clear that some of the attributes associated with being a 'gemmie' in Glasgow remain important to his present self – even though that self is no longer part of a gang. Danny talked openly about the importance he placed on his reputation and ability to fight, and his pride in the fact that his friends would always stand their ground and back him up in any potential altercation.

To Danny, his youthful experiences in the Drummy gang had given him the ability to look after himself and his friends, to build long-lasting friendships forged in the loyalty expected of those in the gang, and to successfully navigate the cultural and social expectations of working-class masculinity in the time, place and historical context in which he grew up. In this way, the gang was a youthful articulation of working-class masculinities in Glasgow, a space for trying out, performing and adopting some of the wider expectations of masculinity in the city rather than a commitment to a particular lifestyle or identity.

FINAL POINTS

Though the imagery projected from the city has changed markedly over the past two decades, most memorably through the 'Glasgow: City of Culture' and 'Glasgow's Miles Better' campaigns – and latterly the rhetoric surrounding the Commonwealth Games in 2014 – it is notable that *No Mean City* remains a touchstone in much media commentary about Glasgow.[70] This chapter has sought to peer beneath this persistent 'hard man' imagery, by bringing forth the voices and experiences of individuals who lived through a crucial historical period in the formation of these stereotypes. There is clear evidence of a street-based culture that privileged a certain form of 'hard' masculinity. In part, this is a reflection of the prevailing norms around machismo in this time and place, with the gang a space in which many young men sought to test out and perform their masculine identities. The form that the gang took in 1960s Easterhouse must also be located within the particular structural and historical context of post-war social housing, in which housing needs were placed above community facilities. As we have pointed out, long-standing notions of working-class machismo interacted with the specific built and social environment to produce the types of masculine characteristics, attitudes and behaviours that were respected by many young boys growing up there – and in other housing schemes – in the 1960s and 1970s. In this way, the gang both reflected and refracted existing forms of masculinity, rather than being a deviation from them.

Moreover, masculinities are not singular; there are multiple forms of masculinity and ways of becoming and being a man open to boys. Many young men who grew up in Easterhouse did *not* join gangs, or participate in gang-related behaviours. As a teenager, one of our interviewees, Ian Monteague, was involved in creating the 'Easterhouse Fights Back' campaign, founded in the late 1960s to try to counter the exaggerated reputation for violence that the area was receiving from the media. He was keen to emphasise that many young people, himself included, were not involved in youth gangs – he was, he emphasised, 'just a normal, ordinary Easterhouse boy'. When asked whether he would like to add anything at the end of our interview, he remarked:

> in a sense it's been good to be able to say no we weren't all running about with chibs and knives and axes, and that's not because we were all wee Goody Two-Shoes, it's because the majority of people were just trying to live their lives and work out some stuff that was going on.[71]

Furthermore, as Danny's narrative demonstrates, for many 'the gang' was a temporary identity connected with peers and local space, rather than a fixed or static characteristic. These insights point towards the importance of understanding not 'the gang' per se, but rather the patterns through which 'hard', violent masculinities are passed on over time – with gang identities one part of this process, one that is still prized by young men in many working-class areas of the city. As has been well established, there is a long-standing connection between 'hardness' and masculine status in working-class culture, despite the uncoupling of heavy labour from the archetypal tough, working-class labourer during the process of de-industrialisation. In this sense, Danny's narrative must be situated within a longer history of masculinities in Glasgow, and the west of Scotland, particularly those involving working-class labour and that form of hegemonic masculinity that values toughness and physical prowess.

The influence of the 'hard man' continues to be cited in relation to the higher rates of violence, murder and mortality rates in twenty-first century Glasgow.[72] A better understanding of masculinities as expressed and enacted through the territorial youth gang could help to explain more about the forms that some working-class masculinities take, as well as why the narrative of the 'hard man' in the 'violent city' has remained so persistent.

NOTES

1. Sean Damer, *Glasgow: Going for a Song* (London: Lawrence & Wishart, 1990).
2. See for example, Alistair Fraser, 'Deviation from the mean? Cultural representations of Glasgow since "No mean city"', in A. McNair and J. Ryder (eds), *Further from the Frontiers . . . Cross-Currents in Irish and Scottish Studies* (Aberdeen: AHRC Centre for Irish and Scottish Studies, 2009), pp. 21–32. Tom McGrath wrote a play on this subject with the convicted murderer Jimmy Boyle – see Tom McGrath and Jimmy Boyle, *The Hardman* (Edinburgh: Fairplay Press, 2011).
3. Alexander McArthur and H. Kingsley Long, *No Mean City* (London: Transworld Publications, 1956); Andrew Davies, *City of Gangs: Glasgow and the Rise of the British Gangster* (London: Hodder & Stoughton, 2013), p. 297.
4. Alistair Fraser, *Urban Legends: Gang Identity in the Post-Industrial City* (Oxford: Oxford University Press, 2015).
5. Linda McDowell, *Redundant Masculinities?: Employment Change and White Working-Class Youth* (Malden: Blackwell, 2003), p. 13.
6. While the focus here is on Glasgow, comparable groups have been documented in other Scottish cities – though notably without attracting a public reputation. For Dundee, see S. A. T. Fitzpatrick, 'Myths and rituals surrounding delinquent gangs in Edinburgh and Dundee' (unpublished doctoral thesis, University of Edinburgh, 1972); for Edinburgh, see P. Bradshaw, 'Terrors and young teams: youth gangs and delinquency in Edinburgh', in S. H. Decker and F. M. Weerman (eds), *European Street Gangs and Troublesome Youth Groups* (Oxford: AltaMira Press, 2005) pp. 193–218. For a broad account of gangs in different cities, see Jon

Bannister, Jon Pickering, Susan Batchelor, Michele Burman, Keith Kintrea and Susan McVie, *Troublesome Youth Groups, Gangs and Knife-Carrying in Scotland* (Edinburgh: Scottish Government, 2010).

7. James Patrick, *A Glasgow Gang Observed* (London: Eyre-Methuen, 1973), p. 150.

8. Patrick, *Glasgow Gang Observed*, p. 123; P. Donnelly 'Evaluating gang rehabilitation and violence reduction in Glasgow's east end', Presentation to 18th UKPHA Annual Public Health Forum, Bournemouth International Conference Centre, 24–5 March 2010.

9. See for example, Andrew Davies, 'Glasgow's "reign of terror": street gangs, racketeering and intimidation in the 1920s and 1930s', *Contemporary British History*, 21:4 (2008), pp. 405–27.

10. J. V. M Shields and J. A. Duncan, *The State of Crime in Scotland* (London: Institute for the Study and Treatment of Delinquency, 1964).

11. Davies, 'Glasgow's "reign of terror"', p. 409.

12. See Davies, 'Glasgow's "reign of terror"'. For more on the response to youth gangs in 1960s Glasgow, see Angela Bartie, 'Moral panics and Glasgow gangs: exploring the new wave of Glasgow hooliganism, 1965–1970', *Contemporary British History*, 24:3 (2010), pp. 385–408.

13. *Glasgow Herald*, 7 June 1968.

14. Bartie, 'Moral panics and Glasgow gangs'.

15. For more on the Easterhouse Project, see Angela Bartie and Alistair Fraser, 'The Easterhouse Project: youth, social justice and the arts in Glasgow, 1968–1970', *Scottish Justice Matters*, 2:1 (2014), pp. 38–9.

16. For a detailed account, see Bartie, 'Moral panics and Glasgow gangs'.

17. On moral panics over youth, see for example Stanley Cohen, *Folk Devils and Moral Panics: The Creation of the Mods and Rockers*, 3rd edition (London: Routledge, 2002) and Geoffrey Pearson, *Hooligan: A History of Respectable Fears* (London: Macmillan, 1983). For exceptions, see for example Stephen Humphries, *Hooligans or Rebels? An Oral History of Working-Class Childhood and Youth 1889–1939* (Oxford: Blackwell, 1981) and R. Hood and K. Joyce, 'Three generations: oral testimonies on crime and social change in London's East End', *British Journal of Criminology*, 39:1 (1999), pp. 136–60.

18. This project, 'Narratives of Glasgow: oral histories of youth gangs in Easterhouse, c. 1965–1975', was supported by a British Academy Small Grant (summer 2011).

19. The pilot study, 'Narratives of Glasgow: oral histories of gangs in 1960s Easterhouse', was conducted by Susan Batchelor, Angela Bartie and Alistair Fraser, and funded by the University of Glasgow Adam Smith Research Foundation Seedcorn Fund (2010).

20. C. Alexander and B. Goldson, cited in Alistair Fraser, 'Street habitus: gangs, territorialism and social change in Glasgow', *Journal of Youth Studies*, 16:8 (2013), pp. 970–85, at 971.

21. See Lynn Abrams, *Oral History Theory*, 2nd edition (London: Routledge, 2016).

22. For a detailed examination of the 'cultural circuit' see Alistair Thomson, *Anzac Memories: Living with the Legend* (New York: Oxford University Press, 1994).

23. See for example Lynn Abrams, '"There was nobody like my daddy": fathers, the family and the marginalisation of men in modern Scotland', *Scottish Historical Review*, 88 (1999), pp. 219–42; R. Johnston and A. McIvor, 'Dangerous work, hard men and broken bodies: masculinity in the Clydeside heavy industries, c. 1930–1970s', *Labour History Review*, 69:2 (2004), pp. 135–152; David Walker, 'Danger was a thing that ye were brought up wi': workers narratives on occupational health and safety in the workplace', *Scottish Labour History*, 46 (2011), pp. 54–70; Andrew Perchard, '"Broken men" and "Thatcher's children": memory and legacy in Scotland's coalfields', *International Labor and Working Class History*, 84 (2013) pp. 78–98; Hilary Young, 'Hard man, new man: re/composing masculinities in Glasgow, c. 1950–2000', *Oral History*, 35:1 (2007), pp. 71–81.

24. Andrew Davies, 'Youth gangs, masculinity and violence in late Victorian Manchester and Salford', *Journal of Social History*, 32:2 (1998), pp. 349–69, at 363.

25. Pierre Bourdieu and Loïc Wacquant, *An Invitation to Reflexive Sociology* (Cambridge: Polity, 1992), Pierre Bourdieu, 'Habitus', in Jean Hillier and Emma Rooksby (eds), *Habitus: A Sense of Place*, 2nd edition (Aldershot: Ashgate, 2005), pp. 27–34.

26. Bourdieu and Wacquant, *An Invitation to Reflexive Sociology*, p. 128.

27. Pierre Bourdieu, 'Masculine domination revisited', *Berkeley Journal of Sociology*, 41 (1997), pp. 189–203, at 199; C. Behnke and M. Meuser, 'Gender and habitus: fundamental securities and crisis tendencies among men', in H. Kotthof and B. Baron (eds), *Gender in Interaction: Perspectives on Masculinity and Femininity in Ethnography and Discourse* (Amsterdam: John Benjamins Publishing, 2001), pp. 153–74, at 155.

28. Holly Thorpe, 'Bourdieu, gender reflexivity, and physical culture: a case of masculinities in the snowboarding field', *Journal of Sport and Social Issues*, 34:2 (2010), pp. 176–214, at 194.

29. Loïc Wacquant, 'Pierre Bourdieu' in Rob Stones (ed.), *Key Sociological Thinkers* (London: Macmillan, 2008), pp. 261–77, at 267.

30. Elspeth King, 'Popular culture in Glasgow', in R. A. Cage (ed.) *The Working Class in Glasgow, 1750–1914* (Beckenham: Croom Helm, 1987), pp. 142–87, at 144.

31. Graham Noble, 'In defence of Easterhouse', *New Society*, 20 (1970), pp. 328–9, at 328.

32. G. Armstrong and M. Wilson, 'City politics and deviancy amplification', in I. Taylor and L. Taylor (eds), *Politics and Deviance: Papers from the National Deviance Conference* (Harmondsworth: Pelican, 1973), pp. 61–89, at 67.

33. Armstrong and Wilson, 'City politics and deviancy amplification', p. 66.

34. Noble, 'In defence of Easterhouse', pp. 328–9.

35. Interview with I. Monteague, 19 July 2011.

36. Damer, *Glasgow: Going for a Song,* p. 200.

37. Interview with DM, 7 July 2011.

38. Armstrong and Wilson, 'City politics and deviancy amplification', p. 67.

39. Ibid. p. 67.

40. Pearl Jephcott, *Time of One's Own: Leisure and Young People* (Edinburgh: Oliver & Boyd, 1967), pp. 98, 139.

41. Patrick (pseudonym) was a twenty-six-year-old approved school teacher, who spent four months undercover with the Young Team, a youth gang based in Maryhill, an older housing area in the northwest of the city. The education researcher, Frank Coffield, has now disclosed that he is 'James Patrick'. The publication of *A Glasgow Gang Observed* was delayed until 1973 to avoid exacerbating the concern over youth gangs in the city. Patrick, *Glasgow Gang Observed*, p. 85.

42. William McIlvanney, 'Where Greta Garbo wouldn't have been alone', in Oscar Marzaroli and William McIlvanney, *Shades of Grey: Glasgow 1956–1987* (Edinburgh: Mainstream Publishing, 1987), p. 18. See also Sean Damer, *From Moorepark to 'Wine Alley': The Rise and Fall of a Glasgow Housing Scheme* (Edinburgh: Edinburgh University Press, 1989), p. 52.

43. In the fiction of James Kelman and in recent film depictions such as *Red Road* (Dir. Andrea Arnold, 2006) and *Under the Skin* (Dir. Jonathan Glazer, 2013), Glaswegian masculinities are portrayed as fragmented and complex. See Fraser, 'Deviation from the mean?'

44. Fraser, *Urban Legends*.

45. Johnston and McIvor, 'Dangerous work, hard men and broken bodies', p. 138.

46. See the chapter on 'Men, masculinity and safety' in E. Stanko, *Everyday Violence* (London: Pandora Press, 1990), pp. 109–xx.

47. Louise Jackson with Angela Bartie, *Policing Youth: Britain 1945–70* (Manchester: Manchester University Press, 2014), p. 100.

48. Jackson with Bartie, *Policing Youth*, pp. 94–5.

49. Simon Winlow, *Badfellas: Crime, Tradition and New Masculinities* (Oxford: Berg, 2001), p. 43.

50. Stanko, *Everyday Violence*, p. 110.

51. These were common expectations and experiences of working-class boys in the late nineteenth century – see Davies, 'Youth gangs, masculinity and violence', p. 363.

52. E. J. Yeo, 'The boy is the father of the man': moral panic over working-class youth, 1850 to the present', *Labour History Review*, 69:2 (2004), pp. 185–99, at 191.

53. Michael Roper and John Tosh (eds), *Manful Assertions: Masculinities in Britain since 1800* (London: Routledge, 1991), p. 13.

54. Interview with DM, 7 July 2011.

55. E. J. Yeo, 'Editorial: taking it like a man', *Labour History Review*, 69:2 (2004), pp. 129–33, at 129.

56. R. W. Connell, *Masculinities*, 2nd edition (Cambridge: Polity Press, 2005).

57. Interview with DM, 7 July 2011.

58. Johnston and McIvor, 'Dangerous work, hard men and broken bodies', p. 142.

59. Interview with DM, 7 July 2011.

60. J. Bannister et al., *Troublesome Youth Groups*.

61. Richard Jenkins, *Pierre Bourdieu* (London: Routledge, 2002), pp. 75–6.

62. Elijah Anderson, 'Jelly's place', in R. Hobbs and D. Wright (eds) *The Sage Handbook of Fieldwork* (London: Sage, 2006), pp. 39–58, at 68.

63. Fraser, *Urban Legends*. On desistance, see for example Beth Weaver, *Offending and Desistence: The Significance of Social Relations* (London: Routledge, 2015).

64. Gail Armstrong interview with DM, 1969. Underlining included in original transcript.

65. Interview with DM, 7 July 2011.

66. Ibid.

67. Anecdotal evidence suggests that there were female gangs in 1960s Glasgow, including in Easterhouse, but no work has been undertaken on this during the period we have explored. For recent work on girls and violence, see for example Susan Batchelor, 'Girls, gangs and violence: assessing the evidence', *Probation Journal*, 56:4 (2009), pp. 399–414.

68. Lynn Abrams, 'The taming of Highland masculinity: inter-personal violence and shifting codes of manhood, c. 1760–1840', *Scottish Historical Review*, 92:1 (2013), pp. 100–22 and Chapter 4 in this collection.

69. Interview with DM, 7 July 2011.

70. Kirsteen Paton, Gerry Mooney, and Kim McKee, 'Class, citizenship and regeneration: Glasgow and the Commonwealth Games 2014', *Antipode*, 44:4 (2012), pp. 1470–89.

71. Interview with I. Monteague, 19 July 2011.

72. In 2013, Glasgow was judged to be the most violent city in the UK by the UK Peace Index Study, with gangs and knife crime highlighted as the major issues. A full copy of the study is at http://www.visionofhumanity.org/pdf/ukpi/UK_Peace_Index_report_2013.pdf (last accessed 29 April 2016).

Index

Act of Union (1707), 59–60, 206
adolescence, 278
adultery, 24, 45, 48, 50, 58, 64, 67, 69,
    101, 134, 140n35, 186, 190–2
Aelred of Rievaulx, 101, 113, 115
affect, 22–3, 25–7, 33, 37n26, 63, 67,
    70, 71, 133, 150, 160–2, 176; *see
    also* emotion
age, 2, 6, 8, 12, 28, 62, 65, 108, 110,
    146, 183, 186–7, 199, 203, 262,
    263–4, 267–70; *see also* life
    course
aggression, 81–2, 88, 161, 203–4,
    208–17, 246; *see also* violence
Airth, John, 10–12, 187–96, 198–9,
    202n65
alcohol, 1, 4, 8, 46–7, 50–2, 58, 64,
    66–70, 73, 85–8, 90, 92, 94, 160,
    193, 224, 229, 231–2, 233, 236,
    237
Alexander I, 104–8, 111, 119n36
Alexander II, 109, 110, 112–14,
    119n34
Alexander III, 102, 105, 106, 109, 110,
    112–14, 124
appearance, 42–3, 47, 55n53, 70,
    84, 88, 105, 106, 107, 110, 111,
    132–3, 224, 228, 229, 230, 244–5,
    247–8, 253–4; *see also* bodies
Aquinas, Thomas, 124–5
assault, 1, 13, 59, 82–3, 86–8, 90, 92,
    207, 249, 261; *see also* fighting,
    violence
Auld Reekie (1773), 70
authority, 2, 8, 9, 11, 26, 39, 42, 43–4,
    48–9, 61, 101–7, 127, 130, 154,

183, 187–8, 194, 196–9, 203, 205,
    207–9, 213–17, 232, 235; *see also*
    patriarchy, kingship
Ayr, the Presbytery of, 44–9

bachelors, 64, 169
Balliol, John, 124–5
Bannatyne, George, 23, 27
Bannatyne manuscript, 21, 23–7, 28,
    31, 32, 33–4
Barbour, John
    The Bruce (c. 1375), 9, 12, 122–38
begging, 10, 12, 142–54
bestiality, 69
Billing, Noel Pemberton, 242–3
bodies, 137–8, 164, 212
    female, 225, 227–30, 236
    male, 7, 21, 24–5, 111, 113, 132,
        167–8, 208, 225, 243–4, 248,
        254
Boswell, James, 8, 9, 58, 63–6, 67, 68,
    72
boys, 4–5, 12, 87, 108, 110, 112, 114,
    183, 196–9, 232, 252, 264–73; *see
    also* childhood, youth
Braveheart (1995), 6
breadwinning, 3, 142, 162, 174, 233,
    242
Brown, George Johnstone, 10, 12,
    160–77
Bruce, Edward, 127–8, 138
Bruce, Robert, 9, 122–38
Buccleuch, Duke of, 150–1
Buchanan, George, 243–4
Burns, John, 225–7, 229–32, 235–6
Burns, Robert, 169, 172, 179n29

camp *see* effeminacy
Campbell, Archibald, 1st Marquess of
    Argyll, 39
Carlyle, Alexander, 61–2, 71
Catholicism, 149
charity *see* begging
chastity, 45, 47, 52
childhood, 2, 4, 5, 28, 39, 41, 44, 110,
    143, 189, 193, 194–8, 226, 228,
    230, 235, 262–5, 269; *see also*
    boys
chivalry, 12, 105, 112–14, 127–9, 131,
    135, 137, 141n37
church, 7, 10, 14, 23, 39–52, 53n18,
    61, 65, 67, 68, 69, 76n46, 88, 107,
    115, 125, 148, 183–99, 216, 249,
    261; *see also* religion
Church of Scotland, 61, 67, 68, 261
civility, 3, 31, 61, 67, 80–2, 91–2, 94,
    205, 209, 217; *see also* politeness
clans, 7, 12, 13, 39, 84–7, 93–4; *see
    also* family
class, 8, 11, 12, 30, 59, 61, 90, 144,
    205, 263
    elite/ gentry, 4, 8, 10, 11, 12, 58–73,
        80–2, 89, 91–3, 108, 111, 113,
        114, 146–8, 150, 154, 205, 233,
        243
    middling/ middle classes, 4, 11, 12,
        59, 61, 63, 67, 68, 80, 82, 84, 91,
        147, 204–6, 208, 213–15, 223–5,
        228, 230–8, 243, 250, 252
    working/ labouring classes, 4, 7, 8,
        11, 80, 81, 82, 92, 94, 144, 146,
        223–5, 227, 231, 232–8, 243, 244,
        245, 252, 258–9, 262–6, 270,
        271–3
clergy *see* occupations
clothing *see* appearance
clubs, 4, 9, 12, 61, 65–6, 68–9, 71,
    167, 224, 234, 248, 260
    Beggar's Benison, 9, 68
    Poker Club, 61, 66
    Soaping Club, 66
    Wig Club, 66
Clydebank, 162–3
Comyn, John, 125, 136
conduct books, 31–2, 34, 147
Connell, R. W., 2, 22, 224, 232, 235,
    236, 250, 267
courtiers, 8, 29, 31, 139n7
courtliness, 24, 30–4, 125, 130–5, 138
courtly love, 24, 134–5, 140n35

courts, 11, 59, 81–3, 87–9, 93–4, 105,
    183–99, 205–9, 212–13, 216,
    217
    burgh, 82, 92, 184, 188, 194, 197,
        199
    church *see* kirk session
    High, 62, 69, 82–3, 245, 248
    police, 204, 216
    sheriff, 1, 82–3, 89, 184, 188, 194,
        199
courtship, 171, 173

daughters, 31, 44, 67, 125, 192, 195
David I, 104, 105, 108, 110, 112, 113
de Burgh, Elizabeth, 130
death, 10, 25, 46, 59–61, 69, 82–3, 89,
    98n36, 136–8, 190–2
debt, 60, 82, 204–6, 209–10, 212–17
desire *see* sexual
deviance, 3, 8, 11, 65, 225, 232, 242,
    245, 246, 248–9, 253–4, 266
Dingwall, 1, 87
discipline *see* masculinity, patriarchy
divorce, 67
domestic violence, 208–9
domesticity, 4–5, 11, 12, 52, 58, 61,
    64, 67, 72, 82, 166, 174, 186, 197,
    208–9, 233, 242, 246, 252
Douglas, James, 9, 122–3, 125–30,
    132–8
drinking *see* alcohol
drunkenness *see* alcohol
duelling, 13, 59–61, 65, 73, 89–90,
    98n38, 214
*A Full and Exact Relation of the
    Duel* (1713), 60–1
Duncan II, 103–4, 107, 111–12

East Lothian, 12, 184–8
Easterhouse, 178n, 259–65, 269–72,
    277n67
Edgar, king of Scots, 104, 106–8, 110,
    119n36
Edward I, 106, 122, 124–6, 136, 138,
    141n42
Edinburgh, 7–11, 13, 23, 27, 58–70,
    81, 204–17, 247–9, 254
education, 7, 44, 144, 147, 162, 165,
    169, 175, 176, 267, 270
effeminacy, 1, 65, 69–72, 242–54
elders, 10, 41, 44, 48, 53n18, 68, 148,
    188–9, 192, 193, 195
emigration, 7

emotion, 5, 8, 10, 12, 22–34, 71, 133,
    145, 152–3, 160–2, 165–6, 169,
    170, 171, 174, 176, 177, 204, 208,
    210, 215, 217, 242, 249
  anxiety, 4, 22, 25, 27, 31, 32, 34, 93,
    94, 129, 168, 172, 227, 250, 260
  courage, 60–2, 125, 127, 128, 130,
    134, 164, 168, 170–1, 203, 246
  crying, 12, 25, 133–4, 137
  fear, 25, 27, 30, 49, 88, 92, 134,
    185, 250, 260, 270–1
  gratitude, 10, 145, 152–4
  love, 10, 24–5, 28, 63–4, 66, 124,
    130, 134–5, 138n, 140n, 150, 160,
    161, 162, 164, 165–6, 169–74,
    176, 245
  shame, 27, 49, 109, 183, 197, 207,
    210
  see also affect
emotional
  community, 23–7, 28, 33
  regime, 23, 28–33
  script, 22, 32
  violence, 204
Empire, 5, 7, 61, 91, 166–7, 168, 242
Enlightenment, 3, 5, 6, 7, 9, 12, 13,
    58–73, 89

Familie Exercise (1641), 40, 43
family, 3, 5, 8, 13, 28, 31, 39, 40, 43,
    46, 47, 49, 52, 61, 67, 86, 145,
    151, 160, 164–5, 169, 172, 173–4,
    176, 213, 242, 244, 246, 252, 267,
    270
  discipline, 40, 43
  feuds, 85–7, 90, 91, 94
  honour, 9, 31, 87
  worship, 42, 49, 50
fatherhood, 10, 12, 22, 28–34, 39–42,
    49–51, 58, 64–5, 87, 102, 113,
    125, 126, 138, 144, 146, 151, 169,
    174–7, 188–90, 193, 194–6, 208,
    267
femininity, 2, 9, 12, 21, 24, 26, 42,
    70, 72, 133, 140, 245, 247–8,
    253, 262, 267–8, 270; see also
    effeminacy
feminism, 5, 142, 232
  antifeminism, 23–4
  see also misogyny
Ferguson, Adam, 61
Fergusson, Robert, 69–70
  Auld Reekie (1773), 69–70

fighting, 1, 13, 50, 51, 73, 86, 88–9,
    90, 91, 101, 103, 108, 128–9, 132,
    134, 136, 137, 193–4, 246, 258,
    264–72; see also assault, violence
fin'amors, 134–5, 140n35; see also
    courtly love, romans courtois
fornication, crime of, 44, 50, 69,
    188–95, 198
friendship, 8, 33, 46, 51, 59, 62,
    63, 70–2, 126, 150, 174, 233,
    250, 251, 264, 270–1; see also
    homosocial
funerals, 3, 88

Gàedhaeltacht, 7
gambling, 51, 64, 92
gangs, 7, 11–12, 160, 258–73
  female, 277n67
'gemmie' see 'hard man'
gender identity, 59, 70, 114, 203–4,
    214
gender relations
  between men, 1, 9–13, 26, 28–34,
    39, 46, 50, 72, 59–61, 62–3, 65–6,
    68–73, 80–95, 130, 133, 193–5,
    196–7, 206, 223–5, 231, 232–6,
    242–55, 258–73
  with women, 9–13, 21, 24–5, 27, 33,
    43–5, 50, 64–5, 66–8, 130–1, 134,
    160–77, 188–93, 195, 226, 228,
    230–1
General Assembly, 42–4, 47–50
Glasgow, 8, 9, 11, 12, 68, 92, 162,
    171, 172, 223–38, 243–7, 251–2,
    258–73
government, 7, 8, 62, 185, 198, 236,
    260

'habitus', 262–5, 271
Haddington, 29, 184–5, 188,
    197–9
Hamilton, James, Duke of, 59–62, 65,
    74n12
Hamilton, Robert, 45–6
'hard man', 3, 88, 160, 258–62,
    265–73
hedonism, 68, 224–5, 232–8; see also
    libertinism
heteronormativity, 3, 72, 135
heterosexuality, 11, 33, 67, 70, 124,
    162, 225, 242, 246, 249–54
Highlands, 7, 8, 9, 13, 61, 80–95, 246,
    270

home, 3, 11, 40, 64, 126, 146, 163, 165–6, 172, 173, 176–7, 197, 208, 267, 270; *see also* domesticity
homophobia, 251
homosexuality, 3, 11, 12, 68–72, 77n79, 242–54; *see also* sodomy
homosocial, 12, 26, 58, 65, 68, 71–3, 133, 137, 174, 234; *see also* friendship
honour, 8, 9, 11, 13, 31, 39, 59–61, 73, 80, 81, 85, 87, 89, 93–4, 134, 183, 190, 194, 203–8, 211, 213–14, 216, 268
household, 7, 8, 12, 13, 31, 40–52, 58, 62, 72, 90, 185, 187–9, 193–9, 203, 206–9, 215
'godly household', 8, 41–52, 183, 185, 186
Hume, David, 61–2, 63, 65, 66–7, 69, 71

illegitimacy, 189, 192–3, 195
imprisonment, 29, 66, 114, 126, 138, 198, 205–6, 212–17, 227, 247, 270–1
incest, 50
independence, 4, 10, 59, 61–2, 71–2, 90, 142–4, 193, 203, 205–8, 214–16, 245
infidelity *see* adultery
insult, 1, 68, 87, 92–4, 188, 194, 206–7, 209–10, 213
intimacy, 5, 12, 68, 70–2, 161–6, 169–74, 176, 243
intoxication *see* alcohol
Inverness, 8, 9, 11, 13, 80–1, 82–4, 90–4

Jacobite risings, 61, 81, 83–4
state response to, 83–5
James I, 28

Kames, Lord (Henry Home), 62, 67, 70–1
Sketches of the History of Man (1774), 70–1
kingship, 9, 21, 101–15, 124, 133, 135–6
and authority, 9, 101–10, 114, 123, 127, 129–30
kinship *see* clans, family
kirk *see* church

kirk session, 10, 43–5, 50–1, 69, 88, 183–99
knighthood, 9, 101–13, 119n36, 122–38
Knox, John, 41

law, 7, 11, 28, 40, 59, 69, 80–3, 87, 89–90, 92, 98n55, 104, 105, 124–5, 136, 184–8, 198, 203–9, 211–17, 243, 246, 249–51, 254
and violence, 211–17
leisure, 4, 50, 63–4, 67, 92, 160, 162, 166, 223, 232, 234, 237, 244, 262–5
football, 51, 162, 167, 172, 175–6, 264–5
music hall, 11, 12, 223–38
sport, 4, 51, 89, 162, 165, 167, 175, 177, 264–5
Leith, 50–1, 190–1, 211
libertinism, 8, 12, 58–73; *see also* hedonism
life course, 10, 11, 46, 184, 268–71
literature, 14, 21, 23, 28, 30, 139n7, 165–6, 170, 175
didactic, 3, 203, 215, 217
periodical, 59
popular, 4–5
love *see* emotion
love lyric, 24–5
lust *see* sexual
Lyndsay, David, 21
Ane Satyre of the Thrie Estaitis, 21

McCall, Danny (pseudonym), 262–73
McCone, John, 46–7
Mackenzie, Henry, 59
Maitland, Sir Richard of Lethington, 22, 29–31
Maitland manuscript, 21, 28–34
Malcolm III, 101, 104, 106, 110, 112, 113, 115
Malcolm IV, 108, 109, 112
manliness, 1, 10, 40, 52, 62, 82, 94, 110, 112, 128, 133, 142, 144, 154, 161, 168, 177, 242
marriage, 2, 4, 12, 24–5, 44–6, 52, 70, 72, 90, 113, 140n, 162, 169, 174, 183, 187, 189–90, 193, 195, 245
companionate, 174
Mary, Queen of Scots, 24, 29
masculine stereotypes, 3, 4, 6–7, 11, 272

masculinity
  alternative, 1, 11, 70, 82, 89, 177,
    224, 236
  complicit, 2, 232
  deviant, 3, 8, 11, 65, 242, 245–6,
    248–9, 253–4
  hegemonic, 2, 22, 27, 34, 102, 144,
    224, 232, 235–6, 250, 267, 273
  historiography of, 5
  ideal, 1, 3, 6, 8, 9, 11–13, 21–3, 32,
    34, 40–2, 44–5, 47, 49–52, 58–9,
    61–3, 65, 67, 72, 94, 101, 106,
    111, 113–14, 123, 129, 135–6,
    138, 144–5, 161, 186, 193, 197,
    204, 206, 208, 246, 263
  marginalised, 2, 232, 235
  practice of, 2, 4, 6, 7, 8, 10, 12, 72,
    82, 94, 144, 210, 217, 258–9, 261,
    265
  representations of, 1, 6, 9, 10, 21,
    25, 31, 42–3, 71, 82, 94, 109, 111,
    113, 122, 130, 174, 183, 246, 250,
    252, 258–9, 261
  subordinate, 2, 3, 22, 27, 232
'mashers', 224–5, 232–8
masturbation, 68
material culture, 114
Melville, James
  A Spiritvall Propine of a Pastour to
    his People (1589), 41
Merrilees, William, 247–8
misogyny, 23, 34, 37n26; see also
    feminism
morality, 7, 8, 11, 21, 23, 28, 30–3, 41,
    44, 67, 69, 70, 89, 149, 183–5,
    193, 215, 223–38, 243–6, 249
  moral panics, 261
  moral philosophy, 59, 61, 62, 68, 71
mothers, 31, 37n27, 60, 104, 134, 163,
    190, 228, 244

national identity, 130–1, 134, 135
Neo-augustinianism, 26
Neostoicism, 26
No Mean City (1935), 258, 260, 264,
    271

obedience, 25, 41, 45, 48–51, 152, 266
occupations
  apprentice, 50, 92, 143, 197, 232–3
  clerk, 92–3, 224
  crofting, 3
  farming, 1, 7, 91, 209

fishing, 3, 84
heavy industry, 7, 266
labourer, 9, 12, 87, 92, 209, 214,
    273
lawyer, 29, 58, 64–6, 91, 209
merchant, 12, 30, 58, 68, 84, 147,
    205, 211–14
mining, 3–4, 160
minister, 8, 40–52, 63, 65, 67,
    190–4, 210, 261
servant, 1, 13, 42–5, 50, 87, 91, 147,
    186, 188, 193, 195–6, 199, 203,
    207, 215–16
shipyards, 160, 252
soldier, 89–90, 101, 162, 166–7,
    209, 242–3, 245–6, 248–9, 254
tailor, 1
tradesman, 91–2, 205, 210–11,
    214
see also work
passion see emotion, sexual
Paton, William, 244–5, 247
patriarchy, 2, 4, 6, 10, 12, 22, 127,
    135, 143, 162, 183, 186–7, 193–7,
    198–9, 203, 206–8, 213, 224–6
  patriarchal authority, 4, 127, 187–8,
    194, 207
  patriarchal dividend, 2, 31, 205, 232,
    235
patronage see begging
piety, 10, 14, 39, 41–3, 47–50, 52,
    102
politeness, 8, 9, 10–11, 58–67, 71–3,
    81, 89, 145, 149, 203, 205–6, 211,
    215, 217; see also civility
poor relief, 143, 145–6
power, 2, 6, 7, 9, 24, 27, 32, 39, 41,
    48–9, 63, 70, 72, 106, 113, 114,
    127, 135–6, 142, 145, 183, 187,
    203–5, 208–12, 214–15, 217, 224,
    232, 235; see also authority
presbyterianism, 7, 54n38, 65, 69, 72,
    224
prostitution, 8, 67
  male, 9, 11, 243–9, 254
  female, 9, 58, 66, 230, 232–3, 248
  Ranger's Impartial List of the Ladies
    of Pleasure in Edinburgh (1775),
    66–7
Protestantism, 5, 8, 40, 42, 149, 224,
    250

querelle des femmes, 23